# NICK CROSSLEY

# Key Concepts in
# Critical Social
# Theory

SAGE

Los Angeles | L
Singapore | V

First published 2005.
Reprinted 2008 (Twice), 2009, 2010 (twice), 2012

SAGE Publications Ltd
1 Oliver's Yard
55 City Road
London EC1Y 1SP

SAGE Publications Inc.
2455 Teller Road
Thousand Oaks, California 91320

SAGE Publications India Pvt Ltd
B 1/I 1 Mohan Cooperative Industrial Area
Mathura Road
New Delhi 110 044

SAGE Publications Asia-Pacific Pte Ltd
3 Church Street
#10-04 Samsung Hub
Singapore 049483

**British Library Cataloguing in Publication Data**

A catalogue record for this book is available
from the British Library

ISBN 978-0-7619-7059-0 (hbk)
ISBN 978-0-7619-7060-6 (pbk)

**Library of Congress Control Number Available**

Typeset by M Rules
Printed and bound by CPI Group (UK) Ltd, Croydon, CR0 4YY
Printed on paper from sustainable resources

# contents

V

vi

# preface

This book is intended to help students who are working with or attempting to read about aspects of contemporary critical social theory. My immediate feeling when the idea of the book was suggested to me was that it might be used as a substitute for 'the real thing' and I was very hesitant about accepting the challenge for precisely that reason. There is no substitute for the real thing. To understand and engage properly with theory it is necessary to hear it from the horse's mouth, that is, from primary texts and critiques. Having reflected more deeply upon the issue, however, I arrived at the conclusion that there is a genuine need for books like this in the present era. The modularization of courses has generated a situation where students often receive less teaching in areas such as theory and where advanced or contemporary theory are taught to students who have had very little introduction to even the basics and who have little time to get up to speed. This makes theory very difficult both to teach and to learn. And that, in turn, necessitates books like this, which seek to explain key concepts and offer some insight into the reasons why theorists have used and developed them. The alternative, I believe, is that theory, which is an essential element of sociology and the other social sciences, becomes so opaque as to alienate all but the smallest clique. My view regarding the importance of primary texts still stands. I would hate to think that a student did not bother reading what Bourdieu himself writes about the habitus, for example, or what Habermas writes about 'colonization of the lifeworld', because my entries on these topics are more accessible. But I believe that this book could be used as an aid by readers approaching these difficult ideas and texts for the first time and I hope that it will be. I hope that students will use this book to check their own understanding of concepts, to fill in gaps and perhaps also to achieve the preliminary clarification that is sometimes necessary for pressing ahead with complex materials.

## PRINCIPLES OF SELECTION

It was suggested to me when I was first discussing the plan for the book that it should reflect my own 'take' on theory, my own range of interests and priorities. Undoubtedly this suggestion found its way into the process whereby I selected concepts for the book, whether intentionally or not. Some of the inclusions that I have made would not have been made by others. I have attempted, however, to be a little more systematic and judicious in my selection. Specifically I have tried to operate according to five principles.

Firstly, I have tried to deal with the concepts of authors who strive to be precise and clear but who are not so clear as to create no need for further clarification. In effect this has meant excluding concepts which are so straightforward as to require no discussion, in my view, but also those which are so opaque or vague as to defy reasonable definition.

This has also meant that I have refused to be drawn in by 'naked emperors'. A great deal of what has come under the banner of 'post' this or that theorizing is, in my view, deliberately obscure, often to the point of incoherence, and very weak or insubstantial. The meaning of complicated sounding concepts vacillates between simple-minded obviousness and obvious simple-mindedness. I refuse to make excuses for theoretical work of this kind or to pander to its pretentiousness. And I advise students to do the same. Writers only try to sound clever and difficult, in my experience, when they have very little of any depth or complexity to offer. One should always approach texts charitably, assuming that the author has something coherent and of interest to say. But that is not always true and when the emperor has no clothes it is as well to recognize the fact. Some of the work to which I am referring may have made its way through my filter and into this book, but not much I hope.

Secondly, I have selected concepts which have a degree of durability to them. Some writers, some of the time, develop throwaway concepts that are intended to serve a specific purpose in a specific argument but are never taken up again after this point. There is nothing wrong with this but I believe that such concepts are best dealt with in their contexts and there is no real need to extract them and discuss them in abstract, in a work such as this.

Thirdly, I have tended towards more sociological theories and concepts. Contemporary critical theory draws upon psychology, literary/cultural studies, philosophy, geography, anthropology, history and other disciplines besides. Indeed, part of what defines it is its interdisciplinarity. It would be impossible to do justice to the input of all of these disciplines however, and my strength is sociology (with some strands of philosophy). So I have opted here, for the most part, to elucidate the sociological input to contemporary critical theory. Or rather, insofar as I have strayed beyond the most central (interdisciplinary) concepts of contemporary critical social theory, I have strayed in a sociological direction. I have tried as much as possible to do justice to the most central concepts of critical theory, as I see them, from whatever disciplinary basis, but where I have gone beyond the absolutely central concepts I have selected from amongst the more sociological strands of theory.

It is important to add here, that my emphasis has been upon theory. Much critical writing emerges out of a practical rather than a theoretical or academic context and most critical social movements (feminist, anti-racist, workers movements, and so on) involve certain sections who emphasize the importance of non-academic writing. They believe, with some justification, that academics obscure issues which, for political purposes, could be relatively clear, and are torn in their priorities between the demands of critique and the demands of the academy. I have not included the ideas discussed in such works in this book as I see no real need for it. These ideas are expressed clearly enough in their primary sources and are not written for the purposes of academic discussion and debate.

Fourthly, having said this, I have tried to select from within sociological theory those concepts which are critical or which belong to projects of critique. This is easier said than done, as different theories work with different definitions of 'critique' and there is certainly one sense of 'critique' which might extend to most, if not all sociology and social theory. 'Critique' can mean something along the lines of 'opening up to investigation and analysis' or 'exploring constituent elements', which covers just about all sociology. Furthermore, as Robert Merton (1964) argued in his response to the charge that sociological functionalism is inherently conservative, any rigorous exploration of social practices and relations tends to disturb the natural 'feel' that such practices and relations can otherwise acquire and is, to this extent, progressive and potentially subversive. This is independent of the fact, also noted by Merton, that the sociological form of politically critical and politically conservative theories can be identical. Radicals and conservatives alike sometimes use functionalist explanations or rational-choice analyses, for example. It is not the sociology that distinguishes them but rather the evaluative accent that is placed upon key claims and findings, or the manner in which concepts are operationalized and used. Finally, there are very few sociologists these days, in my experience, who do not offer a least some sort of 'critical', 'radical' or 'political' gloss upon what they are doing – apart from anything else because the demand by our political and economic masters that we 'make it relevant' forces this issue. Given these arguments, my claim to have selected concepts because they are critical should be treated with caution. I have tried wherever possible, however, to draw upon those theories which offer a relatively well-developed notion of social/political criticism and which put that notion at the centre of their enterprise.

Finally, I have attempted to draw together a mix of contemporary and classic concepts – selecting those classics which continue to have contemporary relevance and which inform more contemporary work. This combination, I believe, maximizes the relevance of my selection.

This book has not always been easy to write. I hope, however, that it is easy to read, and that it serves the intended job of smoothing the passage of students into contemporary critical social theory. As I noted above, there is no substitute for reading primary texts. But with a bit of a leg-up that should not prove too difficult.

X

# Key Concepts in
# Critical Social Theory

# Alienation

Related *concepts:*, **anomie, ideology, recognition.**

The concept of alienation is widely used in a variety of different types of critical social theory. At the most general level it refers to a separation or estrangement of human beings either from each other, from their own life or self, or from society.[1] This separation can be either subjective, in the sense that agents feel alienated, objective, in the sense that they actually are separated from something whether they feel it or not, or both. A number of important social theorists and philosophers have posited theories of alienation, including Hegel (1979) and Simmel (1990). However, much work in contemporary critical theory can be traced back to the specific formulation of the concept in the early work of Karl Marx. In particular Marx's *1844 Economic and Philosophical Manuscripts* offer a detailed treatment of the alienation which, in Marx's view, lies at the heart of the capitalist system (Marx, 1959). I will outline that theory of alienation shortly. First, however, a few scene-setting points are in order.

Marx's model of alienation is centred upon labour and specifically the manner in which workers labour within capitalist societies. His account owes much to Hegel (1979) and specifically to Hegel's treatment of labour in his discussion of recognition (see **recognition**). Marx is equally very critical of Hegel, however, both in this part of his work and elsewhere. There are many aspects to this critique but particularly pertinent here is Marx's objection to the Hegelian idea that human activity expresses the logic of development of an 'objective spirit' which is independent of it. Objective spirit, in the form of culture and society, is the product of human labour, not its cause, for Marx, and the tendency to reverse the equation is in many respects symptomatic of alienation. Alienation, in large part, involves the tendency to experience the world which one produces through one's own labour as an independent entity

3

---

1 Strictly speaking one could be alienated from anything that one could both be 'connected' to or feel connected with but also separated or estranged from.

which controls or at least influences one's action but over which one has no control – which is, more or less, what Hegel's philosophy of history seems to suggest. This aspect of the concept of alienation is not taken up at any length in this entry but has been developed by a number of writers, both within and outside of the Marxist camp, under the rubric of 'reification' (Lukács, 1971; Berger and Luckmann, 1979). Although reification is itself a complex and polysemic concept, it focuses specifically upon the way in which a society produced through the interaction of individuals can appear, for social scientists and lay members of society alike, as a thing distinct from those individuals. Marx is critical of Hegel because he believes that Hegel has been deceived in just this way and has founded his philosophy of history on the basis of this misconception.

At another level Marx's discussion of alienation involves a critique of 'bourgeois'[2] political economy and particularly of all that political economy takes for granted in its attempt to explain the workings of economic life. An analysis of alienation and alienated labour, for Marx, is an analysis of humanly produced and historically specific forms or conditions of labour, forms which constitute the capitalist economic system that the political economists, in turn, assume as an unquestioned starting point in their analysis. What the bourgeois economist takes for granted is, for Marx, precisely that which needs to be explained. Furthermore, in this respect, though it is often convenient to describe Marx's account of alienation as an account of the manner in which labour is alienated under capitalist conditions of production, it is perhaps more accurate to say that his is an account of the manner in which the alienation of labour gives rise to the specifically capitalist form of production.

To understand what Marx means by 'alienation' or 'alienated labour' we must understand first that, for Marx, 'labour' has a much wider meaning than 'paid work'. Labour, for Marx, is the sensuous and embodied practice (what Marxists call 'praxis') through which human beings transform the world around them, in accordance with plans, projects and aesthetic sentiments. Insofar as this involves more than the mere satisfaction of animal need, that it goes beyond securing the basics of survival, he believes that labour raises human beings above our animal nature. To make an object of beauty for the sake of beauty, for example,

4

2 That is, the form of political economy and economics which has emerged in capitalist (that is, 'bourgeois') societies and which, in Marx's view, takes the features of that society for granted, such that it makes those features appear natural and inevitable and thereby legitimates that society, insulating it from critique.

is to transcend the cycle of need-satisfaction which is characteristic of other animals.[3] Furthermore, because it is a transformation of the world outside of us – the world that we perceive sensuously – it effectively serves as a mirror, reflecting our humanity and individuality back to us. By looking at what we have made and recognising it as the product of our own labour, we achieve a form of self-consciousness adequate to our own nature; we see ourselves, truly, as the creative beings that we are. Labour is as much a manner of fashioning our subjective life as fashioning the objective world, from this point of view. This is not a solitary pursuit, however. Like Hegel, Marx believes that human beings only truly and fully recognize themselves in this way when they are recognized and recognize others in this way. Human subjectivities are interdependent, intersubjective. Each depends upon the other for confirmation (see **recognition** and **intersubjectivity**).

Having said that 'labour' is not the same as or reducible to 'paid work', Marx's argument regarding alienation focuses upon the specific conditions of labour constitutive of the capitalist system of production. And here labour is reduced, practically and objectively, to paid work. Workers sell their labour to employers in return for a subsistence wage. Moreover, they work in (factory) conditions, which routinize and deskill their labour, reducing it to basic mechanical actions in a production line process. This, Marx argues, produces alienation on four levels.

Firstly, the worker is alienated from the product of their labour. They do not own it when it is made. Often they contribute to only one part of its production (e.g. sticking on a handle), not even seeing the full process of its production, let alone being involved throughout and certainly not making it in accordance with their own designs and plans. It is a standard object made in accordance with a standard plan and their contribution to it is akin to that of a machine. As such it is an alien thing, a thing which means nothing to them.

Secondly, and in the same way, the worker is alienated from the act of production itself. They do not produce under their own initiative, asserting their own control over the process of production. They slot into that process as a cog in a machine and are estranged from it.

---

3 Marx is quite clear that we are animals. He has no theological or metaphysical view of human beings as being other than animals. His point, rather, is that we, like all species, have certain species specific characteristics – which his analysis seeks to identify. Furthermore, he is also clear that, as animals, we are a part of nature or the natural world. To talk of the way in which human beings 'transform nature', he claims, is therefore, strictly speaking, to talk of the way in which nature transforms itself.

---

Thirdly, they are alienated from what Marx calls their 'species-being'. As noted above, Marx believes that it is the nature of human beings to produce for reasons other than the satisfaction of basic needs, for aesthetic and related reasons, and to discover through such acts of production their own nature. The alienated worker, however, sells their labour as a commodity, precisely as a way of satisfying their basic needs, and there is nothing in the nature of their work that could mirror back to them an image of their creativity or 'interiority'.[4] Their labour assumes only the status of a commodity in the process of production and they therefore receive no feedback from their work environment to suggest that they are anything but a commodity. The human potential to elevate oneself above one's animal nature and (as an essential aspect of that) to recognize oneself as elevated above the animal realm, is not realized.

Finally, in this manner of organizing production, human beings are alienated from one another. Indeed, integral to the claim that human beings are alienated from their species-being is the claim that they are alienated from one another. To live in accordance with our species-being is to live collectively, mutually recognizing one another as specifically human beings and thereby being able to recognize ourselves in this way. If the nature of the conditions of our production do not allow us to elevate ourselves above the basic level of need satisfaction, however, to express our species-being by way of creative praxis, then the basis through which we might be recognized for what we are, or could be, by others, and thus through which we could fully recognize ourselves in this way, are denied to us. When each worker is reduced to a commodity each recognizes self and other in this way.

Marx's conception of alienation is philosophical and 'objective'.[5] It compares what human beings are with what they could be and does not

---

4 I do not mean to suggest by this that Marx believes human subjectivity to be an immaterial inner realm that one can, so to speak, peer into. 'Interiority' is used figuratively here. The point, however, is that our subjective life consists in sensuous and embodied activity which is not, in the first instance, aware of itself in any developed sense. We only become aware of ourselves through our works, through transformation of the world around us, which effectively mirrors back to us what we are like and what we care about.

5 Sometimes we use the term 'objective' to mean 'not a matter of opinion but rather something which is evident and indisputable to all who care to consider the evidence'. This is not exactly the sense intended here. Marx's theory is just a theory and many people might disagree from it. 'Objective' in this sense means that Marx is not interested in the psychology of workers and the question of whether they feel alienated but rather defines alienation in terms which rest upon the conditions in which workers work, whatever they happen to feel about those conditions.

---

focus upon the psychological question of whether workers feel alienated. Some social scientific critiques of alienation in the workplace do shift the concept from its philosophical meaning into a more psychological or sociological register, however, where it is equated with feelings of, for example, powerlessness or meaninglessness. One of the most famous examples of this is that of Blauner (1964). This more social scientific version of the concept is not wrong but it is different from Marx's philosophical conception and it is important that we do not blur the distinction.

In his later work, Marx (1976) introduces a concept of 'commodity fetishism' which reiterates the basic point about the alienated nature of production at the heart of capitalism. The 'fetishistic' nature of the commodity, on this account, resides in the fact that it is seen as an object independent of human life and subjectivity. It is a thing whose being has become disconnected from the human conditions under which it is produced. As consumers we purchase and possess the objects of another's labour but our experience of the object is divorced from any experience of the worker, her labour or the conditions of her labour. We do not recognize the labour of the other in the products that we buy. We take the object as a self-subsisting and independent 'thing'.

As noted above, the concept of alienation, as formulated by Marx specifically, has served as a basis for many further social critiques. There are too many to even begin to unpack here. The critique of the Frankfurt School is worthy of brief mention, however, not least as they traced relations of alienation back through to the consumer, as well as the producer, using the aforementioned concept of fetishism (to which they also added a psychoanalytic element, drawing from the concept of sexual fetishism.[6]) As consumers, they note, we experience products as things, independent of the humans who produce them. We do not recognize products as products of human labour. At the same time, in the 'consumer society' we pursue our own happiness by means of the pursuit of these objects. Goods come to symbolize happiness, in the way that fetishized objects symbolize within sexual fetishism, and we believe that possession of these goods will make us happy or complete. In this respect we are as much alienated in our consumption and leisure as in our work (see Marcuse, 1986; Adorno and Horkheimer, 1983).

6 In fetishism an object seemingly unrelated to the sexual act (shoes are a much cited example) becomes a source of sexual stimulation and excitation, and may, in fact, become necessary to arousal.

Marx's (1959) *1844 Economic and Philosophical Manuscripts* are quite straightforward and there is therefore no reason, in this case, not to go straight to the primary source. Marcuse's (1986) *One-Dimensional Man* is also relatively short and accessible. A similar but independent conception of alienation can be found in the final chapters of Simmel's (1990) *Philosophy of Money*. And no comprehensive exploration of 'alienation' should miss out on the celebrated discussion of 'reification' in George Lukács's (1971) *History and Class Consciousness*.

# Anomie

---

**Related concepts: alienation, colonization of the lifeworld.**

---

Social exclusion?

The concept of anomie is widely used in contemporary sociology. The chief architect of the concept, however, was Emile Durkheim. This entry will focus primarily upon his development of the concept.

For Durkheim society is a moral order. The fact of human beings living together, in groups, he argues, is generative of a range of phenomena which, by virtue of their collective constitution, are genuinely social, and one key set of phenomena generated in this way are 'norms'; that is, shared expectations or rules, some tacit, some explicit, about how one ought to act in particular contexts. In Durkheimian terms, norms are 'social facts'. For our purposes this means four things. Firstly, as just noted, norms arise out of collective life and must necessarily do so; a hypothetical isolated individual would and could not generate a system of norms, nor would they have reason to do so, but at the point that individuals come into interaction norms tend to be generated. In the case of norms this collective nature is partly explained by the fact that they regulate our relationships to one another; they stipulate how we should conduct ourselves in relationship to others. Challenging those moral philosophers, such as Kant (1948; 1993), who believe that the principles governing these rules derive from within ourselves, Durkheim insists that they derive from our relations with others, or rather from the system of relations linking all individuals in a group and constituting that group qua society. Secondly, systems of norms, though intrinsically bound up with the life of flesh and blood societies (that is, with human interaction), may both predate and outlive any given population. In other words, many of the norms we live by today first emerged centuries before we were born and many will continue to exist after we have died. Thirdly, these norms are imposed upon us and constrain us. This can happen in two ways. On the one hand, even if I happen not to agree with a norm or not to be aware of it, it can still exist, embodied in the actions and expectations of my contemporaries, and they will enforce the norm whether I recognize it or not. The norm has a factual existence independently of me. On the other hand we tend to internalize these norms during our infancy and childhood such that they become part of our psychological structure. By nature we are not 'moral' beings, according to Durkheim, and almost by definition we are not 'civilized', but the norms which arise through human interaction take root within our nature, giving rise to a 'second nature' which is both moral and civilized. In this way we are moulded by society, though, of course, we also continue society by way of our (moral and civilized) actions and interactions:

> . . . the individual gets from society the best part of himself, all that gives him a distinct character and a special place amongst other beings, his intellectual and moral culture. [. . .] the characteristic attributes of human nature come from society. But, on the other hand, society exists and lives only though individuals . . . (1915: 389)

Having said this, Durkheim adds that individuals may remain torn between their social and their individual (biological) nature. Natural or selfish impulses can compete with the moral dictates derived from society.

Finally, and most importantly from our point of view, Durkheim believes that normative systems, as parts of society, are interdependent with other parts and thus can be adversely affected by changes or events in those other parts. They might break down, for example, cease to be passed on effectively to new generations or slip out of alignment with the demands and exigencies imposed upon agents by other forces in society. This is particularly likely to happen during periods of rapid social change.[7] It is this breakdown in normative systems that Durkheim refers to as

---

7 During periods of rapid social change individuals' expectations, because they are based upon past experiences, tend to lag behind and thus fall out of alignment with their current situations. Similarly, different areas of life which change at a different pace can fall out of alignment with one another.

'anomie', and he believes that it has drastic consequences for societies and the individuals woven within them.

The obvious example of this in his work is in the study *Suicide*, where anomie is cited as one of the main three[8] causes of high (and rising) rates of suicide in society (Durkheim, 1952). Durkheim's focus in this study is upon 'rates' of suicide rather than individual suicides. That is to say, he is concerned to explain the 'social fact' of variation in suicide rates by reference to other social facts. He is not seeking to explain the individual biographical fact of why this or that person commits suicide. However, in his discussion he reveals just how dependent he believes normal human mental functioning is upon society and specifically upon social norms. In anomic conditions, he argues, individuals are prone towards mental disorientation. Their expectations become unregulated, ceasing to map onto the world they are living within, and they therefore become distressed and, in some cases suicidal. Human desires and expectations, Durkheim argues, are not self-regulating. In the absence of a strong and established system of social norms (which have been internalized by the agent) they are inclined to rise above and beyond what is attainable, and also to become unstable, in both cases leading to disappointment, disillusionment and dissatisfaction. Thus anomie and suicide are closely linked (see also Durkheim, 2002).

As noted above, Durkheim views social change as a key source of anomie, since it dislodges norms and upsets systems of norms as well as generating situations they are not suited to deal with. At a more general level, however, he is equally concerned that the growth of societies, with the concomitant shift from mechanistic to organic forms of solidarity,[9] particularly if that leads to a breakdown of mechanistic forms of solidarity, can generate a tendency towards instability and anomie. This is a theme which has been picked up, in a critical vain, by Jurgen Habermas (1987b) in his work on the colonization of the lifeworld (see **colonization of the lifeworld**). In an argument which closely parallels Durkheim's (1964) argument in *The Division of Labour*, Habermas argues that the expansion of both the market economy and the state, into ever more areas of human

---

8 The other two are 'egoism' and 'altruism' respectively. In effect, these two causes suggest a curvilinear relationship between social integration and suicide. Too much integration predisposes a society towards increased (altruistic) suicide, but so too does too little integration (egoistic suicide).

9 I do not have the space here to discuss these two forms of solidarity (which are posited in Durkheim's first major study, *The Division of Labour* (1964)). Suffice it to say that organic forms of solidarity are less focused upon binding norms and are for this reason more prone to anomie.

---

life, has a tendency to undermine the traditions and norms which previously regulated those areas of life, generating anomie at the social level, and alienation and psychopathology at the personal-psychological level.

### FURTHER READING

Durkheim is a very clear and lucid writer, and is much more sophisticated and nuanced than many critics and commentators give him credit for. *Suicide* and *The Division of Labour* are both fascinating studies and well worth reading first hand. *Moral Education*, though less directly relevant, nicely summarizes some of Durkheim's thoughts on the need for human desire and expectations, as psychological phenomena, to be regulated through (internalized) social norms. The **colonization of the lifeworld** has a separate entry in this book.

# Body-subject

---

*Related concepts: **freedom, habitus, hexis.***

---

The concept of the body-subject is closely tied to the work of the French existential-phenomenologist, Maurice Merleau-Ponty. Although Merleau-Ponty seldom uses this term, it is commonly used by commentators to describe the model of embodied subjectivity he argues for in his central works, *The Structure of Behaviour* and *The Phenomenology of Perception* (Merleau-Ponty, 1962, 1965). Like many of Merleau-Ponty's most interesting innovations, the concept emerges as a dialectical[10] 'third term', mediating between what he takes to be unsatisfactory dichotomies or oppositions within or between the work of other writers. One key

11

---

10 What 'dialectical' means in this context is that Merleau-Ponty formulates his ideas by way of a critique of either opposing philosophical viewpoints or philosophical dualisms which divide the world or some part of it into a binary opposition: e.g. mind/body, subject/object, freedom/determinism. Typically Merleau-Ponty will show how both 'sides' in such oppositions are conceptually inadequate and will seek out a superior position or concept which combines elements of both (a 'third term' as I have called it here).

dichotomy addressed by the concept of the body-subject is that between mind and body ('mind/body dualism'), as famously argued for at the dawn of modern philosophy by René Descartes. Writing in the early 1600s, Descartes (1969) believed that mind and body are two completely different substances and that human beings are composed of these two substances (see Crossley, 2001a). Very few contemporary philosophers advocate mind/body dualism. Merleau-Ponty is hardly unique in his opposition to it. His critique and alternative are relatively unique and certainly interesting, however. We can begin our exposition with this.

Merleau-Ponty (1965) first tackles mind/body dualism in *The Structure of Behaviour*. If we separate mind and body as distinct substances, as Descartes does, he notes, we generate a range of irresolvable philosophical problems; not least of which is that of how these two radically different 'substances' fit together and interact[11] within the context of the whole person, as we know that they do.[12] Monism, the view that we are made up of one substance rather than two, is clearly a more persuasive position. Furthermore, if we agree that we are made up of only one substance rather than two then it is most plausible to suggest that this substance is 'body' since it is self-evident to all but the most sceptical of philosophers that we are physical beings. Merleau-Ponty thus agrees with most contemporary philosophers that human beings are not composed of both a body and a separate mind but

---

11 The body, for Descartes, is a substance which extends into space, is divisible and which obeys the laws of the natural world. The mind does not extend into space, is indivisible, does not obey the laws of the natural world and more positively, it thinks. Defined in this way it is very difficult to see how the two could ever interact. How, for example, is it possible for the body to obey the laws of the natural world but also to interact and be affected by a substance which does not obey those laws? Either the body obeys the laws of nature, in which case it is not influenced by 'spirits', or it is steered by an immaterial mind but therefore does not (always) obey the laws of physical nature. To obey the laws of nature only some of the time is not really to obey them at all, since obeying them means always obeying them and never behaving in other ways which defy them – which is what being moved by immaterial spirits would entail. Similarly it is difficult to imagine how interaction between mind and body could be mediated, given that the body is spatial and moves by way of the application of external force to it, and the mind is not spatial and therefore could not touch or apply force to it. The real problem here stems from the fact that experiences such as perception, which involve both consciousness (mind) and physical parts of the body (sensory organs), clearly indicate that mind and body, in the unlikely situation that they are separate things, do in fact interact. This gives us good reason to reject mind/body dualism. Put succinctly the argument would be as follows. Ordinary experience teaches us that mental and physical processes tend to work together in harmony; therefore, if mind and body are separate substances they must interact; however, the way that Descartes defines mind and body makes it impossible for them to interact; therefore, they cannot be separate in the first place, at least not in the way that Descartes suggests.

12 See above.

---

rather consist of a body only. However, a materialist monism, that is, a monism which claims that all we are is a body, is very problematic if we adopt Descartes' view of the body. Descartes viewed the body as a mechanical object akin to a wind up doll, an object whose movements can be explained in terms of simple, physical cause-effect relationships. The body is an object of perception and action for Descartes. It is perceived and acted upon from the outside. But it is not a subject or site of experience. It does not perceive and act itself. Indeed, Leder (1998) has argued that the Cartesian body is simply 'meat', a 'corpse'. This account of 'the body' does not gel with our experience of our own lives. Neither does it gel with scientific evidence on the behaviour of even quite basic organisms, never mind human organisms (Merleau-Ponty, 1965; Goldstein, 2000; Buytendijk, 1974). And it evidently does not even fit with Descartes' view of human beings, which is why he sought to add 'mind' to his rather impoverished conception of the body in his broader conception of human beings (Husserl, 1970a; Leder, 1990; Ryle, 1949). As he says himself:

I am not this assemblage of limbs called the human body; I am not a thin and penetrating air spread through all these members . . . (1969: 105)

We have a problem then. We cannot say that human beings are composed of two substances, mind and body, as that leads to many philosophical problems. And yet the most likely candidate for a 'one substance solution', the body, does not seem to work either. Or rather, it does not if we stick to Descartes' definition of 'the body'.

The way out of this situation, in the first instance, for Merleau-Ponty, is to argue that the mental life of human beings is not a separate 'substance' attached to the body but rather an 'emergent structure'[13] growing out of the 'whole' constituted by the organism (taken as a whole) in interaction with its environment. The organism-environment forms a whole whose dynamics and properties are best explained on their own level, a psychological level, and which cannot be understood or explained

13

---

13 The concept of emergent structures derives from the philosophy of science. It is used to denote situations in which a combination of distinct elements gives rise to processes, dynamics and effects which can only or at least are best explained by reference to the structure formed by those elements, rather than by reference to the properties of their individual elements. In this case, for example, the various parts of the human body and its environment, as combined by way of behaviour, take on a life of their own, a life which has to be understood on its own terms and cannot be reduced back to individual, biological parts of the body. Merleau-Ponty does not use the term 'emergent structures' but his argument in *The Structure of Behaviour* effectively describes just this.

---

**Body-subject**

if we break the whole back down into its constituent parts. In particular, drawing upon the evidence of the above-mentioned scientific studies, as well as the psychological research of his day, Merleau-Ponty argues: firstly, that the various parts of the body interact in a mutually complementary and systematic way in the context of human behaviour and that this lends behaviour a structure which cannot be explained by reference to atomistic accounts of those individual parts; secondly, that there is purposiveness to human behaviour, a degree of goal orientation, which again cannot be explained by reference to isolated physical parts of the body but only the (whole) body-environment structure; thirdly, that the interaction of organism and environment is mediated by 'meaning' which, in the human case, includes symbolic meaning. The same 'stimuli' can elicit very different responses from the organism, he notes, in accordance with the context in which it appears, and thus the meaning it assumes. Moreover, in the human case the meaning of stimuli is shaped by their encoding within symbolic systems of various kinds, particularly language. Finally, Merleau-Ponty argues that within this dynamic structure the emergent property of consciousness takes shape. The organism perceives its environment. It becomes aware of its environment such that this environment exists for it as an aspect of its experience. This clearly distinguishes living, organic bodies, such as the human body,[14] from inorganic matter, such as a lump of lead – the latter of which would more readily fit Descartes' description of 'the body'.[15] Lumps of lead do just have a 'thing like' existence. They cannot perceive or act on their own account and so on. Like Descartes' 'body' they can only be perceived and acted upon from an external perspective. Organic bodies, by contrast, are aware of their environment and interact with it such that it can be said to exist for them.

The body-world whole that Merleau-Ponty refers to here is not a 'mind' in the Cartesian sense, and that is a good thing since there are many other problems with the Cartesian conception of 'mind' aside from that of its irreconcilability with the body (see Crossley, 2001a). Rather it is a system which gives rise to an agent who is oriented to meanings, animated by purposes and conscious of its world. This embodied agent,

---

14 All animal bodies are different from the Cartesian body according to Merleau-Ponty, simply in virtue of them being alive, capable of perception, action, etc. However, the complexity of their 'structures of behaviour' and thus of perception and consciousness do vary widely, with human organisms being the most complex and advanced.
15 To be fair to Descartes, his concept of 'the body', as I note below, is not intended to refer only to the human body but rather to all material bodies, including inorganic matter. This lack of discrimination on his part is perhaps part of the problem with his account.

a psychological whole greater than the sum of its physical parts, is the first approximation of 'the body-subject' that we find in Merleau-Ponty's work.

In *The Phenomenology of Perception*, Merleau-Ponty builds upon this, developing an argument of the founder of modern phenomenology, Edmund Husserl. Husserl (1970a) observes that Descartes' case for dualism is based upon the fact that he is able, for philosophical purposes, to doubt the existence of his body but not of his mind. It is theoretically possible, he suggests, that he is just a mind who is dreaming or hallucinating that he has a body. Given this, he continues, his body and mind must be different 'substances' – how else could he doubt the existence of one without doubting the existence of the other? This argument emerges in a context where Descartes, troubled by the prejudices which infect ordinary thought and keen to establish a certain basis for science, has elected to doubt the existence of all that he cannot be certain of in an effort to discover an indubitable point of truth on which to ground science and philosophy. To do this, of course, he must stand outside of received scientific and philosophical truths, as well as the common sense of his day, and appeal solely to that which is immediately self-evident. This, Husserl argues, is where his argument breaks down because his doubting of the existence of his body is not based upon an indubitable experience of a disembodied mental life but rather upon a pre-conception of the body, a prejudice which was shaped by both his religious context and the scientific concept of 'matter' which was emerging at the time he was writing (the early 1600s). Both of these historically specific cultural sources define 'the body', as we noted above, in such a way that it excludes much of what we ordinarily associate with mental life and they thereby generate the need for a separate concept of (a separate) mind – which, in the case of religious dogma, already exists in the form of the immortal soul. Descartes is thus insufficiently rigorous in his philosophical reasoning. He lets prejudices about the body shape his reasoning and effectively ends up with a circular argument which uses scientific and religious ideas to ground science. Mind/body dualism is one side-effect of this flawed philosophical venture.

The concept of the body or 'matter' that Descartes borrows is not necessarily wrong, Husserl continues, but it is an abstraction, a partial view which draws certain features of bodies to the fore, in particular features which even the most basic forms of inanimate matter share, to the detriment of others. The key to the problem of dualism, therefore, requires us to rethink 'matter', adding back in those of its aspects which

15

the Cartesian conception neglects – Merleau-Ponty (1968a) begins to address this in *The Visible and the Invisible* where he outlines a concept of 'the flesh'.[16] More importantly, however, on the basis of his own phenomenological analysis of his conscious experience, Husserl (1973) draws the conclusion, contra Descartes, that our conscious life is irreducibly embodied. If we focus in an unprejudiced fashion upon our conscious existence, he argues, then it is inseparable from our bodily life. It is this insight that Merleau-Ponty builds upon in *The Phenomenology of Perception*.

Descartes' philosophy suggests that our bodies are objects, distinct from and experienced by us, Merleau-Ponty notes. We experience our bodies, in the Cartesian schema, as we experience all other physical objects in the world. Such experiences are, of course, possible. By means of mirrors, photography, the fashion industry and the comments and looks of others, we are made aware of our bodies as 'external objects'. Our primary experience of our body is not like this, however. We do not experience our bodies, as such. Rather, our experiences are embodied. Perception, for example, is a sensuous experience. It consists of felt sensations – the discomfort caused by glaring lights, booming sound, red hot chilli sauce and scalding water illustrate this. But our body is the site of these experiences, the subject of them, rather than the object experienced. Or rather, these sensations generate a perceptual subject. What we perceive are objects external to the boundaries of our body. Perceptual consciousness, qua sensational experience, is, in phenomenological parlance, an intentional experience. It is not consciousness of itself but rather consciousness of something outside of itself, something which transcends it. We do not perceive 'sensations'.[17] We 'have' sensations and by means of them we perceive a world outside of ourselves; or rather we perceive specific objects and situations within that world. In this sense, to reiterate, our body is not, as Descartes

16 I am not going to discuss 'the flesh' here because it will unnecessarily complicate things. Suffice it to say that Merleau-Ponty formulates this concept as a way of rethinking the material nature of the world in a manner which transcends Cartesian and related conceptions of 'matter', and more specifically in a manner which captures the 'mindful' and conscious aspects of material/organic life.

17 Even pain conforms to this analysis. Many painful experiences 'intend' an object which is the source of that pain (e.g. the sharp blade which has cut us or the heavy object which has landed on our toe). And even when this is not so, the body does not appear to us in painful experiences as an external agent which somehow acts upon us to cause us pain. Rather, the body is the site of our pain. Although we might say, 'my hand hurts', we do not mean 'my hand is the cause of my pain' (as we do when we say 'these new shoes hurt'), we mean rather that we are experiencing pain in the 'hand region' of our self.

suggests, an object of our experience but rather the very basis and site of our experience. It is our bodies which perceive or rather we are our bodies and it is as bodies that we perceive.

Extending this point further, Merleau-Ponty argues that we perceive objects and situations from the vantage point, the point of view, constituted by our embodied presence and involvement in the world, and that we must necessarily do so. A 'view from nowhere' is inconceivable and certainly does not match anything in our own experience. To perceive is to stand somewhere in relation to a perceived object, at a distance and an angle, differentiating a foreground and a background.[18] Our body is our somewhere. It situates us in relationship to our world such that we can perceive it and, as such, it is integral to our experience.

In a similar vain Merleau-Ponty notes that we do not move our bodies in the same way that we move objects in the world. We do not do anything 'in order' to move them and could not say, for sure, how we move them. I do not know how I move my larynx when I sing in the bath or how I move my hands when typing. They 'just move'. And I am not aware of wanting to do these things and then making an effort to do so. I do not think to myself that I would like to move my legs and then move them. My body just moves or rather I qua body just move. This is quite different from my experience of moving objects in the world, such as tables. When moving objects, especially large objects, I often size them up, plan my approach and of course I do something in order to move them – namely grasp them, lift them, then lug them.[19] Again then my 'experience'[20] of my body is revealed to be quite different from my experience of external objects and Descartes' tendency to think of it as an object is problematized. I do not experience my body in the same way that I experience objects in the external world and the basic assumption of Descartes' argument of dualism is thus revealed, phenomenologically, to be wrong.

---

18 Try to imagine what it would be like to see a three-dimensional object, such as a house, a cube or another person, without doing so from a particular point of view or perspective. That would involve seeing the object from every side at once but also somehow not seeing it with 'sides' at all. If you can, you should perhaps consult your doctor or a contemporary philosopher!

19 This point is not quite so straightforward as Merleau-Ponty does believe that we can develop the same kind of automatic relationship to objects in the world as we have to our bodies but for the present purposes the argument will have to suffice.

20 The term 'experience' is not quite right here, as Merleau-Ponty's point is that we do not experience our bodies as such. Rather, as noted earlier, the body is the site of our experience and our conscious experience, by and large, is experience of a world which transcends our own individual bodily being.

Continuing this point Merleau-Ponty notes how the various 'parts' of the body are co-ordinated with one another and how the body as a whole, in both perception and action, is co-ordinated with its environment. The 'same' action can have very different consequences for an organism depending upon the posture it is in at the time, he notes. What keeps the body in balance in one position might throw it off balance in another. But the body works in an integrated way, the left hand seeming always to know what the right is doing – and what the legs, trunk, head, and so on are doing. If I need to move my arms in a particular way but doing so would throw me off balance, then my legs will move first to give me the posture I need to safely move my arms. And this happens without conscious intervention. This self-possession of the body seemingly works in parallel with the body's grasp upon its immediate environment. If the ground moves beneath our feet, for example, or an obstacle appears before us, we automatically shift our posture. And again this happens without conscious intervention. Body and world work together, independently of conscious/reflective thought, as an integrated system.

In these cases we act, qua bodies, in a meaningful and purposive way without the intervention of reflective thought and often with a form of knowledge or understanding that is not consciously available to us. We do not consciously reflect or think before acting and yet our action betrays a degree of understanding and knowledge (both of the body itself and of the environment) and is quite clearly not a mechanistic reaction to some stimuli. This is a crucial aspect of Merleau-Ponty's concept of the body-subject. Moreover, he extends it to include a consideration of our knowledge and understanding of cultural situations and objects. I do not know in a reflective sense where the various letters are on the word-processor keyboard, for example. I could not tell you, without looking or perhaps trying to type it, where the letter 'K' is. But I can type. Indeed I just typed the letter 'K' without having to search for it. My fingers 'know' the keyboard layout and when I need 'K' one of them heads off in the right direction without my conscious intervention. Obviously I have had to learn this. It is, Merleau-Ponty argues, a 'habit'. And much of the action of the body-subject is habitual in Merleau-Ponty's view. He is very clear, however, to distinguish his conception of habit from the vulgar mechanistic conceptions that figure in much of the literature. Habit is not a mechanical reaction, he argues. It is, as just noted, a form of understanding and knowledge which is utilized in the context of purposive action. To have acquired a habit is to have 'grasped' the principles and prerequisites necessary to participation in a particular mode of activity.

Consider, as a further example of this, a squash player returning a tricky shot in a fast moving game. To play squash an individual must first learn to do so. They must learn what the objective of the game is and what the rules are. They must learn how to hold the racquet, learn a variety of shots (for example, forehand, backhand, overhead serve, 'spin') and develop their hand to eye co-ordination. Within the context of a game, however, they will have a split second in which to race into a position from which they can return the ball, take a shot from that position (a position they may never have tried in practice) and leave the ball, strategically, in a place which is allowed under the rules but which will make it very difficult for the opponent to return the ball. They must act in a way which is skilful and strategic in terms of the requirements of the game, manifesting thus an understanding and knowledge of the game, and they must do so 'without thinking' – since there is no time to think. Of course squash players do this all of the time, as do football players, netball players, and in a different way guitarists, typists, car drivers and even pedestrians (see Crossley, 1995b). As embodied beings we are constantly making our way through physically and socially complex environments which we understand in an embodied and practical way, such that we can act effectively without having to think about them. This capacity and tendency, the combination of acquired habit, defined as practical knowledge and understanding, and purposive action, is integral to the concept of the body-subject. The body-subject is, as Merleau-Ponty also puts it, a 'habit body'.

The habitual nature of the body-subject and its habitual sense of itself, which Merleau-Ponty also sometimes talks about under the rubric of 'the corporeal schema', are often best revealed in instances where they slip out of alignment with objective dimensions of body and world. Iris Young (1998), for example, notes how the rapid bodily changes associated with pregnancy sometimes generate a situation in which a woman's actual bodily size/shape and capabilities do not match her habitual sense of them, such that her attempts to act in particular ways are confounded. She does not slip through a gap that she attempts, and would previously have been able to slip through, for example, or she finds that she lacks the speed or stamina to perform an action that she had not questioned her ability to perform. Her habitual actions still assume that her body is as it was before she was pregnant and the realization that it is not only kicks in, in such contexts, when an action based upon this assumption goes wrong as a consequence of the

19

assumption. In a similar vain, if one buys a new car or another piece of everyday equipment one can experience numerous problems as one's habitual 'feel' for the old is transposed onto the new, where it does not quite suffice. The point here, of course, is that we all rely upon such assumptions and habits all of the time but only realize that we are doing so when unusual circumstances render our habits and assumptions inappropriate.

What Merleau-Ponty is arguing in this respect is also very similar to what Heidegger (1962) talks about under the rubric of 'readiness-of-hand'. Both philosophers want to draw our attention to the very basic, practical grasp which human beings have upon the world prior to any reflective or conceptual understanding. They seek to draw our attention to forms of knowledge and understanding which consist entirely in specific types of practical mastery and which, as such, are irreducibly embodied. The world, they are suggesting to us, is not first of all something that we have reflective knowledge of but rather something that we are practically entangled in and have some degree of mastery over.

Of course much human action is conscious and reflective. However, Merleau-Ponty (1962) argues that reflective activities presuppose the pre-reflective activity of the 'body-subject'. I do not have the space to elaborate at length upon this point here. It must suffice to say that in Merleau-Ponty's view, conscious and reflective activity presuppose perception and the use of language, and that both perception and language use, in turn, presuppose the pre-reflective activity of the body-subject. We first become aware of our thoughts, reflectively, in linguistic form, for example. Thinking is, in a sense, a matter of talking to ourselves. We must speak, without knowing what we are going to say, in order to find out what it is that we want to say – even if we do so sub-vocally, so as to compose our thoughts before inflicting them upon others. This requires a pre-reflective mobilization of our (acquired) capacity to speak. We must, by definition, speak without thinking – and we sometimes become aware that we are doing this, as in cases where we surprise ourselves by what we 'say'. So reflective thought therefore has a pre-reflective, habitual basis. Similarly, numerous studies of perception reveal that it is not a straightforward matter of becoming conscious of what is 'out there' but rests rather upon pre-reflective and habitual interpretative activity by the perceiving agent.

From a sociological point of view it is important to draw out two more features from this account. Firstly, we should note that the body-subject is less an actor more an inter-actor; that is to say, Merleau-Ponty is

**20**

crucially concerned with the way in which human behaviour or action forms a 'system' with its environment. Insofar as other people belong to that environment this is clearly a social system. Agent a's actions are a response to agent b's actions and b's are a response to a's such that the two interlock in an irreducible fashion. Secondly we should note that Merleau-Ponty develops his ideas in what we would now call a 'structurationist' direction. The body-subject, he notes, acquires the competence to act within specific social contexts. It learns the 'rules of the game', as in the squash example. However, as in the squash game the social world depends for its own existence upon the skilled and competent activities of the body-subject. Social agents must learn to play the 'games' which comprise the social world but those games only exist by virtue of the activities of those who play them. Having 'incorporated' the structures of the social world the body-subject then reproduces those structures in its own actions. This is easily demonstrated with respect to sport and perhaps also language (which we must learn in order to speak it and yet which must be spoken in order to exist) but it applies to all structured activities in the social world according to Merleau-Ponty.

Another dualism which Merleau-Ponty seeks to challenge by way of the concept of the body-subject is Sartre's (1969) distinction between being in-itself and being for-itself.[21] Where, for Sartre, human existence is radically distinct from the existence of things, being pure consciousness, transcendence and freedom (see **freedom**), Merleau-Ponty strives for a more balanced view. Our embodiment roots us in the world, he argues, it counterbalances the transcendence that Sartre writes of and makes us vulnerable. In part this is a matter of physical vulnerability. As bodies we are vulnerable to illness, death and injury. Furthermore, our bodies literally situate us physically within time-space and structure our experience and action-potential by virtue of their structure. In addition, however, the body is our way of being in and belonging to the social world. By putting the emphasis that he does upon habit and upon the social nature of habit, Merleau-Ponty seeks to show that we are very strongly rooted in society and history; that is, in particular communities or social groups who constitute the context wherein our habits take

21

21 This concept is dealt with in more detail in the entry on 'freedom'. For present purposes note that Sartre (1969) argues that the way in which human beings 'exist' is very different from the way in which 'things' exist, not least because the world exists for human beings but it does not exist for 'objects'. Clearly Merleau-Ponty agrees that there is a difference but, as noted above, he does not believe that human beings are as different from other 'things' as Sartre suggests.

shape. This does not entail a notion of human beings as 'cultural dopes', mere products of circumstance. As the example of the squash player shows, we behave strategically and innovatively. But as that example also shows, even as we do so we pre-reflectively draw upon acquired skills and a tacit knowledge or understanding of the type of situation that we are in ('the game'). Our action falls somewhere between a mechanical response and a spontaneous burst of free will – see the entry on **freedom** for further elaboration of this.

Merleau-Ponty's account has attracted a number of criticisms, many of which, in my view, miss the mark (see Crossley, 2001d for a brief summary). However, one very important line of criticism has come from feminists who are quite sympathetic to Merleau-Ponty's argument but object to his tendency to assume that his descriptions of bodily experience are gender neutral. Iris Young (1980, 1998) in particular, for example, argues that Merleau-Ponty's account assumes that agents enjoy an unproblematic relationship to their embodiment. This may be true of men, she argues, but it is not equally so for women, whose embodiment is mediated by way of the objectification of the female body in western culture. Women's movements, for example, are much less fluid, according to Young, because women must always seek to protect themselves against unwanted attention. Women tend to minimize their movement and bodily extension in a fashion which can be detrimental to their practical agency because they are made self-conscious by the looks and unwanted attention of men. Moreover, women internalize the tendency to judge and closely inspect the female form, applying this to themselves in such a way that they can never feel comfortable about their bodies, as Merleau-Ponty's account assumes. Similarly Judith Butler (1989) has noted that Merleau-Ponty's account of sexuality (not discussed here but still relevant to his conception of the body-subject) assumes a male, heterosexual subject. It would be incorrect, I believe, to suggest that Merleau-Ponty allows for no bodily differences in his account. He does tentatively discuss class differences, for example, and there is at least an implicit reflection upon disabled or impaired bodies in his account.[22] However, one might extend this feminist critique by pointing to the relevance of 'race' in relation to lived embodiment, as, for example, Fanon (1993) was to do.

22 Merleau-Ponty builds an account of 'normal' bodily experience, in part, through a contrast with the case of 'Schneider', a brain injured war veteran whose experience departs from the norm in important respects. This is a far cry from an engagement with disability and certainly does not engage with the social model of disability (which a comprehensive account should) but it at least indicates an acknowledgement of bodily differences.

Descartes' *Meditations* (1969) are fascinating and very important to the history of philosophy. They are also quite brief and relatively easy to read. Merleau-Ponty's major relevant works, *The Phenomenology of Perception* and *The Structure of Behaviour*, are pretty heavy going by undergraduate standards and presuppose quite a lot of prior knowledge of both philosophy and psychology. Though I will not make a habit of it in this collection I recommend my own book, *The Social Body* (Crossley, 2001a), on these issues, and also my paper, 'Merleau-Ponty' (Crossley, 2001d), for those who wish to set Merleau-Ponty's work in wider context.

# Body-power/Bio-power

*Related concepts: **ideology, power, power/knowledge.***

The concepts of 'body-power' and 'bio-power', along with related terms such as 'anatomo-politics' and 'disciplinary power,' were coined by the French philosopher and historian, Michel Foucault, in his effort both to chart the main forms of power in modern western societies and to challenge the way in which both liberal political theorists and more radically inclined thinkers tend to conceptualize power. For our purposes it will suffice to say that Foucault sets out to challenge two conventions which tend to shape our understanding of power (see **power** for a fuller account).

The first, which is discussed in more detail in the entry on **power**, is the tendency to conceptualize power as a commodity, capacity or 'thing-like' entity which can be concentrated into the hands of such entities as, for example, the state, political elites or the ruling class. Arguing against this tendency, Foucault suggests that we should consider how the effects of power are produced; how, in practical terms, individuals and populations are acted upon so as to fit them to the demands of elites and the status quo more generally. In redefining power analysis in this way Foucault does not mean to deny that some groups do much better out of the status quo than others, but rather that identifying beneficiaries actually does very little to advance our understanding of the workings of power. Furthermore, his hostility towards traditional understandings of 'the subject'[23] incline him to see 'powerful individuals' as products of the various technologies of power. Power, as a property of social relationships, generates powerful agents, not vice versa.

The second notion that Foucault seeks to criticize is the notion that 'power' and social order are exclusively or even primarily secured through 'ideas' or 'consciousness'. Thus, on one hand, he opposes the idea of the 'social contract' advanced by many of the key political theorists of the early modern period and tacitly accepted by many more recent social theorists, such as Talcott Parsons (1951) – that is, the idea that social order and various forms of 'power' (or authority) derive from a consensus amongst citizens with respect to key values and the norms and political goals that should be derived from them. On the other hand he is opposed to those (in his view) 'less sophisticated' theories of ideology which propose that social order is maintained because citizens are duped by powerful groups who propagate various false ideas and beliefs about the nature of the social world. What these two approaches share in common is the view that social order is secured through the conscious consent of individuals. Against this, Foucault argues that power works at a much more basic and pre-conscious level, upon the bodies of individuals:

> I believe the great fantasy is the idea of a social body constituted by the universality of wills. Now the phenomenon of the social body is the effect not of a consensus but of the materiality of power operating on the very bodies of individuals (1980: 55)
>
> . . . one must set aside the widely held thesis that power, in our bourgeois, capitalist societies has denied the reality of the body in favour of the soul, consciousness, ideality [i.e. ideology]. In fact nothing is more material, physical, corporal, than the exercise of power. What mode of investment of the body is necessary and adequate for the functioning of a capitalist society like ours? (1980: 57–8)

What matters, Foucault argues, is not what people think but how they behave habitually, and how the prerequisites of liberal order become engrained in their habits. Power, in the form of a myriad of techniques whose history and effects Foucault unearths in *Discipline and Punish*, invests the body, forming the body in a manner presupposed by liberal societies. The nineteenth century, in particular, saw the growth of a

---

23 In this case, hostility towards 'the subject' is hostility towards any theoretical approach which presupposes the existence of an agent, collective or individual, characterized by properties, including 'power', which are assumed to be or treated as if they pre-exist the situation of that agent in a configuration of relations with others.

---

massive range of techniques for manipulating and managing human conduct, from timetables and new forms of architecture, through 'token economies'[24] and 'scientific management'[25] to 'moral treatments'[26] of madness. Insofar as these techniques seep into everyday life, becoming unnoticed but remaining effective, liberal order is reproduced at a level beyond conscious debate. And debate is thus rendered incapable of levelling a challenge to order. Indeed in *Discipline and Punish* Foucault argues that liberal democracies can only afford to be democracies because the compliance they presuppose for their perpetuation is secured at this microcosmic and habitual level. This moulding of the body at the level of the social microcosm is what Foucault is referring to when he talks of 'body-power'.

Integral to the techniques of behavioural control that Foucault describes are techniques of surveillance. In the ancien régime,[27] he argues, techniques of power worked by means of their own visibility. To be powerful was to be visible and to announce one's presence and power in a visible way, for example, through grand castles or churches which intimidated one's 'subjects'; through the public execution or flogging of those who broke one's rules, a measure which reminded all spectators of the fate of deviants and of one's might; and through portraits and written accounts which recorded and celebrated one's existence and the events of one's life – only the rich and powerful were written about or painted in the feudal era, Foucault notes. In the modern context, however, this situation is reversed. Everybody's life is studied in great detail, examined and recorded. New forms of power function, particularly, by making the

24  Token economies were a common feature in the 'special schools' and mental hospitals of the late nineteenth and early twentieth centuries (they still persist today, though to a lesser extent). They involve the rewarding of good behaviour with tokens and the punishment of bad behaviour by the removal of tokens (a fine). Tokens, in turn, can then be spent once or twice a week on a range of goods from a 'tuck shop' or its equivalent.

25  A technique of management which involves breaking activities down into their smallest elements, working out the most efficient way of performing them effectively, and often timing work to check that workers are keeping pace. So-called 'time and motion' studies form part of this managerial approach. Aspects of the approach are still practised today and have been very widespread in the past.

26  Moral treatments of madness emerged in the late eighteenth and early nineteenth centuries. They were based upon the view, derived in some part from John Locke, that madness derived from faulty learning and that the key to curing it was to 're-educate' the patient. This also often involved an insistence upon 'trusting' the patient to do the right thing and controlling them by means of a reprimanding and watchful look (rather than the whips and chains which were the more usual means prior to the late eighteenth century). In Britain this development was associated particularly with the York Retreat, which Foucault discusses, along with equivalent French developments, in his *Madness and Civilisation* (1965).

27  In the French case this means prior to the 1789 revolution. More generally it refers to the order of the feudal societies of the Middle Ages.

body a visible and knowable object. In part this works by encouraging self-surveillance. Agents internalize external surveillance, such that they become self-policing. In part, however, it is effective to the extent that a powerful body of knowledge for manipulation of the body is generated.

Related to this, body-power is a positive form of power. That is to say, where techniques of power in the ancien régime worked negating the body, denying bodily desires or impulses, inflicting pain or damage and, in some cases, taking life, body-power aims to mould the body in the manner required by society, fostering life and bodily potential. It does not deny the nature of the body – Foucault does not believe in a stable human nature in any case – but rather attempts to shape the body and its dispositions in specific and desired ways. It aims to promote healthy, efficient and effective bodies, relative to the identified needs of society.

Defined in this way 'body-power' is not merely a concept of power. It is equally a concept of the body. For Foucault the body is not a self-contained biological/physiological system. It is historically constituted:

> We believe, in any event, that the body obeys the exclusive laws of physiology and that it escapes the influence of history, but this too is false. The body is broken down by a great many distinct regimes; it is broken down by the rhythms of work, rest and holidays; it is poisoned by food or values, through eating habits or moral laws; it constructs resistances. Nothing in man – not even his body – is sufficiently stable to serve as a basis for self-recognition or for understanding other men. (1980b: 153)

> ... the body is ... directly involved in the political field; power relations have an immediate hold upon it; they invest it, mark it, train it, torture it, force it to carry out tasks, to perform ceremonies, to emit signs ... (1979: 25)

Furthermore, he maintains that the mastery we enjoy over our own bodies and the awareness, the self-consciousness, which reflexively loops us back to our bodies are each effects of the investment of our bodies by power:

> Mastery and awareness of one own body can be acquired only through the effect of an investment of power in the body; gymnastics, exercises, muscle building, glorification of the body beautiful. All of this belongs to the pathway leading to the desire of one's own body, by way of the insistent, persistent, meticulous work of power on the bodies of children or soldiers, the healthy bodies. But once power produces this effect, there inevitably emerge corresponding claims and affirmations, those of one's own body against power, of health against the economic system, of pleasure against the moral norms of sexuality, marriage, decency. Suddenly, what had made power strong becomes used to attack it. Power, after investing itself in the body, finds itself exposed to counter-attack in the same body. (1980a: 56)

**Body-power/Bio-power**

As this quotation also indicates, however, the investment of power in the body can generate resistance. Having become invested in our bodies in a variety of ways, we are then pre-disposed to make claims (for example, upon the state) relating to our investment. Having been made healthy and health conscious, for example, we protest about the way in which aspects of our society are detrimental to our health.

In *Discipline and Punish*, Foucault discusses the technologies and discourses which produce and control bodies at the individual level (or perhaps rather which individualize[28] bodies and construct a sense of 'the individual'). In the first volume of his *History of Sexuality*, however, he begins to explore the same processes as they construct and manipulate whole populations, for example technologies of population control, public health and welfare strategies, census surveillance, and so on (Foucault, 1984). He refers to this higher level network of practices and discourses as 'bio-power'. Where power in the ancien régime was the power to take life, both through execution and by ordering one's subjects to fight for one in war (an obligation which obviously still exists for members of the armed forces and can still be brought to bear upon ordinary citizens who are deemed suitable to fight), he argues, power in modern societies is primarily focused upon preserving and cultivating life, as well as monitoring and recording it. In modern societies, states, as the key agents of bio-power, seek both to manipulate the environment of their citizens, so as to generate health, but also to influence the behaviour of populations, *en masse*, so as to both preserve health and maintain demographic norms.

The concepts of body-power and bio-power are each important and interesting. Some, including myself, however, have criticized Foucault's tendency to view the body as infinitely plastic or, as some see it, to rock between a view of infinite plasticity, on one hand, and Dionysian libidinal excess[29] on the other (Levin, 1989; Burkitt, 1999; Crossley, 1994, 1996b). Although it is possible to read some of Foucault's brief and occasional comments on the 'resistance' of the body to various forms of body or bio-

---

28 In the ancien régime, Foucault argues, 'the people' formed an anonymous mass. They were the crowd who gathered to cheer and jeer at public executions. Modern disciplinary power separates the mass, however, breaking them down into smaller groupings and ultimately to the level of the individual. It 'knows' each body as an individual, with a history, etc. This is integral to its efficacy.
29 Some readings of Foucault (e.g. Levin, 1989; Burkitt, 1999) suggests that he rocks between a historicist view of the body as a tabula rasa, 'totally imprinted by history', and a view of the body as a seat of potentially socially disruptive drives and desires. This latter view is said to derive from the influence of the philosopher Nietzsche upon Foucault.

power as an indication that he does not believe the body to be completely plastic, he fails to consider either the extent of resistance to attempts to mould behaviour or, conversely, the fixed capacities of the body which make it amenable to training in the first place. Plasticity and the capacity to learn are, as Elias (1978) has argued, aspects of human nature qua nature. They make the human body different from other bodies. Furthermore, order cannot be imposed upon a body which does not already manifest some degree of order. It is only because the body is always already co-ordinated and managed that it is manageable. How seriously one takes these observations depends upon one's interests and perspective but they should be taken as a warning to any who would claim, as Foucault does, that the body is a wholly historical phenomenon and has no 'nature'.

## FURTHER READING

Much of Foucault's work is quite easy to read and is certainly easier than that of those who write commentaries about him. For 'body-power' the key references are *Discipline and Punish* (Foucault, 1979) and the various interviews and lectures in *Power/Knowledge* (Foucault, 1980a). Bio-power is discussed in the first volume of his *History of Sexuality* (Foucault, 1984).

# Capital (in the work of Pierre Bourdieu)

28

> *Related concepts:* **fields, habitus, hexis, social capital, social class, social space.**

The concept of capital derives from economics, where it refers to money and property or indeed anything which has a monetary value. Recently, however, thinkers both within and outside of economics have begun to explore different types of 'capital' than monetary or economic capital; that is to say, they have begun to reflect upon forms of resources available to agents whose value is not strictly reducible to money. Within economics, the work of Gary Becker (1996) is central in this respect. Outside of economics, however, the key theorist of these forms of capital is Pierre Bourdieu. It is Bourdieu's work that we will consider here.

Perhaps the most straightforward definition of Bourdieu's capital that I can offer is that the concept categorizes different sorts of resources that social agents can mobilize in pursuit of their projects and which, on account of their value, agents will tend to seek to pursue and accumulate. Another way of looking at it might be to say that the forms of capital are so many axes along which agents can be said to be (dis)advantaged relative to one another. This will become clearer if we consider the four main types of capital identified in Bourdieu's work.

### ECONOMIC CAPITAL

This refers to an agent's income, their accumulated wealth and the monetary value of whatever goods they posses (especially property, land, and so on). This form of capital is generated in and by the economic field[30] but, of course, that field permeates most others making economic capital an important resource in most social contexts. It is also an extremely rationalized form of capital, in the sense that it assumes a quantified (or readily quantifiable) form (namely money or monetary value). This makes it easy, relatively speaking, for analysts to study its exchange, accumulation and so on. Of all of the forms of capital it is easiest to work out what an agent is worth in monetary terms and we can trace flows of economic capital, as well as such economic dynamics as inflation, in a relatively precise fashion.

### CULTURAL CAPITAL

Perhaps the best known of Bourdieu's forms of capital, this concept refers to cultural resources whose possession advantages agents. In an early paper Bourdieu suggests that cultural capital may assume one of three forms. It can assume an 'objectified' form, such as the books, paintings, CDs, and so on that an individual might own. It can assume an 'institutionalized' form, by which he means educational qualifications in particular. And it can assume an 'embodied' form, in the sense that one might have culturally valued competences (the capacity to talk

---

30 The concept of fields is defined elsewhere in the book. For present purposes read 'economy' for 'economic field'.

meaningfully about art, for example) or one might exude a valued cultural bearing in one's 'bodily hexis' or body techniques (see **hexis**), such as speaking with a 'posh' accent and conducting oneself in a 'proper' fashion. In some ways embodied cultural capital overlaps with the concept of the habitus (see **habitus**) but there is a distinction. Insofar as my capacity to understand philosophy and my love of philosophy dispose me to read it, we may speak here of my habitus and its peculiar middle-class structure. Insofar as this love of philosophy secures me further goods than those intrinsic to the enjoyment of philosophy however (such as jobs or high status as a philosophical commentator), we would do better to speak of it as cultural capital. It might be suggested that this distinction is a matter of what Marx referred to as use and exchange value.[31] What makes my embodied competence count as capital, it might be argued, is that I can use it instrumentally to procure further goods, exchanging it, rather than simply enjoying its intrinsic rewards and uses. If I simply enjoy the intrinsic rewards of my competence then this is a matter of habitus but not capital because I do not bring that competence into an exchange relationship. I have some reservations about the use of 'exchange value' in this context, however, and therefore perhaps also about the term 'capital' itself. Unlike objects of exchange, embodied competence and educational qualifications always stay with us. They are never really exchanged or spent. An agent whose 'posh accent' opens doors for them still has a posh accent after they have exploited this advantage, for example, and they can use this resource again and again. Whilst there is a difference between using one's competence for one's own enjoyment and using it instrumentally in social situations, to procure further advantages, therefore, is not quite adequately captured by the concept of exchange and perhaps not by the concept of 'capital' either. 'Resources' might be a less misleading term.

The value of cultural capital is obviously related to the cultural field, as the value of money is to the economic field, but the education system plays a particularly crucial role here. The educational system effectively defines certain cultural traits and arenas as valuable, to the detriment of others. In France in the 1960s, for example, painting and sculpture were

31 Marx argues that the objects which human beings produce can have a use value and also an exchange value. My car, for example, has a value to me on account of its usefulness. It gets me where I want to be, when I want to be there. It also has an exchange value, however, in the respect that I could sell it to make some money if I needed or wanted to. What distinguishes capitalism as an economic system, or at least one of the things that distinguishes it, Marx continues, is the fact that objects are made specifically because they have an exchange value – and not because the person making it needs it.

sanctioned as high and valuable 'arts' by the education system, but not photography or jazz, whose advocates struggled to maintain a 'middle-brow' status for them (Bourdieu, 1990b). Pop music and popular fashion, in further contrast, were not even middle brow. They were looked down upon (ibid.). Moreover, the education system institutionalizes (or rationalizes) cultural capital in the form of qualifications which, in turn, can be used to attain employment and thus money. Those who know about painting, for example, can use their knowledge to obtain qualifications which will get them a good job and a reasonable salary. Much of Bourdieu's critique of the education system is based around this idea. The education system functions to reproduce the class structure, he argues, because of the links between education and cultural capital. Middle-class children have an advantage at school because the forms of culture valued by the school, sanctioned as cultural capital and rewarded with qualifications, are forms which are more concentrated within the middle class and which they inherit from their home background and upbringing. Middle-class children have access to cultural capital from the moment they are born, in its objective form (literary classics, classical music, and so on) and they embody cultural capital in the ways in which they think, speak and act. The school 'launders' or converts this cultural advantage into qualifications which, in turn, helps middle-class children to secure good jobs. Moreover, Bourdieu maintains, both in his work on education and his work on 'taste' (Bourdieu, 1984), that the embodied nature of much cultural capital serves to naturalize and disguise forms of social disadvantage and their reproduction. Cultural acquisitions, embodied and habituated, tend to be mistaken for natural talents and distinctions, and seem therefore to legitimate the social hierarchies which, in fact, they derive from. Some people just seem, paradoxically, to be naturally cultured and thus suited to a high position, when in fact their cultured nature is just that – an outcome of a process of enculturation.

## SYMBOLIC CAPITAL

In essence this means status or recognition. To have symbolic capital is to be valued or highly regarded by others in such a way that one can procure advantages for oneself on this basis. This is much less organized or rationalized than the other forms of capital that Bourdieu refers to and it is difficult to pin it down to one specific social field. In a highly differentiated society such as our own, prestige can be localized within specific domains. One might be a leading figure in microbiology, stamp collecting or bodybuilding, extremely well known and respected within those areas, and yet unknown outside of them, such that one's kudos counts for little in wider 'markets' or fields. However, the existence of such lists as *Who's Who?* and of honours such as Nobel prizes, knighthoods, and so on, not to mention the value of celebrity, all point to the existence of forms of symbolic capital which enjoy at least some degree of general societal value.

## SOCIAL CAPITAL

Social capital is widely referred to in the contemporary literature, and perhaps more frequently associated with the work of Robert Putnam than with Bourdieu (see the separate entry on **social capital**). It is widely acknowledged that, in this broader context of usage, there are at least two different uses of 'social capital'. In both cases it refers to social networks but in the first instance it treats these networks structurally and from the point of view of the network. Analysts studying a particular geographical locale, for example, might examine the extent and intensity of civic, friendship or other such networks within that locale, couching their findings in terms of the social capital attaching to the locale. The second use conceptualizes networks as resources from the individual point of view of their members. From this point of view an individual who has many connections (such as friends or associates) has more social capital than one with only a few friends or associates. This second use is closest to Bourdieu's meaning but the real emphasis in Bourdieu's use is 'friends in high places' and 'old boy' networks. Bourdieu uses 'social capital' to render sociologically meaningful the common-sense wisdom that 'it's not what you know that counts but who you know'. Like the other forms of capital, social capital is not randomly distributed through the social body. Having been to a very exclusive private school, followed by Oxbridge, for example, (or Harvard or an École Normale Supérieure etc.), an agent is far more likely to have 'friends in high places' than one who went to a local state school and left the education system at age sixteen.

In addition to these forms of capital, Bourdieu sometimes introduces others, either as more specialized subdivisions of them or as different types altogether (for example, physical capital, linguistic capital, educational capital, political capital). Often this is related to a more field-specific focus in his work. If we focus upon particular fields, such as professional wrestling, amateur bird watching or sociology, then we increasingly discover a range of goods or resources with a relatively localized value, which have little direct value in the broader social formation. Some of these forms of capital may have an indirect value.

*Capital (in the work of Pierre Bourdieu)*

Certain of the distinctions that allow one to succeed in sociology, such as being networked to its leading figures or being responsible for a devastating critique of a well-known theory, for example, whilst they may have little value outside of sociology, may have an indirect value in the respect that professional advancement and academic titles (professor) have a value in the wider world. Other forms of capital may have no indirect value outside of their field either, however, and may even have a negative value. The distinctions that allow one to rise in the world of snail racing have little indirect value outside of the field itself, for example, since snail racing has little value, and the distinctions which elevate a drug smuggler or paedophile in his field are likely to be vilified in the wider world.

This exposition has tended to consider forms of capital as personal resources. Each individual agent or organization has a stock of various forms of capital which they can use in pursuit of their projects and which, as such, count as forms of personal power. As the entry on **social space** illustrates, however, Bourdieu also has another way of using the concept of capital (see **social space I**). Given that different forms of capital are unevenly distributed through the population of any society or field it is possible, from a more structural position, to locate agents within the social world in accordance both with the overall volume of their capital and in relation to the specific composition of that stock of capital. Some people, for example, are financially well off but not very well educated or 'cultured'. They are rich in economic capital but relatively poor in cultural capital and their power consequently derives from their economic capital. Other people are rich in cultural capital but quite poor in economic terms. Some are rich in all forms of capital, some poor, and so on. Mapping these possibilities and locating agents accordingly is a crucial step to understanding the nature of the social world in Bourdieu's view (see **social space I**).

### FURTHER READING

The clearest exposition which Bourdieu himself gives on these matters is in his paper, 'The forms of capital' (Bourdieu, 1983). *Distinction* is also a key reference for exploring the question of cultural capital (Bourdieu, 1984).

33

# Citizenship

key concepts

34

> **Related concepts: *public sphere, recognition, social class.***

A key reference point for most contemporary discussions of citizenship is T.H. Marshall's relatively early work, *Citizenship and Social Class* (Marshall and Bottomore, 1992) Marshall famously offers a tripartite model of citizenship, the three elements of which, he shows, have developed in distinct and successive stages of the history of citizenship as an institution. Citizenship, for Marshall, is a system of rights and duties, supported by key institutions dedicated to them. In the first phase of its development, which can be broadly (though not exclusively) identified with the eighteenth century, these rights, duties and institutions were developed in the civil domain; that is, the legal domain. Citizens were defined by their legal status and legal rights: for example, the right to a fair trial, protection under law, and so on. In institutional terms this involved the emergence of the early forms of the modern legal system. In the second phase, broadly corresponding to the nineteenth century, political rights were added; that is, 'the right to participate in the exercise of political power, as a member of a body invested with political authority or as an elector of the members of such a body' (ibid, p.8). This involved a reform of key political institutions. Not all groups in society gained these rights at the same time. In particular Marshall is concerned that the working class lagged far behind – women did too but this is not an issue which Marshall takes up (see below). Moreover, he maintains that these rights remained insufficient in the conditions of considerable material inequality and disadvantage, characteristic of the nineteenth century. Proper citizenship was not attained, he argues, until certain social rights, pertaining to welfare, were added to this bundle of rights and duties in the mid-twentieth century:

> By the social element I mean the whole range from the right to a modicum of economic welfare and security to the right to share to the full in the social heritage and to live the life of a civilized being according to the standards prevailing in the society. The institutions most closely connected with it are the education system and social services. (1992: 8)

Much of the emphasis in this account is upon rights. Marshall recognizes, however, as many later commentators, both academic and political, have pointed out, that rights and duties are two sides of the same coin. The rights of any one individual entail duties or obligations for all other individuals. We are required to respect the legal rights and political choices of others, for example, and to pay the taxes required by the system of welfare provision.

For the most part the relationship of rights to duties is complementary and mutually reinforcing. There cannot be rights without duties. Similarly, the three elements of citizenship – civil, political and social – work together in a mutually reinforcing fashion. If taken up, for example, the social right to education empowers the citizen to use their legal and political rights fully and effectively. However, neo-liberal and libertarian[32] writers have been critical of the growth of the welfare state on the grounds, amongst other things, that it interferes with the freedom of the individual. For these writers there is a conflict between the civil and the social aspects of citizenship. Moreover, whilst they do not generally couch their critiques in terms of citizenship, Foucauldian writers and some writers on the left (including Offe, 1993 and Habermas, 1988) echo aspects of this critique. Foucault's various accounts of 'discipline', 'body-power' and 'bio-power' (see **power** and **body-power/bio-power**) clearly focus upon and call into question the practices of the welfare state for example. Similarly, Habermas' account of the **colonization of the lifeworld** is an account of the damaging effect of the extension of the (welfare) state on everyday life, including its damaging effect upon human meaning and freedom. There is room therefore, even within critical social theory, to question the social aspect of citizenship.

Whilst Marshall is generally recognized as an important starting point for conceptualizing citizenship, it is also generally recognized that social changes since his time of writing have challenged and undermined his account in various ways, necessitating a number of revisions. The above mentioned rise of the right-wing critique of welfare and its

35

32 That is to say right-wing political thinkers, including politicians such as (in the United Kingdom) Margaret Thatcher and Sir Keith Joseph, who put a premium, at least in the economic domain, upon the freedom of the individual, freedom of economic exchange and the market, and minimization of state intervention. Some neo-liberals are consistent in their views, arguing that individuals should be free in all respects. These neo-liberals might well advocate legalisation of cannabis or heroin, as well as free market economic policies, as they believe that the individual is or rather should be 'free to choose'. The branch of neo-liberalism associated with Margaret Thatcher and the British 'new right', however, tended to mix a belief in economic freedom with a strong moral authoritarianism. It believed in liberalizing economic relations but more heavily regulating many other aspects of human life.

implementation in practice has been one of the key challenges to citizenship, as both an idea and an institution, in recent years (Roche, 1992). Neo-liberal governments, followed in some cases by 'reconstructed' leftist governments, have begun a process of dismantling (and redesigning) the welfare state, moving it away from the model that Marshall envisaged. Other challenges have also been posed, in Europe, by the growth of the European Union, and worldwide by the emergence of such global institutions of governance as the World Bank, the International Monetary Fund and the World Trade Organization. The emergence of these various international governing bodies has raised questions for critics from all corners of the political map. They appear to wield considerable power over nations, and more particularly the citizens within those nations, without being in any way accountable to those citizens, at least in any direct sense. The political rights of citizens are undermined because they are now governed by international political institutions which are not directly accountable to them. This has prompted academic criticism but also much public disquiet and protest. Citizens of different national societies have begun to work together to demand global citizenship rights from the global governing bodies. This has prompted a number of writers to ponder whether citizenship needs to be rethought (ibid.).

Furthermore, some critics have questioned whether Marshall's tripartite model is sufficiently comprehensive. Specifically, a number of writers have made the case for adding a 'cultural' element to the Marshall model (for example, Stevenson, 2001). In part, the concept of 'cultural citizenship' refers to the cultural underpinnings of citizenship; that is, the various cultural resources necessary to the 'doing' of citizenship, for example, the knowledge and skills necessary to perform the citizen role effectively. In addition, however, the concept identifies wider issues of 'recognition' and cultural diversity relevant to citizenship (see **recognition**). The thrust of this argument is that various groups in society are denied a full sense of social belonging and acceptance, integral to citizenship, in virtue of cultural prejudices and/or differences. The Marshall model, from this point of view, presupposes a specific cultural model of the citizen which no longer holds, if it ever did. I noted above, for example, that Marshall paid more attention to the 'class lag' in terms of the development of citizenship than to the 'gender lag'. The notion of cultural citizenship, though it concerns more than just issues and inequalities pertaining to gender, might be read as a belated attempt to address this and related 'lags'. Just as Marshall argued that civil and political citizenship status are not sufficient to realize citizenship in conditions of social inequality, so too theorists of cultural citizenship are arguing that civil, political and social institutions are not sufficient to realize citizenship for all in a context of cultural inequality and lack of mutual recognition (see **recognition**).

### FURTHER READING

Marshall's *Citizenship and Social Class* is a brief and very readable account. It will be clear from the above that it is a bit dated but it is a classic text and deserves a first-hand read. Maurice Roche's (1992) *Rethinking Citizenship* offers a good account of the challenge to citizenship posed by social and political changes in the latter half of the twentieth century. Bryan Turner's (1986) *Citizenship and Capitalism* offers a strong theoretical exploration of citizenship. Nick Stevenson's (2001) edited collection, *Culture and Citizenship*, offers some useful discussions of the idea of cultural citizenship.

# Colonization of the Lifeworld

> *Related concepts:* **alienation, anomie, citizenship, new social movements, public sphere, system/lifeworld.**

37

'Colonization of the lifeworld' is a key concept in the work of Jürgen Habermas, and is outlined in detail in the second volume of his major study, **The Theory of Communicative Action**. Habermas draws a fundamental distinction in his work between what he refers to as the 'system' element of society and the 'lifeworld' element. This distinction is dealt with in a separate entry so I will not linger on it here (see **system and lifeworld**). Suffice it to say that the **lifeworld** is constituted by way of direct communicative interactions between social agents, which are oriented towards mutual understanding, whilst the **system** is constituted by way of more impersonal and strategic exchanges of money and power, within the context of the economy and the modern administrative state and judiciary. Both system and lifeworld perform essential functions for society, according to Habermas, in particular the lifeworld is a source of legitimate norms and functions to reproduce the cultural patterns upon which society rests, whilst the state and economy function to produce and distribute basic material goods.

The colonization of the lifeworld refers to the imbalance between these two elements in which the system is increasingly impinging upon ('colonizing') and thereby eroding the lifeworld. Much of Habermas' discussion of this process focuses upon the increasing involvement of the state in everyday life. He refers, for example, to a process of 'juridification', a growth in law, which entails both that more areas of life are now subject to legal regulation (the legal system is extending) and that law is internally more complex (law is more intensive). In addition to this, however, he points to the further extension of the economy into everyday life, by virtue of such processes as 'commodification'; that is to say, ever more areas of life are now produced, packaged and sold to individuals as commodities. Our leisure lives, for example, are increasingly structured by a leisure industry and our personal lives and happiness by therapeutic and psychopharmacological industries.

This is problematic in Habermas' view because the impingement of economic and political structures upon everyday life destroys aspects of the fabric of everyday life that those structures are incapable of replacing or replenishing. 'Indigenous' cultures are destroyed and with them go both the narrative structures that lend meaning to people's lives and the normative frameworks they live by. But the economy and the state are incapable of replacing or rebuilding these essential aspects of the lifeworld. 'Meaning' and 'morality' cannot be legislated for or bought and sold. They can only be created by way of communicative actions that are, in Habermas' view, constitutive of the lifeworld. Consequently the colonization of the lifeworld has pathological consequences. At the level of the community there is normative breakdown or anomie (see **anomie**) and this translates at the individual level into alienation (see **alienation**) and psychopathology.

Integral to this process is a 'shrinking of the public sphere'. Again this concept of the public sphere is dealt with in a separate entry and I will not dwell upon it here (see **public sphere**). Suffice it to say, however, that Habermas believes that the process of politics has been radically transformed as the state has expanded and advanced its frontiers. Specifically, he feels that the 'buffer zone' between the state and the private individual, wherein private individuals are able to gather collectively, discuss political issues and generate a pressure for change, has been eroded.

All is not necessarily lost, however. Habermas identifies a possibility for the replenishment of the lifeworld in the form of new social movements such as feminism, ecology, the peace movement, and so on (see **new social movements**). The breaking down of traditions and cultural scripts inevitably generates certain forms of conservative and reactionary backlash, Habermas notes. Groups who have tended to benefit from the status quo ante are prone to protest when the bases of their privilege are eroded. However, the challenge to tradition also raises the potential of a more sustained discursive engagement with the questions (normative and existential) of everyday life, and this is precisely what we find in the activities of the new social movements. The breaking up of the lifeworld affords those movements a space within which to rethink key aspects of what Habermas calls the 'moral grammar' of everyday life. The new social movements are, of course, also prompted by the more direct threats posed by colonization (for example, ecological threats and the above-mentioned problems of anomie and alienation) but the unsettling of tradition by colonization poses this opportunity for transformation too.

## FURTHER READING

Habermas himself is quite difficult to wade through, certainly for readers at undergraduate level. He writes at length and his formulations are often quite complex – although, having said that, he is not deliberately obscure, as some 'critical' writers are, and patient reading is rewarded. The final section of the second volume of *The Theory of Communicative Action* deals with colonization and can probably be tackled independently (although, reading the rest of both volumes is obviously necessary for a full appreciation) (Habermas, 1987). Good secondary accounts are White's (1988) *The Recent Work of Jürgen Habermas*, Outhwaite's (1993) *Habermas*, and (for a psychological perspective on the effects of colonization) Sloan's (1996) *Damaged Life*. I have attempted to update Habermas' account of colonization and new social movements in my paper 'Even newer social movements' (Crossley, 2003a, see also Edwards, 2004).

39

# Crisis

> *Related concepts:* **colonization of the lifeworld, cycles of contention, field, habitus, new social movements, public sphere, social class.**

Critical social theories are very often focused upon situations of domination. They explain how a status quo which from their point of view is unjust and flawed in a variety of ways nevertheless persists through time, reproducing itself and engendering the support or at least the complicity of those involved in it. In this respect we might say that critical theories are theories of how what ought not exist does so and does so quite successfully. If this were all there were to critical theory it would be a rather depressing venture. However, many critical theories, and particularly those stemming from Marxism, tend to see light at the end of the tunnel in the form of crises and crisis tendencies, fault lines in the 'system' which, at the very least, will create opportunities for those who wish to bring about change.

As indicated above, the common origin for many of these theories of crisis is Marx. Here I will outline his approach, the very sophisticated reformulation of the theory of crisis in the work of Habermas, and some of the tantalizing comments about crisis that we find in the work of Pierre Bourdieu. This is by no means a comprehensive survey of the literature on crisis but I believe that it covers the most important and relevant threads.

## MARX

It is well known that, though perhaps the greatest of all critics of capitalism, Marx was also a great admirer of this economic system and of all that it had achieved by his time of writing. It was only because capitalism had created such potential for a better way of living that the socialist alternative was even conceivable, let alone possible, from his point of view. Capitalism is an exploitative system, however, and as such is morally problematic. More to the point, it is a contradictory system, prone to conflict and crisis, which will eventually tumble. The main tension within capitalism, for Marx, is that between the interests of the proletariat and the bourgeoisie (see **social class**). One can only gain at the expense of the other, such that they are in a constant stand off which periodically breaks down, giving rise to open conflict. This is exacerbated, however, in a number of respects, by the crisis tendencies of the economy itself. The key crisis tendency to which Marx refers concerns 'overproduction' and stems from what he calls the 'anarchy of the market'. In markets, he observes, producers bring goods to sell to consumers. The system is in equilibrium to the extent that the amount of goods produced (supply) is equal to the amount of goods either needed or wanted by potential consumers (demand). 'Bourgeois economists' (to use the Marxist language) see the forces of supply and demand as key adjustment mechanisms within the economy and assume that there is a tendency towards equilibrium – supply will meet demand. Marx, however, notes that there is no mechanism to link supply and demand, such that their relationship is haphazard and must occasionally go very wrong. Specifically there are occasions when producers produce much more than consumers are able or willing to consume; they overproduce. The result of this is financially disastrous. Small companies cannot stand the losses and go to the wall. Large companies can withstand the losses but are inclined to make workers redundant to preserve their own financial balance. In either case the net result is an increase in unemployment. And that has the result that demand drops further, sharply and without warning (since the unemployed cannot afford to buy goods), therefore precipitating further overproduction. If such a downward trend were to continue, Marx observes, this could bring the capitalist economy to its knees, whilst simultaneously generating unrest amongst workers who find themselves either out of work or under threat of unemployment and living in worse conditions. The combination of exacerbated class conflict and massive overproduction would spell the beginning of the end of capitalism.

Even if the spiral is broken before the economy hits rock bottom and some measure of equilibrium between supply and demand is restored, overproduction crises tend to lead to a concentration and centralization of capital which Marx identifies with 'late' capitalism: namely capitalism in its final stages and on its last legs. Crudely put, smaller companies are wiped out by recurrent overproduction crises and the economy is therefore increasingly dominated by large companies, which get larger as they buy out the small and medium-sized companies that go to the wall. This tendency towards monopoly is self-destructive for capitalism, according to Marx, since capitalism is a system of competition in the market place between producers. The greater the degree of

41

monopolization, the less competition there is and the less the system conforms to the classic capitalist model. The more, in other words, that it outgrows its own structure. There are still workers and capitalists in such a society, of course, but there are fewer capitalists, and ownership and control are sufficiently centralized and concentrated to make a socialist takeover feasible. Centralized control is now possible. The mechanisms are in place and need only be grasped from the few remaining capitalists by a revolutionary force. Furthermore, concentration and centralization links the working class together and homogenizes their lives and interests, as they become employees of a narrowing range of firms, thereby increasing the likelihood of them recognizing their common identity and interests. Finally, it makes the system as a whole more vulnerable to crises. All of the eggs, so to speak, are in the same basket or at least the same few baskets. If one big firm goes down it takes a large part of the economy with it in a manner which is not true for smaller firms.

Added to this, Marx argues that there is a more gradual tendency within the economy for the rate of profit to decline, thereby driving down wages, polarizing the classes and radicalizing the working class. There is, he argues, a constant drive towards technological advancement within capitalism, fuelled by competition between firms. New production technologies allow products to be produced more cheaply, and firms compete to be on top of whatever technological revolution they are living through. However, keeping up in this way is very costly, does not add to the value of the product[33] and thus reduces profit margins. This prompts employers to keep down wages, at least in real terms, thus immiserating and frustrating the proletariat, and drawing them into deeper conflict with the bourgeoisie.

The path from here to revolution is differently traced by writers in the Marxist tradition. Marx himself is notoriously silent on the matter but many have taken a stance. Some, following Rosa Luxemburg (1986), argue that the proletariat will spontaneously form themselves into a revolutionary force. Others, following Lenin (1918, 1973), argue that workers will only arrive at a 'trade union consciousness'[34] under their own

---

33 This point relates to an aspect of Marxian economics that I do not have the space to discuss here. For a good discussion see Mandel (1970).

34 If left to their own devices, Lenin argues, workers will tend to band together in unions, to bid for improvements to their working conditions and pay. He calls this 'trade union consciousness'. This is different from revolutionary consciousness, however, which entails banding together into a revolutionary force and seeking to overthrow capitalism. Workers will not do this of their own accord, according to Lenin, and therefore need to be led along the revolutionary path by a vanguard party.

---

steam and must be guided into revolution by a revolutionary party. Others still, following Gramsci (1971), argue that crises are really just opportunities which have no necessary consequences and which the politically committed must be prepared to mould to their own advantage.

How well the Marxist theory of economic crisis tendencies bears up to the historical evidence is a matter of debate. Nevertheless, one does not need to probe too far into the history of any capitalist society to find evidence of profound periods of crisis. Nor does one need to probe too far to find evidence of emerging labour movements. The trade unions and labour parties of the present are, of course, the progeny of these more amorphous and often more radical movements. The world moves on, however, and so too does the structure of capitalism, such that some writers have been led to question the Marxist theory of crisis, at least in its classical formulation. One such writer is Jürgen Habermas (1988).

## HABERMAS

The economic conditions that Marx describes, in Habermas' view, are in certain respects specific to the early history of the capitalist system. Crises provide a stimulus to innovation and social learning processes. Human agents spot the problems and institute mechanisms to correct them and avoid them in the future. In the case of the economic crisis tendencies described by Marx this has involved the state assuming far greater responsibility for management of the economy (as well as various marketing mechanisms which link supply and demand in a less anarchic way).[35] The state intervenes in the economy in an effort to offset crisis tendencies. It monitors economic indicators such as inflation and unemployment, counteracting damaging trends by way of policy shifts and manipulation of, for example, the money supply[36] or interest rates.[37] It offers welfare provision which keeps the unemployed out of misery and slows the downward spiral of overproduction by keeping the

43

---

35 Through market research and advertising, for example, firms seek to establish a more predictable relationship between themselves and their consumers.
36 This is the technique of economic management favoured by 'monetarists' in particular and taken up by many of the 'new right' governments of the 1980s.
37 The UK government has recently relinquished its right to alter interest rates, passing this power over to the Bank of England. However, from Habermas' point of view this is not really a big change as the bank will perform the same role in more or less the same way, and it may be regarded as a measure designed to give the state a degree of freedom from economic accountability and thus lattitude in dealing with 'legitimation crises' (see below).

unemployed in the market as consumers, where they contribute to the demand for goods. It funds research and development, thereby absorbing some of the costs of technical innovation. And it has brought the proletariat 'inside' the system by giving them a stake in it (they have more now to lose than 'their chains',[38] they have houses, consumer goods, welfare, and so on), giving them the vote and by accepting their parties (labour parties) and other representatives (for example, trade unions) into the system – a move which has simultaneously served to 'tame' those representatives and teach them to speak the 'language' of the system. These concessions were fought for. They were not given freely by political elites. But it is fair to say that they were given for the fear of the consequences of not giving them and, in this sense, they represent a 'functional adaptation' within capitalism which has offset or at least dampened many of the problems identified by Marx. Class conflict is relatively contained, profit decline curbed and the anarchy of the market sufficiently tamed and supported as to offset major overproduction crises.

However, this has only displaced the crisis tendencies of capitalism according to Habermas. It has not 'debugged' the system completely. In the first instance, the state qua economic manager might fail to balance the books properly, giving rise to fiscal crises of the state (when the state runs out of money) or, more drastically, what Habermas calls 'rationality crises'; that is, crises in the very philosophy of management adopted by the state. The situation in the United Kingdom in the 1970s, when economists informed by the economic philosophy of Keynes[39] found themselves simultaneously faced with economic stagnation and inflation ('stagflation'), a situation which Keynesian philosophy deems impossible, is a key example of a 'rationality crisis'. The managers of the economy were faced with the task of steering the economy through a crisis whose constituent features were not recognized by their system of thought. There is every reason to believe that these fiscal and rationality crises will happen, given the anarchic and conflictual nature of the economic system (as described by Marx) that the capitalist state is required to manage. The job of the state is far from easy, even given the other stabilizing factors that might have emerged in the economic system.

---

38 In the final section of *The Communist Manifesto*, Marx and Engels famously call upon the 'working men of the world' to unite and fight, adding that they have 'nothing but your chains' to lose by doing so.
39 John Maynard Keynes was a leading British economist during the early and mid-twentieth century. His economic ideas were crucial to the economic management of the United Kingdom and other western countries between the 1950s and the late 1970s.

---

The situation is more complex and difficult still, however, because the modern democratic state also has to balance the books, so to speak, with its electorate. Political agitation by the labour and other movements (such as the suffragettes) has been overcome only at the cost of the state claiming to represent its people and claiming to draw legitimacy from its citizens. In his capacity as a political philosopher Habermas claims that the situation is anything but a perfect model of democracy and adds that the system would go into 'legitimation crisis' if citizens demanded true accountability and representation; that is, the 'supply' of democratically accountable decisions would fall well short of 'demand'. The system only works, he argues, because of widespread 'civil privatism'; that is, because modern citizens are disposed to let politicians get on with it and to pursue their own private and domestic pleasures rather than public goods (namely goods that all members of society might benefit from, such as political reform) and true democratic accountability. However, citizens qua clients of the state still make demands for welfare goods and the costs of fulfilling these demands generally conflicts with the savings which effective economic management of the state requires. The state is therefore slave to two competing and conflicting masters: the economy and its citizens/clients. It risks fiscal or rationality crisis on one side and legitimation crisis, that is, withdrawal of the public support it depends upon for its stability and power, on the other.

This situation is further complicated by the party system: namely having different political parties who compete to run the state. On the one hand this system introduces some 'give' into the state as individual parties can take the force of public criticism when things go wrong in political life, thereby shielding the state itself. Public hostility results not in a full attack upon the state but in an attack on a particular party, who are then replaced by another party, leaving the state and political system itself largely intact. Even at times of full-blown rationality crisis this mechanism can come into play, as, for example, when the neo-liberal Thatcher government replaced the failing Labour government in the United Kingdom in 1979, effectively breaking with a paradigm of governance that had been in place since the end of the Second World War.[40] However, the party system can also fuel the problems of the

---

40 Historians of twentieth-century British politics conventionally write of a 'postwar consensus' between 1945 and 1979, shared by all parties and centred upon the mixed economy and Keynesian methods of economic management. In the late 1970s this paradigm effectively went into crises, as already noted in this entry, and the Thatcher government came into power, ushering in a new philosophy of management and breaking with the consensus.

---

modern state as different parties bid each other up with respect to welfare, each promising more than the other, in such a way that the state is led to promise more than it can deliver, risking the wrath of public unrest.

Civil privatism, to some degree, shields the state from these dangers but there is a further crisis tendency to be considered, which concerns the sustainability of civil privatism itself. Civil privatism is one of many cultural dispositions which advanced capitalism presupposes for its effective functioning, according to Habermas, but which this system does not and cannot 'supply' for itself; which it must hope is reproduced in the wider cultural sphere or 'lifeworld', such as in the family, church, media and local communities, as well as the school[41] (see **system and lifeworld**). Another such disposition is the work ethic. If any of these dispositions and competencies were not to be reproduced then the system would face what Habermas calls 'motivation crisis'. Agents' motivations would slip out of alignment with the requirements of society as a social system. It is Habermas' view that the system is in danger of facing precisely such a motivation crisis.

Not only are the state and the economy not capable of reproducing the dispositions that they presuppose for their own survival, he argues, they tend actually to destroy those dispositions. Both systems are inclined to expand and thereby to impinge upon aspects of the social world that they were not previously involved in (in later work Habermas refers to this as 'colonization of the lifeworld' (see **Colonization of the Lifeworld**). The economy expands as a consequence of the pressure to develop new markets and the state expands in an effort to 'buy' more support by providing more welfare services (and by the logic of competing parties bidding up the welfare agenda). As they expand, however, these systems tend to destroy the traditions and customs of the social world. They destroy culture and bring what was previously habitual and taken for granted into question. In the case of the state, moreover, these issues are, at the same time politicized, because they are associated with the state. As Habermas puts it:

---

41 Of course the state does have some control over schools and Habermas' argument that the state and economy cannot create meaning only works insofar as we conceptualize the state from a very narrow point of view. Given the symbolic politics and moral reform that many political parties and actors engage in, it looks plainly silly to say that the state does not create meaning, when viewed from a broader perspective.

---

At every level administrative planning produces unintended unsettling and publicizing effects. These effects weaken the justification potential of traditions that have been flushed out of their nature-like course of development. Once their unquestionable character has been destroyed, the stabilization of validity claims can occur only through discourse. The stirring up of cultural affairs that are taken for granted thus furthers the politicization of areas of life previously assigned to the private sphere. But this development signifies danger for the civil privatism that is secured informally through the structures of the public realm. (1988: 72)

In other words, by intervening further into the social world the state inadvertently brings taken-for-granteds into question and politicizes them. It disturbs established patterns of life, disturbs deep-seated dispositions and makes the private public. As such it engenders the conditions for a 'motivation crisis' which, in turn, engenders the conditions for 'legitimation crisis'. Agents are shocked out of their civil privatism and agitated to a point where they may begin to protest. In later work Habermas suggests that the rise of the so-called 'new social movements' is one manifestation of this legitimation crisis (see **new social movements**). New social movements pick up the issues which the state politicizes and push for an accountability, regarding these issues, which the state, as it stands, is incapable of providing.

Drawing upon a distinction originally posited by David Lockwood (1964), Habermas argues that economic and rationality crises are 'system crises'; that is, crises of 'system integration', crises between 'parts' of the social world which are relatively independent of the 'agreements' of members of society. Legitimation and motivation crises, by contrast, are social crises; that is, crises of social integration; crises which arise when the consensus which otherwise holds society begins to give way. It is integral to his position, however, that system crises generate a tendency towards social crises, since concrete and embodied agents must live through them and experience their consequences (an economic crisis usually means personal financial crisis for many people, for example, making them inclined to discontent and reducing the level of social consensus). Furthermore, when analysing crises he views even 'social crises' from a systems perspective (see **system and lifeworld**). When people cease to 'agree' with the norms/values of their society, he notes, they cease to play their role within the system and the system, in turn, begins to falter.

There is an element of functionalism in this account and one which owes more than a little to the work of Talcott Parsons (for example, Parsons, 1966). Habermas' four crisis tendencies map directly onto the four key functional pre-requisites identified in Parsons' famous AGIL schema. Parsons argues that societies must 'adapt' (A) to their

47

environment, and that the economy is the key societal sub-system in this respect. He argues that they must set and pursue 'goals' (G) and that the state is the key societal element in this respect. He argues that they must be socially 'integrated' (I), and identifies a consensus of norms and legitimate forms of authority as central to this. And he argues that 'latent' (L) cultural patterns, presupposed by the other sub-systems, must be reproduced, citing the cultural domain as the key site for this. Habermas, in turn, identifies each of these elements as a potential fault line. So is Habermas a functionalist? And does it matter if he is? Habermas does get pretty close to Parsons and this leads to certain problems in his position. However, there is arguably an element of functionalism in any account of crisis, since the notion of crisis conceptualizes societies as systems and suggests that those systems can fall out of equilibrium, which in turn suggests that it makes sense to refer to them as sometimes being in equilibrium. This need not commit critical theories to the problematic teleological[42] assumptions of some varieties of functionalism, however, and neither does it mean that critical theories must adopt a positive appraisal of the societies they study, even when those societies are in equilibrium. As Robert Merton (1964) argued many years ago, the most appalling systems of slavery can function very well, from a functionalist point of view, in the respect that they are inclined to perpetuate themselves with little difficulty. This does not mean that we must like or approve of them. There is a difference between approving of them and analysing their functioning, because there is a very big difference between saying that a system functions, from a systems point of view, and saying that it is a good or desirable system. Indeed, we might want to know how a system functions and why it functions so well if we plan to intervene critically, so that we know what we are dealing with.[43] Undesirable 'systems' often function well. If they did not then they would change before we could realistically come to view them as undesirable systems.

Having said this, there are problems with functionalism and systems theory and we do not need to buy into them as fully as Habermas seems

42 A teleological theory is one which assumes that the end result or consequence of a process can be used as an explanation of that process. This assumption is generally rejected by contemporary social theorists because it defies the temporal logic of the concept of causation (events can only cause what comes after them, not what comes before them) and/or relies upon a metaphysical belief of 'purposiveness' in nature which, in the context of other sciences where it has surfaced, has proved more of an obstacle than an aid and has generally therefore been rejected.

43 In the same way that medics want to know how certain diseases work (e.g. how viruses spread and reproduce themselves) and may even marvel at the 'ingenuity' of a disease process, from the point of view that they wish to work out ways of combating it.

to do, to preserve some notion of crisis. The work of Pierre Bourdieu is a useful point of reference in this respect.

## BOURDIEU

Rather than speak of 'systems' or 'sub-systems', Bourdieu conceptualizes different areas of the social world in terms of what he calls 'fields' (see **field**). The concept of a field is much more fluid and dynamic than the notion of a system and arguably admits of a much greater degree of conflict than the concept of system permits. However, Bourdieu still refers to crises within fields and to this extent still assumes some degree of 'fit' between different elements within fields. In this way he allows us to draw all that is useful from the functionalist concept of systems, whilst avoiding what is most problematic about the concept. Furthermore, Bourdieu both takes the idea of crisis into more specific arenas (or 'fields') of the social world, such as the education system, and highlights the interplay of subjective and objective elements in crises. He thus presents us with a more complex and differentiated model of society than the Habermasian tripartite model of economy, state and lifeworld, allowing us to reflect upon conflict and crisis in a wide variety of quite specific areas of social life: for example, education, the family, science, indeed any structured area of social life (any field). And he explores in more detail the preconditions of crisis. Crises occur, Bourdieu argues, when the expectations of individuals, embodied in their habitus (see **habitus**), slip out of alignment with the objective realities of social fields, and particularly the objective rewards agents expect from their participation in those fields. Much of the agitation in the education system in France in the 1960s, culminating in 'Mai '68',[44] according to Bourdieu (1986), for example, was triggered by the mismatch between students' expectations about university life, which were based upon the past state of the higher educational field, and the actual state of the higher educational field as it was in the late 1960s, massively expanded but grossly underfunded and drawn between an old 'elite' model of education and a new 'mass' model. The crisis outgrew this particular mismatch of (subjective) expectations and (objective) realities –

---

44 'Mai '68' refers to a famous uprising by students, who were later joined by workers, in France (and particularly Paris) in May of 1968. For a short period of time it appeared as if the government might collapse, leading the events to pass into legend. Furthermore, the perceived failings of the communist party during this period led to a variety of schisms and innovations within the French left, which still inform radical political thought in France today.

specifically, it was rejoined by striking workers and became a much more general struggle – but that is where it began.

Bourdieu's account is also interesting because he seemingly suggests that the basis of social agency shifts under crisis conditions. Certain of the habits and assumptions which steer action under normal conditions are brought to consciousness, questioned and replaced with a more deliberate and critical mode of relating to the social world. I have argued elsewhere that there are problems in the way in which Bourdieu frames this claim (Crossley, 2002b, 2003b), but it is clearly of importance to our understanding of the nature of crises and must be preserved in some form.

Bourdieu's account of crisis is clearly less developed than that of either Marx or Habermas, and he certainly has less of a grand vision – which may be an advantage or a disadvantage, depending upon one's point of view. Whatever one's position on the latter issue, however, his concepts of **habitus** and **field**, and the idea that they can slip out of alignment with one another, do provide important, empirically operationalizable tools for analysing crises. Furthermore, through his field-based approach to crisis Bourdieu allows us to begin to think about using the concept beyond the parameters of the state-economy-lifeworld model suggested by Habermas.

## FURTHER READING

Although much of Marx's work is relatively accessible, the material on crisis is a little more dense and perhaps less accessible. A good secondary account is Ernest Mandel's (1970) *Introduction to Marxist Economic Theory*. In marked contrast, Habermas' (1988) **Legitimation Crisis** is one of his most concise and clearest works. It pays to read the original here. Bourdieu's comments on crisis are generally just that, namely brief comments scattered through his work. I have pulled some of his ideas on the matter together in my paper, 'From reproduction to transformation' (Crossley, 2003b). There is, however, an extended treatment of the crisis on Mai '68 in the final chapter of *Homo Academicus* (Bourdieu, 1986) which is fascinating and very readable.

# — Cycles of Contention —

critical social theory

> *Related concepts:* **crisis, new social movements, repertoires of contention, social movements.**

The concept 'cycles of contention' emerges out of social movement analysis in the United States and is associated, in particular, with the work of Tarrow (1989, 1998). To understand it we must first grasp the concept of 'contention'. This is a term used by some social movement analysts to widen the scope of their focus beyond 'social movements', to incorporate a range of forms of political activity and protest which might not quite meet the criteria of their definition of social movements but which do not belong to the domain of formal, institutionalized politics either. Social movement formation and activism would be one form of 'contention' or 'contentious politics' but there would be others, such as riots, spontaneous protests and strikes or industrial unrest (see McAdam, Tarrow and Tilly (2002) for a very broad definition). According to Tarrow, social movements grow out of contentious politics and are characterized, relative to other forms of contention, by their relative durability. They are sustained over time:

> Contentious politics occurs when ordinary people, often in league with more influential citizens, join forces in confrontation with elites, authorities and opponents . . . When backed by dense social networks and galvanized by culturally resonant, action oriented symbols, contentious politics leads to sustained interaction with opponents. The result is the social movement. (1998: 2)

There is always some level of contention in any advanced society at any time. However, the concept of cycles of contention suggests that this level varies in a cyclical fashion; that is, it suggests that levels of contention move between peaks and troughs. At some times there are very high levels of contention. Protests are big, frequent and significant. The number of social movements in society increases and the activity levels of those movements is extraordinarily high. At other times, the level drops.

These cycles of 'boom and bust' are not said to be regular. They do not recur like Halley's comet, at set intervals. But it is argued that they manifest a relatively predictable structure. Moreover, the concept of cycles

51

was introduced in an effort to correct the view, evident in some work on political crises or 'moments of madness' (Zolberg, 1972), that these 'moments' can erupt at any time, without prior indication, in the body of previously stable societies (see **crisis**). 'Moments of madness' was an expression coined by Zolberg (1972) to capture those moments in history and politics, such as 'Mai '68'[45] in Paris, when political authorities wobble and anything seems possible. There is a danger with this idea, Tarrow suggests, that we are led to believe that societies pass from perfect stability to near collapse in precisely a 'moment', only then to return immediately to stability. In contrast to this view, the idea of cycles of contention entails that there is a gradual build up and wind down of levels of contention, over a sustained period. Exactly how long is not specified but the implication is longer than the few weeks. Moments of madness, from this point of view, do not emerge out of nowhere. They are the culmination of a much more sustained and gradual build up of levels of protest. Furthermore, as such they might be predicted before the event. The distinction between the concept of 'moments of madness' and the concept of 'cycles of contention' can be illustrated in graphic form, as in Figure 1.

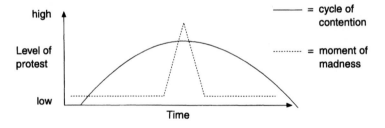

Figure 1 *Cycles of contention and moments of madness*

The key example for most of the work on cycles is the period of political unrest in much of Europe and North America between the mid 1960s and the mid 1970s. This cycle has been studied in great detail, both quantitatively and qualitatively, in a number of national contexts, and has effectively served as the model upon which the concept is based. There are other examples, however, which suggest that the idea has wider applicability (see Traugott (1995a)).

45 'Mai '68' refers to a famous uprising by students, who were later joined by workers, in France (and particularly Paris) in May of 1968. For a short period of time it appeared as if the government might collapse, leading the events to pass into legend. Furthermore, the perceived failings of the communist party during this period led to a variety of schisms and innovations within the French left, which still inform radical political thought in France today.

Many explanations of the comings and goings of cycles focus upon a range of factors which are quite commonly cited in the social movements' literature in relation to the comings and goings of single movements, such as political opportunity structures[46] and frames[47] (see Crossley, 2002a for a more detailed discussion of these and other factors). As McAdam (1995) notes, however, what is interesting about this concept is the fact that it draws attention away from singular groups or movements and requires us to focus upon the interaction between groups and movements over time. It enables us to reflect upon the way in which groups and movements collectively constitute an environment for one another, as well as a provocation and inspiration. Feminist groups might steal the limelight from environmentalist groups, for example, leading the latter to emulate the tactics of the former, until peace campaigners enter the fray with their innovations, forcing both parties to respond, and so on.

As a final point we should note the methodological difficulties associated with the concept of cycles of contention. These revolve around the question of how we accurately measure levels of protest in society at any given time. In practice most theorists of cycles draw upon newspaper reportage; that is, analysts record the number of protests reported in the newspapers over given periods of time as a proxy for the number of protests actually occurring in society at any point in time. There are fairly obvious limits to this source of data, however, as a vast amount of 'protest activity' (itself an ambiguous concept) goes unreported and more importantly the wax and wane of coverage may reflect the wax and wane of journalists or editors' interest rather than genuine increases in protest levels. An increase in reported protests might indicate a media campaign or moral panic regarding protest, rather than a genuine increase, and the media may lose interest in protest or find something else that they are more interested in reporting at just the time that the real level[48] of protest

53

46 The idea of 'political opportunity structures' is that social movement activity is shaped by the opportunities and constraints afforded within the political system of the society in which they emerge and, particularly, that movement activity becomes more likely when opportunities are opening up. For a discussion see Crossley (2002a).

47 It is commonly argued in social movement analysis that individuals are more easily recruited into political action when issues are 'framed' in ways which resonate with their outlook. For example, people might respond more favourably to an issue if it is framed as a matter of 'rights' than if it is presented as a matter of 'power' or 'oppression' because the language of rights is one that they are familiar with and subscribe to. Much of the work of social movement organizations is said to be taken up with attempts to frame their claims appropriately.

48 Obviously protest can be defined and measured in different ways, such that there are, in practice, different 'real rates' of protest. I mean only to suggest here that the level of reporting might move in an inverse direction to the way that it would move if it were motivated by a concern for ascertaining a real rate.

is increasing. Furthermore novel protests are more likely to be reported than standard protests and all forms will become standard and lose their news value over time. There are doubtless ways of getting around these problems. One might argue that the media is a good measure of those protests which really penetrate public consciousness and that this is what is important. Objective rises in protest levels are of little significance, one might claim, unless they get reported and people learn about them. Similarly, one might argue that a build up of protest levels to crisis point will be noted by the media because it will always be newsworthy. Finally, one might argue that cycles will always work through the media, relying upon 'media amplification'[49] for their growth, such that media reporting and actual levels of protest are closely interdependent. I reserve judgement on these matters. It must suffice to say that, though the concept of cycles is fascinating and important, we must be mindful of the methodological difficulties which are sometimes overlooked by its more enthusiastic proponents.

## FURTHER READING

Tarrow first developed the concept of cycles in the context of an empirical study of Italian protest in the late 1960s. This work was published, in book format, as *Democracy and Disorder* (Tarrow, 1989). He also revists this concept in his *Power in Movement* (Tarrow, 1998). Some of the best papers on cycles, including one by Tarrow, are gathered together in Traugott's (1995a) *Repertoires and Cycles of Contention*.

54

# Deconstruction

> *Related concepts:* ***discourse, doxa, ideology, power/knowledge, symbolic power.***

---

49 It is very common in relation to protest, as in other areas of social life, that media reporting of certain events leads to more people becoming involved in those events, thus amplifying whatever tendency is identified in the reports. This is 'media amplification'.

---

Of all of the writers whose ideas are catalogued in this book, Derrida is perhaps the most slippery. Many 'critical theorists' (in the broad sense of the term) seek to challenge the academic establishment in one way or another and Derrida is no exception, but in the case of Derrida the challenge is both performative (that is, practical as much as theoretical) and focused in a very direct and concentrated way upon that most central of academic practices, writing. Derrida writes about writing. He challenges the way in which we write and read, both as academics and more widely. But he also seeks to avoid, in the way that he writes, problems that his work identifies. For this reason it is very difficult to pin down in a short entry the meaning of the 'words', such as 'deconstruction', that we associate with Derrida. Indeed, it is usual to begin accounts of 'deconstruction' with lists of the various possible descriptions of deconstruction that Derrida has, at one time or another, rejected. Deconstruction is not a method, it is not this, it is not that. To my mind deconstruction is best conceived as a theoretically structured way of reading texts, but I say that in full cognisance that, like any definition, it is ripe for deconstruction itself and would never be allowed to escape the constant 'play' and 'interplay' that also seems to define deconstruction as an institution and activity.

Confused? As a useful first step in trying to clarify this confusion it is instructive to reflect upon Derrida's early studies of the phenomenological philosophy of Edmund Husserl (Derrida, 1989, 1973). Derrida is clearly impressed with and influenced by the work of Husserl, but also troubled. Various aspects of the work trouble him but most of his concerns focus upon Husserl's treatment of writing. In his essay on *The Origin of Geometry* (an essay which Derrida translated into French and wrote a long introduction to), Husserl (1970b, also reproduced in Derrida, 1989) arrives at the view that the practice of writing is essential to both the history of geometry and more importantly the constitution of its objectivity – that is, he believes that geometry becomes objective when it is written down and thus made public. But he is troubled by these conclusions and seemingly wishes to resist them. Geometry is a product of the human mind, in quite a specific sense, according to Husserl.[50]

---

50 In Husserl's view, all knowledge derives certain of its parameters from the mind including empirical sciences, but what distinguishes maths and geometry is their purity. They have no empirical part. Their truths are derived by deduction, and their parameters, again, derive from the mind. We do not 'discover' 'right angles', for example rather this is a concept that the human mind has invented. As indeed is the very idea of degrees, angles, etc.

Geometrical knowledge is in no way a reflection of facts about the empirical world 'out there', not least because it deals in pure forms (straight lines and perfect shapes) which are only roughly approximated in the somewhat more messy 'real world'. Writing is essential to the constitution of its objectivity because it frees it from the 'mind' of particular individuals, giving it an independent existence. Geometry ceases to be something 'in the head' of great thinkers when it is written down and becomes part of a shared, intersubjective world. This move beyond the realm of the individual subject, into a shared domain, is essential to objectivity since the very definition of objectivity depends upon phenomena transcending individuals and achieving intersubjective verification and defeasibility.[51] It is also necessary to the history of geometry, as the process of history entails that others will continue the train of thought begun by the hypothetical founder or founders and they can only do this – geometry can only be passed from one generation to another – if it is written down.[52] However, the importance of writing is a problem because it seems to make the truths of geometry contingent. It implies that the laws of geometry would no longer exist if all the people who know about geometry were killed and all of the books which write about it were destroyed, where Husserl believes that there is something more eternal and necessary to geometrical truth. Furthermore, writing separates geometry from the thought which gave birth to it, thereby introducing a certain opacity to geometric ideas, with consequent possibilities for misunderstanding and differential interpretation. Subsequent readers and even practitioners of geometry confront geometric ideas as self-evident finished products and do not have access to the building work which went into them. Finally, writing 'translates' the idea but things can get lost in translation. Like any translation, writing is never perfect or exact.

In his response to Husserl, Derrida formulates certain ideas that would later become central to his philosophy, particularly his critique of

51 Some definitions and particularly critiques of 'objectivity' seem to suggest that the concept presupposes that phenomena are (somehow) known in a way which ceases to depend upon subjectivity at all. This is impossible. One of the more interesting aspects of phenomenology is the way in which it builds up a sense of objectivity as intersubjective. 'X' is objectively known or objectively 'there' because it is not just known by me or there for me but exists for any reasonable person whom I point it out or explain it to.
52 Of course it could be passed on by word of mouth but this system would not permit much expansion of geometry and would be particularly difficult in the case of geometry, which is highly abstract and relates to visible space.

'logocentrism' and 'the metaphysics of presence'.[53] Why, he wonders, does Husserl treat writing as secondary and derivative? Why is writing regarded as a mere translation of speech, which is, in turn, regarded as a mere translation of thought? There is no justification for this in Derrida's view. Writing does not translate something which precedes it. It is an original and constitutive order of meaning in its own right. From this point of view, particularly given that mathematicians often think problems through 'on paper', that they do not first think them then write but rather think by way of writing, geometry is perhaps less a product of the human mind, more a product of the practice of writing. This is not true of geometry alone, furthermore. Writing, for Derrida, is a constitutive activity which brings the phenomena it writes about into being in much the same way that the mind does in the view of other philosophers. In addition, when discussing Husserl, Derrida reflects upon questions of opacity, contingency and interpretation, which later play a great role in his various 'deconstructions'. This point needs to be unpacked.

Truths, whether philosophical or scientific, are written down in our culture. They take shape within written language. And yet outside of literary studies we tend not to notice this, according to Derrida. What he means by this, at one level, is that we tend quite literally not to notice the written inscriptions on the page, finding ourselves moved, instead, by what those inscriptions 'say'. We act, at least when we read philosophy, as if we were confronting 'pure thought' rather than writing. More deeply than this, however, we tend, when reading philosophy and other 'serious' or 'factual' forms of writing, to ignore their inevitable literary aspects: their metaphors, rhetoric, style and stylistic 'devices' (for example, footnotes, quotations, referencing). We are inclined, by force of the habituated norms of the institutions of 'serious writing', to ignore this 'scaffolding' in search of the pure philosophical or scientific thought it reveals. Such details are not incidental, according to Derrida, however. Philosophy is writing and these literary aspects are therefore essential to

57

53 As briefly summarized in this paragraph the terms 'logocentrism' and 'metaphysics of presence' are terms which Derrida uses to denote a tendency to view writing as a translation of thought, which in turn works upon a pure perceptual datum. Much of the thrust of his thought is in opposition to these structuring assumptions. There is no pure point of contact, no moment of self-transparent meaning for Derrida. Meaning always entails reference elsewhere. It is always 'deferred'. This notion of deferral is also central to his concept of 'difference'. This concept borrows from structuralist linguistics the idea that the meaning of any term is always dependent upon its difference from other terms (e.g. 'red' means, amongst other things, 'not blue' and 'colour' means 'not smell') but it adds to this that, for this and other reasons, the meaning of an utterance always depends upon something else, which depends upon something else again, etc. in a chain of endless deferral.

it. They 'make the case' in philosophical argument and they can, for this reason, be used to 'break the case'. In particular Derrida's deconstructions of philosophical texts are famed for picking up and playing with these 'marginal' stylistic elements, showing both how the meaning of the text is dependent upon them but also that and why, because of this, meaning is less certain or stable than might hitherto have been believed. Texts are prised open in such a way that different and sometimes contradictory readings are made possible, or perhaps rather contradictions within the text are revealed. Arguments to show one thing are shown to rest upon images or presuppositions which point in a quite different direction.

Derrida's strategy of reading the 'writing' of philosophical and other texts blurs the distinction between philosophy and literature, between texts which speak of truth (rational or empirical) and texts which speak of fiction. Furthermore, he is particularly concerned with the manner in which such texts often seek to make their case and make sense by using conceptual dichotomies (for example, nature/culture, high/low, truth/falsity) which his playful attention to writing finds ways of breaking down. There is a 'political' element in this for Derrida, in the respect that oppositions are often hierarchical or of a better/worse kind. To question oppositions and textual strategies is to question taken-for-granted value judgements and expose hidden preconditions of (symbolic) power. However, it is never Derrida's aim to simply invert oppositions, nor to completely dissolve them one into the other. His work seeks to problematize but not dismiss or engage in such a way as to suggest alternatives or solutions. Likewise, his blurring of boundaries is never intended to break them down or suggest that they have no meaning. Thus, even as he blurs the boundaries of literature and philosophy, problematizing that boundary, he maintains the boundary and keeps himself on the philosophical side of it.

In many ways 'deconstruction' was one of the buzz words of 'critical theory' (broadly defined) in the last decade of the twentieth century and was taken up (outside of philosophy) by both literary theorists and social scientists. In these contexts it came to mean any of a number things (sometimes only obscurely or nominally linked to what Derrida does). Derrida's philosophical apologists are arguably in a poor position to complain about this. To legislate upon disciplinary or methodological boundaries would seem somewhat against the spirit of the enterprise. From an outsider's point of view, however, that is, from a social scientists points of view, I suggest that there are limits to what we might hope to learn from this undoubtedly very interesting philosopher. On one hand, for example, I suggest that Derrida's insights are very much tied to a specific philosophical concern with writing which does not necessarily transpose readily to other forms of communication, let alone to social practices more generally. On the other hand, and more importantly, Derrida's concern with the text (he infamously claims to focus his critique entirely within the bounds of the text – 'il n y a rien dehors la texte')[54] leads him to ignore factors outside of the text or perhaps invisible at the level of textual exegesis which the methods of social science bring to light and which are important; for example, the material and institutional interests of different types of writer, institutionalized forms of power and violence, poverty. Even when Derrida (1994) deals with Marx, for example, he does not ask the questions of Marx which the social scientist will ask, such as how well does the Marxist account of capitalist societies stand up today. Do social classes, of the sort Marx describes, still exist? Of course there is no reason why he should. He is a philosopher and one specifically concerned with hermeneutic and literary questions at that. But that distinction cuts both ways and, insofar as we might be tempted to deconstruct it, we should be careful not to collapse our own enterprise into his. Social science is a form of writing and sometimes addresses questions of writing. This gives rise to an overlap wherein dialogue with Derrida might prove useful. His is a fascinating account of writing. But we should also follow his lead in recognizing that social science no more collapses into philosophy or literature, than philosophy does into literature. We can, I believe, allow ourselves to be enlightened by Derrida without becoming deconstructionists.

## FURTHER READING

Derrida is extremely heavy going and may prove particularly difficult for social science undergraduates who are not familiar with his philosophical and literary background. Luckily, however, there are some very good secondary texts. Christopher Norris' *Derrida* (1987) is very good. So too is Christina Howells' (1999) *Derrida*. A shorter and more critical discussion (pitched for those who may not be familiar with Derrida's work) can also be found in the chapters on Derrida in Peter Dews' (1987) *Logics of Disintegration*.

59

---

54 'There is nothing', he is often quoted as saying, 'outside of the text'.

Key concepts

# Discourse

Related concepts: **deconstruction, ideology, power/knowledge, public sphere, symbolic power.**

The concept of discourse is used in a variety of different ways in critical social theory and there are a variety of different types of discourse analysis. This variation stems in some part from the fact that discourse can be used as a verb (namely to refer to the activity of discourse) or as a noun[55] (namely to refer to this or that discourse, the discourse of race, the medical discourse, etc.). I will try here to define some of the different uses of 'discourse' and to draw out the significance of the concept for different theoretical approaches in the social sciences.

In some uses discourse simply means speech or communication. To discourse is to engage in communication with others by a variety of means (speech, writing, electronic forms of communication or perhaps even gesture). Discourse analysis, from this point of view, simply is the analysis of the way in which people communicate. It involves, as in 'conversation analysis'[56] for example, a detailed focus upon the way in which parties to a debate organize the timing of their participation (for example, who speaks when?) and the way in which speech draws upon particular conventions and forms of rhetoric to achieve its effects. It is a central claim of this approach that 'discourse' must be organized by the parties to it and that the meaning of what is said is not transparent, if read literally, but rather depends upon both elements of the context in which it is uttered – a context which it creates[57] – and common orientation to

---

55 It is arguable that discourse is always a verb and that reference to this or that 'discourse' is no more than shorthand for the conventions governing the practice of discourse in particular contexts. As discourse analysts would be the first to point out, however, verbal habits shape our ways of thinking about things, such that references to *the* discourse might encourage us to ignore the activity of discourse and treat it as a thing.

56 Conversation analysis is a form of discourse analysis deriving from ethnomethodology. See Sharrock and Anderson (1986) or Heritage (1984) for an account of the wider ethnomethodological context and Psathas (1995) for a more technical introduction to conversation analysis itself.

57 Many discourse analysts, particularly in the conversational analytic tradition, are very much opposed to 'readings' which impute meaning to texts on the basis of contexts without

particular rhetorical and discursive 'devices', which interlocuters may have to subtly point one another towards and which discourse analysts seek to analyse.

Building upon this, some writers use discourse to refer to specific ways of speaking about things which have acquired a largely habitual and taken-for-granted character. To refer to 'medical discourse' or 'racist discourse', for example, is to identify a particular vocabulary, a set of norms or rules for defining (or 'constituting') and making sense of particular objects, and a variety of conventions and rhetorical techniques for settling disputes, making claims, researching issues, and so on. In this context discourse is often used as if it were a noun, for example, 'the medical discourse'. The key critical import of this particular conception of discourse rests upon the assumption that those who partake in it are largely unaware of the system of conventions they habitually use and are perhaps also unaware of specific consequences that their way of speaking may have, such that an analysis which unearths and 'deconstructs'[58] that system has a potentially liberatory value. Social agents are able, reflexively, to recognize that their way of seeing and thinking about the world is derived from a social structure (a discourse) that they have learnt and that they habitually rely upon.

Some discourse analysts who use this definition of discourse focus their analytic attention upon the individual characteristics of particular acts of communication. They analyse speech in action, teasing out the various techniques of sense-making it entails. It is also common, however, to find analysts working at a more general level, focusing, for example, upon media or historical archives and seeking to demonstrate the existence of common patterns of language use across numerous texts in these archives. They analyse, for example, particular 'medical' ways of thinking about and dealing with issues, seeking out what it is that makes medical uses of language distinctive, or perhaps they explore ways of using language which are always applied to certain groups but never others, as in racist discourse. Furthermore, at a wider level still, there is the extremely influential work of Michel Foucault, which not only focuses upon long-term historical changes in internal 'rules of discursive

showing that and how the discourse they are analysing points to or uses that context. What counts as context, it is argued, depends upon how interlocuters interpret their context and communicate their interpretation to one another. Thus discourse analysis has to consider how 'context' is constructed in discourse, so as to thereby lend sense to that discourse.
58 I do not mean 'deconstruct' in a 'Derridean' sense. I just mean forms of analysis which consider how discourses and texts work. See deconstruction.

formation'[59] but equally upon the institutional conditions and social problems which facilitate the emergence, organization and survival of particular discourses. Where some discourse analysts with an interest in 'psychiatric discourse' might examine one or two minutes of dialogue between a psychiatrist and 'her patient', pondering every breathing space, for example, Foucault's (1965) analysis spans centuries, looking both 'inside' the discourse, at such factors as the categories and rules[60] which generate it, and 'externally', at the wider social processes which brought about the institutions which, in turn, provided the social space in which the discourse developed in the first place. Psychiatric discourse only emerged in the way that it did, according to Foucault, for example, after 'the mad' (along with a range of other assorted 'deviants') were locked up in houses of confinement and thereby subject to relatively close observation. The decision to lock them up, moreover, had nothing whatsoever to do with mental health, psychiatry or any such thing. It was simply a measure of social control. Foucault asks why and how we ever came to classify and think about mental problems in the first place; why we have a psychiatric discourse and why it has assumed the form that it has. Moreover, he is concerned with the questions of how, where and when particular forms of discourse came to assume the social importance that they have today. In contemporary society, for example, psychiatry and other 'psy' disciplines play a central role in the regulation of society and Foucault asks how it is that this has come about (see also Rose, 1985, 1989). Finally, because he focuses upon large stretches of history, Foucault is able to explore the periodic disjunctures or ruptures that occur in the development of discourses, how our ways of perceiving and thinking about the world change. This concern with disjunctures is one which he borrows from the French tradition in the philosophy of science, following Gaston Bachelard and Georges Canguilhem (see **epistemological break**).

In sharp contrast to both Foucault and the other approaches cited above, Jürgen Habermas uses 'discourse' as a verb, to denote communicative activities which call norms and assumptions into question. Much of the time, Habermas notes, we go along with norms and allow ourselves to be guided by taken-for-granted assumptions. Some element of this is necessary. We can never totally break free of this

---

59 Analysts sometimes describe the peculiar characteristics of a discourse in terms of 'rules' which, if followed, would produce those particular characteristics: e.g. never use the first person; always refer to x as y and always in the passive form etc. This is not to say that people actually do follow rules in producing specific discourses but it is a convenient way of summarizing findings.
60 See note 59 above.

---

*Discourse*

'background' structure. However, on some occasions we call certain key assumptions and norms into question. This, in Habermas' terms, is discourse. Discourse, from this point of view, is analysis. Habermas credits social agents with the capacity to reflect upon (some of) the assumptions and norms that they ordinarily orient to habitually in their mundane actions. However, he is equally clear in his work both that communication can become 'systematically distorted' (see **ideal speech situation**) and that the role of discourse can be undermined in societies as the public sphere is eroded (see **public sphere**). From this point of view, Habermas' work calls out for some form of discourse analysis.

Critical discourse analysis, as pioneered by Norman Fairclough (1994), can be read, in part, as a response to this need in Habermas' work. Or rather, Fairclough combines aspects of all of the above theories and approaches to discourse in his work. A comprehensive and critical approach to discourse analysis, he argues, must be able to span the continuum from the micro-details of specific exchanges through to the broader social history of the contexts and conditions under which discourse is produced, and taking in the mezzo-level, where these extremes become enmeshed.

### FURTHER READING

The clearest statement of Foucault's method of discourse analysis, or at least the method of his early work, is found in his *Archaeology of Knowledge* (Foucault, 1972). This is quite a clear book. For a shorter introduction see his 'Politics and the study of discourse' (Foucault, 1978). Fairclough (1994) presents the principles of critical discourse analysis clearly in his book *Language and Power*. For a discussion of the role of discourse in psychological analyses see Potter and Wetherell's (1987) *Discourse and Social Psychology*. The best technical introductions to conversation analysis are Psathas's (1995) *Conversation Analysis*, and Hutchby and Woofit's (1998) *Conversation Analysis*. For an account which sets conversation analysis in context see either Heritage's (1984) *Garfinkel and Ethnomethodology* or Sharrock and Anderson's (1986) *The Ethnomethodologists*. Habermas' work on discourse can be found in his *Theory of Communicative Action* (Habermas, 1987b, 1991). This is a very large work and quite difficult by undergraduate standards. Useful synopses can be found, however, in White's (1988) *The Recent Work of Jürgen Habermas* and Outhwaite's (1993) *Habermas*.

# Discourse Ethics

> *Related concepts:* **discourse, ideal speech situation, public sphere.**

Discourse ethics is Jürgen Habermas' attempt to recast the system of deontological[61] ethics posited by Kant (1948, 1993) in a more appropriate and persuasive fashion. Kant famously argued that the way to assess whether a course of conduct is right or not is to ask ourselves whether it could be generalized as a universal norm or rule of conduct – would we want others to act in the same way? This stems in part from his further view that ethical conduct entails treating others as 'ends' rather than means; that is, as beings with their own projects and plans. This is his 'categorical imperative'. The principle of universalization is grounded in this categorical imperative in that it ensures that we grant the same rights to others as we expect for ourselves and impose the same duties upon ourselves as we impose upon them. Kant also argued that legitimate norms can and should be rooted in rationality. They are legitimate if every rational being would agree to them. However, methodologically he did not put this latter clause to the test nor did he suggest that it should be put to the test. He believed that a rational agent, qua rational, would know what was rational and legitimate to other rational agents. Others have questioned this.

In an important essay, George Herbert Mead (1967) challenges the idea, adhered to by Kant, that rationality is a property of individual agents, at least if considered in isolation. Rationality emerges in discourse, or more broadly interaction, he argues, from the discipline of having to meet the objections of others, explain to them, persuade them and most importantly accommodate their (often very different) point of view. Furthermore, he continues, 'what any rational subject will consent to' can only be discovered in practice by seeing what different groups of people, with different points of view, actually do consent to.

---

61 Deontological ethics is a system of ethics focused upon issues of duty – 'deon' deriving from the Greek word for 'duty'. Ethical systems focused upon duty and 'right' can be and often are contrasted with ethical systems, such as utilitarianism, which focus instead upon issues of 'the good'. See footnote 64 for a qualification and further clarification of this.

Any concrete individual only ever has a very limited view of the world and it is only by engaging with others, mutually learning and also thrashing out differences, that they can arrive at a more rational and universal point of view. Assuming to know what other 'rational' agents will consent to fails by the standards of the categorical imperative according to Mead. It does not treat others as beings with their own projects and points of view.

Habermas' discourse ethics builds upon this, claiming also to find a transcendental grounding for it in the pragmatics of speech.[62] Like Mead he believes that 'reason' is necessarily intersubjective or 'communicative' and, like Mead, he believes that moral principles can only aspire to the universality advocated by Kant if agents come into dialogue, overcoming their own particular viewpoints in the construction of a 'higher', synthesized viewpoint. This presupposes that agents are prepared to be proved wrong and prepared to put themselves into the shoes of the other, trying to see the world as they do, but it entails equally that all parties to an argument will do everything within bounds of logical and rational argument to establish the superiority of their argument – only succumbing when they encounter arguments or objections which they cannot meet. From this Habermas draws the conclusion, which forms the basis of his discourse ethics, that 'a norm or moral rule can only be deemed rational legitimate to the extent that all parties affected by it, or their representatives, have had the opportunity to debate it rationally and have given it their considered consent'. Debating it 'freely', in this context, means debating it in such a way that the persuasiveness of arguments is the only force operative in the debate. Bribes, threats, and so on are excluded (see **ideal speech situation**).

There is much about this idea that is impractical and perhaps idealistic. One need only cast an eye around the various 'peace talks' in the world to see that rational argument, even on the occasion that it gets to the table, is often swamped by emotional and strategic[63] considerations that compromise and impede it. As with other aspects of Habermas' theory, however, its 'ideal' nature can serve as a useful yardstick for critical theory, against which a rather more messy reality can

---

62 As noted in the entry on the **ideal speech situation**, Habermas believes that the very act of speech necessarily presupposes certain ideals or norms, from which we can build normative principles for critical theory. Arguments about what must necessarily be the case are one variety of what are called 'transcendental' arguments.

63 'Strategy' is rational in its own way, of course. Habermas makes a distinction, however, between 'communicative rationality' and 'strategic rationality'. See **rationality**.

---

be measured and by means of which it can be criticized – not least because, as Habermas notes, political agents very often do claim to be doing what any reasonable person would do. They claim to be acting rationally. Furthermore, although certain aspects of Habermas' argument are problematic, the basic notion that intersubjective agreement is the only possible rational basis for norms is, to my mind, compelling. Most norms are not derived in this way, but then most norms are not fully rational in this sense.

Some critics have argued that Habermas' schema is, in effect, guilty of one of the same major problems as Kant's, namely, that it is formal. It tells us how to recognize a legitimate norm but it does not have any content. It does not give us any legitimate norms, except for the norms of moral discourse, and does not even hint where this content might come from. In response to this, however, Habermas has argued that the content of norms must come from the lifeworld, from the everyday life and culture of people involved in society at any point in time.[64] Moreover, in his defence we might argue that formalism is the best option for ethics in a multi-cultural context. We have no shortage of claims regarding what is good and proper in contemporary society but these claims are often contradictory and what is needed is precisely a formal means of addressing these contradictions and arriving at acceptable and legitimate conclusions. We might also use this argument in response to those critics who argue that Habermas' universality is, in fact, an imposition of Western standards of reason and morality. That may be so, but Habermas, in my view, can legitimately reply to such objections that competing cultures and perspectives are a fact and that the conflicts between them, if not pursued in discourse, will be pursued in violence and war – which, of course, they often are. From this point of view there is a practical argument in favour of pushing to realize Habermas' ideal in practice. Whether or not all groups affected by the decision to opt for dialogue over violence would indeed agree to dialogue is, needless to say, one which can only be made by those parties.

---

64 More technically – philosophical theories of ethics have tended to divide into those which stipulate what is 'good' and those which stipulate what is 'right', the latter tending to be more formal. In addition, many theorists of the good have argued, following Aristotle, that our sense of the good derives from tradition, culture and collective life. Habermas claims that discourse ethics can take this on board and can integrate a concern for both the good and the right. Traditionally bound and derived concepts of the good, in this schema, are effectively inputs to a discursive process which determines what is right.

Mead's essay on ethics, included in the appendix to *Mind, Self and Society* is very readable (Mead, 1967). So too is much of Habermas' own work on this particular issue. See in particular *Moral Consciousness and Communicative Action* (Habermas, 1992) and *Justification and Application* (Habermas, 1993).

# Doxa

*Related concepts:* **capital, crisis, field, habitus, hexis/body techniques, ideology, public sphere, symbolic power.**

The term 'doxa' can be traced back to the philosophy of Aristotle (1955), where it denotes common opinion or the view of the people and where it stands in contrast to knowledge (episteme). Philosophy, for Aristotle, begins with doxa. It critically engages with doxa in an attempt to establish true knowledge. This engagement is never dismissive. Aristotle does not dismiss the opinions of the people as mere prejudice or superstition as some have done. The practical opinions of the people may lack the refinement demanded by the philosopher, he notes, but they 'work' in everyday life. They have taken shape in real life contexts, where they have played a crucial role in guiding activity, and as such they have been subject to a considerable test. The philosopher whose views were widely at odds with the doxa might have to think very carefully about the wisdom of those views relative to the practical wisdom of everyday life. However, philosophy can improve upon doxa, build upon and question it, and that is its role.

Like many Aristotelian concepts, the concept of doxa appears (in a variety of guises) in the thought of many important philosophers and social scientists. For our purposes, however, it is the appropriation and development of the concept in the work of Pierre Bourdieu that is of particular interest. In Bourdieu's work, doxa is contrasted not merely with knowledge but with spoken opinion. Doxa is what literally goes without saying. It is the taken-for-granted background which lends meaning to what we say but which is not itself spoken. It is tacit and though we orient to and affirm it in our habits, practices and assumptions, we may remain largely unaware of it as we do so.

In *Outline of a Theory of Practice*, Bourdieu (1977) reflects upon the political significance of doxa. The sphere of public political discourse, he argues, is divided between opinions which are 'orthodox' and those which are 'heterodox'. These opinions are but the tip of an iceberg, however, and the deeper and larger base of that iceberg consists in all that we do without thinking, all that we assume without even being aware of doing so; that is, doxa (see Figure 1). There is nothing mechanical or inevitable about this. What is doxic today has often been an explicit topic of contention, argument or conflict in the past:

> What appears to us today as self-evident, as beneath consciousness and choice, has quite often been the stake of struggles and instituted only as the result of dogged confrontations between dominant and dominated groups. The major effect of historical evolution is to abolish history by relegating to the past, that is, to the unconscious, the lateral possibles that it eliminated. (1998a: 56-7)

In this sense the doxa plays a crucial political role. The status quo is only preserved, or at least its appearance of naturalness and inevitability is only preserved, insofar as its historical contingency and the opposition it once attracted are wiped from the collective memory, affording its practices and forms a taken-for-grantedness; that is, insofar as it is doxic. The struggles of the past remain and make their mark upon the present in the form of all that we assume and do habitually but, qua pre-reflective, pre-discursive habits, these sediments of the past can only serve to conserve

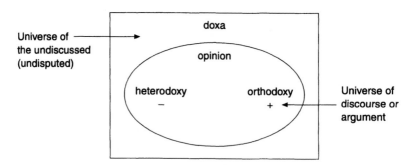

Figure 1 *Doxa, orthodoxy and heterodoxy*
(After the fashion of Bourdieu (1977: 168))

the status quo. In this respect, of course, the doxa also serves the interests of dominant groups, since it naturalizes the conditions of their dominant position:

> Doxa is a particular point of view, the point of view of the dominant, which presents and imposes itself as a universal point of view, the point of view of those who dominate by dominating the state and who have constituted their point of view as universal by constituting the state. (1998: 57)

In this respect, moreover, the concept of the doxa constitutes an important critique of democracy and the **public sphere**. Free speech on matters of public concern poses no threat to central forms of domination and inequality, for Bourdieu, since the interests of the dominant are secured and embodied at a pre-discursive, pre-conscious level. The privileged in particular can afford to be 'open minded' since the questions raised in public discourse have little bearing upon the overall security of their position.

This is not to say that what is doxic now is forever beyond discourse and argument, however. In times of crisis, when the **habitus** of social agents slips out of alignment with the objective structures in which they live their lives, Bourdieu argues, social agents can be prompted to call previously doxic assumptions and states of affairs into question. The world loses its natural feel and at least some of what might have passed without question in the past is subject to argument and debate (see **crisis**). The dominant are forced to defend the practices and beliefs which support and legitimate their dominance, in the name of 'orthodoxy', whilst critical social movements or protest groups are in a position to attack these practices and beliefs in the name of heterodox alternatives (see **social movements**).

In his later work, Bourdieu is keen to identify an affinity between his concept of doxa and the phenomenological concept of the 'natural attitude,'[65] (albeit in a more politicized form) to emphasize its embodied character and to draw out more explicitly its relationship to the practices of the state. Many of the key positions in both sociology and political

---

65 Phenomenologists use 'natural attitude' to denote our usual and mundane way of perceiving and thinking about the world, structured as it is by a range of habits, assumptions and expectations. Phenomenological analysis claims to 'suspend' this natural attitude and to identify and explore the aforementioned habits, assumptions and expectations, reflecting upon the manner in which they constitute the world as it is experienced within the natural attitude. Within sociology the work of Alfred Schutz (1964, 1971, 1972) is the most obvious example of this.

philosophy, he notes, have either assumed that social order is secured through agreement and consensus (whether ideologically manufactured or not) or have puzzled over the way in which the state and other loci of centralized political power secure discursive legitimacy.[66] This is mistaken, however, since the cognitive structures which reproduce the power of the state are 'not forms of consciousness but *dispositions of the body*' (Bourdieu, 1998a: 54); that is, practical ways of perceiving, feeling and acting in the world:

> . . . the social world is riddled with *calls to order* that function as such only for those who are predisposed to heeding them as they *awaken* deeply buried corporeal dispositions, outside the channels of consciousness and calculation. It is this doxic submission of the dominated to the structures of a social order of which their mental structures are the product that Marxism [and other approaches] cannot understand insofar as it remains trapped in the intellectualist[67] tradition of philosophies of consciousness. (1998a: 54–5)

Furthermore, echoing Althusser and Foucault,[68] he argues that in contemporary societies, the state, particularly in the form of the public education system, plays a central role in inculcating these corporeal dispositions. In part he means by this that state education imposes particular schemas of classification and perception in the explicit form of the lesson. Beyond this, however, he argues that rituals of the school, its mechanisms of discipline and regulation, have a crucial conditioning effect. Again this does not preclude crises which facilitate a questioning of doxa. But such questioning does generally presuppose crisis conditions to materialize to any significant degree.

70

---

66 That is, how they persuade people to consciously accept their authority.

67 That is, approaches which make conscious human thought the key to understanding human life. This is a mistake, according to many, for a number of reasons. Firstly, it ignores the fact that agents exist and are involved in the world, practically, prior to any thoughts or reflections they may have. Secondly, thought does not emerge out of nowhere. It emerges out of our practical and sensuous engagement with the world. Thirdly, the point Bourdieu is really driving at here, our conscious and reflective attention is only ever directed towards a very small portion of our lived reality; the rest is a matter of habit, routine and assumptions which are never questioned.

68 Althusser views the educational system as an 'ideological state apparatus' which creates human agents who are compliant and fitted for the needs of capitalism as an economic system. On this see the entry on **ideology**. Foucault sees the education system as part of a broader disciplinary apparatus or carceral network. On this see **body-power/bio-power**, **power** and **power/knowledge**.

---

Aristotle's (Nichomachian) *Ethics* is a fascinating background read from the point of view of many of Bourdieu's concepts, including 'doxa' (Aristotle, 1955). There is no sustained discussion of doxa anywhere in Bourdieu's work but two key works where the concept is used to a significant degree are *Outline of a Theory of Practice* (Bourdieu, 1977) and *Practical Reason* (Bourdieu, 1998a).

# Epistemological Break

> *Related concepts: discourse, ideology, realism, social construction/ constructionism.*

The concept of 'epistemological breaks' is most famously associated, in the context of critical social theory in the English-speaking world, with the work of the French Marxist philosopher, Louis Althusser (1969, Althusser and Balibar, 1979), who argued that the earlier and later work of Karl Marx is separated by one such break. It is also an important concept for understanding aspects of the work of both Michel Foucault and Pierre Bourdieu. I will return to these writers. First, however, we must consider the original formulation of the concept in the work of the French philosopher of science, Gaston Bachelard (1970).

Studying the history of a variety of sub-disciplinary areas of physics and the developments associated with the theories of relativity and quanta in particular, Bachelard arrived at the conclusion that science does not develop by a process of gradual accumulation of observations and experimental findings. Rather it, or rather branches of it, periodically take leaps forward in which their whole conceptual framework, including their norms of reasoning, observing and experimenting, are changed. Scientists begin to perceive and think about their object of study differently, or rather they 'construct' that object differently. In his earlier work, particularly *The Formation of the Scientific Mind*, Bachelard (2002) conceives of this in terms of what he calls 'epistemological obstacles'. The mind of the scientist, like that of anybody else, is structured by a range of largely unconscious habits, assumptions and tendencies which hinder the development of knowledge, he argues, and it is not until these obstacles are identified as such, and/or overcome, that science moves forward. *The Formation of the Scientific Mind* catalogues a range of the key obstacles that, in Bachelard's view, modern science has had to overcome in order to achieve its current, advanced state and the book thereby traces the history of a succession of perceptual/conceptual schemata which structured both early scientific and pre-scientific experiences of the world in the recent history of the west. This is not a matter of new data emerging but rather a matter of new ways of thinking about, observing and treating data, or more importantly, at least in this earlier work, of earlier ways of thinking about, observing and treating data being surpassed.

In Bachelard's later work[69] this is formulated in terms of 'epistemological breaks' which overcome these 'epistemological obstacles'. He uses this concept of epistemological breaks in two ways. In the first instance, the advance of science involves it breaking from pre or non-scientific forms of thought, principally 'common-sense' and philosophy. Science has only tended to make real progress, Bachelard argues, when it has learnt to abandon, in stages, common sense ways of looking at and thinking about the world. The physicist's view of matter, as a structure of interacting atoms, for example, is quite different from our own phenomenological experience of material 'things', and leads the physicist to categorize together 'things' which common sense keeps apart, whilst perhaps categorizing separately 'things' which common sense deems similar. Importantly, this involves science both going beyond what ordinary perception can see, and configuring its perceptual constitution of objects differently. Technologies such as the microscope and telescope, which allow one to see things or aspects of things that are not available to the naked eye, are important in this respect. They afford a different way of seeing. However, Bachelard is clear that these technologies themselves embody theory and are used in accordance with a theoretical framework of reference, such that they cannot be understood simply as extensions of the 'eye'. Theory is as essential to changed ways of seeing as technology and is, in any case, woven into scientific technology. Continuing this point Bachelard argues that many scientific advances have involved a rejection of the standards and evidence of ordinary perception. Science has moved forward by challenging what is obvious and plain to

---

69 The key text, *Rationalisme Appliqué* (Bachelard, 1970) is not available in English translation but see the end of this entry for some English-language commentaries.

see. We are sometimes misled on this count, he argues, because of the similarity between scientific terms and everyday terms. This is misleading because even when science uses words drawn from everyday discourse these words have very different uses and therefore very different meanings. What the physicist means by temperature, for example, is not the same as what you or I (or the physicist when out of role) mean when we talk about temparature, for example in relation to the weather or cooking, and so on.

More dramatically, this also applies to philosophy. There are a number of important instances where what philosophers have deemed undeniable or necessarily true have been debunked by scientific advances (that is by epistemological breaks). Science periodically finds it necessary and proves it both possible and coherent to break rules of thought and reasoning which generations of philosophers have deemed beyond question.[70] Philosophy, Bachelard argues, often presumes to legislate for science, demarcating the boundaries of legitimate thought, but it must not be allowed to do so, at least not in terms of epistemology, ontology or metaphysics.[71] As an exercise of 'pure thought', devoid of 'application' (namely experiments applied to an empirical world), philosophy is inclined to perpetuate and reproduce the common sense of the day, albeit in a logically rigorous fashion.

Importantly, however, Bachelard also notes that scientific perspectives feed back into common sense and modify it. Society incorporates scientific discoveries, both in the form of new technologies and revised common sense. We all wash our hands to clean away bacteria, for example, even though very few of us has ever seen bacteria or really has any independent proof of its existence. On this point we trust to science. Likewise we tend to look to antecedent material causes to explain events in our lives rather than, as our ancestors tended to do, blaming spells, demons or witches. Science changes our view of the world. New forms of reasoning and seeing seep into culture by means of the education system. And of course we all use technologies that are based upon science.

The second use of 'epistemological break' in Bachelard's work refers

73

---

70 Bachelard's key point of reference here is the work of Einstein. Many philosophers were shocked by this work because of the challenge that it posed to previously held views. In many ways, however, the earlier scientific revolutions of the Renaissance and Enlightenment were as shocking, not least because of the challenge which they posed to theological conceptions of the universe.
71 It may be that philosophy is necessary to set ethical guidelines for scientific work, but Bachelard does not consider this and there is no reason why he would be forced to accept this role for philosophy either.

---

to breaks in the history of a branch of science itself, when an old theoretical framework (which might have become an epistemological obstacle, even if once it marked a break) is displaced in favour of a new one; when new ways of looking at and thinking about something, new norms of scientific reasoning emerge. To use a much worn example, the work of Einstein did not so much build upon the work of Newton as effect a fundamental transformation in the way physicists thought and worked. This use of 'epistemological break' parallels Thomas Kuhn's (1970) notion of 'paradigm shifts'.[72] Importantly, however, there is greater attention in Bachelard's work to the manner in which old ideas or observations are incorporated into new 'paradigms', sometimes perhaps as 'special cases'[73] and always in a newly constituted form, such that it is easier to speak of progress in the move from old to newer 'paradigms' (not a term Bachelard uses).[74] Epistemological breaks are more than simple additions to knowledge. Whole frames of reference shift. But there is some continuity and what discontinuity there is allows science to move beyond the obstacles posed by the earlier mode of thought. This is progress – or at least that is how Bachelard sees it.

Bachelard calls his approach 'applied rationalism' (le rationalisme appliqué). The reference here to 'rationalism' implies that the mind plays an active role in constructing knowledge and more particularly in constructing the underlying categories which structure knowledge. In fact, Bachelard suggests that the objects of both everyday experience and science do not exist, as such, independently of the mind and the way in which it constructs reality. The objects of scientific analysis are constructed by the sciences which analyse them. However, he is very critical of the notion of 'pure thought', whether in the guise of philosophy or in the suggestion that scientific knowledge and/or scientific advances are simply a result of the activity of the mind. Knowledge emerges in the interplay between the mind and a world which transcends it, he believes,

74

72 The US philosopher of science, Thomas Kuhn (1970), has also argued that scientific activity (perception, thought, technology, etc.) is structured by underlying and often tacit theories, which he calls paradigms, and he too has argued that these paradigms shift (there is a 'break' in their development) at particular points in the history of science.
73 That is to say, something which was once deemed to apply universally turns out only to be true under certain conditions. In such cases an observation or scientific law is not rejected outright but it is understood differently.
74 Kuhn argues that different paradigms make different assumptions and, as such cannot be evaluated comparatively. In the final instance they are just different ways of looking at the world – at least this is one dominant interpretation of his work. Bachelard, however, seemingly recognizes more continuity across breaks, with the old being incorporated within the new, such that the new can be said to be better than the old. For more elucidation of this point see Gutting (1989).

an interplay which is shaped by (a historically specific) rationality but equally by scientific activity and technologies which embody and realize that rationality in a world which 'resists' it. The world as such is not constructed by the human mind, in other words, only the world as we know it and even then the existence of the world beyond our constructions, reveals itself to us by way of its tendency to occasionally confound our constructions: e.g. when predictions that we make turn out to be false or when closer examination refutes our preliminary models and understanding. Even in these cases, of course, we do not experience the world in an unmediated or unconstructed fashion but there is an intransigence to the behaviour of the world which one would not predict if the world were simply reducible to our constructions of it. To my mind this qualifies Bachelard as a 'realist', at least as that term tends to be used in contemporary philosophy, or perhaps rather it suggests a complementarity between 'applied rationalism' (as an epistemology) and 'realism' (as an ontology)[75] (see **realism**). He was, in fact, an ardent critic of what he called realism but he had a very narrow definition of it which few contemporary realists would subscribe to and his insistence that knowledge emerges from the application of reason and indeed from the sometimes surprising events and observations which such applications throw up, brings him squarely within the realist camp. Like the realist, he puts a great emphasis upon error and the surprises thrown up by errors, in his philosophy of science. It is because we get things 'wrong' and our predictions are not born out, he argues, that science and knowledge are able to move forward. For the realist, similarly, the possibility of error provides the basis upon which we can argue for the existence of a world independent of our knowledge of it (see **realism**).

As noted above, the concept of 'epistemological breaks' really emerged in critical social theory in relation to the work of Althusser (1969, Althusser and Balibar, 1979), who claimed that the earlier and later works of Marx are divided by an epistemological break. The later Marx, for Althusser, is a scientist. He has crossed the threshold of scientificity by breaking with the naïve assumptions or 'ideology' of everyday common sense, 'bourgeois' economics/philosophy and indeed of his own earlier work. In particular, Althusser believed that humanist concepts, which link society and history back to a concept of 'man', impede the science

75 That is, a theory of the world (ontology) and a theory of knowledge about the world (epistemology). See **realism** for a clarification of this distinction and its relevance.

of economy and society, and he believed that Marx had overcome this obstacle by way of the formulation of structuralist concepts which avoid reliance upon 'man' (e.g. mode of production, forces of production). This is an interesting departure because, as McAllester Jones (1991) argues, Bachelard himself was clearly a humanist. It is also a controversial claim which many Marxist theorists have disputed. However, Althusser is a less relevant and less interesting advocate of 'epistemological breaks' from our point of view, than Michel Foucault and Pierre Bourdieu.

Foucault, also via the work of another French philosopher of science influenced by Bachelard, Georges Canguilhem (1991), takes over the tradition of the philosophy of science from Bachelard, applying it to human science. However, there are three clear differences between Foucault's work and that of Bachelard, in addition to the former's turn from natural to social science. Firstly, he is at the very least agnostic about the notion of scientific progress and certainly does not praise science as Bachelard does. Dreyfus and Rabinow (1982) have argued that Foucault's early work is at least compatible with a notion of scientific progress and perhaps even realism (in the sense discussed above). This may be so but Foucault tends not to commit himself on this issue and even in his early work there is a critical edge to his description of modern science that is not evident in Bachelard. Secondly, under the influence of structuralism he removes the humanism of Bachelard's approach, displacing humanist concepts and replacing them with alternatives. Foucault drops references to 'the scientific mind' or 'spirit', for example, in favour of 'discourses' and 'practices'. Thirdly, building upon some of the developments of Canguilhem,[76] he puts a much greater emphasis upon the role which factors external to science have upon its development, and the impact which science, in turn, has upon that world. In practice this means social factors. Changes in science are very often precipitated by social changes and the problems they throw up, in Foucault's account, and the formation of a social scientific discourse is coterminous with the emergence of new practices for the control of those problems (see **power/knowledge**).

---

76 In his history of biological and medical knowledge Canguilhem argues that it is only the problem posed by illness which prompts the emergence of medical discourse. It is only when the 'silence' of the organs is broken that medical discourse begins to take shape. In the social case, of course, the problem which prompts the development of knowledge is often a social problem and may be a problem which emerges only relatively to certain types of social change. 'Madness', for example, only stands out as a problem in need of specialized management in the context of certain types of societies. In some societies it is either tolerated or ignored. Thus the development of psychiatry presupposes certain types of society wherein madness is a problem in need of a solution.

Having said this, references to ruptures or breaks – akin to Bachelard's 'epistemological breaks' – abound in Foucault's work. Indeed, *Birth of the Clinic*, *The Order of Things* and *Discipline and Punish* each begin either with a contrast of two obviously very different rationalities or with a discussion of a way of thinking which is quite obviously very strange from a contemporary point of view – a view we have broken with. What has happened between point a and point b, Foucault asks rhetorically, such that the difference between them should be so great? He then sets about, for the duration of these studies, telling us. The notion of breaks is, in this respect, absolutely central to Foucault's account of both discourses and specific regimes or forms of power and governance. Not just scientific history but social history, as the history of specific regimes of practices, Foucault appears to say, is often the history of breaks or ruptures.

The case of Bourdieu (who was also influenced by Canguilhem, as well as Bachelard) is very different. The need for reflexivity in critical social science generates a need for engagement with Foucauldian type historical studies, he argues (Bourdieu, 1988). Critical sociologists need Foucault et al. to do critical histories of sociology if they are to be reflexively aware of the ground they are walking upon and the effects they have upon it – although we should note that he is also critical of what he sees as Foucault's relativism and occasional irrationalism (Bourdieu, 2000). However, Bourdieu's own appropriation of Bachelard (and Canguilhem) is much more normative. He tends to use their accounts of the development of natural (in Canguilhem's case medical/biological) science as a model for how social science 'should' operate (see especially Bourdieu, Chamboredon and Passeron, 1991). Sociology, for Bourdieu, has yet to leap many of the epistemological obstacles that natural science, in Bachelard's view, leapt many years ago. This is not the place to detail his methodological prescriptions. However, three brief observations are important.

Firstly, explicitly relating his argument back to the methodological prescriptions of Marx, Weber and particularly Durkheim, he argues that sociology has to break from everyday common sense and the 'spontaneous sociology' belonging to it. Everyday ways of thinking about the world might be a legitimate object of analysis, he argues, but they are not a good basis for sociology. Moreover, this means that we should distinguish between 'social problems' and 'sociological problems'; that is, between problems that arise and are defined as such within society, and problems which arise specifically within the sociological field as a result of theoretical and research activity. This break is achieved, for Bourdieu, by 'applied rationalism'; that is to say, it is achieved through the combined result of rational and rigorous theory and equally rigorous empirical research. In places he seems specifically to cite quantitative and statistical work as important in this respect, perhaps because large-scale statistical surveys take us beyond the scale of what is available to individual perception and experience. However, he notes with equal vigour the importance of ethnographic and qualitative methods,[77] and insists that survey work must be informed by a phenomenological sensitivity to lay perceptions and conceptions. The fine line that the sociologist has to tread is between the equally problematic tendencies of simply reproducing, as a model of the world, what interviewees/subjects have to say about it and displacing their conceptual map of the world with one's own. Some of the measures social research will use have no direct bearing upon the way in which 'lay' agents construct their world, Bourdieu notes, but much of what agents do is at least mediated by these constructions – people act in accordance with the way in which they see the world – and the processes of data gathering, analysis and explanation must be sensitive to this if they are to have any validity. The key point here, however, is that the researcher pulls back from the subjectivity of those whom she studies and objectifies that view. Objectification, in this sense, is the key to the epistemological break which, in Bourdieu's view, founds sociology as a science.

Secondly, mirroring a discussion in *The Formation of the Scientific Mind*, Bourdieu calls for an abandonment of 'substantialism' in favour of 'relationism'. This concept is dealt with elsewhere in the collection and I will not repeat myself here. Suffice it to say that critical sociology, for Bourdieu, must abandon the focus upon entities and their properties in the pursuit of a study of relationships. Naïve perception and common sense, Bourdieu claims, attribute properties to substances or entities. Advanced sciences, by contrast, are the sciences of relationships. If sociology is to be an advanced (i.e. worthwhile) science it must therefore do the same and constitute its focus as an analysis of social relationships.

Finally, mirroring natural scientific concerns with relativity but equally engaging the very specific concerns of social science, Bourdieu argues that a critical social science must be reflexive if it is to break free of epistemological obstacles. A point of view which remains unaware of itself

---

77 The philosopher Martin Heidegger (1962) argues that we are blind to both that which is too far away for us to see it and that which is too close. It might be argued that quantitative, historical and comprative work give us access to that which we are too far away from to see, whilst qualitative work allows us to see that which we are too close to see.

as a point of view has failed to sufficiently break free of the constraints of that point of view.

In Bourdieu's work the element of 'realism', that I identified in relation to Bachelard, comes much more clearly into view. One of the two central values of 'applied rationalism', he argues, is 'fidelity to the real' (Bourdieu et al., 1991). To this end social facts must be 'won, constructed and confirmed' (ibid.); that is, they must be developed and redeveloped within a situation where they are tested and might be challenged or refuted by evidence. In particular, contrary to 'conventionalism',[78] Bourdieu argues that:

> The object, it has been said, is what objects. Experiment only fulfils its function insofar as it sets up a permanent reminder of the reality principle against the temptation to yield to the pleasure principle[79] which inspires the gratuitous fantasies of some types of formalism, the self-indulgent fictions of intuitionism or the academic exercises of pure theory. [. . .] Every well constructed experiment has the effect of intensifying the dialectic between reason and experiment [sic.],[80] but only on the condition that one has an understanding of the results, even negative ones, that it produces, and asks oneself what reasons make the facts right to say no. (ibid.: 61)

The simple fact of the facts saying 'no', of the object objecting, are not sufficient to generate an epistemological break and may, in any case, only call for a minor adjustment of minor hypotheses. However, the infidelity of a theory to the real, as revealed in experimental 'objections', clearly does enter into the process whereby shifts are precipitated. It is because reason is applied to a world which transcends it that it is led to transform itself.

78 This term (which Bourdieu does not use) refers to philosophies of science which, contra realism, recognise no reality external to that constructed within scientific theories (or mundane perception and discourse).

79 It is significant that Bourdieu uses the psychoanalytic language of 'pleasure principle' and 'reality principle' here, as much of Bachelard's work on science, and particularly his earlier work uses the language and ideas of psychoanalysis. The gist of Bourdieu's point is that we have to test our ideas against a reality which may throw them back in our face, rather than taking comfortable refuge in the theorists 'arm chair', where sensible or exciting sounding ideas might be embraced purely on the grounds that they sound about right or excite us and confirm our view of the world.

80 I assume that this should read 'between reason and experience'. I think that the problem here with the translation results from the fact that the French use the same word (*expérience*) to denote both 'experience' (in the sense of life experiences) and experiment (in the sense of scientific experiments). On my reading it does not make sense to translate 'expérience' as 'experiment' here – even though Bourdieu is talking about science. 'Experience' makes more sense. Bourdieu would thus be saying that rational models are tested by way of a confrontation with empirical realities as revealed (through experiment) to our experience.

The central text by Bachelard with respect to epistemological breaks, *Le Rationalisme Appliqué* (Bachelard, 1970) is not yet in English translation. His key text on epistemological obstacles, *The Formation of the Scientific Mind*, is now available however, and is a relatively straightforward read (Bachelard, 2002). This was a central text on the French university curriculum. It was read by many key French thinkers and its influence was considerable. For a good introduction to the work of Bachelard see McAllester-Jones (1991) *Gaston Bachelard: Subversive Humanist*. The first chapter of Gutting's (1989) *Michel Foucault's Archaeology of Scientific Reason* also gives a good introduction to Bachelard, and Canguilhem, and it has the advantage of linking these ideas to those of Foucault. Amongst Foucault's own work *The Archaeology of Knowledge* is perhaps the most relevant text (Foucault, 1972). *The Order of Things* is also an interesting text, however, both in the sense that it deals very centrally with breaks and contains a brief critique of the Althusserian claim that Marx's earlier and later works are separated by a break. Foucault configures the history of socio-economic thought differently from Althusser. The most direct reference to breaks, and so on in Bourdieu's work, can be found in *The Craft of Sociology* (Bourdieu et al., 1991) but if we read Bourdieu carefully, particularly his methodological works, the influence of Bachelard is pervasive throughout.

## Field

> *Related concepts: **capital, doxa, habitus, hexis, illusio, relationalism, social space I.***

The concept of 'fields' is one which Pierre Bourdieu uses to capture the differentiation of society into distinct sectors or 'worlds': for example the world of the mass media, the economy, the family, the church, the scientific world and so on. Thus he writes of the media field, the economic field, the educational field and, more specifically, the higher educational field (a sub-field within the educational field). He builds this

key concepts

concept of fields, in a number of contexts, through a series of contrasts with similar concepts derived from other perspectives and through a series of metaphors. In terms of contrasts he seeks to distinguish 'fields', on one side, from Weberian and interactionist conceptions of social worlds which, in his view,[81] either decompose them into the individuals involved in them[82] or focus only upon the immediate and visible logic of interactions, paying insufficient attention to questions of power, inequality and the structural position of agents relative to one another. On the other side he opposes 'fields' to structuralist, post-structuralist and functionalist conceptions, which tend to dissolve agents into structures (e.g. into roles, rules, apparatuses, institutions and so on) thereby ignoring the role of conflict, agency, strategy and innovation in social worlds. There is more to a social field than individual agents in interaction, Bourdieu argues. At the very least agents are positioned in fields, in virtue of their access to power and resources within that field. And what they do and say assumes its significance as a consequence of the structure of the field – its various codes, schemas of categorization and norms. When we view works of art, for example, we do so through a lens which has taken shape in the history of the artistic field. This lens shapes our interpretation both of individual works and of the legitimacy and greatness (or not) of specific artists – such that we might exercise considerable charity in relation to great works which we neither like nor understand. In addition we have differing degrees of access to this lens and to the field as a whole, in virtue of our habitus and cultural capital (see **habitus** and **capital**). Whenever we enter a new field we discover that it has a pre-established and taken-for-granted structure of both meaning and power.

However, any field is dynamic and those involved in it, whether they are new to it or old hands, have different interests which motivate a variety of competing and often conflicting projects. In particular Bourdieu appears to emphasize the importance of younger generations entering fields and attempting to displace the old guard they discover therein. Having said this, he also always emphasizes that such conflicts and disagreements are underwritten by tacit agreements and a shared 'belief in the game' (see **illusio**). If agents did not agree that there was something worth disagreeing about and fighting over then there would be no field

---

81 I do not agree with Bourdieu on this point, at least with respect to the interactionists, but there is not sufficient space here to explore my objections.
82 Weber (1978), of course, argues precisely in favour of this strategy, under the rubric of 'methodological individualism'. 'Rational action theory', or 'rational choice theory' as it is also sometimes known, is another central example of an approach which advocates this strategy.

in the first place, he observes. Art critics might disagree over the meaning of 'art' or 'beauty', for example, but the very fact of their disagreement and the great efforts they go to in order to make their point indicates that they share a common belief that these questions and issues are important and worth fighting about. Furthermore, in more specialized fields it is likely that the stakes and form of conflicts are only a concern for members of the field. Non-sociologists, for example, are largely indifferent to the theoretical and interpretative wranglings of social theorists and their interpreters.

The balance that Bourdieu seeks to strike between agency and structure here is akin to that advocated by Marx. Agents make their own history, Bourdieu is arguing, but not in circumstances of their choosing. They forge their way in a pre-established context of meaning and power, a context shaped by those who have gone before them and, indeed, by their contemporaries.

The first of the metaphors that Bourdieu brings to bear is 'field' itself, a concept he borrows from modern theoretical physics and particularly from Gaston Bachelard's rendering of the concept in his work on the philosophy and history of science. Bachelard (2002, 1984) argued that one of the key 'epistemological obstacles' (see **epistemological break**) physics had to overcome before it developed to its current form was the problem of substantialism (see **relationalism**); that is, the problem of treating objects of study as independent and pre-given 'things' with individual properties rather than as nodes in systems of relations and interaction. The identity and properties of any one 'thing', according to field theories, is a function of its place within a network of relations and interaction. Bourdieu calls for the same innovation in sociology, and appropriating the concept of field, however metaphorically, is his way of striving to achieve it. Thus the meaning and power of any 'thing' in a field (for example, art works, institutions, practices, and so on) is always relative to its position within the field and there is a relational logic and dynamic operative in the field. In the political field, for example, the same policy might, at different times, be adopted by left-wing groups and right-wing groups, both of whom, at the time, will claim it as a left- or right-wing policy. The truth, Bourdieu argues, is that left and right is a structural opposition constitutive of the political field, such that the real meaning of left wing is 'not right wing' and the real meaning of right wing is 'not left wing'. Within this field, any action by one party invites reaction by the other party. Consequently a party may embrace a policy at one point of time and reject it at another, depending upon what the other party or parties are doing.

82

In a slight variation on this Bourdieu seems also sometimes to trade upon the image of 'magnetic fields', making reference to the forms of attraction and repulsion imminent in any field, at any time. For example, where do agents and their resources flow towards, and where do they flow away from? What trends and fashions animate collective action at any particular point in time? What practices attach to which groups or locations in social space? This metaphor is interesting and appropriate, I suggest, as magnetic fields are often referred to in debates in the philosophy of science to illustrate the role of 'unobservables'.[83] They are a key example of the fact that science does not limit itself to the study of phenomena which are directly observable but deals also with phenomena which are invisible and detactable only by way of their effects. This accords with Bourdieu's attempt to get beyond the focus (which Weberians and interactionists are limited to in his view) on the visible and immediate aspects of social relationships and interactions, so as to explore more hidden dynamics and forces.

The second key metaphor that Bourdieu draws upon is that of the 'market'. In each field, as in the economy, agents trade and compete for goods and resources. Consequently, it is possible to identify forces such as supply and demand or inflation within them. When more students are admitted into the higher educational field, for example, the relative value of a degree declines (since more people have one) and access to high social positions therefore comes increasingly to depend upon possession of a higher degree, such as a masters. There is a process of educational 'inflation'. Likewise in the political field, when established parties fail to satisfy their constituencies this generates a demand which other parties and political entrepreneurs are inclined to seek to capitalize upon. Perhaps the far right spot a gap in the market when the main parties ignore particular constituencies, and they move in on that constituency like economic entrepreneurs moving in upon a market niche.

Another integral aspect to this market metaphor is Bourdieu's view that fields involve unequal distributions of the various resources exchanged within them, such that agents themselves might be said to be distributed or positioned within the field in accordance with their access to resources. This can be quite specific and limited in its effects. Certain fields are small and relatively closed, so as to have little effect outside of themselves. Other fields, however, such as the economic and educational

---

83 For a brief treatment of this issue see the entry on **realism**. Magnetic fields are unobservables in the sense that we can only observe them by way of their effects, or techniques designed to demonstrate their effects, never directly.

fields, have a considerable effect upon wider fields and thus upon the power and life chances of agents in relation to those wider fields. Occupying a 'poor' or 'rich' position in either the educational or economic fields has a significant impact upon most aspects of one's life. This point is explored further in the entry on **social space I**. Suffice it to say here that these very important (sociologically and socially) fields collectively comprise what Bourdieu refers to as the 'field of power'.

The third key metaphor that Bourdieu utilizes is that of 'games' – a point not unrelated to the fact that he refers to the habitus as a 'feel for the game' and the illusio as a 'belief in the game' (see **habitus** and **illusio**). The game metaphor preserves the competitive and conflictual aspect of fields noted above, as many games involve conflict and competition, but it adds an important cultural, and culturally arbitrary,[84] element. In games like football, players and teams compete but within a cultural framework which is highly specific. Unlike rugby players, football players cannot pick the ball up and run with it; unlike boxers they are not allowed to punch each other; unlike synchronized swimmers they will receive no marks for elegance. Their aim, which they must pursue without question, is to kick a ball into a space which is demarcated by metal tubes and rope netting. Moreover, when doing this they must orient to certain rules and to a series of social-spatial zones indicated by white lines chalked on the ground. Of course when players play, nothing seems more natural than doing just this. They might bend the rules slightly but only because they believe so strongly in the game and want to win. For the most part they are completely attuned to the game and treat its (from an outside point of view) wholly arbitrary traditions as if they were forces of nature. The same is true in all areas of social life, Bourdieu argues, except that the games of 'real life' are games 'in themselves' rather than games 'for themselves'. They are games that we do not see as such. Unlike football, where the final whistle indicates that the game is over and everyone can relax back into the recognition that it was all 'just a game', fields have no final whistle. Outsiders may experience their arbitrariness but insiders, for the most part, do not. Thus the politician, the artist, the journalist and the sociologist, no less than the footballer, can be viewed as a player in a game. And the point of the concept of the field is to signal this, such that we might study the game-like structure of different arenas of social activity. Again 'relations' are prioritized here, since the player is nothing without

---

84 The concept of the 'cultural arbitrary' is one which Bourdieu and Passeron discuss in detail in their *Reproduction* (1996).

---

the game and acts only in relation to the state of play within the game. Norbert Elias' (1978) discussion of games provides an interesting point of reference here. In a game, he notes, even a simple game with two players, the way one player acts is affected by the actions of another, to whom s/he responds, and the action of that player is equally a response to the actions of the first, such that we cannot understand the actions of either independently of their co-participation in the game.

The metaphor of the game may seem dangerous. Are we really to treat left and right wings in politics as 'arbitrary'? Do we not think that the stakes of politics are more than arbitrary? I believe that Bourdieu agrees with this. However, he believes equally that sociology has to disconnect itself from 'the natural attitude';[85] from what is routinely taken for granted. It has to render the familiar strange. And the game metaphor is a very powerful rhetorical means of doing this which, Bourdieu hopes, will open up previously unseen dynamics of the social world. Borrowing from phenomenology, we might say that this process of stepping back is not a denial or relativization of all that we believe but rather a methodological bracketing of it which allows us to see it and understand it more clearly. The concept of field calls upon us to temporarily suspend our belief in important social worlds but only so that we can study those worlds (because we believe that they are important) and only because we want, in the final instance, to make a positive contribution to them.

Some of Bourdieu's work seems to suggest that all fields have certain characteristic properties in common. I believe that it is important, however, to draw a distinction between established and well-instituted fields which may share a number of generic properties and less established, less institutionalized fields which share only some of the general properties of the former. Much of my own work, for example has attempted to think about social movements in terms of fields (what I call 'fields of contention'). The concept is very useful and works well in this context, I believe, but 'fields of contention' are different from such established fields as the field of higher education, the journalistic field or the artistic field. They are much more fluid; their structure changes more rapidly and they are less durable than more established fields.

---

85  This a concept from phenomenological philosophy. It denotes our habitual way of looking at the world, which is structured by a range of tacit and taken-for-granted assumptions, expectations and affordances. More specifically, it is a perception of the world which remains ignorant of the manner in which it constructs the world as a perceptual object, experiencing the perceived world rather as an entity entirely independent of it.

A field is a 'social space' and clearly need not coincide with a physical space. Agents inhabit both physical and social spaces, of course, but the boundaries of these two types of space need not necessarily map neatly on to one another. Having said this, they do coincide to some degree and in some respects, and this fact opens up important possibilities of researching fields that are hardly touched upon in Bourdieu's own work (although one of his final works, *The Weight of the World*, does begin to open up this issue (Bourdieu et al., 1999). The physical spatialization of aspects of the economic field in ghettos of the poor, 'playgrounds' of the rich and on the floor of stockmarkets, for example, makes that field tangible and researchable in ways which have not been fully exploited yet. The same applies for the physical spatialization of the higher education field in the context of university campuses. There is always a danger in exploring this social-physical overlap that we become overly concrete in our analysis, ignoring less immediately visible aspects of fields that can only be brought to light through a comparative analysis of their various 'positions' and 'spaces'. This does not undermine the potential fruitfulness of a more physically spatial approach however.

### FURTHER READING

Bourdieu discusses fields in a relatively clear fashion in his introductory book, co-produced with Loic Wacquant, *Introduction to Reflexive Sociology* (Bourdieu and Wacquant, 1992). There is also an interesting supplementary essay, 'Some properties of fields', published in *Sociology in Question* (Bourdieu, 1993).

86

# Freedom

---

*Related concepts: **body-subject, habitus.***

---

The concept of 'freedom' can be posed in a metaphysical fashion, as a matter of 'free will', a concept which stands in opposition to and derives its meaning from its opposition to 'determinism'. Alternatively it can be posed in political terms as a matter of liberty, where it stands in contrast to certain forms of humanly constructed constraint or coercion. In the first case being 'free' means that one's actions are not 'caused' by factors or forces outside of oneself. In the second case, being free means enjoying the liberty to act as one would like within the bounds of one's own intrinsic capabilities.

It is usual to further sub-divide the second conception of freedom, freedom as liberty, into negative and positive versions. A negative conception of liberty entails that political freedom derives from the absence of constraint. If I am not stopped from doing something then I am free to do it. Advocates of a positive conception of freedom object that this ignores the resources that are positively necessary to engage in certain types of actions. To use the usual example, a homeless individual is not free to visit the opera or an expensive restaurant, even if they are not barred as such, because they lack the money required to engage in these pursuits. A positive conception of liberty thus focuses equally upon the resources and power necessary to specific forms of action. The two conceptions, positive and negative, often clash in relationship to the issue of equality. From the negative point of view, strategies designed to promote equality, since they can be said to restrict the actions of some (privileged) members of society in a variety of ways, are thereby said to be detrimental to human freedom. Taxation, which is used to fund the welfare system, limits my freedom, for example, because it spends my money for me, preventing me from deciding what I would like to pay for and what I do not want to pay for. Perhaps I have no children and do not want to pay to educate the children of those who cannot afford to pay for private schooling. From the positive point of view, however, inequality in itself is an obstacle to the liberty of the poor and thus one can argue for strategies designed to promote equality both on the basis that equality is a good in itself and from the point of view that it is integral to freedom. Those who cannot afford private schooling are not as free as those who can, according to this definition, and taxation and schemes of economic redistribution therefore serve to enhance their freedom (at the same time as they strive to achieve a greater degree of equality).

In this entry I will focus primarily upon the metaphysical aspect to the freedom debate but, as we will see, this debate can shade over into a more political debate about liberty and its preconditions. My concern is to first highlight why the question of freedom is deemed important and second to put some more meat upon the bones of the idea of metaphysical freedom, specifying more concretely what it means. My discussion will not be comprehensive. Far from it. Hopefully it will be interesting and provocative, however.

The metaphysical debate on freedom arises against the backdrop of determinism and its apparent ubiquity in the world as described by science. Every event, science tells us, has a cause. And as human action is an event, it too must be caused. It does not matter for the moment whether we are referring to physical, chemical, biological, psychological or social causes. The philosophical argument is the same. But does the argument matter? Does it matter whether or not we are 'free' in this sense? There are several reasons why we might think that it does matter and why we might seek to argue that the claim of the determinist is problematic.

Firstly, the claim of the determinist sits unhappily with our own experience. We feel, at least most of us, as if we make decisions and act. We do not feel as if our actions are determined – at least most of us do not, most of the time. This gives us one reason for doubting the determinist and for looking for reasons to reject the deterministic argument. Furthermore, we might even argue that genuine adherence to the deterministic argument would make life impossible for us. We have to assume that our actions stem from our own volitions and decisions, otherwise what is the point? If the determinist is right, should we not just sit down and wait for the inevitable?

This question gives us two further reasons to want to challenge the determinist. On the one hand we do not want to face the consequences of having to live with the belief of what they say because it would make our lives meaningless. On the other it seems implausible that life would continue as normal if we, persuaded by determinism, gave up making decisions and decided to let what will be happen, but that in itself suggests that our thoughts, deliberations and intentions make a difference, such that, at the very least, we have reason to believe that our actions and their outcomes are not determined entirely by factors outside of ourselves – and certain variations of determinism are therefore wrong.[86] The belief in our own freedom, whilst not directly shaping this or that of our actions, nevertheless seems to be an important prerequisite of our acting and choosing in a characteristically human way, and this suggests that what we think and believe makes a difference.

In addition to this, the belief in freedom is essential to our relations with others and to morality. On one hand, our sense that it is right to punish wrong-doing derives from our belief that those who have

[86] Of course some determinists will argue that our thoughts, etc. are caused by 'external' factors, and so the debate continues.

committed acts of wrong-doing were free to do otherwise. If their actions were caused by factors beyond their own, well then it would be wrong to punish them. It would be akin to punishing cars (for example, by withdrawing petrol) for breaking down and about as useful. On the other hand, our respect for others is based, in large degree, on respect for their autonomy. We do not impose our will on others because we believe that they are autonomous agents, with a will of their own and, in virtue of that, a right to decide their own course of action. Again, an adoption of determinism would be disastrous.

Is there a way beyond determinism then? A number of philosophical schools have suggested that there is. We will begin our account with a very radical argument in favour of freedom, made by the existentialist philosopher, Jean-Paul Sartre (1969). Sartre, I believe, is wrong. But through an engagement with his work and with some of those writers who have been critical of it, we can arrive at a more satisfactory position.

Sartre makes a radical distinction between the way in which material objects or things, such as stones and planks of wood, exist, which he calls 'being in-itself', and the way in which human beings as conscious agents exist, which he calls 'being for-itself'. Human consciousness, he argues, is not a 'thing'. You cannot perceive consciousness, like you can a thing, or measure, weigh or smell it. You cannot locate it in space. If you are looking at a boat far out to sea, for example, it is not possible to say exactly where your consciousness is in respect of this situation. Is it far out to sea? On the boat? On the shore? You might say that it is 'in your head' but if I open up your head I will not find it in there. I will find your brain but not your consciousness. And you only say it is in your head by force of convention, since you cannot see inside your own head either. Consciousness is characterized by 'intentionality'; that is, by the fact that it is always consciousness-of objects other than itself, a fact which seems to suggest that being conscious is being outside of oneself, not 'in one's head'. Your consciousness is a consciousness of worldly things which exist (or, as in dreams, virtually exist) independently of you. Importantly this means that your manner of being-in-the-world is very different from the manner of being of a simple material thing. You do not simply exist in the world as a part of it, being knocked about by the physical forces which exist in that world. The world exists for you. You are aware of it. You know it exists. And you are aware of yourself within it.

The difference between existence as a conscious being and the existence of a 'mere' thing is one aspect of the no-thing-ness referred to in the title of Sartre's (1969) classic book, *Being and Nothingness*. Consciousness is not a thing. It is no-thing. Human consciousness is also nothingness for Sartre, however, in the respect that it transforms the world and thereby 'negates' it. It creates but necessarily therefore destroys. In your imagination, for example, you can make bits of the world appear and disappear. You imagine things into existence which do not exist and of course you may actually build them, bringing them into existence. Similarly, you may imagine that actually existing things do not exist, and again in some cases you may take actions to remove them from existence. Finally, you perceive non-existences. You notice that things, perhaps friends, are absent. All of these experiences suggest, for Sartre, that human consciousness is more than a mere reflection of what exists, of being; that it brings non-being or nothingness into being. He sometimes expresses this by suggesting that human consciousness is a 'hole' within being, the important implication of this being that human consciousness thereby breaks the continuous chain of causation and determinism unearthed by science. Consciousness is not determined. It is not the effect of an antecedent cause. As such it is radically free. Following this and more importantly for our purposes, Sartre observes that conscious beings take up projects in relationship to the world. They subordinate the world to their projects, transforming it. They encounter resistance in the world, to be sure, but even this is only ever relative to their freely chosen projects. A mountain is difficult to climb, for example, it resists my attempts to climb it or get to the valley beyond it. But it enjoys this power of resistance only relative to my project of climbing it. What it means for me and the way in which it affects me is always relative to my projects, my freedom.

As consciousness is not a thing for Sartre, as it is radically free, these projects do not belong to the chain of causation either. They too are radically free. Human beings and their projects are radically free. Sartre also refers to this as human 'transcendence'. Human beings transcend the world as it is given; they project themselves forward, freely, into the future.

Elsewhere Sartre (1948) famously argues that his existentialism is a form of humanism. However, where many forms of humanism rest upon a notion of human nature, he, with his concept of human freedom and transcendence, denies that human beings have a fixed nature or essence. Or rather, he argues that human beings make themselves what they are by means of what they do. For the in-itself, Sartre argues, existence entails essence. To exist is to have this or that essence or nature which one is condemned to live in accordance with. In the human case, by contrast, 'existence precedes essence'. Human beings are condemned only to their own freedom and they take on a nature or essence only by means of their own free projects. More to the point, we might elect to change our nature, change our project, at any point in time. At any time the dictator might decide to become a democrat, the loner a social butterfly and so on.

A prisoner, from this point of view, is no less free for being imprisoned because they can choose how to live their imprisonment: whether to resist, to accommodate, and what attitude to take towards their captors. They are free to wish what they want, to dream of being somewhere else. Prison authorities can do whatever they want to the prisoner but they can never imprison the thought and imagination of the prisoner. They cannot constrain the prisoner's consciousness within the prison even if they can constrain his or her body.

However, freedom can choose to negate itself in what Sartre (1969) calls 'bad faith'. We can pretend that we are not free, that some things are necessary. We might say 'I can't help it, I'm just like that', or 'it's in my nature'. We might do this, Sartre argues, because of the anxiety which freedom generates. To know that one is completely free, that every link connecting one to the past can be broken and thus that the future is completely open, is a truly dizzying and anxiety provoking prospect. Consequently we are often tempted to deny this freedom imagining that certain things are necessary and that we are restrained or stuck. This is just self-deception, for Sartre, however. We are free and that means, amongst other things, that we make our own essence, shaping not just our destiny but also our nature.

There is much that is interesting and persuasive in Sartre's account. It has been the focus of a great deal of criticism, however, from both philosophers and social scientists. Some of the most interesting and productive criticisms, to my mind, come from within the existentialist camp itself. Simone de Beauvoir is an interesting case in point.

In her early work she introduces a distinction between freedom and power (de Beauvoir, 1988, 1967). Slaves may be free in an 'ontological' sense because they can choose how to enact their slavery, she argues, but if they cannot change their situation of slavery then they lack the power to carry through their projects in a very real sense. This preserves the essence of Sartre's argument whilst also pointing to a very serious limitation of it. In her later work, however, particularly *The Second Sex*, she effectively does away with the distinction between freedom and power, arguing that slaves and others who are oppressed in some way are simply less free than those who are not (de Beauvoir, 1988). Freedom is not all or nothing from this point of view but rather a matter of degree.

Integral to de Beauvoir's position is the Hegelian notion that true freedom presupposes freedom from the demands of 'necessity'; that is to say, we cannot begin to be free until we have serviced our basic material/biological needs. And some social groups, by virtue of their position in society and the power of others, do not rise above this level. They cannot rise above their 'animal nature', becoming free and transcendent, because their life is such that the satisfaction of basic animal needs is a full-time preoccupation. Furthermore, again following Hegel, she argues that violence and oppression are very real aspects of societies, past and present, and this obscures the possibility for true freedom.

Integral to this, though Beauvoir does not spell it out, is a rejection of Sartre's dualism of being in-itself and being for-itself. In effect she is arguing that human existence is ambiguous, occupying a middle point between the in-itself and the for-itself. We are neither a thing nor a pure consciousness, but then again we are both conscious and thing-like in certain respects. In *The Second Sex*, de Beauvoir expresses this by saying that human 'transcendence' is balanced against what she calls 'immanence'. And she notes that the balance between 'transcendence' and 'immanence' is shaped by social conditions. The body is a key element in relationship to this conception, since the body is both a basis of consciousness (qua perception) and spontaneous action, and a source of our 'thingness'. Our bodies make us vulnerable to illness, hunger, attacks, observation and control by others, as well as death. They locate us in the physical world but equally, as the means of our participation and presence to others, within the social world. And within the social world they are interpreted, classified (for example according to sex) and acted upon in a variety of ways, ways which may remain external to us but which, in some cases, may be internalized as habits or dispositions. To be embodied, to be a body, means that one is inevitably intertwinned with the material world, qua socio-physical entity, in a way not adequately captured by Sartre's dualism.

The notion that human beings fall somewhere between 'being in-itself' and 'being-for-itself' is also integral to the existential phenomenology of Maurice Merleau-Ponty (1962). Merleau-Ponty echoes de Beauvoir's attempt to balance transcendence against immanence, and also her insistence that slaves, prisoners and relatively 'powerless' groups do not enjoy the same degree of freedom as their 'masters'. He pushes further into the heart of Sartre's argument, however.

Merleau-Ponty does not accept Sartre's metaphysical argument that human beings constitute a 'hole' in being. Human consciousness, he argues, arises out of our sensuous, embodied engagement with the world. It takes shape within the world. However, reviewing the psychological and physiological literature of his day he observes that this engagement cannot be reduced down to a level of simple mechanical causation (especially Merleau-Ponty, 1965). The human organism, as it interacts and forms a structure with its physical environment is a whole which is irreducible to the sum of its parts and which must be grasped by means of concepts of meaning, reason and purpose rather than 'cause' (see **body-subject**). This bodily-behavioural structure is structured by the nature of the organism. In this respect human beings are something and not, as Sartre (1969) insists, 'nothing'. But human action needs to be grasped on its own 'human' level. It should not be reduced back to sub-human causes. And we must recognize a 'transcendent' element; that is, we should recognize that human beings transform the world. Furthermore, given that determinism, as Merleau-Ponty understands it, entails outside forces acting upon an object so as to affect it, and given that human beings 'are' their bodies, such that their bodies are not an outside force, he also dismisses determinism. Human beings are not free in the sense that Sartre suggests but neither are we determined. To understand the human condition we go beyond the problematic dualism of freedom and determinism.

Furthermore, freedom from determinism is not adequate as a definition of freedom for Merleau-Ponty. Pure randomness is indeterminate, for example, but we would not take it to be freedom. The concept of freedom entails a notion of 'choice'. Genuine choice, however, entails certain prerequisites which are not themselves chosen and recognition of this fact points us to a less 'radical' and more 'situated' form of freedom than that posited by Sartre. To make a choice we must have certain desires or preferences; we must have an understanding of the situation we are in and the options which are open to us, and for this we must rely upon pre-given schemas of perception and understanding which render the world meaningful for us prior to any conception we form of it; finally, we must have some means or technique of weighing up the possibilities and arriving at a decision (whether that be a dice, a sacred oracle or one of the many modern schemas of cost-benefit analysis). As meaningful 'choice' presupposes these elements, however, they cannot themselves be chosen. They must be given. As such our freedom is anchored in being in ways which Sartre does not recognize.

These anchors of choice are largely habitual and social for Merleau-Ponty. We acquire schemas of perception/understanding, preferences and techniques of decision-making as a function of our (past) experience. And as our experience is, in turn, as de Beauvoir noted, situated within the context of social and political relationships (such as class), they will also reflect the social world(s) to which we belong. Our choices reflect our social location. In this sense Merleau-Ponty very much anticipates the concept of the habitus posited by Bourdieu (1977). Furthermore, he adds that habit is important for anchoring freedom. Sartre's account of radical changes in individuals' ways of being is not particularly convincing, Merleau-Ponty notes. Dictators tend not to spontaneously become democrats. This might be due to inhibiting factors in their situation but it is also due to the force of habit. Deep-seated habits are not easily dispensed with. From this point of view habit looks like a counterbalance to freedom. However, Merleau-Ponty goes on to argue that, in fact, freedom would be meaningless without the 'power of conservation' embodied in habit. That is to say, if my decision to choose a project now is likely to be undone by another burst of free will in five minutes' time then my freedom to choose now is not really meaningful freedom to choose. I can choose but it will have no bearing on my life. It will be like a dream and will not take root in my life. If my decisions are really to take root in my life and to be meaningful then they must achieve a durability within my ways of perceiving, thinking, feeling and acting. It is this power of durability or 'power of conservation' which Merleau-Ponty denotes with the term 'habit' and he deems it central to human freedom since it makes our choices 'stick'.

The social world is important to Merleau-Ponty's conception of freedom, and indeed de Beauvoir's, in one further respect. As his infamous slogan 'hell is other people!',[87] indicates, Sartre saw social relationships as necessarily antagonistic. In essence he believes that we either dominate others, incorporating them in our project of freedom, or we find ourselves dominated. This idea draws from Hegel's idea of a struggle for recognition (see **recognition**) but it is a very partial appropriation of the idea. Both de Beauvoir and Merleau-Ponty are keen to address the other side of the coin; namely that 'heaven' is other people too or more concretely that individual human lives are bound up with each other and that human consciousness only achieves full self-consciousness and satisfaction by way of recognition from others (whom it recognizes in their own right). For both writers this entails that freedom is always necessarily collective or not at all. We are never free alone but only in the context of a community wherein our freedom and potential can be realized. Furthermore, revisiting Sartre's prison and torture scenarios, Merleau-Ponty argues that it is never a bare or pure consciousness which resists in the prison. It is

---

[87] This exclamation is made by one of the characters in Sartre's play *Huis Clos* (Sartre, 1947).

always a being who lives in and through others, and who draws his or her strength from them. Prisoners do not find the strength to survive by looking inwards, he argues, as there is nothing 'inside'. They derive strength from their connections to others and to projects and beliefs in the 'outside' world.

Aspects of Merleau-Ponty's critique of Sartre agree with an important critique by the English philosopher Gilbert Ryle. Suppose we agree that human action is the result of 'inner volitions', Ryle argues, what good would that do us in debates about freedom. The issue would then shift and we would ask if volitions were themselves willed and so on in an infinite regression:

> . . . what of volitions themselves? Are they voluntary or involuntary acts of mind? Clearly either answer leads to absurdities. If I cannot help willing to pull the trigger, it would be absurd to describe my pulling it as 'voluntary'. But if my volition to pull the trigger is voluntary . . . then it must issue from a prior volition and that from another *ad infinitum*. (1949, 66)

It thus makes no sense to invoke 'volition' or 'will' as a purported solution to the question of freedom. Indeed, the very notion of freedom, at least in the radical sense introduced by Sartre (1969), collapses in upon itself. The point, for both Ryle and Merleau-Ponty, however, is not that we should resort to a notion of determinism. Both believe that there is a purposiveness evident in human action which is not captured in simple and naïve accounts of determinism. Human beings are not mere machines and do transcend the given in meaningful and important ways. The point, rather, is that the very language of freedom and determinism is inappropriate; that we should not frame our understanding in this way (because it leads to incoherence). They call for a new way of thinking about human freedom and agency which recognizes the capacity for choice but situates choice within 'the world'; a way of thinking which avoids determinism but not simply by becoming its untenable opposite. It is this notion of situated freedom, I suggest, that provides the most promising basis for critical theory, recognizing freedom and thus grounding its defence and yet recognizing its limits; the manner in which it is both grounded in the world by potentially being compromized by that world.

Having conceded Ryle's point about volition it is important to add both that human beings do have what some philosophers call 'second order volitions' or 'second order preferences' and that these volitions or preferences are very important to what we mean when we talk of human freedom (Frankfurt, 1982; Hirschman, 2002). In other words, human beings can desire to desire things. A smoker, for example, periodically desires a smoke and they act upon this: they smoke. Desires which we act upon in this way are 'first order' desires. However, a smoker may also wish to give up smoking and, to this end, might also desire to be in a state where they do not desire cigarettes. Insofar as they continue smoking and, in practice, craving cigarettes, this desire to give up remains a second order preference. None of this alters Ryle's point, of course, because we need to stop our trail of desire right there. We do not want to ask if they desire to desire to change their desire because that path leads to infinite regression. Equally, Merleau-Ponty's point about habits being hard to break, though complicated in this instance by the possibility of physical addiction, is born out here. We only have second order preferences, arguably, because first order preferences can acquire a stubborn habitual force which is hard to break, even if we want to. Second order desires are important, however, because they indicate that we can be divided against some of our basic inclinations and can, to use Sartre's language, adopt projects which seek to transcend them. We are not mere 'puppets' to our first order desires and preferences.

We can conclude our discussion of freedom with three final points. Firstly, both Durkheim (1915) and George Herbert Mead (1967) offer interesting arguments to suggest that it is our social belonging which accounts for this tendency for us to become divided against ourselves. When we adopt a 'second order' perspective, they argue, we effectively adopt the perspective of our society and we are able to do this because we have internalized the perspective of our society. We have learnt to see ourselves as others see us and thereby to take a backward step from ourselves (metaphorically speaking). Belonging to society cultivates a capacity for reflexivity and, indeed, rational self-deliberation (see especially Mead, 1967). Again then, social belonging is integral to human agency and freedom. Secondly, if some notion of 'rationality' is added to the notion of choice that we have discussed in this entry then, at least by some definitions, it is not incompatible with certain concepts of 'casuation'.[88] From Weber onwards it has been argued that the rationality of human decision-making renders human action predictable, such as is

---

88 This is a different conception of causation from that discussed by Merleau-Ponty and thus, in my view, his argument and this argument are not incompatible. They agree on basic principles, even if the wording that might be applied to this principle would prove a sticking point – not that many philosophical issues do not hang on 'wording'!

presupposed by most concepts of causality. And some writers have pushed this argument forward by arguing that reasons, the external contexts reasons refer to, or both can be regarded as causes of human actions, such that choice or reason and causality are perfectly compatible (see Davidson, 1980; Goldthorpe, 2000). We might say, for example, that the advertized presence of a large great white shark in Blackpool bay caused a drop in the number of bathers there over a given time or caused Jane and Jim to refrain from swimming. But this is not incompatible with the fact that Jane, Jim and others chose not to swim. Indeed the whole point is that, as rational beings, they precisely chose not to swim. The advertized presence of a great white shark in the sea would lead a rational person to refrain from swimming. It would cause a change in behaviour, or perhaps rather it would trigger a choice which, in turn, would cause a change in behaviour. Finally, note that the move from Sartre to de Beauvoir and Merleau-Ponty blurred the distinction between metaphysical and political freedom that I made at the start of the entry. The latter two writers believe that the concept of metaphysical freedom is meaningless in the absence of sociopolitical freedom because human beings live in a sociopolitical world and not, or at least not exclusively, in their own consciousness.

## FURTHER READING

Sartre's *Being and Nothingness*, though very lively and well illustrated in places, is quite heavy going in others – at least by undergraduate standards. The same is true of much of Merleau-Ponty's work. Simone de Beauvoir's (1988) *The Second Sex* is more accessible and is the best starting point for those wishing to tackle primary texts. A good way into Sartre is by way of his novels. *Nausea* and the first volume of the 'Roads to Freedom' trilogy, *The Age of Reason*, both reflect heavily upon the question of freedom and illustrate the radical and individual conception of freedom characteristic of Sartre's early work (Sartre, 1965, 1973). Interestingly, the second two volumes of 'Roads to Freedom', *The Reprieve* and *Iron in the Soul*, chart Sartre's gradual shift to a more social and situated account of freedom, as later emerged in his *Critique of Dialectical Reason* (Sartre, 1976). The same transition is also evident in two early novels of another existentialist writer, Albert Camus. His *The Outsider* explores individuality and freedom, where *The Plague* explores human interdependence and sociality (Camus, 1948, 1982). Simone de Beauvoir explores this shift more reflectively in the course of her autobiographical writings (de Beauvoir, 1967). She identifies the Second World War as a crucial event for pointing out the situated nature of freedom and social interdependence to herself and other existentialists. Merleau-Ponty, who always maintains a more social and situated view, corroborates this account in his essay, 'The war has taken place' (Merleau-Ponty, 1971). An excellent overview of the existentialist debates on these issues can be found in Sonia Kruks (1990) *Situation and Human Existence*, and in Hammond, Howarth and Keat's (1991) *Understanding Phenomenology*. For a good selection of Anglo-American work on freedom and determinism see Watson's (1982) *Free Will* and Honderich's (1973) *Essays on Freedom of Action*.

# Globalization

> Related concepts: **hybridity, new social movements, power, social class, social movements.**

Globalization is a relatively new concept but this has not prevented it from becoming very controversial within both social science and wider political debate. Commentators disagree over its definition, over whether and how much it has taken place and so on. Here I offer my own interpretation of the concept. It is not a particularly original interpretation nor is it intended to be. I believe that it accords with general usage in the sociological community. But it is an interpretation and, as such, it would not be accepted by all commentators in the debate.

The word globalization fairly evidently refers to a process ('ization') which is happening at the world (global) level. It is a process taking place at the level of international, global or world society. A world society arguably comes into being from the point at which different national societies, or rather their representatives or members, come into contact and begin to interact, generating interdependencies and social relationships. By this definition world society is very old indeed and if 'globalization' refers to the process whereby world society comes into being, so too is globalization. However, the term is usually reserved for more recent developments which have effected considerable developments in the nature of world society and, in doing so, arguably made the boundaries of national societies more permeable and blurred, undermining their autonomy and distinctiveness. It is usual to trace these processes along economic, political and cultural trajectories.

At the economic level, two trends, both related to the growth of large multinational corporations, are significant. Firstly, capital and processes of economic production are more mobile. Companies are much less likely to remain in one place or even one national society and are much less likely to have a single national base or location. They are likely to move around the globe, seeking out what from their point of view are the best conditions for their operation. And they are much more likely to spread their production processes geographically – some parts made here, some there, assembled here, stored there, and so on. If the conditions change for the worse in countries where they are currently located then they will move on. Multinationals are, in this respect, nomadic. They do not belong to any national society, have no permanent national location and do not necessarily manifest loyalty to any particular nation. The extent to which this can be done obviously depends upon a variety of factors, including the industry in question and the size of the corporation. However it gives those companies who do it tremendous power and at the same time exercises a considerable 'international' influence on national/local economies and economic policies. The fact that large companies can and will take their business elsewhere if they do not like the conditions in their current location or if other locations offer better conditions, taking thousands of jobs, potential tax revenue and so on with them, exerts a considerable constraint upon representatives of those localities to do all they can to appease these companies – in effect, to give them more for less. Specifically this puts a constraint upon governments since taxation and legal frameworks are amongst the most important considerations taken into account by the corporations. Multinational firms are generally seeking low tax, low wage environments with low (preferably no) levels of unionization and maximum labour force flexibility (freedom to hire and fire, to change working hours, and so on). Furthermore, it introduces uncertainty into the picture for government and economic policy makers, as money and resources flow in and out of their country in a fashion they can neither predict nor control. The success or not of policies depends upon the (unpredictable) activities of the multinationals. All of these factors put a question mark around the idea of a national economy (and national economic policy), at least if we understand by that social structures which are relatively self-contained. Capital flows associated with multinationals tie local and national economies to the global market. The second important point here is that leading multinational companies now have a greater annual turnover than the gross domestic product

99

(GDP)[89] of many smaller nations, making them bigger and often more influential economic actors than those smaller nations. Another way of putting this might be to say that the world economy is no longer decomposable into national economic agents and nations.

One final economic aspect which should be added here is migration. As capital becomes more mobile so too does labour, both in the 'upper' and the 'lower' levels of the market. The labour market is internationalized and workers are, in differing ratios, forced and enticed to migrate.

At the political level this is matched by the enormous growth, since the middle of the twentieth century, in international political and legal institutions (including many which focus upon economic matters) and in the remit of those organizations. An increasing number of political decisions are being taken by international bodies and the degree to which these decisions are binding for nations who are signed up to the agreements which founded those committees is increasing too. Likewise international and (for Europeans) European law is becoming both more extensive and more intensive; that is, it covers ever more areas in ever more depth. At the very least this means that nation states/governments increasingly work within the parameters set by international bodies, bodies on which they are represented and have consented to join up to but which have the power to overrule them and enforce decisions upon them. And in some cases it means that decision-making capacities have passed upwards, beyond the level of the national state.

This is not to say that national societies uncritically accept their place in a global society. Every society argues its corner and to some degree nationalism and unilateralism are heightened by the growing pressure for international agreement and (policy) uniformity. However, from the sociological perspective this looks more like a process of mutual adjustment whereby societies ease themselves into a new and more internationalized political context than a brake or reversal on the trend of globalization.

Political 'globalization from above', that is, at the level of states and inter-state organizations, has also been rejoined by political 'globalization from below'; that is, by the growth of international social movement organizations and alliances (see **social movements** and **new social movements**). The most obvious recent example of such alliances is that

---

89 Gross domestic product: The total value of goods produced and services provided in a country within a twelve-month period.

comprising the global anti-corporate movement, which has involved protest networks and organizations from around the world co-ordinating (amongst other things) enormous protests and debating forums (Crossley, 2002b, 2003; Kingsnorth, 2003a; Neale, 2002; Held and McGrew, 2002). Sometimes these events occur in a single location, often, though not exclusively and less so over time, to coincide with a meeting of one of the above-mentioned international political institutions (the 'legendary' ones include 'the battle of Seattle' and subsequent protests in Prague and Genoa). Sometimes they occur simultaneously in locations around the world (for example, there have been a number of 'global days of action' and 'carnivals against capitalism' of this kind). The anti-corporatists are sometimes dubbed 'anti-globalization' but by my definition this is something of a misnomer since they are responsible for generating a global public sphere and citizenry, and thus are advancing the process of political globalization considerably (see **citizenship** and **public sphere**). In effect they are calling for international political institutions to first prove themselves accountable to the demands and wishes of an international citizenry and second to exercise better and more just control over the dynamics of the global economy. Some of these protesters may not like the idea of a global system or society at all but many do because they believe that global political regulation is the only way to curb the power of multinationals who can otherwise play states off against each other, and the only way to address such global political problems as environmental destruction. Whether or not they support globalization, however, their actions have the consequence of generating global level politics by generating global level political debate and action. Furthermore, these actions embody a 'global consciousness', in the respect that they think through problems, even seemingly very localized problems, in terms of their location within a global system. They recognize that everything is connected to everything else in modern societies, such that problems can only be understood and resolved from a point of view which takes into account the global whole. The aforementioned recognition of the need to curb the power of multinationals and address environmental issues globally are clear examples of this, as is the argument, posited by many anti-corporatists, that poverty in the societies of the underdeveloped world cannot be understood in isolation from the relations of those societies (past and present) with the societies of the developed world (who once colonized them), and cannot be addressed without addressing the disadvantaged position of those societies within the global economy. What this latter issue also particularly illustrates, of course, is the emergence of forms of political and moral solidarity which transcend national borders.

The critical anti-corporate publics also provide one interesting example of cultural globalization. In the context created by these protesters ideas, information, manifestos, identities, and so on all flow freely across international borders. This is not an equal process. There are language barriers and economic barriers to the free flow of culture in this context but these are not coterminous with national barriers. This particular flow of ideas is just one strand of a much wider flow of cultural products which move across national boundaries: for example, TV programmes, films, music, fashion, fast-food chains, urban design, and so on. To some degree this is part and parcel of economic globalization, as many cultural forms are commodified and are sold in the global marketplace. Clearly, however, the growth of new communication technologies including the Internet and satellite television play a very important role. And so too, at least in some places, does migration. Agents find themselves increasingly in contact with representatives of 'other' traditions, either because they have moved or are working with those who have moved to them.

Like the other aspects of globalization, this process is structured by the relative power balance between societies. Many critics, for example, argue that it is western and particularly American culture which has spread more rapidly with the global 'cultural exchange', not least because the west and the United States have spawned most of the global economic and political actors who play a role in distributing culture. Furthermore, it is perhaps in the cultural sphere, above all, where obstacles to globalization are most apparent and most trenchant: languages and cultural values/traditions are arguably more difficult to impose and change than economic and political arrangements because they penetrate more deeply into the very constitution of individuals as social actors – into language, beliefs, identity and deep-rooted lifestyle habits. However, we must be careful not to fall into the trap of adopting a static or monological view of culture. Cultures may be more difficult to impose than either political or economic arrangements but like the latter they are in a constant process of change, not least as a consequence of their coming into contact and dialogue with 'alien' elements which, even as they resist them (if they resist them), they incorporate and accommodate to in various ways (on this see also **hybridity**). We see this quite clearly in the history of any language or culture: there are 'bits' from all over the place, some accepted happily, some absorbed in relations of domination, some incorporated in modified form through the very processes of resisting them. I do not mean to suggest by this that we can expect a homogenous global culture at some point in the future. Diversification too is very common in cultural history. But contact between cultures cannot but have an effect upon them, not least as the agents who embody those cultures attempt to make sense of one another.

Is globalization a good or bad thing? Is it inevitable or do we abdicate our responsibility by supposing so? At a very basic level I suggest that globalization is inevitable, not least because there is nothing natural or inevitable about the natural boundaries of societies as we have come to know them. Societies are constituted out of the interactions, exchanges and relationships of their members, and the social arrangements (customs, institutions, organizations, and so on) those exchanges give rise to. If transport and communication technologies permit those interactions to easily transcend national boundaries then so too will society. There is no reason why, in principle, we should wish to stop this process but if we did we would have grave difficulties because it is very difficult to 'uninvent' technologies and their uses/effects, and because resisting 'globalization' requires a global effort which (if unintentionally) tends to promote globalization. Very obviously, however, globalization might take many different forms, some of which will be much more desirable and just than others. The present form and trajectory of globalization is, arguably, socially damaging for the less powerful members of world society and, as such, unjust (Callinicos, 2003; Danaher, 2001; Wallach and Sforza, 1999). But the very globalization debate itself, and the anti-corporate activism mobilized around it, all suggest that, as in all matters, the future is open.

### FURTHER READING

Waters' (1995) *Globalization* is a good introduction to the issue. Robertson has been a key contributor to sociological debates and his *Globalization* (Robertson, 1992) is an important text. Naomi Klein's (2000) *No Logo* was perhaps the first key (non-academic) book to be written about the anti-corporate movement but there are now a few journalistic accounts and many of the more recent ones are, inevitably, more up-to-date (see Kingsnorth, 2003; Neale, 2002). I have written a couple of papers on the movement from a more sociological perspective (Crossley, 2002b, 2003a) and there are now a few social scientific analyses (for example, Starr, 2001; Smith, 2001). For a discussion which focuses both upon globalization and resistance to it see Held and McGrew (2002) *Globalization and Anti-Globalization*. For a more political engaged discussion of why the protestors protest the early accounts are Klein's (2000) *No Logo*, Hertz's (2001) *Silent Takeover*, and Monbiot's (2001)

*Captive State*. More recent accounts include Callinicos' (2003) *Anti-Capitalist Manifesto* and pamphlets by both Danaher (2001) and Wallach and Sforza (1999). Hilary Wainwright's (2003) *Reclaim the State* is an interesting and strong account on both the political and the more exploratory sides.

# Habitus

> *Related concepts: **body-subject, capital, doxa, fields, freedom, hexis, social class.***

In the contemporary context the concept of the 'habitus' is particularly associated with the work of Pierre Bourdieu, and also perhaps Norbert Elias. However, the concept has a much longer history within sociology and philosophy. It can be found in the work of Husserl (1973, 1989, 1990) and (albeit under a different name) various phenomenologists influenced by him, such as Schutz (1970, 1971, 1972) and Merleau-Ponty (1962); in the work of Weber and of Durkheim's nephew and colleague, Mauss (1979); and more generally in early sociology and the philosophy which shaped it (Camic, 1986). Indeed Mauss (1979) observes that the term 'habitus' is a Latin translation of the Greek concept 'hexis', which is central to Aristotle's (1955) *Ethics* (see **hexis**). In this sense 'habitus' can be traced right back to the very beginnings of Western thought as we know it today.

Both 'habitus' and 'hexis' translate into English as 'acquired disposition' or 'habit'. Insofar as they correspond to 'habit', however, they invoke an older usage of the term than that which prevails today. In a fascinating paper, Charles Camic (1986) argues that the concept of habit used to have a central place in sociological and philosophical discourse, where it was used to refer to a range of complex and intelligent behavioural dispositions, moral sentiments, acquired competences and forms of practical understanding and reasoning. It was only as a result of the somewhat crude model of conditioned reflexes advocated by physiological and psychological behaviourism, he argues, that 'habit' acquired the more limited sense that it has today. And it was because of this degradation of the concept that Talcott Parsons, who, in

**104**

key concepts

the mid-twentieth century largely shaped our sense of the history of sociology, wrote habit out of that history (Parsons, 1968). It is perhaps also for this reason that contemporary sociologists returning to this territory have tended to use the Latin form 'habitus' or 'disposition' rather than 'habit'.

The concept of the habitus, as it is used today, has many layers, and functions differently in relation to a number of different debates. We need to unpick these layers, functions and debates.

## SECOND NATURE, CIVILIZATION AND DISTINCTION

At one level the concept denotes 'second nature', the manner of being that human beings derive from their involvement in the social world and socialization. Unlike many other species, whose members are more or less prepared for the life they will live when they drop out of the womb or break out of the egg, human beings are far from being fully formed at the moment of birth. We are formed and acquire our nature outside of the womb, in a social environment. Our evolutionary advantage lies, in part, in our plasticity; our capacity to learn – in addition to our inventiveness and capacity for intelligent adaptation (Elias, 1978). For many early sociologists, particularly Durkheim (1915), all of what we call 'civilized' about ourselves belongs to our 'second nature', what we have acquired from society; that is, our habitus (see also Elias, 1984). This involves both a positive moulding of our nature but also an internalization of control mechanisms which serve to block certain of the less civilized impulses which periodically emerge from our primary nature, for example, aggressive or selfish impulses.

Elements of our primary nature remain, however, such that our second nature involves a tension between impulses and controls. This tension is evident in both Elias' and Bourdieu's conceptions of the habitus (see also Durkheim, 1973). Both conceptualize the habitus, at least in part, as an internalization of the societal demand for self-control and norm-conformity on behalf of the agent but both also recognize that such restraint co-exists with the periodic impulses it must attempt to constrain and that there may be a genuine battle between impulse and control in some instances, which could go either way or result in any number of compromises. Both thus avoid the 'oversocialized' conception of the agent which Wrong (1961) identifies in Parsonian sociology, a conception which reduces agency to the norms, roles and duties imposed upon the agent.

There is also a sense in the work of both writers that the social demand for control and civilized conduct is fuelled, in some part, by struggles for distinction between social groups. Elite groups have sought to define themselves through a process of self-cultivation that involves them denying and overcoming 'base' impulses, in the pursuit of a civilized alternative. The emergence of the aesthetic sensibilities of the middle class, for example, has involved both an acquired sense of disgust at many of the practices of the working class but also, in relation to the appreciation of art works, a refusal to make judgements of worth on the basis of immediate sensuous pleasures. Art works are judged on the basis of internalized formal criteria and immediate sensuous reactions are neutralized or at least kept at bay. This affects our tastes, what we like and desire, but also what we do and the way in which we do it; our 'body techniques' (see **hexis**).

## SCHEMAS, DISPOSITIONS AND KNOW-HOW

Much of what Bourdieu (1984) writes of the acquired nature of 'taste' can be understood in this light. Our sensibilities, our sense of beauty, disgust and appropriateness, he argues, are all formed in a social-historical context of group division and conflict. In addition to this, however, his conception of the habitus emphasizes the importance of acquired competences and needs, some of which are relatively general but others of which are specific to particular fields. In his work on 'the love of art', for example, he notes how an appreciation of art presupposes a 'trained eye'. Just as we have learnt the English language and must have done so in order to be able to read texts written in English, so too we must have acquired the 'language' of art in order to read and discuss works of art. Principally this means reading art against the background of its history, as that history is understood by the artistic classes, and with a know-how attuned to the artistic game. To read art is to classify or locate it, identifying the principles informing it and by which it can be judged, as well as the alternatives it is defined against. The meaning of art presupposes a hidden background structure of taken-for-granted assumptions which only the trained aesthete has access to. It is not just 'highbrow' comprehension which works in this way of course. To play or watch football one must have learnt the game such that one can grasp the significance of actions and positions. Without the necessary schemas, action on the pitch appears to be a blur of largely incomprehensible movement – an experience we may all have had when watching a new sport for the first time. This is not a matter of knowing theoretically about art or football. It is matter of tacit or pre-reflective knowledge, a form of competence or what Bourdieu calls a 'feel for the game'. This notion of acquired practical competence, the 'feel for the game', to reiterate, is integral to Bourdieu's conception of the habitus.

A feel for the game is acquired through participation, often as a child, in the field in question. So too is the desire for continued participation, the felt 'need' to visit museums, watch football or whatever. The reason that art appreciation remains a middle-class preserve, Bourdieu argues, is because middle-class children are taken around museums, thereby acquiring the disposition (habitus) to continue doing so as adults, taking their own children and so on, perpetuating or 'reproducing' the pattern (see Bourdieu et al., 1990).

## PHENOMENOLOGY, MAUSS AND COLLECTIVE HISTORY

In emphasizing schemas of perception, action and understanding, competence as well as internalized social controls, Bourdieu adds an important 'phenomenological' aspect to his conception of the habitus. Phenomenologists, following Husserl (for example, 1973), have explored in detail the way in which past experiences 'sediment' within social agents and groups in the form of dispositions and schemas which shape the cognition, emotion and action of those agents and groups in a variety of ways. Alfred Schutz's (1972) account of 'types' and 'recipe knowledge' are two very well-known examples of this – and both are prefigured in Husserl's concept of 'habitus'- but Merleau-Ponty's account of the dispositions and habits of the 'body-subject' (see **body-subject**) perhaps resonate more directly with Bourdieu.

The detail and sophistication of the phenomenologists' accounts is greater than that of Bourdieu's and his account can be improved by recourse to those accounts (Crossley, 2001a, b). Where Bourdieu advances upon phenomenology, however, is in his theorization of the collective nature of habitus – an issue only touched upon by Merleau-Ponty and Husserl, and scarcely even touched upon by Schutz (on Merleau-Ponty, see Crossley, 2001d, 2004a). Insofar as one's habitus is a sediment of one's past ('formative') experiences it is as unique as one's biographical trajectory. No two will be identical. Individual biography is an abstraction, however. We do not live and grow alone. We live amongst others with whom we interact. Furthermore, we share a social position with others, finding ourselves in similar configurations of social relationships and thus enjoying/enduring similar sorts of experiences. For these reasons aspects of our habitus will be similar to aspects of the habitus of others in our society and it makes sense to refer to collective habitus; that is, habitus shared by members of a social group or occupants of structurally similar social positions. This point is demonstrated most forcefully in *Distinction* where Bourdieu (1984) locates cultural tastes squarely within the habitus of specific social classes and class fractions. In this study, moreover, echoing some of his work on education, he argues that the habitual and pre-reflective nature of the habitus can serve to lend social differences and exclusions a 'natural' appearance. Social groups appear naturally different from one another, by virtue of their habitus. This is problematic as it can have the consequence of 'naturalizing' social inequality, particularly when powerful groups use their power to define the products of their habitus as superior. If, for example, the refined dispositions of the middle-class habitus are perceived as signs of natural intelligence and sensitivity, then the superior social position of those who have these dispositions can appear justified – they appear to have got where they are by virtue of their intelligence. In other words, the effects of social inequality, manifest in the habitus, can appear to be its (natural) causes, thus legitimating that inequality (see also **hexis**).

In theorizing habitus both in terms of practical competence and in terms of social positions Bourdieu picks up an important thread in the work of Marcel Mauss (1979). Mauss too seeks to use the concept of the habitus as a way of theorizing socially specific forms of practical reason (see **hexis**).

## HABITUS AND AGENCY

The concept of the habitus is used by Bourdieu to challenge a number of alternative conceptions of agency and structure that we find in the sociological literature. In the first instance he is concerned to challenge conceptions of agency which are overly centred upon consciousness and/or are overly voluntaristic. Combating the overemphasis upon consciousness in some approaches, the concept of the habitus points to the pre-reflective nature of much of our action and indeed to the habitual structuration of consciousness itself. How we perceive, think and feel is shaped by sedimented traces of our past experiences which we remain largely unaware of in Bourdieu's view, that is, by habitual expectations and assumptions. When we read a page of written text in our native language, for example, we are struck immediately by its meaning, what it 'says'. We are not aware of any active sense-making process on our own behalf nor of the cultural fit between ourselves and the text. Indeed, as Merleau-Ponty (1962) argues, we scarcely notice language itself, feeling ourselves to be in the presence of unmediated thought. And yet the meanings which flow easily and naturally into our consciousness do so only because, as children, we were trained to recognize the letters of our language, their combination into words and the combination of words into sentences and so on. We think in and by means of a language, automatically and without knowing how we do it,[90] and yet we have had to learn that language over a lengthy period of time. We have learnt to read, to write, to speak and to 'hear' our language, as becomes apparent when we try to learn a new language. What is true of language is true of the other cultural structures which mediate our being-in-the-world. When I swim, play squash, watch a film, cook my tea, invest in the stock market, engage in sociological debate and so on, I always 'read' my situation and then respond purposively to it on the basis of know-how and practical understanding rooted in familiarity with the situation or those similar to it. This may involve some element of reflective deliberation – I'm unlikely to invest without thinking about my options – but, in the final instance, these reflective elements always presuppose and rest upon a bedrock of understanding and competence which extends back beyond consciousness into a pre-reflective realm. To reflect upon investment I must know how to do so; how to read markets and financial pages, how to play the investment 'game'. And as with any game, fluid play requires that I know how to do this without having to think about it. My knowledge must assume a habitual form, beneath the threshold of consciousness. Indeed in some instances reflective thought may be a hindrance. The paradigm case here is sport. When I play sport I have no time to think about how I will act. I must act 'automatically' otherwise the moment for the action will have passed. Having said that, I cannot act mechanically, in terms of a learnt response. I must act in a way which is appropriate to the state of play in the game, as it appears to me, and in a way which serves the strategic advantage of my team. I must act intelligently and purposively, perhaps innovatively and in an improvised manner. And, of course, my actions must remain within the rules of the game. The practical competence which defines the habitus as a 'feel for the game' consists precisely in my capacity to do all of these things without recourse to reflective thought or planning. The structures of the habitus, though they structure perception, thought and thus consciousness, are not conscious themselves, but neither are they

---

90 When we become aware of our thoughts they are already in linguistic form, and we are not aware of putting them in language. Language just seems 'natural' but of course it is not. We have had to learn it.

---

*Habitus*

mechanical habits. They constitute a third position between these two extremes.

This, to reiterate, does not mean that we do not reflectively deliberate and choose. But it suggests that even when we do our choices are underpinned by habitus, as indeed they must be. Choice, as Merleau-Ponty argued, does not emerge out of nowhere or 'nothingness'. It presupposes that we have desires, that we perceive and understand our situation in one way or another and that we have a means of both generating a range of possibilities for action and choosing between them. And these prerequisites of choice, qua prerequisites, cannot be chosen themselves, at least not in the final instance (see **freedom**). They belong to the habitus.

Some writers have suggested that this conception of agency is deterministic. I disagree. Bourdieu is clearly opposed to extreme claims about freedom, such as those of Sartre (see **freedom**). Like Merleau-Ponty, he believes that the structured nature of human action is incompatible with the idea that it somehow emerges out of 'nothing', as Sartre suggests. But neither does he embrace determinism, at least if that means reducing action back to external causes or forces. Again like Merleau-Ponty, he strives for a conception of agency which moves beyond the freedom/determinism dichotomy; a concept which treats them as beings whose actions reflect their purposes, desires and understanding of the world, but who nevertheless belong to the world and reflect their inherence in it in what they do. This is what the concept of the habitus seeks to capture.

## RULES?

If Bourdieu is opposed to conceptions of agency which hinge upon absolute conceptions of freedom, he is equally opposed to approaches, like that of Levi-Strauss (1966), which seek to reduce action to rules and thereby to 'dissolve man'. At one level he is critical of the methodology often used to derive 'rules'. What social scientists are told about rules and norms by their informants very often amounts to an 'official picture' of the world, he argues, which does not correspond very closely to what actually happens. More importantly, however, the concept of rules itself is problematic on a number of grounds. Firstly, with the exception of the explicit 'norms' cited above, 'rules' belong to the conceptual toolbox which analysts use to make sense of the regularities they observe in practice. They are not (at least explicitly) oriented to by social agents themselves, as the concept of 'rule-following' suggests. It is for this reason that agents can be genuinely ignorant of the 'rules' analysts suggest they are following and can be surprised or enlightened when analysts inform them of these rules. All of this suggests, however, that we should be wary of confusing our analytic categories ('rules') with the reality we are observing; that is, it suggests that agents are not really following rules. It would be truer to their experience to say that they have a 'feel for the game'; that their conduct is steered by habitual competence and know-how. Furthermore, the concept of rules cannot fully explain action. As Wittgenstein (1953) noted, the concept of rules threatens constantly to collapse into an infinite regression; following rules, for example, presupposes knowing which rules to follow in which circumstances, but if we invoke further rules to account for this then they too will presuppose rules and so on. To short-circuit this regression we must appeal to some account of a dispositional 'feel' which is strictly irreducible to rules. Similarly, as anybody who has learnt a second language will know, even when we quite explicitly learn a practice by way of its rules, we encounter numerous situations where we are told that 'there is no rule for this, you just have to get the feel for what sounds right'. Finally, rejoining the first point, Bourdieu argues that insofar as there are discernible rules in social life, much human action involves a strategic use of those rules; playful subversion, crafty circumvention and respect in the breech rather than strict adherence. This applies to moral norms which we often bend whilst seemingly to uphold them but it also applies to constitutive rules,[91] as we see in poetic uses of language (to take one example) which play with and bend the shared rules and conventions of language to create an effect. To explain action, therefore, we need to look beyond 'rules' without losing sight of the evident structure and regularity of action. The concept of the habitus is used precisely for this purpose. It is habitus rather than rules which shape human action.

It is not just Levi-Strauss (1966) who Bourdieu has in mind in this critique. In pointing to the role of improvisation, strategy and innovation in practice he is opposing all forms of structuralism and functionalism; indeed all sociological perspectives which seek to 'dissolve man'. We can no more 'dissolve man' than we can make 'man' the generative principle of our studies in Bourdieu's view. We need rather to situate the agent, to

---

91 Constitutive rules are those rules which, if we adopt a rules-based conception, must be followed in order for us to make sense. They are the technical rules which allow us to perform certain activities in a recognizably correct way, whether or not that performance or activity has a moral content.

recognize the ways in which the agent embodies aspects of the social world, and this is what the concept of the habitus does.

## STRUCTURE

The concept of the habitus is not simply a concept of agency, however. It is equally integral to a concept of structure. Indeed it constitutes a hinge between agency and structure. The habitus, Bourdieu argues, is a 'structured structure'. That is to say, it is formed by way of the internalization of structures. My habitus, is formed, for example, by learning a language, learning how to 'play' sociology, how to play 'art appreciation' and so on. In each case I internalize the structure of the game in the form of an embodied disposition. But the habitus is equally a 'structuring structure'; that is to say, having incorporated structures we reproduce those structures through our action. We must incorporate the structures of language before we can speak, of football before we can play and of art appreciation before we can 'critique', but language exists only in speech, football in play and art in the interplay of producers and critical consumers. Structures only exist insofar as agents 'do' them and do so skilfully and inventively. In this sense, Bourdieu argues, the habitus is akin to 'genetic information', necessary for the reproduction of the social world in the same way that DNA is necessary for the reproduction of our biological structure (Bourdieu and Passeron, 1996). Furthermore, as in Durkheim (1915), the relationship of the agent to the social world is thereby conceived in circular terms. Society creates the social agent, who then recreates society. I have argued elsewhere, seeking to draw out Bourdieu's own insistence upon inventiveness in action, that we need to avoid too much circularity here; we need to be able to appreciate that and how the circle is deformed by way of innovative action (Crossley, 2002c). However, this concept of circularity is basically right and is necessary if we wish to understand and explain the nature of the social world.

## FURTHER READING

Bourdieu discusses the habitus in many of his works. I find his discussion in the first section of *The Logic of Practice* particularly useful and interesting (Bourdieu, 1992a) and *Distinction* (Bourdieu, 1984) is still the classic study of class habitus; though sometimes heavy going, it rewards close reading. Bourdieu's most updated thoughts on the habitus can be found in *Pascalian Meditations* (Bourdieu, 2000). Elias uses the concept in a number of works. Although the concept is not used explicitly in *The*

112

*Civilizing Process* (or rather the concept is not translated as 'habitus' in the English version) his discussion of the moulding of nature in that work is perhaps the key reference point for his work. *The Germans* and *The Society of Individuals* are also useful reference points in this connection. On the history of the concept, Camic's (1986) article, 'The matter of habit', is excellent. For some discussion of phenomenological versions of the concept see my *The Social Body* (Crossley, 2001a) or my paper 'The phenomenological habitus and its construction' (Crossley, 2001b).

# Hegemony

Related concepts: *crisis, doxa, ideology, power, social class.*

Although the term is used by Lenin, it is in the work of the Italian Marxist writer, Antonio Gramsci (1971) that the concept of 'hegemony' is developed into the powerful intellectual tool that we know today. Gramsci was imprisoned by Mussolini, on account of his 'dangerous mind' and the threat it posed both to fascism and capitalism. Consequently most of his ideas were written in prison, where he was denied access to Marxist and other communist writings. The deprivation did not prevent Gramsci from making many important innovations within Marxism, however, including the concept of hegemony.

Like Marx, Gramsci believes that capitalist societies are founded upon class domination; the bourgeoisie dominate the proletariat (see **social class**). The very nature of the relationship between the bourgeoisie and the proletariat, in which the latter sell their labour to the former (who appropriate the 'surplus value,[92] of that labour) in return for a subsistence wage, is a relationship of exploitation and subordination.[93] Again like Marx, however, Gramsci recognizes that this enconomic arrangement is

---

92 As noted in the entry on **social class**, 'surplus value' is the difference between the value produced by the labour of the working class and the value they get back in the form of wages, a difference which is appropriated by the bourgeoisie, such that their relationship to the proletariat may be described as one of exploitation.
93 Because the bourgeoisie appropriate the surplus value produced by the proletariat – see **social class**.

only one element in the relationship of class domination, not least because, other things being equal, the proletariat may refuse to accept their economic exploitation and domination, and may seek to change their situation. One way in which this can be prevented is by way of coercion. If the bourgeoisie not only own and control the means of production but also control the state then they can use the powers of the state (law, the police, the army) to quell uprisings and enforce conformity. This is still quite a fragile a situation, however. If the proletariat, who by definition are the majority in capitalist societies, spot a weakness in this system of constraint and coercion, which there will surely be on some occasions, they are likely to take their chances and rebel, and they may overthrow the state. What is needed, if a relationship of domination is to be rendered relatively secure, Gramsci argues, is intellectual and moral leadership. The bourgeoisie must win the hearts and minds of the people, persuading them (without even seeming to do so or to need to do so) that the status quo is natural and inevitable, beneficial for all, and inducing them to identify with it. Although the term 'hegemony' is sometimes used by Gramsci to refer to domination in general, it is usually taken to refer to situations where this intellectual and moral element is in place. A group which has secured a relationship of hegemony has won the hearts and minds of the people. It exercises intellectual and moral leadership.

What Gramsci says here accords with the more general emphasis upon ideology within Marxism. In contrast to many variants, and particularly structuralist variants of Marxism, however, which appear to suggest that ideological domination emerges automatically and is secured as a 'superstructural effect'[94] of the economic base, Gramsci emphasizes agency and openendedness. Domination has to be won, he argues. Moreover, this requires that groups competing for hegemony must be prepared to form alliances that may not, from their own point of view, be 'natural' or obvious. They must be prepared to engage with the ideas, beliefs, customs and practices of other groups, irrespective of how alien those customs and practices may seem to them. To secure hegemony, contending groups must seek to build bridges with already existing organic cultural configurations. Otherwise these will prove a very stubborn obstacle. Furthermore, it is these organic cultural formations

---

94 Structuralist versions of Marxism sometimes divide society into a 'base', comprising the economy, and a 'superstructure' comprising culture and the state. There are then various competing versions of what the relationship of the one to the other is. Most, however, suggest that the superstructure is determined by the base. See **ideology**.

---

which provide the key to lending a sense of naturalness and inevitability to (historical and contingent) situations of domination. The obvious example of this, in Gramsci's context, was the contrast in both strategy and success between the fascists and the communists in Italy in the 1920s. In many respects the country was ripe, in economic terms, for a leftist revolutionary uprising. In actual fact the fascists took control. Why? Because the fascists took it upon themselves to engage with Italian culture and folk traditions, whilst the communists derided folk tradition (including the Catholicism that was central to the identity of many Italians) as 'bourgeois ideology'. The fascists won the war of hearts and minds because they engaged hearts and minds on their own terrain, creating a situation in which fascism began to seem like a natural extension of what people already believed and aspired to. Fascism seemed like 'common sense' because it managed to enmesh itself within the common sense[95] of the people.

A very similar analysis to this was offered in the British context during the 1980s, by authors associated with the *Marxism Today* magazine and particularly by the sociologist Stuart Hall (1987). Why, these authors asked, was the hold of the Thatcher government so strong, even amongst the working class, when from a leftist point of view its new and radical policies were so obviously opposed to the interests of the working class. And why was the Labour Party faring so badly? The left, they argued, had to learn both from Gramsci and indeed from Margaret Thatcher and her government. The British general public were not greatly interested in abstract political theory and ideology, nor in gloomy and turgid economic analyses. Furthermore, their 'interests' were not fixed or given, certainly not at the subjective level of what they took to be their interests (and insofar as 'interest' necessarily involves a subjective element, thereby not at all). The success of the Thatcher government was based upon the fact that it took account of this. It connected with popular symbols (such as the union flag, the royal family and the church) and popular sentiments (for example, aspirations, ambitions, intolerance towards difference and anxiety regarding the post-1960s 'moral decline'), and as such it was able

---

95 Sometimes we use 'common sense', in everyday parlance, to refer to what we believe is obvious. To say, 'that's common sense' is effectively to say, 'that's irrefutable'. In critical social theory, by contrast, it is argued that much 'common sense' is actually quite historically specific; what seems obvious to one group of people, at one point in history, is anything but obvious to other groups, in other eras. What seems 'natural' to one society would seem immoral or artificial to another. And what one group does without thinking, another would never even think of doing. If one group wishes to communicate with another however, and a fortiori to win their hearts and minds, it becomes expedient to build bridges across these gaps in common sense.

to 'interpellate'[96] British citizens, that is, to communicate the message 'We are like you. We express what you think. You are already Thatcherites and were before we came along. So support us'. The left, meanwhile, hammered on about economic ideas which were alien to most members of the public, which they could not always understand and which they were not therefore inclined to care about.

The implication of Gramsci's concept, however, and particularly the idea that hegemony is won, is that the working-class movements of the left can fight to win back hearts and minds, to secure their own hegemony. In this connection Gramsci refers to what he calls a 'war of manoeuvre' and a 'war of position'. The former applies to societies where intellectual and moral leadership by the dominant group is weak, where coercion by a strong state is the chief means of securing order but where there are visible cracks in the power of the state. It involves a quick assault upon the state. This is not applicable in most western democracies, most of the time, as 'consent' (another key term used in debates on hegemony) is secured in these contexts, moral and intellectual leadership has been won, and repressive state actions, at least on any large scale, are the exception rather than the rule. What is called for in these contexts is a 'war of position'. Oppositional groups, adopting a longer term strategy, must operate on the terrain of culture and public institutions, learning what is important to people and building bridges with it. Like Margaret Thatcher, they must interpellate citizens such that those citizens begin to identify with oppositional projects and feel a natural affinity with them.

Another important point in Gramsci's discussion of the 'war of position', which has been taken up in recent work, concerns the need to draw together a range of oppressed and excluded groups. The tendency in more rigid variations of classical Marxism is to assume that the proletariat and they alone are the agents of change, such that other struggles (for example, gender, sexuality and racial struggles) are at best reducible to class struggle, at worst irrelevant bourgeois distractions. Gramsci by contrast recognized that effective opposition requires coalition. Diverse oppositional and oppressed groups must be brought together, brought to identify in a common oppositional identity which respects their differences. For him this was primarily a matter of

---

96 An Althussarian concept which is added into many contemporary discussions of hegemony. It entails that agents come to identify themselves in accordance with the way in which they are addressed by others, specifically powerful 'others' in positions in authority. For a brief outline of the concept see the entry on **ideology**.

persuading the industrial proletariat of Northern Italy to identify with the plight of the peasantry of Southern Italy, forming a coherent oppositional block. In more recent work, however, and particularly Laclau and Mouffe's (1986) influential book, *Hegemony and Socialist Strategy*, the idea is applied much more widely. There are multiple struggles in contemporary capitalist societies, Laclau and Mouffe argue, and there is no necessary connection between them, but connections can and should be built if an effective opposition is to be mounted.

### FURTHER READING

Gramsci's own reflections on hegemoney are distributed through his work and there is no obvious brief essay that I can single out. *The Prison Notebooks* are fascinating, however, and repay close reading (Gramsci, 1971). Stuart Hall's (1987) 'Gramsci and us' offers both an interesting brief introduction to Gramsci and a good argument for the contemporary application of Gramscian thought, particularly the concept of hegemony. For a slightly longer introduction see Grehan's (2002) *Gramsci, Culture and Anthropology*.

# Hexis/Body Techniques

The body is man's first and most natural instrument. Or more accurately, not to speak of instruments, man's first and most natural technical object, and at the same time technical means, is his body. (Mauss, 1979: 104)

The concept of body techniques was introduced to the literature by Marcel Mauss (1979) and is based, in the first instance, upon his observation that human bodily 'doings' (for example, walking, swimming, speaking, eating, dancing) manifest a social variability; that is to say, the way that they are done varies across societies, through history and between different groups within society. Mauss claims, for example, that there is a difference between the way in which the Americans and the French walk, and he notes how swimming styles have changed within his own lifetime; that is, the same stroke is now performed differently. This, Mauss argues, reveals that the 'use'[97] of the body is as much a social as a biological or psychological process. How I use my body depends upon my location within the social world and social changes bring about changes in the way we use our bodies. Biology and psychology are involved. Limits are set to what we can achieve with the body by virtue of its biological architecture and uses of the body certainly reflect individual psychological attitudes, as in the case of an arrogant strut. Indeed, one of the significant factors of body techniques is that they illustrate how biology, psychology and society interpenetrate (see also Levi-Strauss, 1987). However, the social nature of body techniques is very important to Mauss, and he thus defines them as 'ways in which from society to society men [sic] know how to use their bodies' (1979: 97).

Mauss was a Durkheimian. In fact he was Durkheim's nephew. And his demonstration of the social nature of body techniques can be read in terms of the Durkheimian notion of 'social facts' – albeit 'total social facts' which incorporate biological and psychological facts. Body techniques are social facts and demonstrate how minute details of bodily life, as social facts, are open to sociological analysis. They pre-exist and will outlive the specific individuals who embody them at any point in time and they constrain individuals, at least in the respect that they are difficult to change or shake off.[98] Mauss is also adding an important rejoinder to the Durkheimian notion of 'collective representations', however. Alongside representations, he is arguing, societies have collective forms of embodied reason. This is what 'body techniques' are. They are not just 'movements' or even 'embodied styles' but are methods for understanding and engaging with situations. They are skills and competencies; forms of practical reason. More to the point, they are forms of practical reason shared by social groups and derived from collective experience – hence their social pattern of distribution. Mauss uses the term '**habitus**', a Latin rendering of the Greek term 'hexis', which Aristotle used to denote practical competencies, to capture this:

> . . . I have had this notion of the social nature of '*the habitus*' for many years. Please note that I use the Latin word – it should be understood in France – *habitus*. The word

---

97 I find the expression 'uses of the body' somewhat problematic as it implies that the agent is in some way distinct from their body. It would be more appropriate, though admittedly more cumbersome, to say that body techniques are ways in which the body uses itself.
98 Mauss tends to overdo 'constraint' in his account and to underplay the possibility of flexibility and change (see Crossley, 1995b, 2004b). Techniques can be difficult to change or drop from our repertoire however.

translates infinitely better than 'habitude' (habit or custom), the 'exis', the 'acquired ability' and 'faculty' of Aristotle (who was a psychologist). It does not designate those metaphysical *habitudes*, that mysterious 'memory', the subject of volumes or short and famous theses. These 'habits' do not vary just with individuals and their imitations; they vary between societies, educations, proprieties and fashions, prestiges. In them we should see the techniques and work of collective and individual practical reason rather than, in the ordinary way, merely the soul and its repetitive faculties. (1979: 101)

Mauss' work on body techniques was an important influence on the work of Pierre Bourdieu. Bourdieu uses the concept of body techniques. He argues, for example, that language is a body technique, a socially structured, expressive use of the body. And, of course Bourdieu takes up the concept of the habitus too, to the point that many commentators treat this concept as his alone (see **habitus**). Interestingly, however, Bourdieu uses both the Latin 'habitus' and its Greek equivalent, 'hexis' (sometimes translated as 'exis'). The former has a very broad application in his work but the latter is used more narrowly to denote the stylistic dimension of particular body techniques. In particular Bourdieu is keen to draw out differences in bodily style between social classes and across gender, for example, an individual's linguistic accent, their manner of comportment, facial expressions and posture. Consider his reflections on stylistic uses of the mouth in speech and eating:

Language is a body technique, and specifically linguistic, especially phonetic, competence is a dimension of bodily hexis in which one's whole relation to the social world, and one's wholly social informed relation to the world, are expressed. [. . .] The most frequent articulatory position is an element in an overall way of using the mouth (in talking but also in eating, drinking, laughing etc.) [. . .] in the case of the lower classes, articulatory style is quite clearly part of a relation to the body that is dominated by the refusal of 'airs and graces' [. . .] Bourgeois dispositions convey in their physical postures of tension and exertion . . . the bodily indices of quite general dispositions towards the world and other people, such as haughtiness and disdain. (1992: 86–7)

. . . the whole body schema, in particular the physical approach to the act of eating, governs the selection of certain foods. . . . fish has to be eaten in a way which contradicts the masculine way of eating, that is, with restraint, in small mouthfuls, chewed gently, with the front of the mouth, on the tips of the teeth (because of the bones). The whole masculine identity —what is called virility – is involved in these two ways of eating, nibbling and picking, as befits a woman, or with wholehearted male gulps and mouthfuls, just as it is involved in the two (perfectly homologous) ways of talking, with the front of the mouth or the whole mouth, especially the back of the mouth, the throat (in accordance with the opposition, noted in an earlier study, by the manner symbolized by *la bouche* and *la guele*). (1984: 190)

This is not merely matter of style, however. In these quotations Bourdieu seeks to link style back to deep-rooted attitudes towards the world, ways of being-in-the-world which vary across social groups and types. The petite bourgeoisie, for example, are 'up tight' in his view. Their refinement involves an excessive degree of self-control and an insistence upon control. And this manifests very directly in their 'tight lipped' use of the mouth in speech. There is almost a sense here that Bourdieu sees a link between being careful about money (being 'tight'), a bourgeois disposition perhaps traceable to the Protestant work ethic, and being 'up tight' in one's use of the body. Both, for him, are instances of a more deep-rooted disposition. Interestingly, this very restrained, tight lipped and controlled manner of being is a feature of femininity also, according to Bourdieu, and it is for this reason that men might struggle eating foods –like fish in the above example – which must be eaten in a refined and 'picky way'. The virile man shovels food in with vigour and gusto, much as he approaches any other situation, and has difficulty accommodating food which requires 'feminine tact'. It is arguable that Bourdieu trades in caricatures here rather than realistic accounts. Fishing, for example, is a very traditional masculine occupation and in fishing ports working-class and masculine men have traditionally eaten fish in large quantities. However, there is clearly something resonant about these claims. At the very least they should provoke more thought on the values and ways of being embodied in different forms of hexis.

Bourdieu is not only interested in the form of different types of hexis and the underlying attitudes they embody, however. He is interested in the functions of hexis. Two points are important here. Firstly, the right hexis is a prerequisite for getting on in middle-class society. It opens doors and is a necessary resource – a form of embodied cultural capital (see **capital**). George Bernard Shaw's play *Pygmalion* and the popular musical, *My Fair Lady*, which is based upon it, illustrates this very well. The play concerns a young woman, Eliza Doolittle, who sells flowers on the street but who wants to work in a 'posh' flower shop and who, with the help of two well-to-do men, sets about learning to be a 'lady' in order that she can fulfil her dream. Eliza cannot work in a 'posh' flower shop because she lacks the genteel manner required in such establishments and must acquire the required hexis before she can fulfil her dream. Secondly, because hexis attaches to the body and because it is learnt, nature tends to be forgotten, it naturalizes social inequality. Embodied differences generate a situation in which members of different groups seem naturally to belong to those (different) groups. They seem almost to belong to a different 'species'. Furthermore, insofar as the hexis of dominated social

*Hexis/Body Techniques*

groups is read, as it often is, as a sign of fecklessness, dishonesty or low intelligence, the social hierarchy is legitimated. The effects of social inequality are perceived or 'misrecognized' as its cause and a contingent state of social domination thereby assumes the appearance of a natural hierarchy. Those who lack the motivation, intelligence or honesty to succeed are at the bottom of the pile, where they should be, and the intelligent, honest and motivated take their place in the upper echelons. Again there is an element of caricature involved here. Eliza Doolittle and her benefactors belong to a bygone age and many of the traditional myths of natural superiority have been displaced. However, like any caricature there is also an element of truth that is worth teasing out in its more complex form.

## FURTHER READING

Mauss' (1979) essay 'Body techniques' is a slightly strange and far from convincing account but is very important and interesting. It is well worth reading. Bourdieu's references to hexis are dispersed throughout his work. However, the first half of *The Logic of Practice* provides an important and interesting discussion of Bourdieu's general attitude to these matters (Bourdieu, 1992a). In addition, *Distinction* is a central reference point for all discussions of this issue (Bourdieu, 1984).

# Humanism and Anti-humanism

121

Related concepts: *alienation, body-power/bio-power, freedom.*

In the context of critical social theory 'humanism' refers generically to theories of society, economy, history, culture, knowledge or ethics which are grounded in a conception of human nature or essence, that is, in a concept of species-specific human capacities, tendencies or needs. Anti-humanism, to risk stating the obvious, refers generically to those theories which oppose this grounding for whatever reason – although anti-humanism, in the present, tends to be associated with structuralist and post-structuralist thought in particular.

Recent debates on humanism stem from its rediscovery by social and political critics in the mid-twentieth century. Following the carnage of two world wars and the growing suspicion, eventually born out, of the atrocities being conducted in the Soviet Union – which some believed to be related to the dehumanized and mechanistic version of Marxism subscribed to by the Soviet Communist Party – many critical theorists were prompted to rediscover and advocate humanism. Mechanistic, scientistic or metaphysical theories of society which delete 'man' and thereby fail to engage with the question of human nature, they argued, often lose sight of human values and also human need and thus fail to achieve the promise of critical theory.

One important source for this humanism was Marx's early work, particularly the *Economic and Philosophical Manuscripts of 1844* (Marx, 1959). In this work, Marx develops an understanding of the essential nature of human beings, describes the manner in which that nature is alienated under capitalist conditions of economic production, but also insists that society (and thus capitalist conditions of economic production) is a human creation (see **alienation**). Human beings have made a society in which their essence is denied or alienated, he claims, but they can remake it.

Another important source was the work of Jean-Paul Sartre, and particularly his essay, 'Existentialism and humanism' (1948). Sartre's version of humanism is a slightly odd one, in the respect that he explicitly rejects the idea of a pre-given human nature or essence. 'Existence', Sartre famously claims, 'precedes essence', that is to say, our essence or nature is not given by the fact of our existence. To the contrary, we are what we make ourselves by way of our actions, according to Sartre, and our actions take shape in conditions of absolute freedom (see **freedom**). This is not an invitation to do whatever we want, however. The core of Sartre's humanism is ethical. When we act, he argues, we act for everyone, we affect everyone, and this prompts the moral question of our relationship to others. This is fuelled, furthermore, by his atheism. If there is no God then there is no plan, order or guarantee of meaning and truth behind that which human beings have created for themselves. To think otherwise, Sartre argues, is to alienate our own freedom, taking refuge in 'bad faith' (see **freedom**). Our task is to realize our freedom and to make the morality and meaning of the world in which we want to live.

The challenge to Sartre's humanism was more or less immediate and came from within the existentialist camp to which he himself belonged. On one hand he was challenged by Heidegger (1978). Heidegger's critique is complex and very much tied to a deep reflection upon issues raised by his own version of existentialism, as outlined in *Being and Time* (Heidegger, 1962). In essence, however, Heidegger is opposed both to the ahistoricism which he discerns in humanism, its tendency to abstract human essence from the movement of time, and more particularly to what he takes to be the metaphysical framework within which the question of humanism is posed. It is less the 'answers' that humanists provide than the questions they are addressing and the framework out of which those questions arise that is problematic, for Heidegger, a framework structured by assumptions that he finds problematic. Specifically, the question of human being, following a tradition of philosophy which dates back to the later and better known of the ancient Greek philosophers, glosses over the deeper question of the nature of being which, for Heidegger, is the proper philosophical question. To some degree I think that we can read this critique as a critique of scientific conceptions of what human beings are (science here meaning both biology and social science) and of the dominance which these scientific conceptions come to play within philosophy itself. Science, for Heidegger, operates by bracketing certain questions out of consideration, is unreflexive and fails to locate either itself qua activity or the objects it studies within a broader historical perspective. What human beings do and think now, for example, tends to be universalized and taken as an indication of human essence, when in fact it might reflect only what human beings are now – not what they might have been in the past and might be in the future. Sciences freezes time. There is more to Heidegger's view than this and putting it this way sells it short, not least because it is not very defensible as a view of either biological or social science,[99] but it at least gives us some sense of what Heidegger is driving at.

Heidegger does acknowledge Sartre's departure from mainstream humanism, his challenge to the notion of a fixed human nature, but he claims that this challenge still works within the framework of that which it challenges, much as Sartre's atheism, as a position on the question of the existence of God, might be said to work within a 'theistic' or religious framework – to say 'no' is still to remain within the framework of the

123

---

99 Within biological science, for example, evolutionary theory is obviously focused upon change. And many sociological theories too emphasize the historical nature of both society and the individual.

---

question, not yet to explore and move beyond that framework. Furthermore, borrowing from this same logic, Heidegger is clear to argue that his own opposition to humanism is not an embrace of the inhuman or a justification of inhumanity. On one hand he claims to be working beyond the binary opposition of human/inhuman. On the other hand, though his argument is anything but clear, he appears to suggest that humanism sells human beings short and that the possibilities for human life might be better if pursued within a post-humanist frame.

It should be pointed out here, though it will be controversial to do so, that Heidegger's personal record with respect to ethics and humanity is considerably tarnished by his apparently enthusiastic embrace of Nazism during the Second World War. This has been the subject of several major academic works, some of which at least have debated the question of the association between Heidegger's philosophy and his politics. This is not the place to debate that point. Needless to say, however, this is not a good advertisement for anti-humanism and one is forced to wonder whether a humanistic philosophy might have better placed him to resist Nazism. Furthermore, from the point of critical theory it is problematic to divorce life and work, since if academic work does not address real-life situations and represent the political/moral viewpoint that one would adopt towards 'real life' then it has little claim to be 'critical' in the moral and political sense of that term implied in 'critical theory'.

In a very different vain, Simone de Beauvoir and Maurice Merleau-Ponty, anticipating the turn of Sartre's own later philosophy, outlined the basis for a more critical form of humanism. Merleau-Ponty tackled the ethics of humanism head on in a reflection upon both the Moscow Trials, which involved certain 'counter-revolutionaries' being executed for their crimes against the revolution in the former Soviet Union, and the question of collaboration with the Nazis, which was very central in French intellectual life in the period immediately following the war (Merleau-Ponty, 1969). In essence he sought to challenge what he saw as the naïve humanism which abstracts the individual from history and puts them, morally, before the collectivity. Individuals who act against the flow of history or find themselves out of line with that flow, he argues, must face the consequences of doing so. We all belong to history and are not detachable from it. The details of this argument are less important, however, than his attempt, which parallels that of de Beauvoir, to address the weaknesses in Sartre's understanding of freedom (see **freedom**). Simone de Beauvoir focuses primarily upon gender and Merleau-Ponty upon class, but both seek to temper the Sartrean concern with 'pure consciousness' and 'radical freedom' by reference to the embodiment and social situation of human beings. Our bodies and social situations are not external conditions to our consciousness, and certainly not to our freedom, they respectively argue. We are our bodies and our social situations; they shape what we are and what we become. We are never 'nothing', as Sartre (1969) suggests, but always something – as defined by our body, our habits or internalized culture, and by the relations which bind us to others. If we make ourselves, as Sartre suggests, it is only in and through these conditions of our situation.

The position advocated by de Beauvoir and Merleau-Ponty is not anti-humanist but what Merleau-Ponty calls 'critical humanism'. If by humanism we mean a philosophy which focuses upon 'the inner man' and abstracts human beings from their situation in the messy complex of historical relations, he argues, then humanism is a poor philosophy. A critical humanism is one which studies human beings in their situation, giving due complexity to the 'weight' of their situation, both external, internalized as habit and in the form of the body as a lived condition of our existence (Merleau-Ponty, 1964).

This definition of humanism corresponds, in many ways, to the definition of 'real humanism' which Marx appears to embrace in his early work; namely, a humanism which treats 'man' (and woman, as de Beauvoir adds!) as an 'ensemble' of 'social relations'. Human beings become whatever they are, according to this definition, through their relationships with other people, and their nature can never be adequately described in abstraction from the particular configuration of relationships in which they are enmeshed. This definition of humanism is also contemplated by Louis Althusser (1969), a central Marxist critic of humanism. For Althusser, however, this statement was really a transitional one within Marxism, marking the beginning of the epistemological break which separates Marx's earlier 'ideological' work from his later 'scientific' work (see **epistemological break**). If we take seriously and elect to carry through consistently the idea that 'man' is an 'ensemble of social relations', Althusser argues, we end up displacing man in favour of a consideration of these relations – an outcome which he views positively, as a gain in scientificity.[100] And this is exactly what the later (scientific) Marx does in Althusser's view. He drops the language of 'man' in preference for the language of forces of production, relations of production, modes of production, social formations, superstructures,

---

100  It is interesting that Althusser, to some extent, declares his anti-humanism in the name of science, where Heidegger, to some degree, declares his in opposition to science and the pollution of philosophical thought by science.

ideology, and so on. The argument here is akin to that which we find in Levi-Strauss, whose focus upon structures led him, ultimately, to 'dissolve man'. The concept of 'man' has no use in social science, for Levi-Strauss, rather we should focus upon underlying structures.

This structuralist displacement or dissolution of 'man' is, in effect, the basis of much of the anti-humanist emphasis in recent critical social theory. It is anti-humanist in the respect that it deems 'man' an 'epistemological obstacle' (see **epistemological break**) to a proper understanding of the social world and, indeed, 'the human condition'.

This argument was also taken up and extended in the work of post-structuralist writers; particularly Foucault. In *The Order of Things*, Foucault traces the history of the discourses which have given rise to a concept of 'man' as both a subject and object of knowledge, identifying what he believes are the contradictions of this concept and noting, in the form of structuralism, what he believes to be a new break in discourse which will mark the end of 'man' as a concept. The larger part of Foucault's work, however, is focused upon the way in which knowledge of 'man' has emerged in the context of technologies for the control of man; technologies in which knowledge (in the form of human science) and power interact in a mutually reinforcing fashion (see **power/knowledge**). Knowledge of man, as it has unfolded historically, Foucault argues, has been normative and normalizing. In saying what man is, we have specified what man should be and this has been related to a variety of forms of exclusion and control which seek to check that those norms are adhered to and that those who deviate are identified and brought back into line with the ideal:

Humanism invented a whole series of subjected sovereigns; the soul (ruling the body but subjected to God), consciousness (sovereign in the context of judgement but subjected to the necessities of truth), the individual (a titular control of personal rights, subjected to the laws of nature and society) . . . (1980b: 221)

Like other anti-humanists, Foucault claims that his stance is related to a greater respect for humanity, and greater love of freedom, than humanism makes possible. Sounding rather like Heidegger, he claims that:

What I'm afraid of about humanism is that it presents a certain form of ethics as a universal model for any kind of freedom. I think that there are more secrets, more possible freedoms, and more inventions in our future than we can imagine in humanism.' (1988: 15)

The challenge of anti-humanism is fascinating and important. In the final instance, however, it is my contention that it tends to throw the baby

*Humanism and Anti-humanism*

out with the bathwater. We would be better, in my view, to look for a contemporary reworking of the critical humanism of Marx, de Beauvoir and Merleau-Ponty, albeit one which is cognisant of the critiques of writers such as Althusser and Foucault. For present purposes it must suffice to make three points in respect of this critical humanism. First, contra Althusser and Levi-Strauss, the effort to displace 'man' by way of 'structures' is far from satisfactory on scientific grounds alone. It oversimplifies the complexity of social practices and underestimates the role of (acquired) human competence, innovation and improvization in the reproduction of the social world, not to mention in social change. Merleau-Ponty understood this. Reflecting upon Levi-Strauss' early work he draws the conclusion that it not only decentres man, by identifying collective rules and resources which shape action, but equally reveals that 'the social finds its centre only in man', since social structures depend upon the innovative action of agents for their existence. In effect, he argues, 'we are in a sort of circuit with the socio-historical world' (1964: 123). This point receives a much stronger and more developed formulation in the work of both Giddens (1984) and Bourdieu (1984, 1992a: Bourdieu and Wacquant, 1992) and is, I suggest crucial. We should not try to understand human beings independently of their location in social contexts and relationships but neither should we seek to explore those contexts and relationships as if they had a life of their own. Furthermore, it is important to recognize that human beings are able to have this 'sort of circuit' with the social world because of our 'nature', because it is our nature to innovate and habituate, learning from others, from experience and from our own mistakes (see Elias, 1978).

The second problem with anti-humanism is that, like Sartre's humanism, it is insensitive to the vulnerability of human beings and the conditional nature of our freedom; both of which form a meaningful basis on which to talk about human need. As de Beauvoir noted, we are not in a position to begin to 'invent ourselves' until our more basic needs have been taken care of, and perhaps even in 'inventing ourselves' we need the recognition of others to give meaning to what we are doing. If we abandon notions of human nature, and with them notions of need, we have very little leverage with which to argue for the importance of social provisions and institutions which cater for these basic underlying needs. There are many challenges and challengers to this provision outside of critical theory and the job of critical theory, in part, should be to defend it against these challenges.

Thirdly, although Foucault is right to point to the link between humanism and certain forms of power, it is often far from obvious that the forms of power and control that he points to are a bad thing. For example, the idea that power in modern societies, in the form of bio-power (see **body-power/*bio-power***), serves to prolong life seems like quite a good idea. Similarly, although surveillance, which Foucault talks about at length and links to the rise of the 'sciences of man', can be abused, it can equally serve to protect us in a variety of ways and is certainly not inherently bad in all cases. In places Foucault seems to recognize this, arguing that his critiques do not aim to say what is wrong or right so much as to let us take a closer look at the forces which impinge upon and shape our lives. This is surely a good thing. Critical humanism must be reflexive. But that is not, or at least need not imply anti-humanism. Furthermore, Foucault concedes that there is power in all societies, and that the idea of a society without forms of power is a myth. The question then is whether this or that form of power is appropriate. This, it seems to me, is perfectly consistent with critical humanism and certainly gives one no reason to abandon humanism. We can accept that humanism emerges within a particular configuration of power/knowledge without concluding that we should therefore abandon humanism, particularly if we accept that power is an inevitable feature of all societies. Perhaps the humanist regime is preferable to others. Furthermore, using Foucault's critique we may seek to disarm the less desirable forms of power associated with humanism whilst holding onto a more critical form of humanism in the process.

### FURTHER READING

Sartre's essay, *Existentialism and Humanism*, is very interesting and engaging (1948). It is also quite straightforward. Heidegger's 'Letter on humanism' is very difficult to follow but not the most difficult of his works and merits reading (Heidegger, 1978). There are a couple of papers in Althusser's (1969) *For Marx* which address the question of humanism, both of which are quite straightforward. There is no obvious point of reference for Foucault, de Beauvoir or Merleau-Ponty but the issue is sufficiently central to the work that any good secondary account should provide further elucidation.

# Hybridity

Related concepts: **orientalism, racism.**

The concept of hybridity or cultural hybridity emerges out of postcolonial literary studies, that is, out of the study of literature produced in former colonies, literature which often reflects back upon and bears the stamp of the culture of the colonial nation. In his seminal study, **Orientalism**, Edward Said (1978) explored the manner in which various western textual forms, including literary forms such as the novel, contributed to the construction of the 'orient' as a specifically western object of experience (see **orientalism**). Through the novels of, for example, Joseph Conrad, readers, past and present, experience the colonies as culturally constructed by the literati of the colonial era and class. In these literary works a relatively clear distinction is preserved between the 'cultured' or 'civilized' European and the savage or barbarous 'oriental'. Indeed, the savagery of the oriental is invoked in order to affirm the cultured nature of the European and the two are kept strictly separate.

Colonialism brings cultures into contact, however. Dialogues are effected and hybrid cultural forms, identities and experiences begin to emerge. It is these mixed forms that the cultural theorist Homi Bhabha (1994) refers to by the term 'hybridity'. The hybrid is neither one thing nor the other but somewhere in-between. Given the power relation between colonizer and colonized this in-between usually involves the mimicry of the 'master' by the 'slave'. Colonized people absorb the language and culture of their colonizers, combining it with their own and producing their own hybrid forms.

This can lead to difficulties for the hybrid agent who, as Franz Fanon (1993) notes in *Black Skins, White Masks*, finds their self caught between cultures (see also Fanon, 1986). They are fully accepted and recognized by neither side in the (post) colonial situation and perhaps are internally divided against their self. Fanon describes, for example, the situation of the black person who reads the racist fiction of a colonial power, identifying with the white European protagonist against the barbarous 'other', only to discover that, in the eyes of their white contemporaries, they are the barbarous other. They are not 'Tarzan', as they had imagined and fantasized their self to be, but are rather identified as belonging to one of the barbarous tribes that this hero of western literature struggles against. Furthermore, some of the discussion in postcolonial literature describes the situation of becoming a stranger within one's native culture, returning to it, having been away and having internalized aspects of another culture, such that one no longer fits into one original life and culture any longer.

Bhabha sees hybridity as a source of resistance against colonial power, however, not least because it challenges the neat distinction between the culture of the master and the culture and slave. The betweeness of the hybrid challenges the categorical boundaries of the colonial discourse and the sharp distinction which it draws between self and other. Furthermore, as a 'repetition' it undermines the authority and authenticity claimed for the 'original'. The cultural 'mask' of the hybrid reveals culture (in the sense of 'high culture') to be a mask. And European culture finds itself outside of the complete control of Europeans.

Much of the work on hybridity is conducted within literary studies. Analysts have looked both at the way in which specific literary forms manifest aspects of hybridity and also at the way in which the issue of hybridity is tackled within texts; that is, how do different authors manage the hybridity of their characters. The concept of hybridity can be extended beyond literary studies, however, and indeed beyond the postcolonial context. Indeed, the debate on hybridity in some ways parallels sociological (as well as literary) analyses from the 1960s of the mixing of the classes brought about, for example, by the entrance of working-class pupils into the (middle-class dominated) grammar school and university. Analysis of this situation typically focused upon the cultural betweeness arrived at by the agent in question. They gained enough middle-class culture to find themselves shunned by their native working-class commuity and to feel themselves a 'stranger' therein, but not enough to find themselves accepted or to feel at home within the middle-class. This could be a source of **alienation** for them but alternatively, or perhaps as a consequence of this alienation, it could also be a source of resistance and subversion. Work on 'the stranger' by both Simmel (1971) and Schutz (1964) also echoes some of these themes and illustrates their wider sociological application and relevance.

### FURTHER READING

Bhabha (1994) discusses hybridity in *The Place of Culture*. I find this an odd and difficult text, neither persuasive nor particularly coherent, but it is worth examining it first hand. Many introductions to postcolonial literature have sections on hybridity. Fanon's (1993) *Black Skins/White Masks* is a very interesting study, which is written in a straightforward and accessible style.

# I and Me

Related concepts: *id, ego and superego, identity, intersubjectivity, relationalism.*

There are many different definitions of 'I', 'identity' and 'self' in the social sciences and philosophy, not to mention further afield in the religions, popular psychologies and mystical belief systems of the world. One particularly important conception from a sociological point of view, however, derives from the work of G.H. Mead (1967). Mead's influence can be felt in much of the important work on self and identity within symbolic interactionism and related branches of sociology (for example, Becker, 1984, 1993; Goffman, 1959, 1968; Strauss, 1997; Blumer, 1986), not to mention recent developments within German critical theory (Habermas, 1987a and Honneth, 1995).

Self-identity, for Mead, is a reflexive process. It arises when the social agent turns their perception back upon their self in an effort to inspect, evaluate, prepare, and control their self, and so on. The image of a dog chasing its own tail is a useful one here, both because it reminds us that the reflexive relationship of self to self unfolds through time (it is an activity and thus processual) and because it illustrates a central tenet of Mead's theory, namely that the self will never catch up with itself. Every step that the dog takes in anticipation of getting closer to the tail necessarily whips the tail around, further away. So it is with the self. Note, however, that this is not because the self is mysterious in any way – we are likening it to a dog's tail after all! – but rather because of the simple logical impossibility of thought thinking about itself. When I reflect upon my activities, my life, self or thought, I necessarily take a step back from them. I cease doing them in order to do something else – to reflect. And I cannot reflect upon my reflection without stepping back from and ceasing to do that too. My reflections upon myself are never quite up-to-date then because they never

131

include themselves, the activity I am involved in right now, as I am doing it, in the picture. Like the dog, I slip away from myself through the very act of trying to catch up with myself. Putting that another way and drawing a further implication from it, I can only ever know myself in the past tense, since the act of reflecting upon myself in the present necessarily eludes my view. Or rather, since I can project imaginatively into the future, I can only see myself either in the past or the future tense but never in the present.

The individual features twice in this reflexive process. They are both the subject who reflects or looks and the object which is reflected about or looked at. When I look in the mirror, for example, I split into two, metaphorically speaking, becoming both a subject who perceives an image and the image which is looked at. Similarly, when I think about myself, I am both an agent who thinks and an object which that agent thinks about. And when I tell a story about myself, either to another person or to myself in the course of recollection and memory, I thereby occupy the role of both storyteller and character or protagonist in the story. Mead refers to these two elements in the reflexive process as the I and the me. The I is the active agent who perceives, thinks, tells the story, and so on and the me is the image which is seen, the character who is thought about or whose story is told. I and me are, of course, the same person but to reiterate the argument above, the reflexive process effects a temporal separation. The I belongs to the present, the me to the past or future, and the two can never coincide. The I never coincides with (sees or reflects upon) itself qua I. It has access to itself only as me. As Mead himself puts it:

> [the I appears as me] but it is a me that was an I at an earlier time. If you ask then where directly in your own experience the I comes in, the answer is that it comes in as a historical figure. It is what you were a second ago that is the 'I' of the 'me'. [the I] is not directly given in experience. (1967: 174–5)

This temporal dimension is central. Some have interpreted I and me spatially, as parts of the self, arguing, for example, that the I is our biological nature, akin to the Freudian Id, and that the me is an internalized mechanism of social control, akin to Freud's superego (see **id, ego and superego**) (for example, Giddens, 1991). This is a poor interpretation in my view. There clearly is a sense, for Mead, in which the reflexive process of the I and the me introduces a social control element into human agency, in a fashion perhaps similar to Freud's model of the superego. I discuss this shortly. However, the key to the split is temporal.

It is not spatial. And the I is not a biological agent, set against a cultural restraint ('me'). The I is everything that I am currently as a social agent and the me is everything that is included in the image that I have of myself. I and me are not 'parts' of the self but rather 'tenses' of the self, 'moments' in a temporal process. The 'me' does not control the 'I'. Insofar as 'self-control' or 'impulse-control' is at issue, the I controls itself but fashions a 'me' in the process.

Mead's insistence that the I and the me do not coincide, that the dog never catches up with its tail, can be read as part of a more general critique of the Cartesian view of the self, that is, the view of the self advocated in the seventeenth century by the French philosopher, René Descartes (who is generally regarded as the father of modern philosophy) (Descartes, 1969). Descartes famously argues that he knows his mind in a qualitatively different and superior way from the way in which he knows about other things in the world. To know the outside world he must rely upon his senses (such as his eyes and ears), which he knows to be limited and sometimes unreliable, but to know himself he need only look inwards, by means of introspection. By way of an inward glance his own soul is laid before him. Other philosophers, famously David Hume (1969), challenge this, claiming to have searched deep within themselves and found only a meaningless flow of sensations. The self, Hume argues, is a fiction or perhaps at best a memory trace. When Mead says in the above quote that the I is not given directly in experience he echoes this. He agrees that an attempt to 'look within himself' reveals nothing corresponding to a self. Furthermore, he develops an interesting critique of the idea of introspection. Like other important philosophers of his generation (such as Merleau-Ponty, 1962, 1965; Ryle, 1949, Wittgenstein, 1953), he believes that we are mistaken if we think that we learn about ourselves from looking inwards. There is nothing to see 'inside our heads', he believes. Our consciousness comprises perceptions, which are perceptions 'of' an outer world, dreams which simulate an outer world, and sensations, which we make sense of by reference to the outside world. More to the point, most of what we know of ourselves we know by reflecting upon our actions, contexts of action and action-dispositions – aspects of ourselves which are at least potentially available to the perceptions of others. To say that a person is jealous, caring or in love, for example, is to report upon how they act or are prone to act in particular situations, and whatever 'sensations' might be experienced in these situations can only be meaningfully interpreted in light of these actions and situations (Coulter, 1979; Crossley, 2001a). A hot flush might indicate anything from passion, to anger, through food poisoning to the onset of the menopause, for example, and one cannot decide which of these it is by reflecting upon the flush itself – a flush is just a flush. One must look to the context of the flush. Is it occasioned by an amorous exchange, an insult or a mouthful of vindaloo? Introspection is a reflection upon our lives and actions as they unfold in the real world, a world we share with others. Unlike Hume, however, Mead does not dismiss the idea of the self. The temporal, processual relationship which the individual (qua I) develops with their self (qua me) is a very real basis for self-hood according to Mead. More to the point, he is critical of the idea that the self derives from 'within' because he believes that it takes shape within the social world, in the context of social relations. This point needs to be unpacked.

One way in which the self is socially produced, as Mead's colleague, Cooley (1902), first argued, is by way of the mirroring action of others. There are lots of aspects of myself that I am not aware of and/or cannot see, both in terms of physical features and personality traits, but which other people can see and can tell me about, formally and informally. Others generate a feedback loop which 'puts me in touch with myself'. Perhaps I am unaware that I look foolish when I dance, for example, and it takes a friend to tell me. Perhaps I do not know that I'm a bit arrogant, and, again, I need to be told. Perhaps I smell but do not know it. Cooley captures this process is his description of the self as a 'looking glass self'. The self is formed within social relationships which reflect images of self back to self, he argues. Following Mead's terminology we might say that others reflect an image of 'me' back to 'I'. This is not to say that I am forced to agree with what others say about me, of course. It does not deny that I can argue my corner or, as Goffman (1959) famously shows, 'present' myself in specific ways in the hope of being seen in those ways. Even in these cases, however, there is no internal arbitration and the 'court of appeal' for definitions of the self is always the social group. To establish that I am not arrogant it is not sufficient to say that I do not feel arrogant (what would it be to 'feel arrogant' rather than acting in an arrogant way?). I must rather attempt to persuade others to see my actions in a different light and I can only do this by reference to aspects of my context – perhaps my apparent 'arrogance' is a response to an earlier snub and thus defensive retaliation rather than genuine arrogance.

Related to this, certain of my attributes are relational and only make sense in the context of others. Being 'tall' is not an intrinsic property, for example. It is a comparative attribute and is always relative to others who are shorter than me, so too for being rich, male, working-class, a fast runner and many other qualities. These are all ascriptions that function by means of comparison and, as such, I could only learn about them by comparing myself or being compared with others.

Mead pushes this argument further. Through our interactions with others, he argues, we learn to take their roles and thereby to 'see' ourselves from their point of view. When the I turns back upon itself to view itself, as me, it does so by assuming the role of another person. A child, for example, may see itself as its parent sees it, or from the point of view (the role or perspective) of a friend. Like actors, we get 'outside of ourselves' and experience the world differently by playing the role of others. We become other to ourselves. We learn to do this in childhood, first as the unintended effect of role play, which transports us into the role of specific other people, then later as the unintended effect of game playing, which leads us to view ourselves from the point of view of the 'generalized other' (that is, the point of view of a whole group or community and its abstract norms, values and standards). By the time of adulthood this process has assumed a truncated habitual form. We no longer play at being our parents, donning their clothes and aping their gestures, but we still look upon our own actions through their eyes and reprimand ourselves as they would. And we continue to internalize the perspectives of both specific significant and generalized others, judging, assessing and making sense of ourselves from their point of view. It is this process of becoming other to ourselves, paradoxically, which gives us our sense of self. Hume was right that we do not find a 'self' within ourselves but if we have a means of getting outside of our self (for example, by adopting the role of the other), we can put our self (past or future tense of course) into perspective and get a handle on ourself.

This process is essential to social life, for Mead. It allows us to fit our life and actions to that of our social group. Moreover, because we 'take the role of the other' (both specific and generalized) our actions have a moral flavour. We judge ourselves both from the point of view of others and from the point of view of abstract norms. In this sense there is some parallel with the Freudian picture of the id and the superego, especially as the tendency to reflect upon our lives and actions, controlling immediate impulses, becomes habitual.[101] To reiterate, however, this is a reflexive, temporal process, not an interaction of separate spatial parts of 'the self'.

135

---

101 I have argued elsewhere that it is also possible, given Mead's view that the self (I) does not coincide with itself (me), that there is some room to develop a specific version of the concept of the unconscious in relationship to Mead's view (Crossley, 2001a).

---

**I and Me**

Much of Mead's (1967) argument in his central work, *Mind, Self and Society*, is tied up with debates in psychology and sociology which a contemporary reader is unlikely to be familiar with. Furthermore, the book is composed from posthumous notes. For both of these reason it is not always an easy read. However, the middle section of the book, entitled 'self', is very good and I recommend giving it a go. Blumer (1986) is perhaps Mead's most famous commentator. His discussion of Mead is reasonable on some points but I believe that much of the richness of subtlety of Mead's approach, particularly its philosophical subtlety, is lost. A much stronger account is given in Joas (1985) and I like Honneth's (1995) account. I have written about Mead on a number of occasions and, needless to say, am quite keen on these expositions too (Crossley, 1996a, 2001a, 2002).

# Id, Ego and Superego

> *Related concepts: imaginary, symbolic and real, mirror stage and the ego, repression, unconscious (the).*

136

The id, ego and superego are the three interacting parts of the personality as theorized in psychoanalysis. The founder of psychoanalysis, Sigmund Freud, actually posits two (overlapping) models of the psyche in the course of his work. In his early work he distinguishes between consciousness, the pre-conscious and the unconscious, only turning in his later work to the id, ego and superego (see **unconscious, (the)**). The former typology is dealt with in the entry on the unconscious in this volume. Here I will deal only with id, ego and superego, although I will attempt also to deal slightly with the overlap between the two schemas.

The id is the locus of human drives and desires, many of which, in Freud's view, are socially unacceptable because they are either aggressive/anti-social in nature or directed toward forms of sexual release which are prohibited. It is an irrational element in the psyche in the respect that it tends towards instant gratification and recognizes no boundaries, either social or natural, between itself and desired objects. We might recognize it within ourselves in those moments where we act upon impulse, without thinking or assessing consequences. In much of his work Freud implies that the id is largely biologically rooted, at least in its basic structure. It is what we are 'by nature'. Moreover, much of it is unconscious, not least because our less acceptable desires and drives are 'repressed' and thereby kept out of consciousness (see **repression** and **unconscious, (the)**).

In direct contrast and opposition to the id is the superego. The superego, in effect, is constituted from the internalization of social norms and demands, and the pressure they put upon the psyche to conform. It is formed in early childhood, particularly during the oedipus complex (see **unconscious, (the)**), where the child is forced to submit to the authority of their father (or parental authority figure), who in turn represents the demands and standards of wider society. In some of his work Freud suggests that this process of formation involves a part of the id being turned back upon itself. In effect the energy and aggression of the individual, which might otherwise be directed outwards towards the world, is redirected within the psyche as a means of the individual exercising self-control.

Part of the superego is conscious. We are all aware, at times, of being torn between what we would like to do and what we feel we ought to do, or again between a rule or interdiction and a desire. Similarly, we are all familiar with the various emotions generated by transgression of social norms or perhaps even just the thought of transgression: for example, guilt, shame and fear of reprisal. In these cases we are aware of our super ego. Part of the superego is also unconscious according to Freud, however. There are desires and prohibitions which would be distasteful to our consciousness if we knew about them, which operate below the level of our consciousness and beyond our conscious reach. Our self-control and self-censorship are so strong in some cases, in other words, that we are not even aware of them.

Freud defines 'the ego' differently at different points of his work. If we start with the definition associated with the id-ego-superego triumvirate, however, then it is that part of our psychological make up which both mediates between the id and the superego, as a 'referee', and puts the compromise arrived at in the struggle into action, taking into account the circumstances we find ourselves in. The development of the ego, in effect, involves an infant learning how best to act so as to maximize its interests and desires in socially acceptable ways. At one level this entails the acquisition of the basic sensory-motor schemes necessary to effective agency but it also entails the internalization of such principles of action as, for example, looking before one leaps, delaying gratification to maximize rewards and not always showing one's hand immediately unless it is expedient to do so. Although it is not always clear in Freud, there is good reason to believe that this aspect of the psyche is composed both of innate and acquired capacities (and also perhaps innate tendencies that presuppose specific environmental conditions to develop properly), and that aspects of its operation might function at either the unconscious, preconscious or conscious levels.

Human agency, for Freud, arises out of the interaction of these three elements, id, ego and superego. The 'ideal' situation is one in which the ego maximizes the satisfaction of the desires of the id, within the framework of acceptability set by the superego, which in turn is set by wider society. The ego thus adapts the agent to (social) reality and fits them to take their place in society. However, the tension between the elements can become too great, or alternatively one element in the triumvirate can become too strong/weak,[102] unbalancing the personality. In any of these cases we would expect the agent to suffer psychological problems and, as a consequence of this, perhaps also to become defined as a social problem on account of their 'lack of fit' with the demands of social reality.

Many contemporary appropriations of psychoanalysis within critical social theory, particularly stemming from the work of the French psychoanalyst Jacques Lacan (1989), have been critical of this focus on the adaptive (or not) ego within psychoanalytic theory, particularly as it has been developed in the US context. American psychoanalysis, it is argued, has become too preoccupied with 'fitting' or 'adapting' the ego to reality and is thereby diverted from the task of challenging the nature of (social) reality. It would be foolish to reject this way of thinking altogether, however, and it has been connected to certain interesting developments in social theory. Much of the psychoanalytic influence on the work of Anthony Giddens (1991), for example, derives from the 'ego psychology' (and also 'object-relations')[103] branch of psychoanalysis.

---

102 Obviously strengths and weaknesses are relative in this context. One might equally say that one part of the personality is too strong as say that another part is too weak, e.g. saying that a person's id is too strong is tantamount to saying that their superego or ego are too weak to control it, and saying that the superego is too strong is akin to saying that it overpowers the ego and id (and thus that they are not strong enough).

103 Even if we draw a quite tight and specific boundary around 'psychoanalysis' there are numerous schools and developments, some of which have departed quite markedly from Freud's own original position. 'Object-relations' is a branch of psychoanalysis which focuses particularly upon the role of internalized relationships upon the psychological life of the individual. How individuals form relationships with significant other people ('objects') and represent those objects and relations internally is said to be crucial to the functioning of their psyche.

---

Similarly, the work of Norbert Elias (1984) draws very strongly upon the dynamic of id-superego impulse-control.

An alternative conception of the ego in Freud's work, which has been particularly popular amongst critical social theorists who follow Lacan, focuses upon the self-identification of the individual, the way in which, through such psychological processes as identification, they build a sense of their self. The ego, from this point of view, is a representation which the individual has of their self and the feeling they develop for this representation. This sense perhaps comes closest to the everyday use of 'ego' (for example, 'he's got a big ego') as it concerns the narcissistic[104] relationship which an individual forms with themselves. The ego, defined in this way, develops out of relationships which the individual has with others, according to Freud. Lacan offers a slightly different and complementary account, however, in his analysis of the 'mirror stage' (see **mirror stage and the ego**), a stage of development not noted in Freud and perhaps occurring earlier than the processes of ego development described by Freud.

The critical aspect of this definition of the ego, at least as defined by Lacan, is twofold. Firstly, he believes that the ego, as a representation, is a misrepresentation or misrecognition of what we are really like. Specifically we tend to represent ourselves as coherent wholes when, in fact, the reality of our unconscious psychological lives is far from this and our consciousness itself is split off from and ignorant of this other dimension. Our psychological life is anything but unified. This view leads Lacanians to be both critical of liberal political theories, which also presuppose a stable and coherent self, and to recommend the practice of psychoanalysis as a personal means of ridding oneself of such misrecognition. Secondly, Lacan argues that the structure of modern societies induces an obsession with the ego or self and that many contemporary social and psychological problems stem from this fact. Psychopathology in modern societies is dominated by narcissistic and paranoid, self-oriented conditions (see **mirror stage and the ego**). In this respect his argument overlaps in an interesting way with arguments about egoism and its (self) destructive consequences in Durkheim's (1952) analysis of suicide.

---

104 'Narcissism' generally implies 'self love'. In this context, however, it applies more generally to the preoccupation of the individual with their self and the affective relationship they develop with their self. Self-hatred, from this point of view, might be 'narcissistic' if it involves excessive self-preoccupation. Even 'normal' ego development entails some degree of narcissism from the psychoanalytic point of view, however.

---

Some later psychoanalysts, particularly Lacan (1989), are very difficult to read, not least because they do not present their ideas in the form of clear, rational and coherent arguments. Freud, by contrast, makes strong, rational arguments in defence of his views and is very easy to follow. One might not agree with him but his work is very enjoyable to read and very engaging. The main text for 'id, ego and superego' is *The Ego and the Id*, which is included in Volume 11 (*On Metapsychology*) of the Pelican Freud Library (Freud, 1984). For a further exploration of the tensions between the id and society see 'Civilization and its discontents', which is published in Volume 12 of the Pelican series (*Civilization, Society and Religion* (Freud, 1985)). These ideas are given an interesting sociological development in the work of Norbert Elias. See particularly his *Civilizing Process* (Elias, 1984).

# Ideal Speech Situation

*Related concepts:* **discourse, discourse ethics, public sphere, rationality.**

The 'ideal speech situation' is a much maligned and misrepresented concept formulated by Jürgen Habermas (1970a, b) in his early work. It is his first theoretical attempt to explore the notion and possibility of a form of discourse composed of the exchange of reasons and steered by the force of the better argument alone: an exchange of views and reasons in which the best argument wins and does so only because it is the best argument. What constitutes the best argument, in these cases, will vary according to the balance of cognitive, moral and subjective claims involved: cognitive claims are truth claims about the external world which must be supported by reference to evidence, theory and the logic of inference; moral claims are claims about what is right and require rational justification; and subjective claims are claims about truthfulness and sincerity which can be confirmed or disconfirmed in various ways. Notwithstanding these differences, however, the point is that in ideal speech situations interlocuters are called upon to provide evidence or justification for their claims, or for the inferences deducible from their claims, are required to reason logically and are required, by these means, to generate a situation in which their alter cannot rationally disagree with them. Perhaps they will take certain of the other's beliefs and show how their own claim is logically and irrefutably deducible from those beliefs, for example, 'you believe that Socrates is a man, you believe that all men are mortal, so you must agree that Socrates is mortal!' Perhaps they will point to aspects of their interlocuters' arguments or actions which undermine their claim to sincerity, for example, 'you say that you are committed to world peace but you keep bombing other countries!' What they will not do in an ideal speech situation is try to bribe, blackmail or intimidate their other into acceptance. They will not lie or deceive. And they will not bypass the need for argument by recourse to coercion or power.

To dispense with certain of the silly criticisms of Habermas first, this does not mean that people involved in the dialogue necessarily like each other or are keen to please each other and agree. It does not mean that argument is a harmonious affair. And neither does it mean that passions are left 'at the door'. Arguments might be quite combative and heated. All that matters is that the 'weapons' used in these exchanges are those of reason, rhetoric and argument alone. Similarly, although Habermas is not quite so clear on this issue, there is no need to assume that these situations are free of power and restraint. Power and restraint, or perhaps incentives and rewards, might be necessary to make people abide by these conditions of discourse.[105] Power and restraint only become a problem when they 'distort' communicative processes and prevent the better argument from winning out. More to the point, Habermas does not believe that we live in a world replete with ideal speech situations. The ideal speech situation is precisely an ideal and one seldom even approximated in contemporary societies. It is not an arbitrary ideal, in Habermas' view, however, not a figment of his philosophical imagination. Importantly, he claims to have derived this notion, transcendentally, from the universal pragmatics of communication. This point needs to be unpacked.

A transcendental argument is an argument which deduces claims about what must be the case because one could not coherently think otherwise or because the world could not be as it is if it were not so. In modern philosophy Kant (1933) is the key example of a philosopher who

---

105 This point is closer to the view of Pierre Bourdieu (2000) than to Habermas himself but I see no reason why we cannot adopt it in this context.

---

uses these types of argument, and Habermas is influenced by him. Where Kant makes transcendental arguments which focus upon and concern the individual subject or ego, however, Habermas focuses upon communication and speech between people – intersubjectivity rather than subjectivity. More specifically, he focuses upon the pragmatics of speech; that is to say, the norms, assumptions and procedures which shape speech concretely and make it possible. At this level, he argues, one can see that the 'ideal speech situation' is an ideal which is concretely, necessarily and therefore universally embodied in all speech acts. The very process of arguing and reasoning, in other words, embodies the ideal speech situation as an assumption. If it did not we could not coherently argue in the first place – why would we bother? When we set out to argue and debate there are certain things that we cannot logically say without involving ourselves in a 'performative contradiction', that is, without contradicting what we say in the very act of saying it, for example, 'nothing I say is true'[106] or 'all truth is relative'.[107] By reflection upon these contradictions we are able to arrive at certain 'ideals' which must necessarily be embedded in speech practices. The ideals of the ideal speech situation, according to Habermas, belong to this category. When we set out to argue, we necessarily presuppose them and must necessarily do so if we are to avoid self-contradiction, even if we do not generally live up to them. In other words, Habermas claims to have deduced the ideal speech situation from an analysis of the (necessary) assumptions of ordinary speech. The ideal speech situation is not his theory, he therefore tells us, but our theory, a theory we necessarily ascribe to when we speak and particularly when we argue with others.

The importance of the idea, for Habermas, derives less from its actualization in contemporary societies, more from its moral and critical potential. As noted above, he admits that, in practice, most communication is far from ideal. We do, in other words, contradict ourselves and/or transgress the normative ideals necessarily embodied in our speech acts. As a necessary moral ideal and model of speech, however, the ideal speech situation provides him with a basis from which to identify and criticize the 'systematic distortions' which corrupt many of the speech situations of everyday life, including and perhaps particularly speech situations which have a powerful influence on our lives, for

106 This is self-contradictory because to be true it would have to be untrue.
107 This is self-contradictory because it presents itself as a universal truth ('*all* truth is relative') yet claims that there can be no universal truth (since it deems truth relative to certain particular conditions).

142

example, in the public sphere (see **public sphere**), in parliaments, in the meeting between political and business elites. More specifically, it facilitates 'imminent'[108] critique. Habermas can claim to criticize people on the basis of their failure to realize their own ideals and values, rather than values which he, as a critical theorist, imposes upon them. Furthermore, this is a critique which points to a better world, a utopia or ideal. Or rather, it is a critique which draws upon a utopia which, it claims, we are already subscribed to in any case.

Needless to say my defence of Habermas' concept deals only with the crudest criticizms of it, those based more upon misunderstanding than genuine, reasonable objection. My purpose here is not to defend the idea, however, merely to provide a fair exposition of it. And, in this case, a fair exposition involves fending off obvious misrepresentations.

### FURTHER READING

Habermas visits and revisits these themes at various points in his work. The classic papers (in English translation) are 'On systematically distorted communication' and 'Towards a theory of communicative competence' (Habermas, 1970a, b). A relatively brief introduction to Habermas' 'universal pragmatics' can be found in the first two chapters of his *Communication and the Evolution of Society* (Habermas, 1991a). A good secondary discussion on these and related issues can be found in Cooke's (1997) *Language and Reason: A Study of Habermas' Pragmatics.*

143

---

108 An imminent critique is a critique which works by criticizing an argument, social groups, society or whatever, by its own criteria or values. This stands in contrast to a form of critique which imposes its own values and criteria upon whatever it criticizes. The advantage of this form of critique, or at least one of them, is that the party criticized cannot reject the criteria against which they are being compared without falling into self-contradiction.

---

*Ideal Speech Situation*

# Identity (personal, social, collective and 'the politics of')

> *Related concepts:* **I and me, intersubjectivity, social movements.**

The concept of identity has emerged as a key theme in social science in recent years and there are many competing definitions of it. I give my preferred theory of identity under the heading 'I and Me' elsewhere in this collection. Here I want merely to state the 'bottom line' on identity, flag up some debates and map out some the different types of identity referred to in the literature.

At its most basic 'identity' refers to the ways in which we demarcate and make sense of ourselves. It generally entails locating oneself within a range of categories (male, old, British) or formulating a description and account of who and what one is. Furthermore, by definition this entails a demarcation of what one is not, a marking out of 'the other' and of one's difference.

Defined thus, identity implies reflexivity, that is, the capacity to turn back upon oneself, to 'inspect' oneself. Beyond this formal capacity for self-perception, however, the concept of identity implies substantive content, that is, that an agent views their self in this or that way, as this or that type, belonging to this or that category or group. Studies of identity are interested in the types of identity that people adopt and perhaps the ways in which dominant forms of identity change over time (see below). They are interested in the ways in which identities are 'defended' when attacked, built up and performed or enacted. Moreover, some studies at least are interested in the uses or functions of identity, that is, the role which formulations of identity play across a range of situations. Individuals could potentially define themselves in a multitude of different ways and the question thus arises of why they define themselves in the specific ways that they do. What purposes are served by me defining myself in 'this' way when I could equally define myself in 'that' way?

It is common in much work to draw a distinction between personal and social identity. Generally speaking 'social identity' refers to forms of categorization which link an individual to a broader social grouping, for example, 'women' or 'the working-class', whilst 'personal identity' refers to the various ways in which the individual demarcates their self, or is demarcated, as a unique being with a distinct body, biography, situation, and so on. Both forms of identity are 'social' in the respect that they are negotiated in interaction, draw upon linguistic and other schemas from a socio-historical stock, and so on, but where 'social identity' tends to link the individual to this or that group, 'personal identity' generally seeks to differentiate the individual from the group by locating elements of difference.

Much debate on identity in recent years has focused upon the issues of fixity (or lack of it) and contextuality. One line of argument runs that we 'do' our identities differently in a multitude of different contexts, in accordance with the dynamics and demands of those contexts, such that it makes little sense to refer to a deep underlying identity. Sometimes I describe and distinguish myself this way, other times that way, with no fixed point or underlying 'master description'. Others, however, argue that we do have an underlying sense of who and what we are, a 'deep self', beneath this flux. My own view is that identity is always relational; that is, we always define ourselves relative to others and to contexts of interaction, in accordance with the demands of those situations. But claims that we are therefore 'fragmented' or 'schizophrenic', which some advocates of the contextual approach make, are overdone. Agents generally strive towards coherence, juggling their various identities, social and personal, and attempting to pull them together into some form of meaningful whole. There is no grand meta or master description which might pull all of this together, and there is no need for one as identities are practical and relational phenomena, constructed for the purposes of making life possible and workable. But the construction of multiple identities is, in the case of each agent, the work of an underlying organically individuated being, the parts of whose life must, at one level, fit together. And the work of identity is as much about the pulling together of these threads as it is multiplying them across social contexts.

Not that the individual is necessarily always the object of identity work. Individuals can locate themselves, qua individual, within a group, constructing a social identity. Or they can be located in that way by others. Furthermore, groups too sometimes strive, collectively, to construct an identity, often in opposition to an identity which has been foisted upon them or perhaps as a way of consolidating a network based upon issues of common interest or concern, but always in 'opposition' to others, since demarcation of self or identity necessarily identifies 'not self'

145

or other. Identity, to reiterate, is relational. One cannot have self without other, anymore than one can have left without right.

Much recent work in social movements analysis has focused upon processes of collective identity building, particularly following the seminal work of Alberto Melucci (1986). This work looks at how groups strive to achieve solidarity and collective coherence. We can see, for example, how groups develop new terms to describe themselves, or perhaps seek to alter the connotation of old terms (the appropriation and transformation of 'queer' by gay rights activists and 'nigger' by black activists being obvious examples of this). The formation of collective identities involves the generation of narratives of collective history and rituals which develop strong emotional bonds (what Herbert Blumer (1969) calls an 'esprit de corps') between their members.

All social movements, including the archetypal social movements of the early industrial era, engaged in identity work. A social movement, arguably, cannot cohere and therefore cannot exist without some degree of identity work. There must always be a sense of 'we'. However, whilst all social movements engage in 'identity work', only some movements take identity, as such, as the focus of their struggle. Workers' movements, for example, formulated the identity 'worker' as a means of calling their potential members to order but their main concern was with pay and work conditions rather than the identity 'worker'. Other movements, by contrast, are much more focused upon the nature of their identity itself and the way in which they are regarded and categorized in wider society. Struggles around sexuality and ethnicity are sometimes of this order. It is arguable that these types of struggles are more predominant now than in the past (although see Calhoun, 1995; Tucker, 1991), and on this basis some have argued that we live, or have been living in, a period of increased 'identity politics' (Woodward, 1997).

Another point, related to this, concerns the focus of social identities in contemporary societies. The argument, basically stated, is that the basis of social identity is changing. Where agents used to identify with their work and involvement in the production process (for example, as 'working-class' or 'a miner' or 'a doctor'), it is claimed, they are now more likely to identify in accordance with their consumption activities (for example, as a 'music buff' or more specifically a fan of this or that type of music, or perhaps as a 'Marks and Spencer' type of person). This shift, insofar as it is born out by the evidence, and that is disputed, might be explained both by the relative shrinking of the labour movement and trade unions (with their various activities of collective identity building) and the rise of consumer culture, with the correlative emergence of a powerful advertising industry. Many modern manufacturers do not merely produce and sell material goods. They sell symbols and identities.

### FURTHER READING

Goffman's work, particularly *Asylums* (1961), *Stigma* (1969) and *The Presentation of Self in Everyday Life* (1959) remain classic texts on identity and are very accessible. Giddens' (1991) *Modernity and Self-Identity* offers both a psychoanalytically informed account of the nature of identity and an interesting and accessible reflection upon the nature of identity in the modern world. Melucci (1986) is probably the key reference for identity, social movements and identity politics. Good discussions of theories of identity are found in Burkitt's (1991) *Social Selves* and Jenkins' (1987) *Social Identity*.

# Ideology

*Related concepts: crisis, discourse, doxa, power, power/knowledge, social class.*

The history of the term 'ideology' can be traced back to the work of Destutt de Tracy (1754–1836) in the late eighteenth and early nineteenth century. Tracy coined the term to denote the new science of ideas which he was seeking to develop. In this context 'ideology' was a positive term. One did ideology as one might do any other science and doing it was a good thing. Over a relatively short period, however, and not least as a consequence of Napoleon's pejorative use of the term, 'ideology' acquired a negative meaning. It gradually came to refer to bodies of ideas which, in the view of those referring to them as ideological, are false or unrealistic and yet, because believed to be true, have (again from the critics' point of view) negative political consequences. More specifically, it came to mean systems of belief, often tacit and taken-for-granted, which serve to legitimate unequal forms of social relations, usually class relations, to the disadvantage of the poorer and less powerful party to those relationships. There are, of course, other uses of the term ideology. Political scientists, for

Key concepts

example, sometimes use the term to mark out different sets of more or less explicit political beliefs or belief systems, for example, conservativism, socialism and liberalism. From this point of view, although one may disagree with a specific ideology, ideology per se is not a bad thing. Indeed, it is the kind of thing that a politically inclined individual might be proud of 'having'. In the context of much critical social science, however, the focus has been upon the less explicit beliefs, assumptions and taken-for-granted conceptions which legitimate, often by naturalizing them and thus making them seem inevitable, situations of domination which are deemed by the theorist of ideology to be neither natural nor inevitable.

The nineteenth century was not the first to discover the potential political function or use of false ideas. As Larrain (1979) notes, the work of Machiavelli (1469–1527) is a good example of a conception of this kind from a much earlier historical period. It was the nineteenth century, however, which put the name 'ideology' to this phenomenon and, in doing so, set a ball rolling that was destined to have a considerable impact upon critical thinking in social science.

The main source of most contemporary discussions of ideology is the work of Karl Marx. As Michèle Barrett (1991) has noted, however, there are many distinct theses on ideology in Marx's work (she identifies six), with different and perhaps inconsistent emphases. Sometimes, for example, Marx appears to emphasize the illusory or distorted nature of ideology, whilst on other occasions it would be difficult to read him in that way. Sometimes he appears to regard ideology as a mere product of the economic system, other times not. Sometimes he appears to identify different ideologies with different classes, other times he appears to suggest that the ideas of the ruling class are imposed upon the working-class (who are forced to accept them) such that there is only one (or at least one dominant) ideology in society at any point in time. Underlying this, I suggest, is a consistent emphasis on the socially and materially rooted nature of ideas, their investment by forms of class-based power and their contribution to the securing of social order. Nevertheless, the manner in which these themes are drawn out does vary and this variation has arguably been one major source of much of the controversy and debate surrounding ideology ever since. Successive factions in the Marxist camp have sought to carve out a distinctive position on ideology, drawing upon different passages from Marx or different interpretations of vague passages to establish the authenticity and authority of their particular version of the theory of ideology.

Debates on ideology have also been fuelled by historical events, however, or rather non-events. The failure of Marx's predictions regarding proletarian revolution (see **crisis** and **social class**) and the apparent incorporation of the working class and their parties and unions within the capitalist system, as a relatively compliant and contented group, prompted many Marxists to ponder the mechanisms that brought about this compliance. Why would a group of people whom Marxist theory deems to be objectively exploited not seek to overthrow the system which exploits them unless their view of society were not distorted? And what could possibly lie at the source of this distortion if not ideology?

The list of writers, following Marx, who have contributed to the development of the theory of ideology is potentially very long. Key contributors include: Engels, Mannheim, Goldmann, Adorno, Horkheimer, Marcuse, Gramsci, Barthes and Althusser. There are far too many contributions to even attempt a synoptic overview. Elsewhere in this collection I offer a separate entry on Gramsci's key contribution to the debate, his concept of '**hegemony**'. Here I will seek to briefly outline some of the key points from Althusser's (1971) theory of ideology. Althusser is a useful point of reference because his work, firstly draws out some of the key issues that have emerged in relationship to the theory of ideology in recent years, and secondly, draws together some of the key innovations in ideology theorizing from the wider Marxist tradition, and thirdly paves the way for some of the later 'post-ideological' theories of discourse which tend to predominate in the contemporary literature.

## ALTHUSSER

Society consists in three[109] levels of practice for Althusser (1969): the economic level, the political level and the ideological level. Many Marxists writing before him referred to the economic level as 'the base' and argued that the political and ideological levels constitute a superstructure founded upon and determined by that base (see Figure 1).

Ideological and Political superstructure

Economic base

Figure 1 *Ideology as a superstructure*

---

109 Strictly speaking Althusser identifies a fourth level, the level of (his own) 'theoretical practice' and science. I am not going to muddy the water by discussing that here.

In a functionalist vain, it was also sometimes argued that the superstructure provides for the functional prerequisites of the base and is best explained by reference to these prerequisites. For example, the education system is said to reproduce the necessary (skilled) labour power required by the economy, as well as the attitudes required of a disciplined labour force and is explained, qua social institution, by reference to these functions. It is argued that we have an education system of the kind that we do because capitalist society needs an institution which cultivates skilled labour, and so on. Althusser famously challenges this on two grounds. Firstly, he argues that political and ideological practices have their own internal logic and dynamics and, as such, are 'relatively autonomous' from the base. Relative autonomy is an infamously tricky concept but it represents Althusser's attempt to avoid the equally unsatisfactory alternatives of arguing either first that ideas develop in a vacuum, entirely by way of their own internal logic, or second that ideas are nothing more than effects of economic dynamics. It would be silly, for example, to reduce the products and workings of the literary world to the functional prerequisites of capitalism and/or to suggest that they are mere 'side effects' of the economy. The literary world has a specific structure and dynamics of its own which we need to understand if we are to understand literature sociologically. On the other hand, it would be equally silly to suppose that the structure and dynamics of the literary world were completely autonomous and free from the influence of the economy.[110] The economy impinges upon literature in all manner of ways. Books are produced in factories then sold; writers are paid, as are critics and publishers, and so on. Furthermore, the rise of the capitalist era ushered in certain underlying models of social organization and values which arguably structure much of what we do in most domains. Thus the literary world (and we could have focused upon any 'world') is neither totally shaped by the economy nor totally autonomous. It is relatively autonomous.

---

110 There is a sleight of hand here in the argument. It would make more sense to say that 'everything is connected to and affects everything else' rather than singling out the economy as a structure affecting all others. Why say that the economy, specifically, affects the literary world and not, for example, the political world. The reply to this might be that the economy is a far more powerful social structure than any other. There is no a priori reason to believe this however. It is an empirical claim which would need to be tested against the evidence in every case. Althusser's work is perhaps the most sophisticated attempt within the body of Marxist literature to address this question of the 'primacy of the economic' and he makes interesting headway in his discussion of it. His ultimate conclusion, however, is vague and something of a fudge. After seeming to concede in a variety of ways the relative autonomy and determining power of other structures, he concludes that the economy is determinate 'in the final instance'. I try to explain briefly what this means later in this entry.

---

Secondly, Althusser argues that different social structures may be dominant in the organization of society at different points in time. To give a very crude and slightly oversimplified example, the economy is arguably the dominant force, the structure in dominance within capitalism, but in feudal societies, where economic production is subject to the will of the monarch, the political structure of society dominates, as it did in the communist era in Eastern Europe. And even within a given 'mode of production' (see **social class**) there may be historical points at which different structures take the lead in motivating society and dominate the others. In times of political crisis, for example, political considerations and dynamics may override all others. As with relative autonomy, this idea of structure in dominance sophisticates Marxism and mitigates against crude economic determinism.

However, Althusser qualifies and ultimately confuses this position by arguing that the economic base always determines the ideological and political superstructure 'in the final instance'. The meaning and coherence of this claim were a subject of great debate amongst Marxists in the 1970s (for example, Cutler et al., 1977). Just what is determination 'in the final instance' and why should we accord the economy this privilege? There may be reasons to do so but what are they? It must suffice to say here that what Althusser appears to mean is, firstly that the superstructure is always only ever relatively autonomous, and secondly that other structures only ever become dominant in situations where economic exigencies and dynamics require or dictate this. Whether he can justify this position is a question we cannot address here except to say that even many paid up members of the Althussarian camp came to the view that he could not (see Hindess and Hirst, 1977; Cutler, et al., 1977). It is perhaps also worthy of note that, in the case of British sociology in particular, the breakdown of this Althussarian model was closely associated with the breakdown of Marxist theorizing in general and with a shift to post-structuralist and particularly Foucauldian models. Smart (1983) gives a good account of this.

Althusser presents much of his more mature reflections on ideology in the key essay 'Ideology and the state ideological apparatus' (in Althusser, 1971). Here these reflections are presented in the form of a series of propositions. We can best grasp his theory by way of a brief examination of each of these propositions:

## Ideology is material

Althusser wants to dispense with the idea that ideology consists of free floating 'ideas' or indeed of an immaterial 'ideational' realm, such as would be incompatible with his (and Marx's) 'materialism'.[111] Against this he wants to argue that ideology is composed of apparatuses (see below) and practices. What he means by this is that we should act the way in which 'ideas' are embodied. This might mean looking at the ways in which we speak and write but it also entails a focus upon habits, rituals and other ways of acting which embody ideas and beliefs. Religion, for example, is not a disembodied set of ideas which float into consciousness and persuade us to accept our lot – as Marx's famous definition of religion as 'the opium of the people' might suggest. Religion involves us going to church, getting on our knees to pray, repeating prayers and singing songs. We 'do' religion, routinely partaking in its practices and rituals in the course of our everyday life (that is, if we are religious) and that is why and how it affects us.

### Repressive and ideological state apparatuses (ISAs)

This notion of practices is complemented by a notion of 'apparatuses'. Capitalism survives, despite the obvious misery it causes for many and the exploitation it involves, Althusser argues, by virtue of the action of the state. And the state operates in two ways. It involves a series of 'repressive state apparatuses', such as the army and police, who enforce order when conflict emerges, for example, during riots, strikes and demonstrations. Repressive state apparatuses 'fight fire with fire'. However, if repression were the sole tool at capitalism's disposal, order would be fragile indeed. Much more effective is the fact that capitalism secures 'consent' for order by way of a series of 'ideological state apparatuses', for example, the family, church, media and school. These apparatuses are sites of practice where human subjects or agents are, in effect, shaped as compliant and willing members of (capitalist) society. That is, they are the sites of practices which form us as human agents, making us what we are and, more importantly, making us 'in the image' of capitalist society.

---

111 Materialism, in this context, is the idea that everything in the world is physical. It contrasts with, amongst other things, the notion that human beings have minds which are not made of physical matter. Materialism can be fairly crude, seeking to reduce the world to very simple mechanisms of physical causes and effects. Marx, however, seems to at least gesture towards a more sophisticated form of materialism which focuses not upon inert physical substances but rather sensuous and embodied human praxis. Human beings do not have a separate immaterial mind, from this point of view, but neither are they 'lumps of wood'. Rather they are very complex and intelligent physical organisms who, by way of their embodied physical activity, bring ideas, etc. into being. Thought, in this sense, does not belong to 'another realm' but to the realm of sensuous praxis or, to use an equivalent expression, embodied practice.

## Ideology has no history, it is necessary

Specific ideologies have specific histories (mostly shaped by the dynamics of the economy and class struggle). Any given religion, for example, has a potentially traceable history, as do the ideological practices of the media and sporting worlds. However, ideology as such has no history according to Althusser. What he means by this is that 'ideology', in the way he understands the term, is a necessary and inevitable feature of human societies, such that there must always have been ideologies and there always will be ideologies. Given the way that Althusser understands ideology, what he is effectively suggesting is that there cannot be a society without language, normative systems, cultural practices and beliefs, and so on. In this respect it is difficult to disagree with him – although note that in agreeing with him we are conceding at least something to functionalism.[112] Saying this, of course, does not mean that any specific ideological formation is either necessary or good. As a Marxist Althusser was opposed to the central ideological structures of capitalist societies and looked forward to the superior ideological structures which, again as a Marxist, he believed would characterize the impending socialist societies of the future.

## Ideology interpellates individuals as subjects

Ideology shapes what and who we are, and who we believe we are, by virtue of the fact that we live in it and enact it. It consists in practices that we do, and which thereby shape our thoughts, beliefs, perception and action. On this point Althusser quotes the philosopher Pascal (1972), who argues that human beings do not kneel down to pray because they believe in God but rather believe in God because they kneel down to pray. Religious thoughts and beliefs are shaped by (immersion in) religious practices in Pascal's view, and Althusser believes that extends to all aspects of ideology. Beyond this, however, Althusser also believes that subjects are constituted in ideology by way of what he calls 'interpellation'. 'Interpeller' is a normal French verb which means to address or call out to somebody or, as Althusser puts it, to 'hail' them. In a more technical sense, however, Althusser uses the term 'interpellation' to describe a

153

---

112 We are agreeing that there are certain things which are necessary for a society to be possible – although note that we are not arguing that the fact of the necessity of those things is a cause of those things appearing. The 'teleology' of full-blooded functionalism would lead us to suggest that society's need for, for example, language is sufficient to bring about the emergence of languages. We can argue, by contrast, that societies do need languages but that it is a contingent matter whether languages (and thus societies) ever emerge.

process whereby individuals come to think about and conceptualise themselves in accordance with the manner in which others conceptualise them, which is itself conveyed in the manner in which they are addressed (or hailed) in the context of ideological practices. More succinctly, people form a conception of themselves in accordance with the way in which they are treated. In capitalist societies this means that we come to view ourselves as free and rational individuals who choose how to live our lives and indeed have chosen the life that we lead because this is the image of lives and ourselves that is reflected back to us in the family, school, media, and so on. From before we are born we have a place in the world, Althusser argues (for example, parents often have a name for their children prior to birth, and have plans for them). Others 'know' who and what we are. Interpellation is the process whereby this is communicated to us and we come to accept it. Crucially, Althusser believes that this is how we are formed as 'subjects', that is, self-aware and conscious beings capable of making choices and acting upon them. And it forms part of his (infamous)[113] critique of those social theories which start from 'the subject' and seek to reduce social life to the projects of such subjects. We cannot reduce society back down to individuals, Althusser believes, because (amongst other things) individuals are formed by society. They are interpellated by ideology and shaped by ideological practices which constitute the milieu of their life.

### Ideology is a 'representation' of the imaginary relationship of individuals to their real conditions of existence

Many theories of ideology suggest that it is a misrepresentation of the real conditions in which people live. Althusser challenges this. Insofar as ideology involves 'representations', he argues, it correctly represents imaginary relations to real conditions rather than straightforwardly misrepresenting real relationships. This is a difficult point to grasp and Althusser does not discuss it in any detail. He appears, however, to draw from the psychoanalysis of Jacques Lacan (as indeed he does in his account of interpellation), who argues that human relationships to 'the real' are always mediated by way of imaginary and symbolic structures

---

113 Althusser's work was a central element of the structuralist theory which swept across the social sciences in the 1970s and, amongst other things, sought to challenge social theories which rooted or reduced social life to apparently autonomous human activity and/or fixed human attributes. In many ways Althusser was the most vehement advocate of this aspect of structuralism and was well known for it. See the entry on **humanism and anti-humanism**.

(see **imaginary, symbolic and real**). As the notion of interpellation suggests, we are formed as conscious beings within the structures of ideology, such that the very core of our subjectivity is 'ideological' and we cannot have unmediated relationships with others or the world. We might shed some light upon this by reference to the role theories which are common in sociology. A role is a real social relationship, it relates us to others, but a role is equally an 'imaginary' structure. Husbands and wives really exist, for example, but their existence depends upon agents playing those roles and putting themselves into role; a husband, for example, must act and think like a husband. We 'play' a role and it entails that we imaginatively put ourselves into it (although note that 'imagination' and the Lacanian concept of 'the imaginary' are not directly equivalent terms – see **imaginary, symbolic and real**). Insofar as ideology is a representation it is a representation of these imaginary relations.[114]

Althusser's work has attracted a great deal of criticism. Many people have argued, for example, that his theory does not leave much room for individual agency or subjectivity, tending to see agents merely as effects of ideological mechanisms. On the other hand, it has been pointed out that his account of interpellation, though it claims to explain the formation of the subject, actually presupposes the subject. It presupposes that we are beings capable of recognizing images of ourselves as they are communicated back to us (Hirst, 1979). In itself, of course, this is not problematic. Any theory which denied that we are capable of this would fly in the face of what is evidently true. However, it does introduce inconsistencies into Althusser's argument and that is very problematic.

In a different vein, some critics have argued that Althusser's work is implicitly functionalist in many places, in a strong and problematic way. That is, it does not just note that different parts of the social world play a role in relations to the whole, which may be true and can be defended as a legitimate form of observation, but rather seems actually to explain those parts in terms of their overall functional role. He explains ideology, for the most part, for example, in terms of its overall functional value for capitalism. Functionalist 'explanations' of this kind are termed 'teleological' and are generally deemed highly suspect in social science. The effect of a social practice cannot be regarded as the cause of that

---

114 This is an extremely slippery aspect of Althusserian theory, and I think that there is a slippage in his use of ideology here because the emphasis of much of what he writes is that ideology is not a representation in the first place – it is a set of practices. The Lacanian terminology, in my view, obfuscates this all the more; firstly, because Althusser does not bother to explain how he is using it, and secondly because Lacan is far from clear himself about what he means and tends to slip and slide all over the place.

practice, it is argued. This puts the cart before the horse, seeming to run causal relations backwards. Furthermore, most 'functional explanations' break down on close inspection and more conventional, forward running causal relations can generally be found.

Finally, as noted above, the ideas of 'relative autonomy' and 'economic determinism in the final instance' proved very difficult to run together in practice, leading many Althussarians to abandon them in favour of post-structuralist alternatives.

In certain respects Althusser was the last great theorist of ideology. After his work, critical theorists have tended to abandon the concept of ideology in favour of concepts of discourse, practice, power-knowledge, and so on (see **discourse, power, power/knowledge, doxa**). However, the spectre of Althusser is often to be found in these more contemporary formulations, at least amongst those who lived through the Althusserian era.

## FURTHER READING

Marx's own work on ideology is spread far and wide. The student edition of *The German Ideology* (Marx and Engels, 1970) is a useful starting place, however, as it contains both an abridged version of this central text, as well as the famous 'Introduction to a critique of political economy', which many discussions on structuralism and Marxism draw upon, and the 'Theses on Feuerbach', which is the classic statement on materialism within Marx's work. Althusser's (1971) 'Ideology and ideological state apparatuses' is quite accessible – notwithstanding one or two paragraphs which are a little difficult to fathom – and this is certainly a classic essay which should be read. For an overview of theories of ideology Larrain's (1979) *The Concept of Ideology* and Barrett's (1991) *The Politics of Truth* cover the ground in interesting and complementary ways.

**156**

# Illusio

> *Related concepts:* **capital, doxa, epistemological break, field, habitus, hexis, recognition.**

Like many before him, Pierre Bourdieu utilizes a metaphor of 'games' in his attempt to elucidate the nature of the social world. On one hand, for example, he explicitly compares 'social fields', that is the various differentiated sub-worlds (for example, of religion, politics, art and education) which comprise the social world, with games (see **field**). Any social field is, he argues, from an outsider's point of view, structured by a range of seemingly arbitrary conventions and goals which, like the rules and goals of a given game, have no ultimate rational foundation. Conventions and goals might be supported by a variety of 'internal' justifications, that is, justifications which are compelling if one 'buys into' the wider conventions of the game itself, but if we question these wider conventions and keep questioning in pursuit of a final bedrock of justification the best we will come up with is that 'that's just how it's done'. The structure of any field, like that of any game, is, in the final instance, 'culturally arbitrary'. Similarly, participation in any field, like participation in any game presupposes acquired abilities, techniques and know-how. We learn how to play games, developing a 'feel' for them which allows us to play without even having to think about how we do so and the same is true of 'playing' or participating in social fields. Bourdieu's famous conception of the habitus seeks to capture this phenomenon. In fact, he sometimes even describes the habitus as a 'feel for the game' (see **habitus**).

This vision of the social world begs the obvious question of the 'point' of participation in social fields. Why do agents bother if fields are culturally arbitrary and without foundation? This is a question raised in the work of some existentialist philosophers, notably Heidegger (1962) and more directly Albert Camus (1975), who writes of the 'absurdity' of life and our need to construct a world of meaning upon it. Bourdieu does not answer the question directly, nor does he address it philosophically, but his concept of the 'illusio' represents a sociological approach to this issue.

The illusio is the 'belief in the game' which binds agents, individually and collectively, into both games and social fields. We can best illustrate this by reflecting briefly on 'real' games. Consider, for example, a card game like poker. For the duration of a game of poker pieces of paper with numbers and pictures on them (namely cards) acquire an almost magical power over players. As the cards are dealt, exchanged and laid out, for example, players are affected by them, sometimes deeply. Heart rates rise, players sweat and adrenalin is pumped into circulation. Players are captivated and the turn of the cards assumes central significance. How do fifty-two pieces of paper manage to have this effect? It's not the properties of the paper as material which have the effect, of course. Effects may be physical but their causes are not. It is their meaning, a meaning conferred socially by the game, which generates these effects. The turning of the card bearing the 'Jack of Hearts' impacts upon the players, for example, because of what it means in the context of the game, both generally, in terms of the rules of the game but also more specifically in terms of the state of play of the particular game in progress. And this, in turn, depends upon the power of players to somehow put themselves into the game so that they are taken over by it; upon a form of 'make believe' which remains unaware of itself for the duration of the game to the point that players believe very strongly in what they are playing at and can thus become very 'worked up'.

This is a temporary effect. After the game, when somebody has won, the cards lose their 'sacred' status, becoming 'profane' ('just pieces of paper') again and players regain the critical distance which allows them to recognize that it was 'just a game'. There are instances, of course, when games can get out of hand. Players become agitated to the point of aggression and are prepared to raise 'the stakes' of the game above that prescribed by the game. Card players in the 'wild west' begin shooting each other, for example, and footballers sometimes end up brawling. They have to be told that 'it's just a game'. But most of the time, most of us realize the fact.

Fields are slightly different. Whilst poker is, to use Bourdieu's (1992a) terms, a game 'for itself', that is, a game which, at least when we are not in the thick of playing it, we recognize as 'just a game', social fields are games 'in themselves'. What Bourdieu means by this is that they are games that we do not recognize as games. We regard them as 'real life' and, as such, tend to contrast them with 'mere games'. However, these games in themselves, these games of 'real life', require the same degree of 'magic' as games for themselves, according to Bourdieu. 'Players' have to be taken over the game, attributing meaning to actions, agents and objects in accordance with the structure of the game; 'believing' in it in the sense of failing to recognize the arbitrariness of its conventions and goals and rather feeling those conventions and goals as forces of natural necessity. They must 'make believe' in a way which involves a systematic failure to recognize that this is what they are doing. And they must desire to play and to succeed within the game. Without this, the field in question and its power over human conduct would disintegrate; the crucifix would be an odd shaped stick and the cassock a silly frock. Paper money would be mere paper –akin to Monopoly money – and the rituals of parliament and the courts would lack the legitimacy that is the basis of their power. The structure of social life would fall apart, overwhelmed by the absurdity that writers such as Camus' (1975) claim lies just under the surface of the social world and by the anxiety which these writers claim is kept at bay by belief and meaning.

The illusio, to reiterate, is the name which Bourdieu gives to this 'belief in the game'. In some ways the naming of the concept is unfortunate because it sounds like 'illusion' and seems thereby to undermine the meaning and value of the social world. This is not Bourdieu's intention, in my view. Firstly, he is not suggesting that there could be a social world or field not rooted in misrecognized arbitrariness. To identify the illusio belonging to a particular field is not to criticize that field or the players in it. It is not to say that agents are deluded. There is no 'authentic' reality to contrast with the present – except perhaps a world which has learnt to live with its own arbitrariness.[115] More to the point, however, the arbitrariness of the social world, as revealed in philosophical/sociological analysis, is in certain respects an artefact of the 'analytic viewpoint' of the theorist and one which the analyst deliberately effects in an effort to 'make the familiar strange' and thereby to objectify the social world in order to study it. In order to constitute the world as a possible object of scientific analysis, Bourdieu believes, it is necessary to distance oneself from it, and particularly from its 'obviousness', to step back. The metaphor of the game and the concept of the illusio provide ways of doing this. They effect an epistemological break (see **epistemological break**). Whilst convenient for social analysis, however, this is an impossible attitude for lay members of society to adopt, or indeed sociologists when they are not doing sociology. It is an attitude which works for social analysis but not for everyday life. Finally, I would suggest that the word 'illusio' is best understood alongside the concept of 'disillusionment' rather than 'illusion'. We are all familiar with the process of disillusionment, when a once meaningful activity or pursuit ceases to be so for us. People become disillusioned with work, with politics, with family life, indeed any and all aspects of life. This fact of disillusionment is important because, qua dis-illusio-nment, it reveals the 'illusionment'

---

115 In certain respects this is what Heidegger (1962) understands by authenticity. There is no lifestyle which is 'authentic' as such for Heidegger. Rather, living authentically entails living with the knowledge both that ways of living are arbitrary and that they will come to an end (death) – but still choosing to live and make a path for oneself through all of this. Insofar as one can detect a view on such matters in Bourdieu it is that one needs to believe in the social world in order to act in it such that one could not live as Heidegger suggests. However, at the same time Bourdieu sees sociology as a form of enlightenment which will lay the social world bare to its members, in all of its arbitrariness, so perhaps there is a Heideggerian element to his thought.

or 'illusio' which preceded it. It reveals that our enthusiasm and interest in social fields is variable, that the magic animating our social involvement can dry up. It is against this background that the concept of the illusio begins to make sense.

In some of his later work Bourdieu attempted to explain this in terms of the psychoanalytic concept of libido, that is, the sexual energy which psychoanalysis deems central to our mental life and which, psychoanalysts claim, is 'sublimated'[116] into non-sexual areas of life on account of the repression of sexual drives necessary to a stable and civilized society:

> One of the tasks of sociology is to determine how the social world constitutes the biological libido, an undifferentiated impulse, as a specific social libido. There are in effect as many kinds of libido as there are social fields: the work of socialization of libido is precisely what transforms impulses into specific interests, socially constituted interests which only exist in relation to a social space in which certain things are important and others don't matter and for socialized agents who are constituted in such a way as to make distinctions corresponding to the objective differences in that space. (1998a: 78–9)

This formulation is interesting because it uses biology, rhetorically, to further effect sociology's epistemological break, rendering the familiar strange. The various cultured interests of human beings, ranging from high art or haute couture through science and mathematics to football begin to pose fascinating scientific questions when we ask how it is that we acquire the passion for them. How do we get from being 'mere organisms' with a desire for food and other 'base' pleasures to the dizzy cultural heights of avant garde literature, professional chess tournaments and 'key concepts in critical social theory'? What biological advantage could possibly be derived from a penchant for twentieth-century French sociology? The point, of course, is that biology does not explain these things and that we must look to the ways in which society transforms the biological organism, lifting it above its biological nature and into the civilized social world. I am not very convinced with Bourdieu's allusions as to the manner in which this happens however (see also Crossley, 2001a). This is not the place to spell out the problems in detail. A few brief points must suffice.

160

116 Sublimation is a psychoanalytic concept. It entails sexual and aggressive drives being redirected and finding expression/satisfaction in activities far removed from their original goal, which nevertheless substitute for them. Academic and artistic activity, for example, are often claimed to be sublimated forms of sexual release. They are the result of redirected sexual energy (apparently!).

Firstly, the concept of an undifferentiated biological libido is highly problematic (Goldstein, 2000). It does not make much sense in either biological or sociological terms. Of course human beings have (physical) energy which they expend in a variety of different types of pursuit, and of course we develop commitments, interests (both subjective and objective) and enthusiasm, but the concept of 'libido' does more to mystify and reify this than to elucidate or explain it. The idea of libido, at least as used in this context, seems to me a relatively meaningless label which makes us believe that there are real mechanical processes going on with human beings which determine our behaviour in some way. It detracts us from empirical analysis of the rather more messy and plural ways in which agents' interests are shaped and their commitment formed.

Secondly, Bourdieu's account has a 'once and for all' character to it, where other sociological accounts, including that of Bourdieu's protégé, Wacquant (1995), suggest that human commitment is constantly being negotiated in interactional contexts. Social agents, individually and collectively, ask themselves 'Why am I doing this?' at various points in their 'career' of doing whatever it is and they devise various ways of boosting their own morale and keeping both self and other 'on side'. These various techniques and strategies of preserving interest make more sense of the idea of the illusio than the channelling of libido and are easier to analyse as they are potentially visible to the social scientist in the form of symbolic exchanges between players in a particular game.

Thirdly, related to this, there are other, more parsimonious concepts in the sociological literature that make sense of the way in which agents become subjectively attached to particular (sometimes seemingly arbitrary) pursuits. Howard Becker (1960), for example, notes how involvement in an activity sometimes leads agents to put more of their 'eggs' into its particular 'basket', such that more of their needs and wants become tied up with that activity, making them both more subjectively and objectively 'interested' in or committed to it. In order to tie ourselves into something that we fear we might not stick to, he notes, we often make 'side bets'; that is, we tie the activity into the attainment of something that we know will genuinely motivate us to complete it. We might literally make a financial bet, for example, therefore generating a financial incentive for us to do whatever it is we are trying to do. But this process of making 'side bets' can also happen in unintended ways, as a consequence of involvement in an activity, with the same effect. Each step along the path of a 'moral career' raises stakes in a variety of ways.

From a slightly different point of view, Goffman (1959) describes the process whereby 'playing at' an activity by assuming a particular role can lead to a situation whereby an agent effectively internalizes and becomes the role that they are playing. They lose their distance as they become comfortable in and adjusted to their role. Interestingly, this actually coincides with something which Bourdieu himself writes in *The Logic of Practice* (Bourdieu, 1992a). The body, he claims, 'believes in what it plays at'. In other words, at the most basic pre-reflective level of our agency we are capable of acting imaginatively, putting ourselves into a situation and playing a role, in a manner which is free of the critical distance that reminds us that this is 'just a role'. Again these explanations are both more parsimonious and more researchable than notions of libido and, for these reasons, are preferable.

Finally, if we are looking for an underlying 'drive' to explain social commitments then the 'desire for recognition' makes far more sense than the idea of an 'undifferentiated biological impulse' (see **recognition**). Basically, the idea here is that human beings desire to be recognized, that is, desired, respected and esteemed by other human beings whom they respect and thus deem worthy of recognizing them. In most accounts of this desire it is acknowledged that it often works through the mediation of symbolic goods. One achieves the recognition of the community by obtaining or achieving goods that the community collectively values, such as big cars, political office, good qualifications. Anything might become an object of desire and commitment from this point of view, if it becomes entangled in a struggle for recognition. The everyday expression 'pissing contest' sums this up. Agents (males specifically in this case) will compete over anything, even who can pee highest up a wall, not because peeing is important but because it becomes a vehicle through which competitive urges or desires for recognition can be played out. Social fields are 'pissing contests' in just this sense. What is competed over within them is often secondary to the underlying dynamic of competition and a struggle for recognition. It is the desire to win, to be recognized, which gives meaning and importance to the various symbols and stakes of the field. This is not to say that such competition cannot give rise to end products which will be highly valued on intrinsic grounds. But it suggests that their initial importance to social agents may have a broader basis.

### FURTHER READING

There is no obvious single reference for the concept of the illusio in Bourdieu's work, although *Practical Reason* (Bourdieu, 1998a) perhaps discusses the concept in more detail than any other works. Loic Wacquant's (1995) 'Pugs at work', which discusses the 'collusio' (a version on the same theme) in the context of an ethnographic study of boxers is also a good source. Some of the themes discussed here in my entry are also explored by Bourdieu in *Pascalian Meditations* (Bourdieu, 2000).

# Imaginary, Symbolic and Real

---

*Related concepts:* **id, ego and superego, mirror stage and the ego, recognition, repression, unconscious (the).**

---

In the version of psychoanalysis developed by Jacques Lacan (1989) the imaginary, symbolic and real are three dimensions of psychological life or perhaps rather three modes through which the individual relates to self, other and world. The former two emerge at particular points in child development, according to Lacan, but all three are intertwined in adult psychological life.

As the name suggests, the 'imaginary' is that dimension of psychological life consisting of perceptual images, imagination and the internalized representations of significant others from early childhood that psychoanalysts sometimes refer to as 'imagos'. More crucially, however, it is bound up with the ego and the processes which give rise to it, particularly the 'mirror stage' (see **mirror stage and the ego**). When the child 'identifies' with itself in the mirror stage, (mis)recognizing itself, developing a narcissistic attachment to itself and thus developing an ego in the Lacanian sense (see **id, ego and superego**), its relationship to others and to the world is transformed. It begins to seek recognition from others, whom it also now sees as separate, and its experience of the world is increasingly mediated through its newly developed sense of self. Frustrations can be experienced personally, as assaults upon the self, for example, and the context in which basic needs are satisfied by a parent or guardian figure becomes a context in which the child demands love. Feeding, for example, is no longer simply a matter of the infant's physical need for food and the parents' act of satisfying that need, at least not from the child's point of view. It is a matter of demonstrating love and recognition. The child does not just want to be fed. It wants to be loved, recognized and affirmed by the parent. And food and the act of feeding the child are two amongst a number of ways in which this recognition is demonstrated. They are symbols of love. They have an 'imaginary' significance.

We should note here that the ego, for Lacan, is never a stable structure. Its very construction gives rise to insecurities and a demand for recognition. Furthermore, within the imaginary at least, its boundaries are never tightly drawn or intersubjectively 'balanced'. Thus it can be that individuals experience events in the world in an overly personalized or ego-focused fashion, as in paranoia. Everything that happens around them is experienced as if it were focused upon them, as a form of persecution. Perhaps they feel that strangers laughing in the street are laughing at them and talking about some shameful act from their youth. Perhaps they feel that the bus is late because the driver knows they have an important meeting but does not like them and wants to inconvenience them. Alternatively, individuals may have too little self-awareness, such that they are insufficiently sensitive to the personal significance of events. They might fail to realize that people are talking about them, perhaps subtly trying to make recommendations to them, when in fact that are trying to do this. Finally, the boundaries of self and other can become blurred by means of what other schools of psychoanalysis[117] refer to as 'projection', 'introjection', 'identification' and 'projective identification'. They can attribute certain of their own desires and dispositions, which they disavow in themselves, to others (projection). They can attribute the qualities, desires and dispositions of others to themselves (introjection). They can take over the role or persona of those around them whom they love and respect or perhaps hate and fear (identification). And they can accept or identify with the attributes which others project on to them (projective identification).

The symbolic, which the child 'enters'[118] upon acquiring language,

117 The concepts listed here (projection, introjection and projective identification) derive particularly from the 'object-relations' and ego-psychology forms of psychoanalysis, which derive from the work of Melanie Klein (1993) and Anna Freud (1968) respectively. Lacan seldom refers to these writers or indeed these concepts but he was certainly aware of them and they often appear to underpin what he says.

118 Whilst the symbolic is a part of the individual's psychological make up, it is formed through the internalisation of social structures which can be regarded, in some respects, as 'external' to the individual (see the note below). There is thus some sense, if only metaphorical, in saying that an individual 'enters' the symbolic, as indeed it enters them. In effect the child's entrance into the symbolic is its entrance into society as an agent capable of operating in that world.

imposes order upon this chaos. It is best considered, in my view, as the normative order of society or perhaps rather as the core of norms or rules necessary to society and social order, which the child internalizes. It is equally an order of symbolic meaning, however, consisting of the structure of language (with the various norms and rules that entails). Lacan draws heavily from structuralist writers in his analysis of this 'order'. On one hand, for example, he views language as a central aspect of 'the symbolic', drawing from the work of the structuralist linguists, Saussure and Jakobson. Language, from this point of view, is a social institution or social structure, 'external' to the individual in a Durkheimian[119] sense and consisting of rules which infants must internalize to the point that they become automatic. On the other hand, he draws together Freud's account of the oedipal stage of development[120] with Levi-Strauss' (1969) structuralist analysis of the 'incest taboo' (a taboo which is evident in all known societies, according to Levi-Strauss). The incest taboo is a basic functional prerequisite for all societies, according to Levi-Strauss, since it assures the movement of individuals outside of the family unit. Without the norm stipulating that individuals must marry or form sexual attachments outside of the primary group of the family, given the strong emotional bonds within families, (sexual) relationships might very well remain internal to the family, such that society effectively dissolves into a cluster of distinct but unrelated family groups. It is with this argument in mind that Lacan views the oedipal moment as the point at which the child

119 There is a great deal of misunderstanding of the Durkheimian notion of 'externality' within sociology. In one respect, of course, language, society, etc. are in no way external to us. They exist in and through what we do. Language, for example, does not exist independently of the human activities of speaking, listening, reading and writing. It exists only in and through these activities and if human beings were to stop doing them then language would cease to exist. Durkheim recognizes this. What he is drawing our attention to is the fact that, for example, the English language existed before anybody alive today was born and will outlive us all too. In that sense it is external to us. Furthermore, it involves all manner of rules which none of us invented, which we had to learn. Indeed, when we are first learning a language (particularly a second language that we are aware of learning as such) it may strike us as an alien thing external to ourself. Finally, any language imposes certain constraints upon us, as the act of translation often reveals; what one can say in one language isn't always easy to say in another, even if one is perfectly fluent in both languages. Lacan is particularly interested in the constraints imposed by language, although in his case it is not translation of one language to another which is of interest but what we might call translation of the 'language of desire' or the 'language of the unconscious' (that is, our feelings, desires, fantasies). In his view our unconscious desires seldom break through into language proper, largely because of the normative censorship built into the structure of language. Our unconscious desires do not translate easily into our social language.
120 That is, the stage where, according to Freud, the child, who has developed a sexual love for the mother, is torn away from their sexual object by the father, and internalizes this incest prohibition along with other aspects of the morality of their society (see **unconscious (the)**).

enters the symbolic. It is, in effect, the point at which the child acquires the moral dispositions which prepare it for life in wider society, and which compel it to seek (sexual) satisfaction outside of its family of origin, within society. It is also the time that the child is forced to express itself in the language of the outside world, following the rules of that language and any other number of standardized rules and criteria which govern public and social (but perhaps not family or intimate and personal) life.

Although Lacan does not follow Freud's gendered understanding of the oedipal conflict exactly,[121] his language is gendered. The rules and norms of the symbolic are 'the law of the father' and whoever enforces them plays the father role. The gender politics of this aspect of the theory are far from clear but it is important to observe the implication that the symbolic is a patriarchal order. This observation might be deemed useful from the point of view of feminism, insofar as it connects to feminist concerns with patriarchy (see **patriarchy**) but given that Lacan deems the symbolic necessary,[122] sticks doggedly to his gendered understanding of it and makes no common cause with feminists, it might equally be deemed problematic from the feminist point of view.

The entrance into the symbolic is also the moment at which the unconscious, as Lacan understands it, takes shape, since the unconscious consists in all that the symbolic represses (See **unconscious (the)** and **repression**). Lacan seemingly understands this as a process of alienation and, as such, it can be seen to continue a process initiated during the mirror stage and the formation of the imaginary (see **mirror stage and the ego**). The formation of the 'I' in the mirror stage is a form of alienation since the infant relates to and identifies with a reflected (external) image of itself. It becomes other to itself.[123] This alienation is continued when the child's mental functioning is made to conform to the demands of society, and when its contact with itself, its presence to itself, is mediated by way of the social institution of language. From Lacan's point of view language forms a barrier within the individual between their conscious thoughts and their (now unconscious) desire. Pre-linguistic desires and

**166**

121 Freud suggests that children develop a sexual love for their mothers and that it is fathers who break up this relationship, where Lacan suggests, in effect, that these are roles which anybody can fulfil (perhaps the same person playing both).
122 What lies outside of the symbolic, Lacan seems to argue, is psychosis, and he believes that children who do not enter the symbolic fully will become psychotic. In addition, there are at least hints in his work that social organization necessitates the symbolic – indeed, without that central pillar of the symbolic, the incest taboo, society would collapse back into incestuous and self-contained sexual units (in the world according to Lacan).
123 There is a fascinating parallel here with G.H. Mead (1967), who in my view has a much stronger and more persuasive version of the same idea. See **I and me**.

wishes are channelled into language (itself an inhibition of the earlier tendency of infants to act immediately upon them) where they are expressed but only in a censored form, in accordance with norms rooted in language. Language is the medium through which we know our own subjective life but it is not a transparent and neutral medium. It reflects the normative order of wider society, rules and prohibitions, such that we are denied access to a part of ourselves – the unconscious. Like Freud, however, Lacan believes that the forces of the unconscious occasionally burst through this order, in the form of slips, metaphors, and so on. Indeed, he argues that the desire (for recognition) which is at the heart of our unconscious lives is the ultimate motivation behind speech. In and through speech we seek out recognition from others. In his early work Lacan seemed to suggest that this recognition can actually be achieved in speech relations. Through speaking and listening, forming genuine communicative relations, we achieve mutual recognition. In his later work, however, he becomes more focused on the ambiguities of speech and is inclined to argue that these ambiguities prevent proper recognition. Even when somebody tells us that they love us, for example, there is always the possibility that they do not mean it. Language conceals as much as it reveals.

Very little is clear in Lacan's work. He is hopelessly vague and one is forced to be extremely charitable to rescue even a semblance of sense in much of what he writes. This is particularly true with respect to his concept of the real. What I take him to mean by the real, however, is the realm of events beyond or outside of the imaginary and the symbolic which impact upon the psychic life of the individual but which can only be experienced through the mediation of the symbolic or the imaginary. As a living organism, for example, the individual has needs (for example, for food), is vulnerable and will die. These are facts of life which hold whether or not the individual is aware of them, and which have an impact upon the individual. And yet, insofar as the individual confronts them they always do so by way of either the imaginary or the symbolic. In other words, all that affects human beings cannot be reduced to social or psychological constructions, and yet human beings cannot access these things other than by means of social and psychological constructions. Furthermore, as I said above with respect to food, the basic needs and vulnerabilities of human beings acquire a social and psychological significance in the human context, which they cannot be disassociated from. Food, warmth and shelter, for example, whilst real human needs, are seldom just organic needs. They assume various layers of significance in the interplay of imaginary and symbolic relations, and our pursuit of them cannot be distinguished from these various layers of meaning.

*Imaginary, Symbolic and Real*

Lacan is a notoriously difficult writer. He writes in a very imprecise and vague fashion, sometimes not seeming to make any sense at all and never presenting his ideas in the form of rational/coherent arguments. Personally I regard him as a dreadful writer and, though his ideas are sometimes interesting, I could not in good conscience recommend that students read him. Inevitably this also applies to some of Lacan's followers. Fortunately, however, not all Lacanians are taken in by this pseudo-intellectualism and some endeavour to state his ideas clearly. One very good account, in my view, is Benvenuto and Kennedy's (1986) *The Works of Jacques Lacan*, as is Bowie's (1991) *Lacan*. Of the social theorists using Lacan's work Peter Dews is by far the most persuasive (and the clearest). In his earlier work, *The Logics of Disintegration* (Dews, 1987), he approaches Lacan, along with other post-structuralist writers, from a sympathetic but critical perspective. In his later work, *The Limits of Disenchantment*, he is more concerned to develop Lacan's work and its implications and seems generally more committed to the approach (Dews, 1995).

# Intersubjectivity

*Related concepts: I and me, recognition, relationism.*

As the term suggests, 'intersubjectivity' denotes the existence of a between-world, connecting individual human subjectivities. Theories differ on the precise details of how this between-world is constituted. Here I will focus upon two broad approaches. The first, which I call the 'egological' approach, is wrong in my view, if taken as foundational, but aspects of it can and should be included in our overall understanding of intersubjectivity. The second approach, which I have referred to elsewhere as 'radical' (Crossley, 1996a), and which is in fact more sociological, offers a much better foundation but it can benefit from some dialogue with the egological approach.

For the egological theorist the key question underlying the concept of intersubjectivity is as to how, as an individual consciousness or ego, one can know that others are conscious subjective beings and know the contents of their conscious, subjective lives. Consciousness, it is argued, is something that can only be known from the inside. Indeed, in a sense it has no 'outside' and thus cannot be experienced from the outside. Only you have your thoughts, perceptions, feelings, and so on, so how can I ever know what they are or that you even have any? All that I see is your body, from which I infer that you have a conscious subjective life, but how do I know and/or why do I infer this?

Some versions of this thesis are posited in a sceptical mode; that is to say, they are posited in a way which asks whether other people than the author really do have thoughts, feelings, and so on. The sceptic will say, 'You may say you have feelings and thoughts but how do I know that you are not just a cleverly designed robot programmed to say these kinds of things?' The point of this is not necessarily to deny that others have a subjective life but to ask what proof we have that they do. How do we know? Or more to the point, do we know? Such scepticism, in this as in other philosophical questions, is difficult to satisfy. The best we can do in relation to hard-line scepticism is to take the view that we have less reason to believe that other people are simulating machines than genuine subjective beings, that is, that our knowledge of the subjective lives of others may be shaky but nowhere near as shaky as the view that others are machine simulations of consciousness, such that, on balance, the existence of 'other minds' is the best bet. In addition we might argue that the view that other minds do not exist, at least insofar as people bother to write and speak about it, involves a 'performative contradiction'.[124] Why write books and give lectures if you do not believe that there is somebody out there to appreciate and reply to them? The more the sceptic tries to persuade you that they do not believe that you are a conscious, subjective being like them, the more they contradict themselves through their actions.

Another way in which the question of intersubjectivity is posed, however, still within the egological mode, is to suspend the question of whether other subjectivities exist, focusing instead upon the question of how it is that we come to experience and 'know' the subjectivity of others. This is the approach of the phenomenological philosopher

---

124 That is, a situation in which an individual seemingly contradicts what they are saying in the very act of saying it. Other examples are 'everything that I say is a lie' – to be true this would have to be false (i.e. a lie). The example of the philosopher who tries to convince others that he does not believe that they exist is perhaps not quite contradictory – s/he could claim to be talking to him or herself – but it is at the very least unusual.

Edmund Husserl (1991). He notes a number of ways in which we appear to experience the subjectivities of others. On one hand, he says, we believe that we know the thoughts, feelings, and so on of others. When we make strategies, for example, we attempt to second guess the strategies of others, thereby presupposing that they too are thinking about how to act. Similarly, we commonly 'read the minds' of others, noting that they are happy, for example, or sad and asking why. Perhaps more mysterious, however, is the way in which we sometimes seem to experience their experience. For example, we sometimes feel ourselves to be looked at, that is, we appear to feel ourselves caught up in the visual field of other. We feel eyes burning into our back as we walk away from an argument, for example, and we feel ourselves dissected when we enter a room and all eyes turn towards us. Furthermore, we experience the world as visible to others. The case of Raskolnakov in Dostoevsky's (1951) *Crime and Punishment* provides a dramatic example of this. The character can see evidence of his crime all around him but more importantly he feels that others see it too; that is, that their eyes are drawn to the same perceptual objects as his and that they too read these objects as evidence. The drama of the situation rests upon the fact that we, as readers, know that they do not yet suspect him so do not read these objects as evidence, if they notice them at all. We suspect that he will give himself away by virtue of his conduct. Raskolnakov experiences the world as one experienced in the same way by other people as by himself. Somewhat less dramatically, we all treat the world as one others experience. We are, for example, genuinely shocked if somebody who has been at an event with us does not report seeing and hearing the same things. And we routinely point these things out to others in the expectation that they are capable of experiencing them as we do.

Pushing this one step further, Husserl argues that our very sense of objectivity and rationality depend upon this basic experience of intersubjectivity. To say that something is objective, he notes, is to say that it exists independently of my perception of it, which ultimately boils down to the fact that others can experience it too. When I say 'this is objective' I mean, 'anybody else looking at this would see the same thing as me'. Of course we do experience the world as objectively existing beyond us, as there when we are not thinking about or perceiving it, such that all of our experiences have this intersubjective aspect to them. We experience our world as a shared world. Similarly, rationality implies that what we do and say will make sense to others. To say, 'that is rational' is effectively to say, 'other people would reach the same conclusion, do the same thing', and so on. So again, our sense that things can be rational and that we are rational belies a deeper sense that we live amongst a world of likeminded consciousness. The question is, however, how do we arrive at this intersubjective sense given that, as the sceptic points out, all that is given directly to our (perceptual) consciousness of others is their body.

In an effort to answer this question and explain intersubjectivity, Husserl (1991) enlists a number of key concepts: 'analogical apperception', 'pairing' and 'habitus'. By 'apperception' Husserl denotes the manner in which our perception always contains more than we actually see. A simple example of this might be our perception of a house. The size and shape of a house necessitates that I cannot see all of it at once. I can only see the back, one of the sides or more usually the front. My experience is not of a 'house front', however. At the very least I say that I see a house 'from the front' but more usually simply that I see a house. And this is genuinely how I experience it. As far as I am concerned I see a whole house. This is why, in Hollywood films or even cartoons, we are genuinely shocked when 'houses' turn out to be just 'house fronts' with no back, sides or interior. In such situations we are inclined to take a second look, not certain that we can trust our eyes. Similarly, if I pull a 'book' from my friend's shelf only to find that it is a book spine glued to a wooden block – a 'book effect' – I am genuinely jolted by the experience. The world has not turned out to be as I expected and I am momentarily disorientated. The reason this happens, Husserl argues, the reason I can be shocked and disorientated by such events, is that my perceptions are always embellished. I see what I see but then unbeknown to myself I add in hidden dimensions or aspects. I see the front but 'add in' the back, see the 'spine' but impute the whole book. This process of embellishment is apperception. But why do I do this? The answer, for Husserl, lies in our prior experience. In the past 'fronts' have been linked to backs, spines to whole books and I habitually 'pair' past experiences with present experiences, taking signs of similarity as my cue. Likewise my current experiences sediment, in the form of what Husserl calls a habitus (see **habitus**) and will shape my future experiences. This happens all of the time, of course, even if I only notice it when things go awry. In my life I am constantly coming into contact with objects and situations which, strictly speaking, are unique and new to me, but I am not usually aware of this because I habitually 'pair' them with similar objects and experiences from my past. To use the language of Alfred Schutz (1972), who developed Husserl's insights, I 'typify' experiences and use a stock of taken-for-granted and 'recipe' knowledge to render the world familiar and manageable. I have never seen your car before, for example, but when you lend it to me it does not strike me as a unique object. I see it through the type 'car' and, on that basis, impute and attribute any number of qualities and features to it on the basis of my past experiences of 'cars'. I may be wrong. I may reach for fifth gear only to find that one is not there. I may put the car into reverse by accident because your reverse is where my first gear is. But it is only then that it begins to strike me as unfamiliar and perhaps strange. Prior to that I assume and expect that it is a car like any other and I treat and perceive it as such.

The importance of the concept of apperception is that it highlights how we see hidden aspects behind or beyond what is strictly perceptible. As such, it promises to be able to account for how we are able to experience the consciousness of others, which, as we have said, is hidden from us. There is a problem, however, because the tools which Husserl uses in his account of apperception (pairing, typification, and so on) all presuppose that we have prior, first-hand experience of what we apperceive. I apperceive the back of a house when I see it from the front because, in the past, houses that I have seen from the front have turned out to have a back attached to them and I have seen those backs when walking around the house. The problem with the consciousness' of others is that I have never seen one. If I had, there would be no philosophical problem of intersubjectivity in the first place. Husserl addresses this problem by recourse to the one experience of consciousness that he does have: his own. He has experience of his own consciousness, he argues, and he experiences it as attached to his body. He also has experience, from without, of the bodies of others, and he notes that they look and act very similarly to his own. Given this, he continues, it seems likely that he pairs them with his own and habitually attributes a subjective life to them on the basis of his own. He knows, for example, that he laughs when he is happy, so when they laugh he is able to attribute the experience of happiness to them, on this basis. He apperceives their subjective life, via his habitus, on the basis of his own subjective life. Our experience of others, therefore, is effectively an imputation onto others of our own subjective life. We make this imputation of an 'inner life' because we see that others have a body like ours (more or less) and we know that our body is connected to an inner life, so we pair the two bodies and transfer the attribution of internality. It is important to add here that this is not scepticism. Husserl is not saying that others do not have a subjective life. Neither is he saying that our perception is a mere projection of our mental life. In the first case we only use our self-knowledge to 'read' others. We do not simply 'lump' any old mental baggage onto them. Thus, I do not attribute happiness to a person who is shaking his fist at me – unless I believe that he is joking or acting. I use my knowledge of anger, its causes and its outward manifestations in an effort to make sense of his state of being. More to the point, however, the context of Husserl's project is not a psychology but rather an epistemological project, run along very similar lines to that of Kant (1933), which seeks to explore the basic preconditions of certain forms of knowledge and the constitutive role of human consciousness in that process. Husserl is not out to rubbish our sense of objectivity, rationality or empathy for that matter, but to explore their conditions of possibility, as experiences, within our own ego.

There are further aspects to Husserl's account. He builds his account to consider how we reconcile the fact that others are in a different position to ourselves (we are 'here'; they are 'there') and he attempts to build up from one-to-one situations to a sense of the whole community. We can halt our exposition at this point, however, and turn to some of the problems of Husserl's position.

Husserl's account is problematic on many grounds (see Crossley, 1996a; 2000; Schutz, 1971; Levinas, 1989). I do not have space to detail these criticisms here but I will briefly note three points. Firstly, Husserl starts from the point of view of the isolated individual who apparently encounters others, as a visual datum, from afar. He precisely adopts what I have called an egological viewpoint. Secondly, he assumes that he knows himself 'from within', so to speak. Thirdly, he assumes his sense of self, prior to his sense of 'the other', as pre-given. Each of these assumptions is problematic and unpicking them allows us to move towards a more radical and sociological sense of intersubjectivity. Starting with the self, Schutz (1971) has noted that the concept of 'self' only makes sense as a corollary of 'other' and argues that we can only experience 'self' relative to an experience of 'other', such that the two must arise simultaneously. There is no 'self' without 'other' because 'self' is a relational concept and experience, dependent upon 'other'. Furthermore, as sociologists and social psychologists, at least since George Herbert Mead (1967) have observed, our sense of both self and other emerges, in the course of our early childhood, as a function of our social experience. In other words, we interact with others before we even have a sense of self or other and it is out of this interaction that we develop a sense of self and other. This suggests, contra Husserl, that our sense of self cannot be the prior basis of our sense of the other. Furthermore, in contrast to Husserl's emphasis, where the individual comes prior to the group and its interactions, it suggests that the group and interactions come first, and that a distinct individual emerges out of that interactional context as an effect of it. We are enmeshed in interaction from the moment we are born, long before we have any conscious sense of self and other but we can become aware of self and other by means of interaction.

Is this interaction 'intersubjective'? Before we can answer this question we need to turn to a further issue. Husserl seems to imply that the meaning of subjective states originates 'inside' human beings and that we enjoy a privileged access to our own subjective states, so defined. It is because I understand 'love' from the inside, for example, that I can attribute 'love' to others, and I do so on the basis that they behave as I behave when I am in love. There are many good reasons to believe that the actual order of events is rather different. To continue the example, the word 'love' belongs to a public language and as such the rules and criteria underlying its proper use must therefore be public too. Insofar as the word 'love' refers to anything (and clearly it may be used to do many more things than simply 'refer')[125] it must be to public behaviours. To be in love is to 'do' certain things which, at least in principle, are visible to other people. How could one ever learn or teach the meaning of the word love, as is necessary to the words in a public language, if that meaning depended upon something essentially private? One could not point to it or explain it. The words in a public language depend exclusively upon public criteria for their meaning (Ryle, 1949; Wittgenstein, 1953; Crossley, 1996a, 2001a). One learns to use the word, both in relation to self and other, in a public context where it is used in connection with such behaviours; perhaps one's peers tease one for being 'in love' or perhaps one is exposed to the antics of other 'lovers'. This is not to say that private 'sensations' are not involved but they are not a primary referent upon which the meaning of the term 'love' rests and through which it is learnt and known (ibid.). Furthermore, there is no 'sensation' which is either necessary or sufficient to the meaning of 'love' – or any other subjective state. As with the behaviours of love, the sensations, if there at all,[126] vary across contexts and derive their meaning from their occasioning contexts including the presence of the individual who is loved, of course. A 'racing heart' may be a sign of love but only in certain contexts. It may be a sign of lots of other things too (for example, fear or an impending heart attack). And there are many other signs of love which are similarly context specific (such as we are happy but only when our lover is happy, sad when they are sad, and so on). The logic of love, as a subjective state is bound up with social contexts and to know that we are 'in love' is to have learnt to read our own behaviours and sensations in light of these contexts, according to a schema which is public and social in nature, that is,

---

125 If I say 'I love you' to somebody, for example, I am not describing or referring to something. I am declaring my love – something which lovers are inclined to do.
126 Emotions such as love are generally deemed to have a longevity not shared by tingles, for example. I might have loved you for the last ten years but that does not mean that I have been experiencing a weird tingle or sensation throughout that period.

which is originally intersubjective. Finally, note both that we can be 'in love' without knowing it, such that others point it out to us first, and that we can argue meaningfully with others over the question whether we are 'really' in love. Again, only I 'have' my sensations but what they mean, if anything, is derived from their connections to the way in which I act within (potentially) public contexts, such that my subjective state, qua meaningful phenomena, is a public and intersubjective matter. What is true of love is true of any subjective state and we can, on this basis, reverse Husserl's argument. I do not begin with knowledge of myself, which I then project on to others. I first interact with others and, on the basis of doing so, learn to make sense of myself. Subjectivity develops in and through intersubjectivity. Although, of course, as subjectivity develops intersubjectivity is developed too. The infant is an entirely public and intersubjective being. Its feelings and intentions are all expressed 'out loud' and noisily, if somewhat vaguely and imprecisely. Part of its development involves a sharpening of intersubjective bonds. It learns to control its behaviours and formulate its expression in socially specific forms; readable and thus intersubjectively meaningful 'natural outbursts' are sublimated into socially acceptable and more precise forms. Part of its development, however, entails a privatization of thought and experience that leads in the direction of the more private ego described by Husserl (Elias, 1984; Crossley, 1996a, 2001a).

It is important, in this context, to add a few brief remarks on language. Much of the sense of our subjective life takes shape within language. Our reflections, even in their most private form, take shape within language. But language is, of course, a public, social institution which we have learnt to use by way of interaction with others. Furthermore, even when we 'talk to ourselves', as Mead (1967) notes, a coherent stream of thought generally takes the form of a dialogue and thereby assumes a form borrowed from the social world. We learn, as he puts it, to 'take the role of the other', to anticipate their likely input and responses to our proposals, and then to form our own responses to their responses. What we see here, again, is a way in which individual subjective life is fashioned from the materials of an intersubjective domain.

Part of the problem with Husserl's argument is its residual Cartesianism.[127] Although Husserl does not explicitly align himself with Descartes' vision of a mind distinct from and privileged over the body,

175

---

127 Cartesianism is the philosophy associated with René Descartes. Although the link with Descartes is not particularly strong in much of Husserl's work, his main work involving a discussion of intersubjectivity is *Cartesian Meditations*, a work which retraces and works over the finding of Descartes' (1969) *Meditations*.

which is best known from within, much of his argument presupposes aspects of this vision. Husserl begins his exploration of intersubjectivity, explicitly following Descartes, with the contemplative individual. Then, breaking with his own key tenet of the intentionality of consciousness, which implies that consciousness is always consciousness of something outside of itself, and is not given to itself directly, qua object, he claims to discover a meaningful inner realm of experience which he has privileged access to. Finally, he is prepared to treat bodily behaviours as mere side effects of this 'inner realm', unjustifiably abstracting inwardly felt sensations and privileging them over embodied actions. A much more satisfactory starting point is one which recognizes embodied action as the basis of subjective life, rather than a mere puppet controlled by an inner being, and which recognizes that this 'body-subject' is always already enmeshed in interactions with others (see **body-subject**). There is no 'before interaction'; that is a philosopher's fiction.

With this said we can now proceed to argue that intersubjectivity, in its primary and most basic (radical) form, is best conceived not from an egological point of view, as the perception and interpretation of 'other' by self, but rather from an interactionist and relational point of view, as a fabric of social life into which individuals are born, in which they take shape as individual egos, but in relation to which they are always decentred qua 'node' in a 'link'.

Does that mean that intersubjectivity is, in some sense, a basic and given state of our being? I suggest not. Intersubjectivity is a constant flux, a fabric of 'social becoming', rather than social being (Crossley, 1996a). It entails constant and ongoing interaction. Furthermore, 'shared meaning', 'agreement' and so on take work. As conversation analysts and ethnomethodologists remind us, even the most basic human interaction, to the extent that it succeeds (from the point of view of its interlocuters) is an achievement of great skill, often requiring considerable reparation work (Sharrock and Hughes, 1986; Heritage, 1984). But these interactions are not those of previously or otherwise isolated monads and there is no 'outside' to this flux of interaction. One can interact poorly but one cannot cease to interact. As Merleau-Ponty (1962) says, even the refusal to communicate is an act of communication – often a profound one.

## FURTHER READING

Husserl's (1991) *Cartesian Meditations*, the fifth of which outlines his theory of intersubjectivity, is not an easy read but it is quite short and offers quite a good introduction to phenomenology overall, so it is worth tackling. An excellent critique of this position is to be found in Schutz (1971). It is difficult to pin Mead down on this issue but Joas (1985) offers an interesting account, which sets Mead within his philosophical context. My own views on intersubjectivity are set out in my *Intersubjectivity: The Fabric of Social Becoming* (Crossley, 1996a). This book offers more extended discussions of Husserl, Mead and many others, and an earlier but more elaborated version of the argument concerning radical and egological forms of intersubjectivity.

# Knowledge Constitutive Interests

> *Related concepts:* **epistemological break, ideal speech situation, ideology, power.**

In his early study, *Knowledge and Human Interests*, Jürgen Habermas (1972) critically reflects upon what he understands to be the subordination of questions of epistemology to those of the philosophy of science. Philosophers with an interest in knowledge and epistemology, he argues, are increasingly tending to narrow their focus to 'scientific knowledge' and the question of how (not whether) it can lay claim to superiority over other forms of knowledge. They are seemingly losing sight of wider forms of knowledge as well as broader epistemological questions about the origins of knowledge and the conditions under which it emerges. In an effort to address this deficiency and at the same time lay the epistemological foundations for critical theory – which at this time he conceives of as an opponent to (positivistic)[128] conceptions of science – he outlines a theory of 'knowledge constitutive interests'.

---

128 Positivism has been defined in many different ways (see Halfpenny, 1982). In a strict sense it derives from the philosophies of August Comte and (in the case of logical positivism) the Vienna Circle. As Habermas uses the term, however, it refers more generally to the view that society and social relations can be studied in a scientific manner, much as the natural world is studied within the natural sciences.

The pursuit of all forms of knowledge, he argues, derives from one of three basic interests which have been, and to the present remain, central to the human condition: control, understanding and emancipation. We will consider each of these in turn but first it is important to distinguish between these basic, and to some degree fixed, needs, and the more specific and variable interests that each of us may be attributed in accordance with our social circumstances. By 'knowledge constitutive interests' Habermas does not mean the specific interests that might motivate particular groups or agents in society to pursue specific types of solution to particular types of problem or question; for example, the interest that pharmaceutical companies have in finding pharmacological solutions to the problems of modern life, or the interests that clothing companies have in new forms of fabric production. These are specific interests deriving from specific social positions and situations. Knowledge constitutive interests are more basic than this and more general. They are interests which all human beings have, even if they might find different forms of expression amongst different groups. We might express this by saying that they are transcendental rather than empirical interests.

The first knowledge constitutive interest that Habermas describes stems from the human need to control the environment and render it predictable. From the moment we are born, he argues, we attempt to exert some form of control over our immediate environment. And this requires that we devise means for predicting how it will behave. The 'schemas' of which Piaget writes in much of his celebrated work on cognitive development in childhood exemplify this perfectly (for example, Piaget, 1962). From the first attempts of the child to grasp the objects in its reach, it attempts to know, in order to both predict and control, its environment. Its development trajectory is, at one level, marked by the emergence of schemas which function precisely to secure this control and prediction. And the history of human societies, at least insofar as that it is history of technologies and modes of belief about the nature of the universe, can equally be read as a succession of collective schemas oriented to this same goal. The history of human societies is, in part, a history of attempts and struggles to render the world more predictable and to exercise control or mastery over it. From the taming of fire and early hunting techniques through to the computer and alternative forms of energy, this knowledge constitutive interest is clear.

Many forms of human activity manifest this interest in prediction and control, Habermas observes, but in modern societies it assumes a concentrated and specialized form in science. Or to put that the other way round, science is a specialized extension of our everyday ways of attempting to make the world predictable and controllable and is, as such, an expression of the 'knowledge constitutive interest' in prediction and control.

To some degree, given that Habermas concedes that control and prediction of the environment are necessary for human beings (as a matter of survival), he concedes also that this mode of knowledge is necessary. However, part of his opposition to positivistic models of social science is clearly premised upon the over-extension of this interest in prediction and control to the case of human life itself. Indeed, in revealing the underlying interest of science in control Habermas is hoping to alert us to what he believes to be the dangers of a scientific approach to social analysis. Effectively he here rejoins Adorno and other writers of the first generation Frankfurt School,[129] who view 'positivist' social research as a technology of social control masquerading as neutral investigation (see Adorno et al., 1969)

The second knowledge constitutive interest of which Habermas speaks is 'understanding'. This interest stems from the fact that human beings live in societies, with others, using various symbolic systems of communication. In order to live in social contexts human beings must develop their tools of understanding and interpretation. Again we might cite the child development literature. Just as children must learn to render their immediate environment relatively controllable, so too must they learn both to understand others and to make themselves adequately understood. And again this process of individual human development is paralleled in collective, social history, for example, in the history of languages and forms of communication. As with the interest in control, this interest has been channelled historically, in more specific ways. The specialized forms of study of legal and religious texts, what Habermas calls legal and religious hermeneutics, which are evident in even quite early societies, provide one example of this. They effectively formalize techniques of reading and interpreting. More recently, however, these narrow forms of hermeneutics have been rejoined with the broader swath of cultural and philosophical hermeneutics[130] which Habermas himself

129 The Frankfurt School were a group of philosophers and social scientists associated with the Institute for Social Research at the University of Frankfurt. Habermas is often regarded as belonging to the second generation of this 'school' (see Held, 1980; Jay 1996).
130 Hermeneutics is a branch of philosophy devoted to the analysis of the process of interpretation and understanding. Often this means interpretation of texts of various sorts but for Habermas, as for others, it applies equally to those more philosophical approaches in social science which address questions of interpretation and understanding: e.g. phenomenology, ethnomethodology and interactionism.

is partly associated with and which he further identifies with some of the more interpretative branches of social science. Weberian and interactionist sociologies, insofar as they seek to 'understand' social actors (and particularly when they contrast their 'understanding' with 'explanation'), constitute branches of hermeneutics in this respect. The human need for understanding both self and other has both everyday and more specialized expressions.

However, hermeneutics is not a proper basis for the study of social life either, according to Habermas, not least because, in its quest to understand, it manifests a conservative instinct to preserve. Hermeneutic inquiry seeks to clarify forms of life and traditions but in doing so tends to leave them unchallenged. The epistemological basis for critical theory must rather be sought in the final knowledge constitutive interest in the inventory: emancipation. Human history, Habermas argues, is a history of struggle and conflict waged by oppressed groups in pursuit of their liberation from dominant groups – a view which echoes both Hegel (1979) and Marx (Marx and Engels, 1967), whose work was very influential upon Habermas at this point in his career. We may, again, see this in child development, in the struggle that children wage with their parents in their quest for autonomy. However, the historical examples are clearly of more relevance. One of the key drives behind human knowledge has been the drive for emancipation and this is evidenced in the various critiques and cultures of resistance generated by, for example social movements. Knowledge is not just for controlling or understanding but equally for criticizing and, as Nietzsche somewhere puts it, 'cutting'.

This is the model for critical theory. Habermas' discussion of it goes via a discussion of psychoanalysis, however. Psychoanalysis, he argues, effectively offers a prototype of knowledge rooted in this emancipatory interest that critical theory can draw upon. This need not involve an acceptance of the content of psychoanalysis (libido theory, the oedipus conflict, and so on) but is rather a matter of extrapolating the form of psychoanalytic criticism. Psychoanalysis works by identifying 'systematic distortion' in the communicative life of the analysand, which it then traces back to the effect of events and institutions in the history of the individual. These events and institutions manifest as unconscious forces inhibiting the liberty of the analysand, which must be identified and worked through if that liberty is to be attained. Critical theory, Habermas argues, can and should do the same with respect to public discourses and culture. It must effect a critique of ideology, uncovering the unconscious forces which distort popular culture and inhibit the autonomy of the members of contemporary societies.

Critique is different in form from both the explanation sought by the scientists and the understanding sought within hermeneutics. However, it also, in some measure, draws from both. Although Habermas is critical of Freud's occasional scientism, there is nevertheless a recognition in his work that critical theory is a 'mixed discourse' which seeks to explain, on the path to correcting, the systematic distortions which render our self-understandings problematic, distorted and preclusive of the proper development of autonomy.

There is much that is problematic in this account, not least its very caricatured and simplistic view of science and its failure to engage with the view that science itself is an emancipatory force.[131] However, it stands as one of the most interesting and suggestive attempts to spell out and ground critical theory (of whatever epistemological persuasion). Moreover, what I find particularly attractive about it is the fact that Habermas locates specialized forms of knowledge, including the specialized knowledge of the social critic, in relation to lay versions of the same type of knowledge. There are potential problems with this, at least if we are not attentive to the 'epistemological breaks' that often separate lay from specialized forms of knowledge (see **epistemological break**). However, there is an important corrective here to those forms of critical theory which pay insufficient attention to the capacity of lay members of society to develop a critical voice of their own. Critical theory does not invent social criticism. It continues, advances and specializes it. Furthermore, as the (albeit also problematic) psychoanalytic metaphor suggests, critical theory cannot dictate its interpretations back to the lay public, expecting either that this will lead to emancipation or that they will even accept it. Rather it must engage in a dialogue with the lay public until such a point as a mutually acceptable interpretation has been reached.

### FURTHER READING

*Knowledge and Human Interests* is a relatively straightforward text. For further commentary, however, see Jay Bernstein's (1995) *Reclaiming Ethical Life*.

181

---

131 Many conceptions of science, contra Habermas, portray it as a critical project, devoted to smashing myths and liberating human beings through the advancement of knowledge. In recent social science this view was advanced by Norbert Elias (1978) and Pierre Bourdieu (e.g. 1993, 1998a, 2000), the latter of whom in particular emphasizes the socially critical nature of social science. Roy Bhasker (1989) also offers an interesting critique of Habermas' view of science in his *Reclaiming Reality*.

---

# Lifeworld

> *Related concepts:* ***body-subject, epistemological break, habitus, intersubjectivity.***

The concept of the lifeworld has at least two distinct formulations, one in the work of the phenomenologists, following Husserl (1970a), and one in the work of Jürgen Habermas (1987a). In this entry I will deal with the phenomenological version of the concept, beginning with an outline and then discussing the potential critical import of the concept. Habermas' version of the concept is discussed in the entry on **system and lifeworld**.

The concept of the lifeworld was developed by the pioneer of phenomenological philosophy, Edmund Husserl, in his later writing. It is particularly associated with his *Crisis of the European Sciences and Transcendental Phenomenology* (Husserl, 1970a) but it is also discussed, either implicitly or explicitly, in certain of his other key texts of that later period of his work. In essence, the concept refers to the world as it is given to human beings in their most basic and fundamental experiences, the world as it is 'lived'. The lifeworld is the lived world. As such the concept connects directly with the broader phenomenological mode of philosophy which Husserl originated. The basis of this philosophical approach can best be explained, for our purposes, by reference to Husserl's critique of the work of Descartes and particularly his retracing, in *Cartesian Meditations* (Husserl, 1991), of Descartes' path of philosophical inquiry in *Meditations* (Descartes, 1969).

Written in the mid-seventeenth century, Descartes' (1969) *Meditations* aimed to establish a point of certainty upon which knowledge, and specifically the emerging science of the day, could build. The knowledge base of his society was contaminated by all manner of superstitious and magical belief, Descartes believed, and science could only progress, liberating human beings from their ignorance, if true and erroneous beliefs could be separated. To achieve this, he argued, he must turn over the apple cart of knowledge, throwing out all beliefs of which he could not be certain until he found at least one of which he could be certain. This 'Archemedean point', he continued, would provide him with a solid foundation from which to generate veridical knowledge. He therefore elected to doubt everything which, to his mind, it was possible to doubt. This included the external world, his own body and even certain truths of logic and reason. Particularly pertinent to our purposes here is his doubting of the external world, a doubt rooted in his experience of dreams and hallucinations. He has, he remembers, had very realistic dreams in the past which he has only come to recognize as dreams after he has woken up. So how does he know that he is not dreaming now? His whole life could just be a dream! Similarly, he is aware that some people experience hallucinations which they cannot distinguish from veridical perceptions. Again this casts doubt upon his own perceptions of the world. How does he know that he is not hallucinating? What Descartes found that he could not doubt, however, was his own existence as a thinking being. Even if everything that he thought was wrong, he would still exist as a thinking being. Thus he arrives at his famous dictum: 'cogito ergo sum' ('I think therefore I am').

Having established the certainty of his own existence as a thinking being and diverted through a theological argument in which he 'proves' the existence of God, Descartes begins to establish arguments to reinstate his various beliefs in the existence of the external world and the veracity of logic. We need not follow him down this path. What is more important from our point of view is the rather different path which Husserl adopts. In *Cartesian Meditations* he follows Descartes down the path towards the cogito. All of which we can be certain, he agrees, is our existence as thinking and experiencing beings. Moreover, he at least enjoins the spirit of the Cartesian project, with its quest to establish sure foundations for knowledge and other intellectual endeavours. However, Husserl is critical of Descartes' attempt to prove the existence of an external world beyond his own (perceptual) experience and knowledge. We cannot, by definition, know that which lies beyond our own knowledge, Husserl observes, nor can we claim to know that which lies beyond our own perceptual consciousness (since 'knowing' something implies consciousness of it). Descartes' 'realism'[132] is therefore doomed from the start. However, the further implication of this argument, in Husserl's view, is that it makes no sense to doubt the existence of this world either. It only

183

132 It is important to note here that what Husserl calls Descartes 'realism' is only one species of realism and has little to do the philosophical position more often referred to as realism. We should also note that some realists, as the entry on **realism** in this book suggests, would claim to have a 'transcendental' proof of the existence of the world beyond their own consciousness of it, based upon the capacity of 'the world' to resist certain of their attempts to explain or interpret it. If the world did not exist beyond our own perceptions of it, these realists argue, our perceptions and interpretations would never prove wrong – but of course they all too often do!

makes sense to doubt that which could potentially be proven or refuted, he argues, and as the existence of a world beyond our consciousness of the world can be neither proven nor refuted it makes no sense to doubt it either. Philosophy must therefore give up upon the fruitless task of attempting to match our world of experience, that is, the phenomenal or phenomenological world, with a second, 'real' world which is alleged to lie behind it. It should concentrate rather upon examining the nature of the phenomenological world, the world as it is given to experience and the nature of that experience itself. Specifically, at least in *Cartesian Meditations*, Husserl is concerned to investigate the manner in which experiences are ordered and embellished with tacit attributions, in ways which, in his view, can only be properly explained by reference to the constitutive activities of the human subject. Of particular interest to us is his use of the concept of 'habitus' (see **habitus**). Any examination of human experience, he suggests, reveals that we always tend to perceive, in any situation, more than is actually given to experience. Our perceptions are effectively shaped by a habitual stock of schemas and forms of tacit knowledge.

The concept of the lifeworld maps on to this project of phenomenological philosophy. If the task of philosophy is to explore the basic nature of human experience, then the lifeworld, the world as lived and experienced, is its primary datum. The lifeworld is the world as we experience it, a world constituted within our experience by means of the habitual schemas, fore-knowledge and know-how that we bring to bear upon it. And analysis of the lifeworld is analysis of this process of habitual constitution.

This is only one half of the story, however. The concept of the lifeworld also functions to differentiate out the world of our lived experience from the world as it is conceived in science. The latter, for Husserl, is an often erroneous and potentially dangerous world of abstraction and generalization and the analysis of the lifeworld is envisaged as a means of criticizing it. To explore this further we must briefly consider the habitual constitution of the lifeworld in a little more detail.

An analysis of the lifeworld and specifically of the role of the habitus in its constitution reveals that our experience always contains a degree of generalization and abstraction. One aspect of our habitus, for example, consists in perceptual 'typifications' which lead us to perceive specific and unique objects as members of a class. If I were to enter a friend's house for the first time, for example, I would see many objects which, in a strict sense, I have never seen before (because I have never been in the house before). Insofar as they are standard household items, however, I would undoubtedly experience them all as familiar and, were I to use any of them, would do so without question. I would perceive my friend's toaster simply as a toaster, for example, 'pairing' it with all other toasters I have experienced in my life and, by force of habit, 'transferring' everything I know of toasters to it. I would have certain habitual and tacit expectations about it, for example, such as that it will have a slot for bread, a button to turn it on and that, in all probability, it will either lightly warm the bread or burn it to a cinder (because that is what toasters, in my experience, do). None of my assumptions will be revealed to me if this toaster is indeed like those I have known. I will only become aware of my 'habitual constitution' of the toaster if for some reason this toaster is different. It may turn out, for example, that it is actually a bread bin in the shape of a toaster. If this is so, I may experience something of a shock when I get up close to it and attempt to turn it on. My expectations and perceptual schemas are revealed to me because they are confounded. My perception is shaped by such expectations and habits all of the time according to Husserl, however. I just tend not to notice this because my expectations and schemas are habitual and, most of the time, they are not confounded. The lifeworld is a habit-world, a world of experience structured through our habitual ways of perceiving, understanding and acting in it.

Pushing this point further, Husserl notes the centrality of language to the lifeworld. Language is, in effect, a socially shared stock of habitual 'typifications'. It pairs new experiences with old, imposing generalized categories and schemas of understanding onto new and unique situations, rendering them familiar.[133] However, there are differing degrees of abstraction at which this operates, moving from the less abstract level of our ordinary lived experience, to the much more abstract level of science. Science builds upon the everyday lifeworld, Husserl argues, as it must, but it effects ever further levels of abstraction and generalization. More importantly, its conceptual schemas are highly selective, bracketing out much of what is ordinarily given to our lived experience. Science has a narrow lens. Specifically, it tends to delete the 'point of view' of the individual subject and to bracket out the moral and aesthetic 'halo' that surrounds our everyday experience of the world. The human body, for

---

133 'Uniqueness' and 'particularity' are used in very strict sense here. Husserl is not suggesting that our lives leap from one novel and completely different situation to another. The point rather is that we use knowledge gleaned from previous experience to make sense of present situations – situations which, by definition, we have never lived through before. From a practical point of view most of the situations are very much like ones I have had in the past, involving very similar objects, and that is why I both can and do apply previous experience to them, but that does not alter the fact that there is an interesting process of 'sense making' to be grasped here and that is what Husserl is directing us towards.

example, is no longer viewed as an expressive embodiment of another person, potentially beautiful (or ugly) and demanding of moral consideration. It is viewed as a collection of physical 'bits' which are causally related to one another. The moral, aesthetic and existential meanings of the body are stripped away to reveal an abstract and bare physical core. In itself, Husserl argues, this can be dangerous and problematic. As he suggests in *The Crisis of the European Sciences and Transcendental Phenomenology*, however, these intrinsic dangers are heightened by the fact that the scientific 'construction' of reality has been elevated above our everyday constructions, such that the world of science is taken to be more real than the world of our everyday experience, our lived world or lifeworld. Bodies, for example, are viewed to be 'really' collections of physical bits linked by causal relations, and our aesthetic and moral apprehension is deemed, at best, secondary to this 'underlying' reality – an ordering which, from Husserl's point of view, is the wrong way round. This happens at an institutional level, by means of the status and material resources we invest in science, but it also happens at a more local level, of the individual, when we defer to science and substitute its definition of reality for our own. The effect of this, Husserl argues, is to generate a 'fact-minded' culture which is incapable of dealing with moral, existential and aesthetic issues. We narrow our horizons and thereby incapacitate ourselves. Phenomenological arguments regarding the primacy of the lifeworld and the derivative and limited (albeit interesting and useful within its limits) purview of science, combined with specific phenomenological studies of aspects of the lifeworld, are a crucial counter-weight in this respect. They bring into view all that science represses and rediscover the moral, aesthetic and existential texture of human life. For example, a phenomenological investigation of the body as it is lived, such as that conducted by Merleau-Ponty (1962), exposes the very one-sided nature of scientific, physiological views of the human body, retrieving the existential, aesthetic and moral dimensions of the body which are excluded from scientific accounts and demonstrating the foundational and irreducible nature of these dimensions.

The substitution of the scientific view of the world for that of the lifeworld is not only evident in everyday contexts, Husserl continues, but in philosophy too. At this level it generates all sorts of problems and difficulties, and is again dangerous. Descartes' mind/body problem[134] is

---

134 Descartes famously argued that mind and body are distinct and separate 'substances'. Having separated them, however, he could not come up with a satisfactory account of how they co-exist and interact within human beings, and neither could anybody else – a problem which led most writers to reject the view that they are separate in the first place.

one example of this. Descartes claims to arrive at the mind/body distinction on the basis of the fact that he can doubt the existence of his own body, without thereby doubting his own existence, such that he is forced to conclude that his own existence must consist in something other than his body. This, he concludes, is his mind. In response to this, Husserl questions the possibility that one can doubt the existence of one's body. In our own everyday experience our mental life is not divorced from the bodily realm. Our experiences are sensuous experiences and our body is quite clearly not an external object or appendage. Furthermore, we experience the mental life of others through their embodied gestures, expressions and behaviours. To separate out mind and body as Descartes does, Husserl argues, presupposes a prior abstracted conception of the body as mere 'matter', devoid of spirit. This is exactly the conception of matter that the scientists of Descartes' day, following Galileo, were developing, Husserl notes, and Descartes unconsciously substitutes this abstract scientific model for his own more basic lived experience of embodiment. This is clearest when Descartes actually spells out the distinction between mind and matter, as his definition of matter (and 'the body') is precisely that of Galileo. For this reason Descartes' *Meditations* fail in their stated task of establishing a foundational ground for science, since they include scientific conceptions amongst their basic presuppositions. And perhaps more seriously, they generate a pseudo basis for what has become a perennial problem of philosophy ever since, mind/body dualism.

Descartes' *Meditations* are not radical enough Husserl concludes. They remain trapped within the abstract conceptual framework of science, failing to dig beneath that level to the more primordial level of the lifeworld. Consequently they fail in their task. They sell us short by deferring to science (albeit unwittingly) and they sell science short too in the respect that they fail to provide it with the indubitable basis it requires. The Cartesian foundation for science is circular because it presupposes concepts from the sciences it purports to ground.

There is a twofold 'radicalness' to phenomenology and its excavations of the lifeworld, in this respect. Phenomenology is philosophically radical, in a way Descartes intended to be, insofar as it seeks to penetrate beneath the abstractions and generalizations of science and a culture dominated by science, to reveal beneath that a much richer world of lived experience. But in doing this it is also socially and politically radical, since it necessarily challenges both the hegemony of science and the details of the predominant scientific worldview.

In certain of his later studies, particularly *Experience and Judgement*,

Husserl increasingly emphasizes the embodied nature of our primary experiences and thus the embodied nature of the lifeworld. Amongst other things, this entails a direct challenge to the primacy afforded to reflective thought in the Cartesian system and, specifically, the cogito. Our primary manner of being in the world is not, in the first instance, 'I think', Husserl argues, but rather 'I can'. We are practical beings whose primary experience of the world consists in what Heidegger (1962) referred to as its 'readiness-to-hand'.

This more 'embodied' phenomenological trajectory is often associated with the work of Merleau-Ponty, particularly his *Phenomenology of Perception* (Merleau-Ponty, 1962). Merleau-Ponty considerably advances the notion of a 'lived body', challenging crude materialist reductions of the human body to mere matter and, in the process, he offers extremely illuminating phenomenological challenges to a variety of objectivist and scientific constructions (see **body-subject**). Against objectivist constructions of space, for example, which equate it with 'space' as conceptualized with geometry, Merleau-Ponty argues for the primacy of the 'lived space' of our bodily being (see also Husserl, 1970b). Our immediate experience is not that of the straight lines and perfect right angles, he argues, nor is our grasp of space at first reflective and intellectual. Rather we occupy an oriented and perspectival space of ups and downs, nears and fars, and our grasp upon space is precisely that, a practical competence at moving in and utilizing the area around us. When an infant takes its first steps or begins to reach for and grab objects, for example, it manifests an awareness and understanding of space, but this is not space as Euclid understands or theorizes it. It is practical conception of space from a particular point of view, a conception manifest in mastery over space.

Within sociology and social theory this specific Husserlian conception of the lifeworld has tended to go in two directions. Some of the early Frankfurt School members, most notably Marcuse (1968), offer a further exploration of the relations between science and the lifeworld, extending Husserlian themes by way of the various other concepts of their critical theory. Habermas too follows this through in some of his earlier work (Habermas, 1987a). Alternatively, in a less critical vain but connecting with many of the wider themes of Husserl's approach, Alfred Schutz undertook to explore the social world and our experience of it by way of this concept of the lifeworld (for example, Schutz, 1972). Schutz maps the insights of Husserl onto the basic concerns of Weber's interpretative sociology, suggesting that the Weberian concern for adequacy at the level of meaning can only be fully achieved through an appropriation of phenomenological concepts. In effect this amounted to a sociology which focused upon the various 'typifications' and forms of habitual knowledge by which agents construct their experiences of each other and of the broader social world.

We have insufficient space here to consider in any detail the criticisms that might be levelled against the Husserlian perspective. It is at least worth noting, however, that certain other perspectives, most notably that of Gaston Bachelard (for example, 1970, 2002), offer a very different view. The relationship of Bachelard's philosophy to that of Husserl is complex. For our purposes, however, suffice it to say that he calls into question the primacy which Husserl wishes to afford to the lived world. Reflecting in particular upon the 'epistemological break' effected by the work of Einstein (see **epistemological break**), Bachelard notes how scientific work radically challenges our common sense conceptions of the world, changing the way in which we perceive the world and, in effect, thereby changing the very nature of our subjectivity. There is something too static in the notion of the lived world, for Bachelard, something backward looking. Furthermore, whilst he agrees with Husserl that our basic experiences of the world are shaped by scientific discourses and typifications he sees this as positive (because he views science positively). I cannot address the myriad of issues this raises. I mention Bachelard here simply to indicate the existence of a possible counter-current to this important Husserlian notion of the lifeworld.

### FURTHER READING

Husserl's work is generally fairly heavy going. However, *Cartesian Meditations* (Husserl, 1991) and *the Crisis of the European Sciences* (Husserl, 1970a) are perhaps the two clearest works (particularly the latter of the two), and are certainly the easiest entry point to Husserl's work as a whole (and the most relevant from a social scientific point of view). In addition, Schutz's work, which takes up and develops the idea of the lifeworld is very clear and engaging. The best entry point for this work is perhaps *The Phenomenology of the Social World* (Schutz, 1972). However, there are a number of shorter and interesting pieces in his three volume collected works (Schutz, 1964, 1971, 1973).

189

# Mirror Stage and the Ego

> Related concepts: **id, ego and superego, imaginary, recognition, symbolic and real, unconscious (the).**

The concept of the mirror stage was first formulated in the psychoanalysis of Jacques Lacan. It has subsequently been used and alluded to in the work of number of writers, including Maurice Merleau-Ponty, Franz Fanon, Louis Althusser and Julia Kristeva. Lacan's (1989) paper on the concept remains the classic statement of it, however.

Lacan's perspective is complex and often seemingly contradictory. The concept of the mirror stage emerged very early in his career, however, before many of the other key ideas of his approach and perhaps also before he had adopted certain of the more controversial stances for which he is known. It emerged at a time when his work, though already resolutely psychoanalytic, was also influenced by phenomenology, animal ethology, Gestalt psychology and the work of Hegel (which had been popularized in France of the 1930s by the lectures of Alexandre Kojève (1969)). All of these influences inform the concept of the mirror stage but, with the exception of the basic psychoanalytic framework, non so much as the Hegelian notion of the desire and struggle for recognition (see **recognition**).

The basic presupposition of Lacan's claim is that human beings begin life, subjectively, in an undifferentiated state. That is to say we lack (mature) self-consciousness. We are not conscious of ourselves as such. According to Hegel (1979), who shares this view, awareness of self only emerges through desire. The infant experiences itself, as indeed animals do, through and as privation, lack, for example, of food. Feelings or pangs of hunger are, in effect, experiences of 'self' or rather of an absence (of food) at the heart of self. Ordinary animal desires are readily satisfied by eating, however, such that they can only give rise to temporary glimpses of self. Given that mature human beings have a stronger sense of self than this, therefore, Hegel postulates that there must be a further desire in human beings, an insatiable and peculiarly human desire which accounts for human self-consciousness. The candidate he proposes is a desire for recognition; a desire, as Kojève (1969) puts it, 'for' desire, a 'desire to be desired'. Integral to this claim is the idea that human beings can only become conscious of themselves by becoming aware of the consciousness of others and of the fact that they exist as objects in the consciousness of others. Self-consciousness, at least in the absence of full recognition, is 'alienating' in this respect and human beings experience themselves as 'captured' or 'caught up' in the experience of others. Jean-Paul Sartre's (1969) concept of 'the look' provides a good illustration of this. Sartre describes in detail the anxiety-raising experience of feeling that one is being looked at, feeling that one's actions and being are not one's own.

These ideas are explored in more detail elsewhere in this book (see **recognition**). For the moment it must suffice to say that Lacan (1989) is very much alert to the fact that self-consciousness, which he refers to variously as 'the I' or 'the ego', emerges in the context of what he refers to as 'the dialectic of identification with the other', that is, through our relations with others. Moreover, this process is further extended for Lacan, through the infant's acquisition of language. However, the 'dialectic of identification with the other' is precipitated and even facilitated by an earlier experience according to Lacan, an experience which occurs between the age of six and eighteen months.

During this time, he notes, children seemingly become capable of recognizing themselves in such reflective surfaces as mirrors. This is, to some extent, a process of 'derealization'; that is to say, the infant learns that the image in the mirror is not real. It is not a real other person but rather a reflected image of their self. Other mammals, including chimpanzees, get this far. When they realize that the image is not real, however, they tend to lose interest in the image. The human infant, by contrast, does not. At a cognitive level it seemingly recognizes the image as its own. At a more affective level, however, it becomes fascinated by the image, deriving great pleasure from playing in front of the mirror: manipulating its appearance and delighting in the visual effects of this. Furthermore, Lacan argues, it 'identifies' with the image in the psychoanalytic sense; that is to say, it internalizes the image and takes over the properties of the image in its sense of itself.

It is important to be clear about what is being argued here. Before the mirror stage the child has no real sense of itself. It is aware of the world around it and is involved in that world as far as its still quite underdeveloped state will allow, but it is not conscious of itself as a part of the world. It is only when it catches sight of its own reflection that it becomes an object for its own awareness and, as Lacan argues, pleasure and even love. The relationship which the infant forms with itself is alienating for Lacan, however, in the same way that we said above that relations with others are alienating. The child identifies with an external image of itself. Moreover, the child's recognition of itself is, in Lacan's view, a misrecognition. What he means by this is multi-levelled. At one level, the mirror image tears the infant out of its prior, more immediate relationship to itself and its lived relationship to the world. The infant takes an outside view upon itself, facilitated by the mirror image, but in so doing it becomes an outsider to itself. It is estranged from itself and hence alienated. Furthermore, since what it identifies with is its own exteriority, it also misrecognizes itself. It identifies with the image 'over there', an image to be looked at, rather than the lived, perceiving body 'here'. What also concerns Lacan, however, is the discrepancy between the 'perfect' whole which the infant perceives in the mirror and the rather more fragmented state which the infant is living at this point in its development. The mirror stage takes place at a time when the infant still lacks basic motor co-ordination and proprioceptive organization, he notes, and even before the neuronal development which makes this possible is complete. Insofar as it identifies itself with the 'whole' that it perceives in the mirror, therefore, it misrecognizes itself. This misrecognition, Lacan argues, prefigures the basic misrecognition constitutive of the adult ego. We take ourselves, our 'I', to be a coherent and organized author of our actions and experiences but this is little more than a convenient fiction which we employ to make sense of our experiences, a fiction that begins life in the mirror stage. We are not coherent wholes, in Lacan's view, but rather deeply divided or fractured beings who incorrectly identify with a sense of ourselves as unified and coherent.

What Lacan terms the 'I' or 'ego' here is clearly intended in the psychoanalytic sense. Indeed, the mirror stage can be regarded as Lacan's own account of the stage in ego development that Freud referred to as 'primary narcissism', a stage in development where infants take themselves as their own love objects. As Grosz (1990) argues, however, Freud posits different versions of what the ego is at different phases in his work, or at least he manifests considerable shifts in emphasis, and Lacan's account only maps onto one of these versions, which is by no means the best known (see **id, ego and superego**). Indeed, it is quite clear in Lacan's account that he opposes the more popular account of the ego in Freudian psychoanalysis, an account which suggests that the ego is essentially a system of perception and consciousness which allows the individual to adjust to the world they find themselves in and balance the demands of that world with the demands constituted by their desires. Certain other strands of psychoanalysis, particularly the American strand of 'ego

*Mirror Stage and the Ego*

psychology' focus centrally upon this adaptive conception and argue that the aim of therapy is to strengthen the ego to allow it to cope with the demands of reality. Lacan eschews this on account of its political conservativism and, given his rather different view of the ego, suggests a different aim for analysis, namely to unravel the self-deceptions that make up the ego. Furthermore, he suggests that it is the ego, the narcissistic relation of the individual to the image of their self, which stands in the way of analysis and often motivates the attempt to block it with 'resistances'. The individual defends the narcissistic image they entertain of themselves, against the intrusions of the analyst.

The mirror stage is the first stage in a process of ego development for Lacan. It prepares the way for the next stage of 'dialectical identification with the other'. However, it also sets in place the 'aggression' that psychoanalysts sometimes describe under the rubric of the 'death drive'. It is very difficult to pick out from his account exactly how Lacan conceives of this link. However, the following quotation provides some indication of what he means:

> It is in this erotic relation, in which the human individual fixes upon himself an image that alienates him from himself, that are to be found the energy and the form on which this organization of the passions that we call the ego is based.
> This form will crystallize in the subject's internal conflictual tension, which determines the awakening of his desire for the object of the other's desire; here the primordial coming together is precipitated into aggressive competitiveness . . . (1989: 19)

It is the subject's love of themselves, in other words, which lays the foundation for their desire to become the object of desire of others, a desire which inevitably leads them into conflict with others and thus generates aggression. In many respects desire is always already 'aggressive' in the view of the philosophical tradition that Lacan is drawing from here (for example, that of Hegel (1979)). It is always the desire to consume and thereby annihilate its object. Hunger, for example, is only satisfied through the annihilation of objects (by eating them). And in Hegel the desire for recognition drives subjects into a 'battle for the death' with the other as each attempts to 'prove' him or herself to the other (see **recognition**). Lacan is clearly building upon this here, however, by introducing an account of the origin of a form of self-love which, in his account, drives subjects to seek recognition from others.

A further clue to the link that Lacan identifies between the mirror stage, the ego and aggression is also to be found in his numerous remarks on the 'paranoic' structure of the ego as constituted through the mirror stage. Paranoia involves an enlarged or overextended sense of oneself, a tendency to over-perceive self-relevance in events. Moreover, it often involves feelings of persecution, feelings of being watched, followed or talked about. It is a disturbance in one's relations with the world and specifically with other people that can result in hostility towards them. As such it is an extreme, outside of the 'normal' human range. However, Lacan claims that this is only a more extreme version of a form of 'egoism' that is normal in human beings and is generative of aggression. The usual state of the ego is 'paranoic', at least in a moderate way, for Lacan.

In much of his work Lacan appeals to social factors in the constitution of human psychological life, without reference to historical factors, that is, he seems to believe that the human psyche develops in a social context but he does not particularly relate it to factors in the social world which, in his view, vary over time. However, in his essay on aggression, from which some of my comments here are taken, he does seem to suggest, much as Durkheim (1952) does, that egoism is exacerbated in modern societies and with negative consequences. Citing both the erosion of tradition and ritual and the abolition of the 'male and female' principles through the 'battle of the sexes', he argues that:

> It is clear that the promotion of the ego today culminates, in conformity with the utilitarian conception of man that reinforces it, in an ever more advanced realization of man as an individual, that is to say, in an isolation of the soul ever more akin to its original dereliction. (1989: 27)

And

> In the 'emancipated' man of modern society, this splitting reveals, right down to the depths of his being, a neurosis of self-punishment, with the hysterico-hypochondriac symptoms of its functional inhibitions, with the psychasthenic forms of its derealization of others and of the world, with its social consequences in failure and crime. It is this pitiful victim, this escaped, irresponsible outlaw, who is condemning modern man to the most formidable social hell, whom we meet when he comes to us [i.e. for psychoanalysis]. (1989: 28–9)

Lacan's line of argument is interesting here. He clearly positions himself as a critique of modern society or, as he also puts it, with reference to Freud, 'civilization', but his critique has an interestingly conservative or perhaps rather reactionary twist to it. He believes that contemporary societies exacerbate the 'pathologies'[135] of the psyche that he analyses in

---

135 Of course in a sense these are not 'pathologies' at all for Lacan as they are statistically normal.

194

his work – narcissism, aggression, egoism, paranoia – but the way in which he frames his critique is as a lament for the past, for tradition, and this even extends to an apparent hostility towards the critique of traditional sex roles that was beginning to take shape (for example, in the work of de Beauvoir (1988)) at his time of writing. I do not mean to suggest that Lacan's conservativism is wrong. That is a separate question. It is, however, interesting; not least on account of the kudos his work has attracted amongst feminists and other 'critical'[136] theorists.

### FURTHER READING

I noted earlier in the book that Lacan is extremely unclear in what he writes. In actual fact, the paper on the mirror stage in his *Écrits* (Lacan, 1989) is one of the clearer chapters, as is the chapter 'On aggressivity' which follows it. Both are also quite brief and would constitute a reasonable choice for anybody wishing to read primary materials by this often very obscure writer. Good secondary sources are Benvenuto and Kennedy's (1986) *The Works of Jacques Lacan*, Bowie's (1991) *Lacan*, and Elizabeth Grosz's (1990) *Jacques Lacan: A Feminist Introduction*.

# New Social Movements

**195**

*Related concepts:* **crisis, cycles of contention, repertoires of contention, social class, social movements.**

The definition of 'new social movements' can be broken into two parts: a definition of 'social movements' and a definition of specifically '*new* social movements'. I deal with the general concept of social movements elsewhere in this book (see **social movements***)* and will focus here on the 'new' bit of the definition.

In essence the label 'new social movements'(NSMs) is used to refer to those social movements which rose to prominence in the political

---

136 I place 'critical' in scare quotes here because it is by no means clear that these writers are very critical in a social sense – even if they are aesthetically or theoretically challenging.

upheavals of the late 1960s, maintaining a high profile in the 1970s, 1980s and 1990s, such as the student movement, environmentalism, feminism, pacifism, animal rights and so on. That much is uncontroversial. The question of what is specifically 'new' about these movements is rather more problematic, however. Many critics have assumed that the alleged 'newness' of NSMs derives from the issues they tackle (for example, the environment, gender issues, and so on), the tactics (of direct action and protest) they employ, their scepticism with respect to the 'usual channels' of politics and their opposition to the grand revolutionary schemas characteristic of Marxist movements. And these same critics systematically attack the idea of the NSMs on the grounds that none of these characteristics of the movements of the 1960s and 1970s is particularly new. They can be identified much earlier, in the nineteenth century, in certain strands of the labour movement (Tucker, 1991; Calhoun, 1995). Although it is argued that the NSMs might have revivified earlier political currents, this is the extent of their 'newness'. All of their significant features echo those of significant political movements of the past and, in particular, the early labour movement – which is the archetypal 'old social movement', in contrast to which the NSMs are deemed 'new'. For these critics then, the label 'new social movements' is a misnomer.

These are important points and we need to be mindful of them. We need to push the argument and the definition a little further however. Most of the theorists of the NSMs, in my view, do not define these movements by reference to specific issues, tactics or even their tendency to work 'outside the system'. Neither do they suggest that there is anything completely new about such features of movement politics. Indeed, most recognize that there are considerable overlaps between the early activities of the labour movement and the current activities of the NSMs. Their argument concerning NSMs is less that the movements themselves are new, although some claim that the class base and recruitment pool of movements have changed,[137] more that the structure of society and its fault lines have shifted, so as to shift the central lines of division and conflict in society. Furthermore, their argument is a call for new theories of social movements and social division to replace the Marxist models

196

---

137 The archetypal 'old social movement' was the labour movement. It recruited disproportionately, as one would expect, from amongst the working class. The new social movements are alleged to recruit from a wider basis (students, housewives, scientists, public sector workers), but it is noted that the working classes are often poorly represented within them, whilst members of the educated 'new middle classes' tend to be over-represented. Many studies conducted since the 1960s have noted this pattern of over-representation (see Bagguley, 1995; Rootes, 1995).

which prevailed within critical social science (at least in Europe)[138] for many years until quite recently. These points need to be unpacked.

Like Marx, the NSM theorists believe that, whatever the diversity of contentious issues in society at any point in time, there is an underlying 'fault line' which defines the key areas of contention and conflict. For Marx that fault line was the relationship between capital and labour and the crisis tendencies of the economy (see **crisis** and **social class**). And for Marx the labour movement, the movement of the working class, was the key movement emerging out of this fault line. However many movements and campaigns we identify in society at any point in time, from a Marxist point of view, the labour movement is the movement of capitalist societies and it is constituted as such by the basic structures and structural contradictions of capitalism. Theorists of NSMs disagree. Social transformations during the late nineteenth and early twentieth centuries, they argue, have altered the structural conditions and contradictions analysed by Marx and reduced or contained their impact. Interventionist economic policies have sought to manage what Marx identified as the anarchic and crisis ridden economy and social policies, specifically relating to the welfare state, have softened the impact of economic dynamics and divisions, lending society a more egalitarian appearance and putting the proletariat in a position where they have more than 'their chains'[139] to lose by engaging in political action. Furthermore, the labour movement has been brought into the political system as an institutionalized part of it. In the course of the late nineteenth and early twentieth centuries, NSM theorists argue, labour movements narrowed their focus. They dropped both the revolutionary and the ethical lifestyle elements of their struggle in favour of the pursuit of more narrow, utilitarian and material goals (namely higher wages, better health care, and so on for workers). In addition they became increasingly co-opted into the political system, in the form of labour parties and bureaucratic trade union organizations. In this respect the class struggle theorized by Marx is over. History has moved on.

However, this has not 'solved' the problems identified by Marx, according to NSM theorists. It has merely displaced them. The fault line has opened up elsewhere. In particular the main theorists of the NSMs

---

138 Social movement analysis has, until recently, followed two quite distinct trajectories in the United States and Europe (see Crossley, 2002a).
139 In the closing paragraph of *The Communist Manifesto*, Marx and Engels (1967) famously argue that the workers should join together in a revolutionary struggle because they have nothing and thus 'nothing but your chains' to lose.

(Touraine (1981); Melucci (1986, 1996) and Habermas (1987b)) claim that conflicts now emerge out of the growth of a vast planning and programming apparatus (in the form of the state) which imposes itself upon everyday life, disturbing life forms and reducing, by way of bureaucratization, possibilities for autonomy and the pursuit of meaning. Habermas (1987b) captures this with the phrase 'colonization of the lifeworld', though he adds, importantly, that the expansion of capitalist markets contributes significantly to this colonization also. Everyday life is undermined by the expansion of state surveillance, bureaucracy and law[140] and by increased market penetration and commodification. This, Habermas argues, is the fault line of contemporary societies, and this is the 'strain' to which the NSMs respond. Other theorists of the NSMs are perhaps less attuned to economic dynamics, and less explicit in identifying 'the state' as the cause of the new problems, but the general picture holds for most of them. Touraine's (1981) claim that NSMs respond to the problems of the 'programmed society', for example, clearly indicates that, for him, the 'fault lines' of our society centre upon attempts to manage or 'programme' it from above.

There is much that it is interesting and persuasive in these accounts. However, there are many problems. One key problem with the concept of NSMs is its ethnocentrism. It focuses upon the impact of what is effectively a world capitalist system on those countries in the west who tend to benefit most from it. There are two problems here. Firstly, it ignores the extent to which economic dynamics and inequalities, capital and labour, remain a key fault line in many developing societies – and in fact these issues, if they ever really went away, are beginning to emerge in societies of the first world again too (see below). Secondly, it ignores tensions and strains constituted at the global level through the interaction of states and large (multinational) economic players, tensions and strains which play back within specific national territories to varying degrees. Another key problem is that the theory reflects the 'postwar welfare consensus' of economic and political governance which was evident in many western societies from the 1950s through to the late 1970s, but which was challenged in the 1980s by the rise of neo-liberal movements and was largely displaced. The effort of neo-liberals to both 'roll back the frontiers of the state' and 'liberate' the market has significantly altered the economic and political dynamics of societies throughout the world,

198

---

140 Law is becoming both ever more extensive, according to Habermas, in the sense that ever more areas of life are subject to legal regulation, and ever more intensive, in the sense that each area of the law is becoming more complex and internally differentiated.

including the west, and has arguably shifted the fault line again – perhaps reactivating certain of the dynamics and problems noted by Marx.

The emerging anti-corporate movement[141] illustrates these points in many respects. Certain of the issues and players of the NSMs remain salient within it but they stand alongside archetypal 'old social movement' activists, pursuing newly energized 'old issues', not to mention a strong array of groups addressing issues prompted by the rather chaotic and unequal state of play in global society and the flows of money, people, information, and so on, circulating within it. First and third worlds, right and left, old and new, secular and religious, all seem somehow to converge in this 'even newer' anti-corporate space. Furthermore, the 'fluffy'[142] approach to politics sometimes deemed central to the NSMs, whilst in some ways more evident than ever, has been rejoined by a variety of 'hate' movements prepared to advance their cause through violence against both people and property. The involvement of the various so-called black-block anarchist and far-right groups are the most obvious examples of this. Furthermore, in the wider context, the emergence of Islamic and other forms of terrorism all indicate that the present context of movement politics is far from fluffy.

Should we then speak of 'even newer social movements'? This is not the place to open that Panodora's box, nor indeed to attempt to untangle what is going on within the world of social movement politics today. It must suffice to say that the ground of social movement politics does seem, once again, to have shifted.

### FURTHER READING

Touraine's (1981) *The Voice and the Eye* is a classic statement on NSMs (though I find it an odd book which drifts off in different directions and isn't always that easy to follow). Melucci's (1986) *Nomads of the Present* is another classic and a 'must read' for this issue. Habermas (1987b)

199

---

141  For discussions of this movement see Crossley (2002a, 2003a), Edwards (2004), Hertz (2001), Klein (2000), Smith (2001).

142  Emerging in the 'peace and love' era NSM politics are sometimes associated with very peaceful 'hippy' tactics, such as the famous attempt to levitate the Pentagon through collective meditation. In fact, there was a great deal of political violence towards the end of the 1960s by such groups as the Red Army Faction, the Black Panthers, the Angry Brigade, the Weathermen, etc. Furthermore, although there has been some violence associated with anti-corporatism, there has been quite a lot of fluffy stuff too, in the form of, for example, protest samba dancing and so-called 'guerrilla gardening'. Indeed, some anti-corporatists have explicitly taken the view that the best way to defend themselves against possible police reprisals is to go fluffy!

discusses NSMs at the very end of the second volume of his *Theory of Communicative Action*. Fortunately, however, this section has been published separately as an article, simply titled 'New social movements' (Habermas, 1981). Again I would say that this is a classic statement on the subject. The anti-corporate movement is very active as I write and as yet there is not a great deal of good analytic literature on it. However an interested reader, besides reading the newpapers, might consult: Crossley (2002b, 2003a), Edwards (2004); Hertz (2001); Klein (2000); Smith (2001).

# Orientalism

> *Related concepts:* **discourse, hegemony, hybridity, power/knowledge, racism.**

Although the term 'orientalism' has a long and varied history of usage, its use in critical theory can be traced back to Edward Said's (1978) book, *Orientalism*. Said defines 'orientalism' in different ways at different points in the book and is clear that he does so. One of the clearest and most comprehensive of his definitions, however, describes it as a discursive field, in the Foucauldian[143] sense, comprizing three levels or elements. The first level, closest in meaning to older and wider uses of the term 'orientalism', refers to the network of academic disciplines and sub-disciplines devoted to the analysis of the orient,[144] the key texts and authors within that network and also its norms, methods and incentives of study, in fact the whole cultural and institutional formation of

---

143 Elsewhere in this book I have defined the concept of 'field' as Pierre Bourdieu uses it. On my reading, Foucault never really develops a systematic concept of 'fields', and that is why I have not endeavoured to explain his version of the concept. For present purposes I think that it will suffice to say that, for Foucault, a field is a social space of interacting and interrelated practices and discourses. The Foucauldian texts that Said specifically references in *Orientalism* are *Discipline and Punish* (Foucault, 1979) and *The Archaeology of Knowledge* (Foucault, 1972).
144 'The orient' refers generally to societies of the east, including some African and all Asian societies. Said's particular interest, however, is in the Middle East.

---

'oriental studies'. These elements, Said argues, interact to form an orientalist field. The second and broader level refers to a much wider network of writers, texts and cultural products/producers who in some way either draw upon or contribute to the constitution and representation of 'the orient' within the west (the Occident). Said's central concern in *Orientalism* is with the way in which cultural production within the west has effected a binary distinction, separating occident and orient, and has built up a concept of the orient as other, sometimes romantic and exciting, sometimes dangerous, usually backwards and barbarous. Specialized studies of the orient, included at level one of his definition, have played a large role here but so to have works of art, literature and philosophy, which allude towards the east to varying degrees and in different ways, drawing upon its meaning/status as 'other' and thereby reproducing that meaning/status. From the late eighteenth century onwards, Said argues, we can identify a tradition amongst artists, novelists and philosophers, including some whom we tend to think of as critical and radical (for example, Marx), trading upon images of the orient or orientals which 'other' this part of the world and its inhabitants, for purposes of advancing their projects. Individual authors/artists and works are important here, and Said is careful to draw a distinction between his own concern for the author and the principled rejection of concern for the author in the work of Foucault, who is in other ways a great inspiration for him, but what is also important is the underlying structure of assumptions and norms that these writers draw upon. The succession of writers Said considers in his study do not each reinvent orientalism ex nihilo, even if they do contribute to its reproduction. They draw upon established, if 'unconscious', cultural conventions and assumptions.

Finally, Said expands the meaning of 'orientalism' one step further to include the practices and forms of power and control involved in the west's material relationship with and governance of (parts of) the east. This is a crucial point in Said's argument. Orientalism is not simply an 'idea' of the east. It is a relationship between parts of the world which has both material and ideational aspects. Moreover, drawing both upon Foucault's ideas of power/knowledge and Gramsci's ideas of hegemony, Said is interested in the interplay of forms of knowledge (and imagination) and forms of domination and control (see **hegemony** and **power/knowledge**). Knowledge and imagination of the East does not arise out of nowhere or out of a neutral intellectual encounter, he argues, but rather out of an encounter which is already political and economic. It arises in a context of material and political domination and is shaped by that context. Access to the orient is always accessed by means of the forms of control on the ground. At the same time, however, knowledge and images of the orient can contribute to forms of domination, insofar as they both inform and legitimate disciplinary controls and other strategic advances. Said's concern in *Orientalism* is to attempt to unpick this complex field of interacting elements or at least aspects of it.

It is not Said's intention to argue that all western literature, philosophy and social science can be read as orientalist, or as contributing to domination of the East. Nor is it his intention, in talking of the cultural constitution of the orient within the west, to ignore or deny the indigenous cultures of the east. 'Orientalist' discourse emerged out of a confrontation of eastern and western cultures; it was not an act of pure imagination on the part of the west. Furthermore, his analysis suggests that it was the British and the French, in particular, who were responsible for the creation of orientalism in its early stages, this mantle having now passed to the United States.

## FURTHER READING

*Orientalism* is a fairly straightforward and very engaging read – it is also obviously the best text for following up this context. The same applies to Said's later work, which deals with similar issues. See particularly *Culture and Imperialism* (Said, 1994).

202

# Patriarchy

---

> *Related concepts: **performativity, sex/gender distinction.***

---

The concept of patriarchy, developed by feminist critics in an effort to denote and explore relations of gender domination, is used, theorized and explained in a diverse number of ways. For some 'patriarchy' is a descriptive term denoting any or all of a wide range of situations in which men are advantaged over and/or dominate women. For others it denotes an ideology, a cluster of ideas and practices, embodied in those situations, which shape them and legitimate the domination they entail. For others still 'patriarchy' is a social system, a 'mode of production'[145] or something akin to a mode of production, which shapes wider society in the way Marxists claim the capitalist mode of production has. Notwithstanding these differences, however, there are a range of common themes which overlap in different combinations in different accounts of patriarchy. We can briefly unpack some of these themes.

Many accounts point both to the system of patrilineal descent, whereby ancestry is traced through the male line and women assume first their father's then their husband's name, and to the system of patrimonial descent, less common now in the western context, where property and privilege pass from father to son and perhaps to a son-in-law, but not to a daughter. These systems of descent, it is further argued by some, reflect a basic structure, famously described by the anthropologist Levi-Strauss (1969), in which society is based upon the exchange of women by men. Groups exchange their female members, in the form of inter-group marriages, as a means of stabilizing relations between themselves and generating a society beyond the realm of the immediate domestic group. The situation Levi-Straus describes is obviously not that of the developed West. Nevertheless, his account is held, by some writers, to capture an underlying structure which lies at the heart of the contemporary system of gender domination. Women are 'goods' or 'property' exchanged amongst and between men.

At a further level, many accounts of patriarchy point to the dominant pattern of relations which structure domestic work and which then spill over into paid work within the wider labour market. Women, it is noted, assume the largest portion of domestic work. They cook, they clean and they care for family members. And they are expected to do so because that is 'women's work'. This is deemed an inherently unjust situation, if only because it denies women the opportunity of not taking on this role if they do not wish to do so. But it also generates difficulties for

---

145 'Mode of production' is a Marxist concept. It captures the economic structure of society which, for Marxists, is the centre or 'base' of society itself. A mode of production comprises 'means of production' (for example, factories, mines or agricultural land and practices) and 'relations of production' (that is, a system of social relationships through which the organization of the use of the means of production is achieved). Some groups (for example, slaves or the working class) are disadvantaged in this system of relations relative to others (for example, masters or the bourgeois class who own and control the means of production). In the case of patriarchy the analysis is often focused on the means and relations of domestic production, including sexual reproduction and the various forms of domestic labour necessary to the reproduction of the household. Women, it is argued, are subordinated within this arrangement and their subordination herein contributes to their subordination beyond the boundaries of the home.

women in the wider labour market, firstly, because their 'responsibilities' in the home compete with any they might wish to engage outside of it and secondly, because the conception of 'women's work' spills over into the wider labour both in relation to the types of work women are likely to be offered (for example, cleaning or caring work which mirrors their 'domestic duties') and in the respect that employers and colleagues (actual and potential) are inclined to view their commitment to work as a secondary concern, relative to their domestic concerns, whether or not this reflects their own subjective assessment of their priorities. Women are positioned within patriarchy as domestic carers and workers.

Another very common theme in studies of patriarchy is violence and its role in the founding and reproduction of relations of gender domination. Feminists have analysed such physical forms of male-on-female violence as rape, domestic violence, (varieties of) child abuse, and also symbolic forms of violence such as pornography[146] and other forms of representation which constitute women as objects for male consumption and pleasure. These instances of violence, it is argued, constitute very concrete and material ways in which women are subject to male wishes, punished for transgression of gender expectations or male desire(s) and positioned in accordance with such desire(s) within patriarchy. Indeed, as a system in which the wishes of men are imposed upon women, patriarchy is violence and these are only its most visible and obvious forms.

Finally, much attention has been focused upon representation and even language itself. Men, it argued, have traditionally controlled the 'means of representation' (literature, art, film, TV and language itself) within society and, as a consequence, dominant representations of gender reflect and reinforce male domination. Much contemporary analysis has focused on this aspect of male domination. Interestingly, the term 'patriarchy' appears to have been dropped in much of this work, and there is a notably more

---

146 The debate on pornography is often framed, particularly in the mass media, in terms of the question whether pornography affects the way in which men behave towards women, whether it encourages rape and sexual assault, etc. Some feminists, however, have argued that, irrespective of these effects, pornography is, in itself, a symbolic degradation of women and should be challenged on this basis (Kappeler, 1986). Feminists have been divided on the question of how to address this problem. Some argue that pornographic images should be banned and that feminists should therefore campaign to get them banned. Others, by contrast, argue that censorship, both in itself and because of the complicity with the state that it involves, is an unacceptable strategy for feminists (on the range of views see Chester and Dickey, 1988). One of the key feminist texts on the question of pornography is Andrea Dworkin's (1981) *Pornography*.

'literary' reference base to it.[147] However, the import of the analysis is much the same, as are many of the themes.

The concept of patriarchy was seemingly introduced or at least achieved prominence in what has become characterized (albeit with a fair degree of reductionism and caricature) as a debate between 'socialist feminists' or 'Marxist feminists' and 'radical feminists'. The stereotypical socialist feminist argues that capitalism needs both a 'reserve army of labour'[148] and a domestic labour force to service and soothe the (male) workforce, at as small a cost as possible. And women, they continue, play exactly that role. Indeed, as wives, mothers and housewives they are free labour for capitalism, absorbing the emotional strains which it generates and which might otherwise threaten it, physically maintaining workers, giving birth to and nurturing new generations of workers, and, qua consumers, keeping demand for capitalist goods high. Thus capitalism is said to 'explain' gender domination. The stereotypical radical feminist, by contrast, does not accept this. She wants to know why it is women particularly who play this role within capitalism – what does 'capitalism' care if it is women or men who form the reserve army and provide domestic services as long as the job gets done? Furthermore, she is concerned that this does not account for all aspects of female domination within capitalism (for example, male violence) and does not account for female domination in societies which are not capitalist in form. Finally, she worries that an exclusive focus upon the ills of capitalism might lead to a situation wherein those ills are addressed but basic gender inequalities, being in fact relatively independent of capitalism, persist. Indeed, she may not be a socialist (the relationship between feminism and socialism is by no means necessary) and/or she might want to forge political alliances with other women who are not socialists and are 'put off' feminism by its socialist links. Consequently, the stereotypical radical

205

147 As opposed to earlier work which was often social scientific (sociological, historical, anthropological and economic) in focus.
148 Capitalism famously moves between periods of boom and bust. As such the demand for labour within it is variable. It too moves in cycles. Consequently, some Marxists argue, the system presupposes and requires a section of society who will move into the labour market when they are required and out of it when they are not, that is, a 'reserve army of labour'. In addition, this reserve army is of value to employers because their willingness to work is a willingness to take the jobs of those currently employed, and as such they pose a threat to those currently in employment which gives the employer leverage in minimising their concessions to workers – 'if you don't like these conditions, leave because there are plenty of people willing to work!' This notion has also been used by some Marxists to explain the structural nature of employment in capitalism; there will always be unemployment in capitalist societies, it is argued, because capitalist labour markets need and generate a 'reserve army'.

*Patriarchy*

feminist wants a theory of gender inequality and domination which stands alone, that is, a concept and theory of patriarchy.

Insofar as this nice and neat division ever existed it did not last long. Certainly in the late 1970s and early 1980s we see a succession of theories which seek in various ways to reconcile the notions of capitalism and patriarchy (whilst, of course, many accounts of capital and labour persisted in making no reference to gender relations and some feminist theories of patriarchy continued in a 'purer' form, making no reference to class or capitalism). Amongst the hybrid forms were the notion of 'capitalist patriarchy' or 'patriarchal capitalism', the notion that capitalism and patriarchy are 'analytically distinct'[149] whilst concretely and historically inseparable, and the notion that capitalism and patriarchy are separate social structures which are 'articulated' in a specific (and historically variable) fashion; that is, are combined in a fashion whereby they are complementary and each contributes to the shaping and operation of the other. Sylvia Walby (1986) gives a good account of these various combinations, and also presents a strong version of the latter type.

'Patriarchy' is used as a form of explanation in some cases. In particular, for example, new social developments which manifest gender inequalities might be explained by a system of patriarchy which pre-exists it and which, qua system of unequal opportunities and/or entrenched cultural expectations and norms, shapes those new developments. For the same reason inequalities in 'this' aspect of the social world (such as paid work) may be explained by reference to inequalities in 'that' aspect (for example, the family). Much work on patriarchy, however, sought not to use it as an explanation but rather to explain it. Why do we have patriarchy? As noted above, theories vary. There are too many and they are too diverse to attempt even an overview here. However, given the controversy it has attracted, it would be instructive to conclude with a brief note on debates concerning the place of biology in the explanation of patriarchy.

Theories of patriarchy, qua gender inequality, necessarily touch upon

---

149 To say that two things are analytically distinct is to say that, for the purposes of analysis, one can distinguish or separate them out, although in practice they are indistinguishable and inseparable. Usually theorists who talk of entities being 'analytically distinct' concede that scientific concepts simplify reality by abstracting and drawing only certain of their features into the foreground for analysis, the implication being that another concept might abstract different features of the same 'thing' such that we have two concepts which denote different aspects of the same thing. Critiques of the many dualisms which plague social thought sometimes draw upon this idea of analytic distinctions. Dualisms, it is argued, arise when analysts mistake analytic distinctions for distinctions between real things. They mistake two distinct levels of description (of the same thing) for descriptions of two different things. This type of mistake of reasoning is referred to as a 'category error'.

questions of sexual difference. Patriarchy, qua system, systematically disadvantages 'women' and social agents are (usually) assigned to the category 'woman' on the basis of certain basic biological markers of sexual difference. From the very earliest attempts to deal with that fact, such as Simone de Beauvoir's important account in *The Second Sex*,[150] great care has been taken to distinguish between the fact of biological differences and the way in which those biological differences are understood and implications (about social order and desert) drawn from them. There is always a slippery territory to be negotiated, however. Both de Beauvoir and after her Firestone, for example, point to the social understanding of women's reproductive capacity as the original source of gender inequality, claiming that this gives, and historically has given, men leverage to effect a system of inequality. Women, in effect, must carry children during pregnancy and this creates a situation in which men are inclined to impose the other domestic duties upon them. Many critics of both writers, however, feel that this boils down to a biological, or perhaps an overly biological explanation. Furthermore, many have argued that it, and perhaps the concept of patriarchy too, is not sufficiently sensitive to the many variations in gender relations that historical research has identified.

The concept of patriarchy seems less often used these days, particularly amongst the key theorists of gender difference. The apparent rise to dominance of post-structuralist theories in feminist theory and writing has seen the emergence of a new language and new concepts within feminism (see **performativity** and **sex/gender distinction**). In many ways, however, debates revolve around similar issues. For example, how important is biological sex to gender inequality? What place can economic accounts of gender inequality have in broader accounts? What is the role of capitalism in all of this? In this respect, given also the stubborn persistence of all of the forms of domination and inequality covered by the concept of patriarchy, the debate continues.

### FURTHER READING

Sylvia Walby's (1986) *Patriarchy at Work* gives a good overview of some of the main theories of patriarchy, as well as the author's own position. The full range of contemporary approaches and issues is covered in Kemp

---

150 Note that de Beauvoir's account predates theories of 'patriarchy' as such, although she was an important source of inspiration for early theories and still is an important resource for feminist writers and activists.

and Squires (1997) *Feminisms*. Although outdated in certain respects and written prior to the birth of patriarchy as a critical, feminist concept, Simone de Beauvoir's (1988) *The Second Sex* remains a classic text.

# Performativity

> *Related concepts:* **humanism and anti-humanism, patriarchy, power/knowledge, sex/gender distinction.**

Deriving from the work of Judith Butler (especially 1990), in the context of her attempt to rethink certain central aspects of feminist theory, this concept grows out of a critique of substantive understandings of gender as a property that one either has or is. Butler suggests, alternatively, that gender is something one 'does', that it is a social structure which, like all social structures, must be repeatedly 'performed' in order for it to exist. Gender, from this point of view, consists of the various ways we have of perceiving, speaking and thinking about it, as well as the various gestures, manners and more generally the behavioural patterns we associate with it. Traditionally, Butler argues, these behaviours were conceived of as 'expressions' of gender; that is, gender was conceived of as a substantial and perhaps even metaphysical essence which both lies behind 'gendered' activities and expresses itself through them: for example, such that I might claim to express my masculinity by strutting as I walk, growing a beard, dressing as I do, and so on. Against this she suggests that gender is nothing but the cumulative effect of these various behaviour patterns, that it exists entirely through them and, as such, is 'done' by them. It is performed and exists only in this performative mode. More to the point, because it exists only in the 'doing' it is never 'done'. It is never completed but must rather be continually repeated. For example, I never become 'male'. I just keep on 'becoming' male or, rather, I keep on 'doing' my masculinity and 'my masculinity' consists entirely in this process of doing. This is what is meant by performativity.

This can be a difficult concept to comprehend. To get a grip on it one might try to imagine what would be left of gender, or say of femininity, if the actions associated with it were stripped away. Butler's argument, in effect, is that there would be nothing left recognizable as gender if we did this. In common with a number of post-structuralist critics and critics of metaphysics, she believes that western thought has been hampered by a problematic tendency of imputing essences or forms behind appearances, depths behind surfaces. Against this, to reiterate, she maintains that surface acts and expressions are not expressions of something deeper or essential. Rather, they are the very doing of that which they 'express'.

In the discussions that this way of conceptualizing gender has generated, a key theme which has emerged has been the degree of 'choice' involved in the performativity of gender. Butler links her conception to a form of feminist politics which, as one might imagine, centres upon the possibility of disrupting and subverting gender performances. Gender norms can be challenged and transformed in Butler's view and much of her work is devoted to emphasizing this and exploring certain examples of it. Nevertheless, some appropriations of her work have been criticized for misconstruing her conception of performativity in a humanist fashion, so as to refocus it, inappropriately, around the concept of 'choice'. We perform our genders, according to Butler, but we do not choose to. Two points are important here.

Firstly, just as Butler seeks to challenge the notion that there exists a substantive gender behind the various performances of gender, the former being expressed through the latter, so too she opposes the notion of a substantive agent or subject existing independently of or behind their 'acts'. There is no substantive subject or agent lying behind action, for Butler. Rather, the agent or subject is coterminous with and produced by and through their actions. They too are 'performative'. She generally elaborates this by marking out a distinction between 'performance' and 'performativity':

> . . . it is important to distinguish performance from performativity: the former presumes a subject, but the latter contests the very notion of a subject. (1994: 33)

Many appropriations of her work have confused these two, Butler continues, and have consequently arrived at an overly voluntaristic account of gender. They have assumed that agents in some way knowingly 'perform' gender, acting out a role or 'putting on' a 'performance', and they have further assumed, by implication, that agents can change their gender by dint of an unproblematic choice. This is not what is meant by 'performativity'. Insofar as there is choice, for Butler, 'performativity' precedes it and escapes its immediate purview, operating at a pre-reflective, pre-conscious level. I do not think that this excludes the possibility of choice for Butler, or indeed the possibility of (feminist) choices about gender. She would insist, however, that choice itself is a 'performance', such that performance always precedes choice, and she would also assumedly insist both that the performativity of gender generally eludes conscious reflection and would prove a 'stubborn' object for change or transformation.

Secondly, Butler argues that performances of gender are shaped by what she refers to in *Gender Trouble* as the 'heterosexual matrix', a matrix of discourse and power within society, akin to the ensembles of power/knowledge described by Foucault (see **power/knowledge**),[151] which categorizes individuals sexually, prescribing the ways in which they must act and enforcing those prescriptions in a variety of ways. The precise nature of this heterosexual matrix is not spelt out in very much detail by Butler but it is evident that the practices and discourses she is referring to extend from the everyday to more specialized, scientific and artistic forms of representation and control. It is by dint of the power of this 'heterosexual matrix' which begins work on the performances of individuals from the moment of birth and perhaps even before (as parents prepare to bring a child of a specific gender into the world), that performances of gender take shape independently of choice. Social agents perform their gender without even realizing that they are doing so. Moreover, they may have learnt to perform certain aspects of their gender before they have even learnt how to choose. In her later work Butler deliberately drops the term 'heterosexual matrix' because, she claims, it sounds too static and immovable (see Butler, 1994). She replaces it with the concept of 'heterosexual hegemony'. This concept arguably allows more leeway for change, since 'hegemony' is a historical specific and achieved balance of power which must be continually reproduced and nurtured (see **hegemony**). However, the basic point is the same. Gender is performed within the context of relations of power which shape and constrain it in various ways.

The main elements of this concept of 'performativity' were introduced by Butler in *Gender Trouble* (Butler, 1990). Since that book she has developed the concept in a number of ways (see Lloyd, 1999; Bell, 1999). Two are particularly noteworthy. First, she has developed the concept through a more sustained engagement with psychoanalytic theory and what we might call 'philosophical psychologies' of power (for example, the Hegelian account of the master/slave dialectic (Hegel, 1979) and Nietzsche's (1967) reflections on conscience) (Butler, 1993, 1997a). The

---

151 Butler's work is very strongly influenced by Foucault, especially her earlier work – where she outlines the concept of the heterosexual matrix.

precise status of these other theories in relation to her own remains unclear. However, what Butler seems to be attempting to draw from these theories is a more extended account of the manner in which relations of power invest and construct human subjectivity and, by the same token, how relations of power assume a subjective form. This development, though often difficult to pin down, allows Butler considerable scope for distancing her position from the overly voluntaristic caricature painted by some of her critics. She effectively explores the psychological dynamics that, in her view, drive the repetitious reproduction of gender. The second line of development in Butler's work has been to return, in a more focused way, to the 'performative' account of speech acts offered by the British philosopher, John Austin[152] (1971), in his *How To Do Things With Words*, and the various critical developments of that account that are to be found in the work of Jacques Derrida and Pierre Bourdieu (Butler, 1997b). Derrida's essay on Austin seems a likely source of inspiration for Butler's own use of the term, 'performativity', although she does not address Austin and his somewhat more specific notion of 'performative utterances' until her more recent work. In this more recent work Butler has begun to engage with the various implications of the notion that speech is an act. In particular she has sought to problematize certain strains of feminist argument which call for greater legal restriction on pornography (and the expression of racist views) on the grounds that these speech acts are indeed 'acts' and not simply expressions of views. The context for much of this debate is the US constitution whose First Amendment, crudely put, provides for the right of free speech. If pornography is more than simply free speech, the argument follows, then it cannot be defended under the First Amendment and legal restriction of it may therefore be constitutional. Butler's critical analysis of this line of argument is complex. An integral part of her argument, however, focuses upon the way in which declarations of homosexuality are prohibited in the US military on what seems to be much the same grounds, namely, that saying one is homosexual is itself a homosexual act.

This later work on speech and censorship represents, in certain respects, a shift in Butler's use of the term 'performativity'. As noted

---

152 Although Butler's (1997b) *Excitable Speech* admittedly comes closer, on my reading of both her early work and the work of Austin, these two philosophers use the concept 'performative' in very different ways, for very different purposes and thereby give it a very different meaning. The main thrust of Austin's work, as the above-mentioned title of his book suggests, is the argument that words do not merely describe the world but, in the context of their exchange, 'do' things. 'I proclaim this parliament open', assuming that it is uttered by a head of state, for example, has the effect of opening parliament.

above, she seems to move closer to the earlier philosophical uses of the term that are to be found in Austin (albeit whilst remaining critical of Austin). In addition, it also marks a more decisive engagement, on her part, with normative[153] theorizing. Nevertheless, this context also proves to be an interesting terrain for exploring the implications of the 'performative' approach, and warning (as Butler has throughout all of her work) against oversimplistic appropriations of the concept. As Butler shows, a 'gung ho' adaptation of the notion of 'performativity' can lead one in a normative direction that one may not wish to go.

The concept of performativity is clearly a very thought provoking and interesting one. What degree of originality Butler can claim for this view of gender is an open question but even as she revisits older critiques she invests a new energy and insight into them. To my mind the key problems with the concept are, firstly, that its details tend to be fleshed out only by way of detailed philosophical/literary exegesis,[154] such that they are far from clear and, in my view, can only appeal to the authority of philosophy (Hegel or Nietzsche for example) for their own authority. We are encouraged to accept a theory as true because it can be inferred from the writings of Freud, Foucault, Lacan, Hegel or Nietzsche. Critical theory effectively becomes a self-referential philosophical game, insulated from the demand for empirical testing or verification. This is problematic given that the concept claims to offer us a purchase upon an empirical domain – gender and the lives of women. Secondly, it is by no means clear that the various philosophical authorities Butler cites can be coherently combined, at least without a considerable amount of argument (which she does not offer). At the very least, for example, her respective engagements with both Hegel and psychoanalysis appear to run contrary to the more Foucauldian aspects of her work. Foucault was, after all, very critical of both Hegelianism and psychoanalysis.

### FURTHER READING

Like many post-structuralist writers Butler is notoriously difficult to read. And as in the case of many post-structuralist writers I believe that this is not due to the complexity of her ideas but rather to her involvement in

153 That is, theory which makes moral claims and posits theoretical justifications for those claims.

154 That is to say, Butler appears to make empirical claims about the world but then rather than referring to studies which have investigated the world in a systematic fashion, or conducting such work herself, she seeks out verification through a process of interpreting works of literature or philosophy.

a specific philosophical 'game' wherein clarity is disvalued and pretension and (pseudo) profundity admired. Having said that, there is a very good interview with Butler in the *Radical Philosophy* magazine (1994, issue 67, pages 32–9), where she discusses the key ideas from *Gender Trouble* and *Bodies That Matter* in a fairly straightforward manner, addressing the sorts of objections and questions that philosophers and theorists from outside of the post-structuralist camp are inclined to raise. In addition, there is a good special issue of the journal *Theory, Culture and Society* (1999, 16(2)), edited by Vicki Bell, which contains some interesting and again relatively clear and well written articles on the concept of performativity (there is also a further interview with Butler which discusses some of her work written after *Bodies That Matter*).

# Power

---

> *Related concepts:* **body-power/bio-power, ideology, power/knowledge.**

Virtually every school of critical social theory (and many others besides) posits a theory of power. There are far too many competing theories and concepts for me to offer even an overview here. There is a useful distinction to be drawn, however, between theories which focus primarily upon 'who' questions and those which focus primarily upon 'how' questions, that is, between theories which address the question of who has power and theories which focus upon the question of how 'power', as a property of social relationships, is generated.

### HOW VS WHO

Some advocates of the 'how' camp, who have also sought to criticize 'who' theories (for example, Foucault, 1982) have argued that the 'who' question naively assumes power to be a resource or capacity which some agents possess and others do not. Power, as conceived in this straw model, is a fixed capacity which enables an agent or set of agents to impose their will on another agent or set of agents, with or without the consent of the latter. It is defined as a capacity to secure given outcomes (see also

Hindess, 1982). Against this it is argued that attempts at subjugation, control and/or the imposition of will are always subject to potentially innovative acts of resistance by seemingly 'weak' groups who, under favourable conditions, can succeed in either blocking the actions of the 'powerful' or at least forcing some sort of compromise, such that talk of 'power' as a fixed 'capacity' is inappropriate. Whether or not 'powerful' groups succeed in imposing their will is not a matter of any 'capacity' on their own behalf but rather of their relationships to and interactions with 'powerless' groups – who, it turns out, are never completely powerless. Outcomes depend upon the reaction and strategies of subordinated groups, the conditions under which agents struggle at a particular time, the 'social space'[155] in which they are struggling, the intervention (or not) of third parties and so on. Barry Hindess (1982) cites the resistance of the Vietcong to the United States as one example of this. Prior to the Vietnam war, he argues, one might have regarded the military power of the United States as absolute, such that they had the capacity to impose their will upon whatever nation they wished, overthrowing and dominating less powerful states. The actual practice of war, however, was by no means so straightforward. The Americans were out-manoeuvred in Vietnam and undermined by western protest such that, in effect, their power was anything but a fixed capacity to secure their will. The Vietnam war was an 'arena of struggle' in which any number of contingencies beyond the control of the Americans came into play and affected their chances of imposing their will. The concept of power, Hindess concludes, needs to be rethought in terms of this concept of arenas of struggle. The notion of power as a possession or fixed capacity is simply unrealistic.

214

Vietnam is admittedly an exceptional case and should not detract us from recognizing the existence of relatively stabilized situations of domination in which one group tends to come off better in its interactions with another group. However, even if exceptional it serves to remind us that 'outcomes' are dependent upon both the ways in which agents act and interact and the balance of a variety of factors in their field of interaction or 'arena of struggle'. Insofar as one can talk of 'power' from this more critical point of view it is not a capacity of any one agent or group but is 'relational', a property of the relationships between agents or groups and an effect of their interactions.

---

155 The outcomes possible within a 'legal battle', for example, are different from those of a 'media battle', a war or an industrial conflict. Any 'arena of struggle', as Hindess (1982) refers to these social spaces, is limited in the range of outcomes possible within it.

Norbert Elias (1978) develops a very similar idea to this in his sociology. Whenever two or more people interact, he notes, each affects the action of the other in some way. In this respect all social relationships are power relationships. Furthermore, as each party to a relationship can affect the actions of any other, power is not held by one party or another but rather consists in the balance or ratio between parties, a ratio which may change over time. To give an example used by Elias, a newly born child, though very much dependent upon its parents and thus subject to their power, can exert considerable influence upon their behaviour, not least because they love it and want it to be happy. To that extent it too has power. Moreover, as it grows up the power balance will change. It will become less dependent upon its parents and they might even become dependent upon it – although note that they will not become powerless if this does happen as the child's love for its parents will generate a lever through which they can influence it. At any one point the balance will tend to lie in one party's favour but it is always a balance and is always conditional upon factors which might change.

## BLURRED BOUNDARIES

This is an important line of criticism but we need to be careful in our appropriation of it, (Elias is, but others are not). It tends to caricature 'who' theories of power, simplifying and misrepresenting their position. Not all 'who' theorists have a naïve 'capacity-outcome' model of power. Indeed, they may have a relational concept. Many Marxist theories of power, for example, are preoccupied with demonstrating that, sometimes contrary to appearances, power is 'concentrated in the hands' of the bourgeoisie. The bourgeoisie 'have' power in Marxist accounts. The very definition of 'bourgeoisie' is relational, however. The bourgeoisie are defined by their relationship to the means of production and, via the means of production, to the proletariat (see **social class**). The 'power of the bourgeoisie', as discussed by Marxists, is therefore often shorthand for 'the power emerging out of the relationship between (and constitutive of) the bourgeoisie and the proletariat, which allows members of the bourgeoisie, in many instances, to impose their will upon the proletariat'. It is clear why one might sometimes opt for the shorthand! Furthermore, Marxist writers generally believe that the proletariat, when they become conscious of their position and band together in an effort to overthrow capitalism, will be successful in doing so. In this respect 'the power' of the bourgeoisie is conditional upon the fragmentation and false consciousness of the proletariat, such that talk of 'the power of the bourgeoisie' is, again, shorthand for a conditional and contingent balance of conditions in their relationship with the proletariat which is (at least as far as Marxists are concerned) relatively durable in the short-term but temporary in the longer term. Finally, we should note that 'who' theories of power are often attempts to go beyond the basic (relational) mechanisms of power, to explore the interests served by those mechanisms, often contrary to appearances. They claim, for example, that contrary to its claim to neutrality and democracy, the state often serves the interests of elite groups in society. The power of the state may well be relational from this point of view, that is to say, dependent upon the legitimation bestowed upon it and the obedience to it by 'the people', and so on. But the point is that the reserve of power generated in these relations is then more easily accessed by some groups than others or perhaps automatically serves the interests of some groups over others. To use the example of the power of the bourgeoisie again, claims that this social class 'have power' are often shorthand contractions of a more sophisticated claim that the relational practices constitutive of the state tend to function to support the interests of the bourgeoisie – perhaps because politicians and top civil servants tend to be recruited from amongst the ranks of the bourgeoisie, perhaps because of the very form of the state itself and the wider structural constraints within which it operates.

It would make sense to briefly unpack the 'who' and 'how' theories of power a little more by reference to the main claims of a key representative of each. To this end I will outline the key claims of Steven Lukes (1974, 1986), on one side, and Michel Foucault (1979, 1982, 1984) on the other.

## LUKES' 3-D WHO APPROACH

Steven Lukes is an important representative of the 'who' tradition of power theory. In an introduction to an edited collection on power published in 1986 he defines the central questions of power analysis and in each case this is a 'who' question – 'Who can adversely affect the interests of whom?', 'Who can control whom?', 'Who can secure the achievement of *collective goods*?' (1986: 9–13). Furthermore, in a very useful and important text from 1974 he develops what he calls a three-dimensional methodology for power analysis (again focused upon 'who' questions), which he contrasts with earlier 'two' and 'one-dimensional' methodologies. Each of the methodologies focuses upon decision-making bodies who are sanctioned to pass binding decisions (for example, within a nation, locality, organization, and so on) and the decisions they arrive at.

Each varies, however, in the approach it adopts. The one-dimensional approach, which Lukes associates with the work of Dahl (1961), focuses only upon those decisions reached by decision-making bodies and upon the interested parties who have expressed an opinion relevant to the decision. In essence, the researcher considers who has expressed what opinions in relevant policy forums and compares this against the final decisions reached by the policy-making body in question, searching for systematic bias. The results of such studies, Lukes argues, often serve to support 'pluralist' theories of power, that is, theories which claim that power is distributed through a wide range of groups in society, rather than a select elite. In most cases there is no one single group who benefit from even the majority of decisions taken. The outcome of such studies is an artefact of the methodology adopted according to Lukes, however, and he therefore calls for a more sophisticated methodology. The two-dimensional approach, which Lukes associates with the work of Bacharac and Baratz (1970), is better in his view. Rather than focusing only upon decisions which have been made, this approach focuses equally upon potential decisions, posited by various agents and groups, which do not make it onto the decision-maker's agenda. When these non-decisions or suppressed possibilities are taken into account, Lukes argues, the evidence tends to point more in the direction of 'elite' theories of power, that is, theories which suggest that power is concentrated in the hands of a specific group or groups. Studies like that of Bacharac and Baratz suggest that some groups are systematically advantaged relative to others in terms of the policies and decisions of official decision-making agencies. There is much greater homogeneity in the interest base served by the exclusion of issues from decision-makers' agendas than we find in relation to decisions actually taken. In his three-dimensional approach Lukes seeks to advance this one step further. Both one and two-dimensional approaches are locked into a behaviourist-positivist model of research practice, he notes, and as such work strictly with 'observables'.[156] Bacharac and Baratz are only prepared to speak of non-decisions, for example, in cases where they have been able to observe evidence of opinions aired which have not made their way onto official agendas. It is often assumed, Lukes observes, that scientific analysis can only work with observables and that to invoke non-observables is necessarily to give way to speculation or fancy. This is not so. Power analysis can and should work with non-observables. As an

---

156 Positivist philosophies of science argue that concepts which do not refer to observable (and often measurable) entities are strictly meaningless. For further discussion of this claim and its problems see the entry on **realism**.

example he cites work by Crenson (1971) which examines levels of environmental/anti-pollution protest in American towns, comparing those towns whose chief polluter was a large firm which was the major employer in the town and had a reputation for its power, with those towns whose chief polluter was one amongst a number of employers and/or had a lesser reputation for power. Each of the towns had equal cause to be concerned about pollution and the environment, Lukes argues, and there was no visible evidence of environmental issues being knocked off political agendas, but the study indicated that protest was much less evident (if evident at all) in those towns where the chief polluter was also the single major employer and enjoyed a powerful reputation. Lukes interprets this as an indication of the power of major employers to reduce, if not eliminate, all observable traces of protest or dissent – perhaps unintentionally by the force of their reputation alone. In other words, the very fact that nobody protests or visibly dissents, in conditions where otherwise they would, indicates the hidden, non-observable workings of power. This is the essence of Lukes' three-dimensional approach to power. Or rather his approach incorporates all three of the dimensions just outlined. It focuses upon decisions reached, suppressed agenda items and invisible restraints upon the airing of opinions. This approach is more likely still to point to a concentration of power into the hands of a few and thus to support an elite model.

Totalitarian states, such as the world conjured up in George Orwell's *1984* offer a useful thought experiment that further exemplifies Lukes' point. There is very little visible resistance to such regimes, such that the two-dimensional power researcher might be inclined to conclude that they are quite consensual and show little evidence of elite formation. The truth, however, is that the threat of repressive sanction, combined with their means of ideological persuasion or mystification, quell resistance – often before it has begun. There are problems with the 3-D approach. The concept of 'interests', for example, raises many difficulties (see Hindess, 1982). My aim here, however, has simply been to lay out one strong example of the 'who' approach.

## FOUCAULT'S HOW APPROACH

The key contemporary representive of the 'how' approach is Foucault. Like Lukes, Foucault is critical of the liberal and democratic pretensions of modern western societies. In contrast to Lukes, however, he turns his focus away from the activities of decision-making bodies to focus upon the 'micro-mechanisms' of power which operate, often unperceived, in everyday life and which, in his view, underpin the liberal order. Modern western societies can afford to give their citizens freedom of speech and rights of assembly and suffrage, he argues, because the basic preconditions of order are secured at a grassroots level by a network of practices and institutions which mould individuals as efficient and effective citizens, workers, parents, children, and so on.

Underlying this is a conception of power very different from that of Lukes. Power, for Foucault, is the effect of a variety of different types of social 'technologies' or 'techniques' which function to administer, regulate and mould human beings in a variety of ways – albeit often prompting resistance. Just as societies or the agents within them invent new ways of, for example, producing and transporting material goods, so too they invent new ways, and new rationales[157] for managing and organizing human beings such as new 'technologies of power'. Thus societies at different times manifest different technologies of power, as indeed they manifest different productive technologies.

This is very evident in *Discipline and Punish* where Foucault (1979) traces the transition in modes or technologies of power from the ancien régime into modern societies, focusing specifically upon what he calls 'disciplinary' technologies of power. I do not have the space to elaborate upon this mode of power here but a few points of contrast will briefly illustrate the gist of Foucault's argument. Firstly, where power in the ancien régime worked by means of its own visibility (for example, in the form of large castles and churches, public ceremonies and public execution and torture), effectively threatening those subject to it with violence and force, disciplinary power works by making those subject to it visible. It entails surveillance and is achieved by way of techniques, specifically forms of architecture and spatio-temporal organization, which individuate the masses and render them observable. This renders individuals more knowable and thus more controllable and, at the same time, insofar as they are aware of and internalize the surveillance mechanism, it encourages self-policing and self-regulation. Secondly, and related to this, where power in the ancien régime was bound up with religious knowledge and legitimation, power in modern societies is intimately bound up with the human sciences (see **power/knowledge**).

---

157 Foucault's work on power grows out of his research on the history of (human) science (see **power/knowledge**) and, as such, is very much focused upon the ideas and forms of rationality embodied in different types of social practice (that is, different technologies of power). The idea of 'forms of rationality' is derived from the work of Gaston Bachelard, whose approach to the history of science suggests that different sciences, at different points in this development, manifest distinct, localized forms of rationality.

Thirdly, where power in the ancien régime was overwhelmingly 'negative', in the sense that it focused upon prohibitions and served to punish (sometimes by death) those who transgressed these prohibitions, power in the modern era is generally 'positive'. It is less focused upon punishing wrong-doing, more focused upon cultivating desired forms of behaviour. It entails numerous régimes and techniques of 'training' which nurture efficient and compliant beings. Indeed, even where it is forced to confront transgression and disobedience it does so with 'punishments' which rehabilitate more than they 'hurt'. For example, an individual who does something wrong is required, by way of punishment, to repeat the act over and over again in the correct way, until the correct way is instilled as a habit. Finally (at least for our purposes),[158] where power in the ancien régime rested in the person of the monarch, power in the modern régime is dispersed throughout the social body in a capillary network, functioning at the mundane level of everyday life. The disciplinary mechanisms that Foucault identifies are to be found, for example, in schools, army barracks, prisons, hospitals, lunatic asylums, and even beyond these institutional barriers in the ways in which we all deal with each other in our personal lives. In political reality, Foucault argues, we 'cut off the head of the king' more than two centuries ago, that is to say, we replaced the absolute power of the king with a more impersonal and administrative form of power, which controls everybody and has no centralized source or 'holder'. Political theory still tends towards 'sovereign' models of power, however, and it is time that we cut off the head of the king in theory too, recognizing power as a relational effect of a network of localized social practices which shape the conduct of everybody but belong to nobody.

Foucault draws the starkest contrast between modern (disciplinary) and ancient forms of power at the very start of *Discipline and Punish*, where he contrasts two punishment régimes, separated by only 80 years, on either side of the French revolution. The history of forms of power, he seems to suggest, is subject to radical ruptures just like the history of sciences (see **epistemological break**). Much of the analysis in the book suggests that the various elements comprising disciplinary power had different and sometimes much longer historical trajectories, however, and Foucault is keen to emphasize the contingent basis upon which these elements came together. There is no 'big story' about functional necessity

---

158 The list could go on, not least as Foucault formulates his concept of disciplinary power, differently, in a number of different contexts. My purpose here is merely to give a flavour of the way in which he develops the idea of 'technologies of power'.

---

or historical dialectics to explain disciplinary power. Just a story of local events and chance occurrences. Furthermore, though the time period studied by Foucault hinges upon the French revolution (of 1789) he refuses to read the emergence of discipline as a consequence of the revolution – except to say that discipline is very much characteristic and indeed constitutive of the post-revolutionary order. 'Liberty, fraternity and equality' are possible only at the price of discipline but neither they nor the needs of the liberal society which valorizes them 'explain' discipline.

Disciplinary power may work more to the advantage of some than others, Foucault admits. It may even be used by 'ruling' groups. But it cannot be reduced to an account of powerful groups. We must explain power from the bottom up. Discipline was not invented or imposed by powerful groups. It emerged at the ground level and, if anything, perhaps erected the basis of order upon which dominant groups emerged. Furthermore, removing 'elites' by way, for example, of a revolutionary seizure of the state and production processes, will do little to change relations of power if disciplinary mechanisms remain in place. Indeed, the state socialist societies characteristic of Eastern Europe during the mid-twentieth century were as much, if not more 'disciplinary societies' than the capitalist societies of the west.

The theories of Lukes and Foucault are so different, in my view, that it makes little sense to ask which of the two is better or more correct. Each is problematic and invites further investigation but each asks a very different question of power, and from the point of view of a critical social theory there is no reason to suppose that either question should be privileged (in all cases) over the other. As with so many conceptual disagreements in social science, the preference for one over the other must be determined by the purpose at hand.

## FURTHER READING

Both Lukes and Foucault are relatively clear and straightforward to read. The key reference for Lukes is his (1974) *Power: A Radical View*. For Foucault see his *Discipline and Punish* (Foucault, 1979), *Power/Knowledge* (Foucault, 1980a) and perhaps also 'The subject and power' (Foucault, 1982), which deals with the who/how question most straightforwardly. For a very good overview of theories of power see Clegg's (1989) *Frameworks of Power* or Westwood's (1999) *Power and the Social*. Hindess' (1982) paper, 'Power, interests and the outcome of struggles', is a useful reference on the who/how question and Elias' (1978) discussion of power in *What is Sociology?* is a useful contribution also.

# Power/Knowledge

Related concepts: **body-power/bio-power, discourse, epistemological break, ideology, power.**

The concept of power/knowledge is formulated in the work of Michel Foucault. It is intended to designate the manner in which specific forms of power and specific forms of knowledge, characteristic of the modern era, interact in a mutually reinforcing manner. Foucault writes about this in the middle period of his writing, primarily in *Discipline and Punish* (Foucault, 1979) and the essays and lectures comprising the *Power/Knowledge* collection (Foucault, 1980a). Certain of the ideas captured in the concept are explored in his earlier work, however, particularly *Madness and Civilization* (Foucault, 1965) and *Birth of the Clinic* (Foucault, 1973).

To grasp the concept of power/knowledge it is essential to begin by recognizing that Foucault's early work was rooted in the tradition of the history and philosophy of science, particularly as shaped (in the French context) by the work of Gaston Bachelard (1970, 1984, 2002) and Georges Canguilhem (1991). Like these writers, Foucault was concerned to trace the history, or perhaps pre-history, of specific scientific discourses, focusing in many cases upon the ruptures or breaks which punctuate the trajectory of these discourses (see **epistemological break**). Unlike Bachelard, whose primary focus is physics, however, Foucault is focused upon the human sciences. And unlike Canguilhem, whose focus is biological and medical science (although see Canguilhem, (1980), Foucault's remit within 'human science' often extends to the more 'social' and epistemologically/politically controversial human sciences. In addition to medicine (Foucault, 1973), he studies psychiatry (Foucault, 1965), sexology (Foucault, 1984) and the social sciences more generally (Foucault, 1970, 1979).

The history of human science is clearly a history of discourse and the underlying schemas of classification and 'historical a priori'[159] which

---

159 'A priori' truths are those whose truth value is believed to be logically or rationally necessary – usually because they deal with what is true by definition (e.g. 2+2=4) and not

shape them. Thus, in *The Order of Things* we find Foucault (1970) examining transformations in the deep categorical schemas, what he calls the 'episteme',[160] of western culture. Shifts at this level, he argues, gave rise to the concept of 'man' as a centring principle of knowledge and this was an essential precondition for the emergence of the sciences of man. Furthermore, again following Bachelard, Foucault emphasizes that specific discourses constitute their objects, and he seeks in various ways to examine the manner in which discursive shifts and disjunctures facilitate such processes of constitution.

Discursive shifts alone do not explain the rise and history of the human sciences according to Foucault, however. On one hand, a point we will return to later, he follows Bachelard in maintaining that knowledge presupposes specific techniques and technologies of investigation – what Bachelard (1984) calls 'phenomeno-technics'. These techniques and technologies embody discourses and localized forms of rationality but at the same time they extend and reconfigure 'the gaze' of the scientist. They facilitate new and different perceptions of the world, allowing the objects of discourse to be perceived and measured in various ways. The obvious examples from natural science are microscopes, telescopes, dissection techniques, thermometers, barometers and ECG scanners. On the other hand, drawing more upon Canguilhem, Foucault focuses upon the social problems and issues which bring potential objects of scientific inquiry into focus. In *The Normal and the Pathological*, Canguilhem (1991) made the point that medicine only developed because human beings experience bodily disorder and present themselves as such, that is, because people sometimes feel sick or experience pain. Medicine and biology, in this respect, are tied to the everyday world. They do not arise out of idle curiosity or abstract meditation but rather in response to perceived and experienced problems. In Foucault we find this point extended to the social realm. He shows that and how social problems generate potential objects for social scientific analysis.

To give an example, 'madness' did not become an object of scientific

---

dependent upon empirical observation or fact. Generally these truths are assumed to be universal; that is, true at all times and in all places, irrespectively of whether people recognize them as such. Bachelard (2002) in particular challenges this, however. Einstein's physics challenges many truths believed formally to be a priori, he argues, and effects a shift in rationality which forces us to concede that even 'a priori' truths are historical in nature. Foucault seizes upon this in his own work.

160 The term 'episteme' is generally reserved in philosophy to designate rationally and rigorously derived knowledge, and is contrasted with the 'doxa', which is common opinion (see **doxa**). The fact that Foucault elects to study historical shift in the episteme indicates, I suggest, his commitment to the idea that even the most fundamental truths are historical.

---

knowledge until such a time as it became a social problem. The first stage of this process, what Foucault calls 'The great confinement',[161] involved the mad as just one element in a heterogenous grouping of 'undesirables' being locked away in large houses of confinement, on account of the threat they posed to the newly emerging social order of the late middle ages. Society was changing and, as a consequence, groups who had previously blended in and fitted no longer did so. In the context of these houses of confinement, however, the specific difficulties posed by the mad stood out from the rest, such that they began to emerge as a distinct (adminstrative) category. It is against this backdrop, Foucault (1961) argues, that they emerged as an object of scientific analysis. They become a visible problem which calls for a solution.

A similar point might be made about any of a number of early developments in empirical[162] social science and this is one crucial dimension of interaction between power and knowledge. Possible objects of social scientific knowledge often emerge against the backdrop of social problems which, in turn, are problems of social order and control, that is, problems of 'power'. In the *Archaeology of Knowledge*, Foucault (1972) refers to these contexts as 'surfaces of emergence'.

A further point to note here is that the process of locking up the mad in houses of confinement functioned simultaneously as a technique for controlling the mad, a 'technology of power', and a way of making them observable in significant numbers and under controlled conditions, such that they could become an object of study and knowledge. This would be true even if the mad were simply locked up as a way of keeping them off the streets. However, Foucault extends the point in two respects. Firstly, he notes that the rational administration and control of the mad within public institutions came increasingly to depend upon the separation of different types and degrees of madness, thus creating a need for new

---

161 'The great confinement' was arguably specific to France. Andrew Scull (1993), for example, notes that, though the beginnings of confinement were noticable in England at the time Foucault is referring to, the English Civil War put an end to any such grand 'top down' political initiatives. Consequently confinement of the mad in Britain began with the development of very small private madhouses, only later giving way to a very large system of public asylums (Scull, 1993; Porter, 1987; Busfield, 1989). Although this point is significant it does not detract from the general outline of Foucault's argument.

162 Nikolas Rose (1985), who applies these principles to the history of psychology, makes the point that it is specifically empirical disciplines that develop in this way. One can, he notes, trace the history of theoretical speculation about the nature of human beings back into the depths of human history for as far as one wishes and one will not necessarily always be able to tie these down to the same 'political' conditions in the same way – although, of course, much philosophical speculation on human beings has been motivated by historical problems and events.

schemas of classification and measurement. These schemas functioned within the administrative régime as an organizational principle (power) but they also laid the foundation stones for later schemes of psychiatric categorization (knowledge). Secondly, Foucault argues that power in the modern era is increasingly based upon surveillance (see **power, body-power/bio-power**). Power works by making individuals visible such that they can be corrected when they step out of line and such that, aware of this surveillance, they come increasingly to police their own conduct. Again power and knowledge work in a harmonious relationship here, since the surveillance techniques that make individuals visible serve simultaneously to control those individuals and to make them possible objects of knowledge. This is one of the key points in Foucault's (1979) famous analysis of the Panopticon.[163] The Panopticon is at once a machine for making people knowable and rendering them controllable. And the same basic point applies to the many wider instances of 'panopticism'[164] he refers to. One might argue, for example, that early (questionnaire) 'surveys' of the populations of western Europe were simultaneously tools of administrative control and the databases of the newly emerging social sciences. Even when the pioneers of social science did not administer these surveys themselves they drew upon them as databases and it was arguably the existence of these databases, derived from attempts to administer the population more effectively, which made the social sciences possible as empirical disciplines.

We should refer back to Bachelard here. I noted above that Bachelard claims that new technologies which reconfigure our ways of looking at the world or objects within it (what he calls 'phenomeno-technics') play a crucial part in the constitution of objects within science. Foucault is making the same point about questionnaires, public institutions and architectural designs. They make human beings visible in a fashion inaccessible to 'the human eye' before that time, thereby constituting

163 The Panopticon was a prison design, drawn up by the well-known philosopher and prison reformer, Jeremy Bentham. Had it been built it would have allowed firstly, a guard in a central watchtower to observe any prisoner at any time, without the prisoner knowing whether they were actually being watched at that time or being able to return the gaze, and secondly, a prison inspector to enter the prison and view the conditions in which the prisoners were being kept within a matter of minutes, thus effectively keeping prison staff under surveillance too (concern about mistreatment in madhouses, prisons and workhouses was rife at the time). The Panopticon was never built, as such, but the plans for many prisons and public buildings of the eighteenth and nineteenth centuries, which were built, incorporated its central principles. In addition, Foucault is interested in it because, in his view, it captures perfectly the 'rationale' of the main techniques of control of the day.
164 Panopticism is the term Foucault uses to capture the general emphasis upon surveillance and self-surveillance in techniques of power. See the point above.

human beings as objects in new ways which, in turn, facilitate new forms of analysis and knowledge. His point, however, is that in the case of the human sciences these phenomeno-technics are also intimately interwoven with power. They are techniques of power. The prison, like the madhouse, simultaneously renders its inmates knowable and controllable, and in both cases it does so by making them visible and keeping them captive.

The relationship between power and knowledge is a two-way street for Foucault, however. It is not simply that strategies and technologies of power facilitate and generate knowledge. At the same time knowledge becomes the basis and principle of power. On one level, for example, the scientific study of human variation gives rise to statistical norms which, in turn, often become 'moral' norms which inform controlling interventions. Nikolas Rose's (1985, 1989) important work on the history of British psychology, for example, notes that the measurement of human beings by psychologists –in the form of IQ tests, stages of development, personality tests, and so on – gave rise to various 'norms' against which we are still compared today, with deviants being duly subject to intervention and treatment. Strategies of power, in this respect, are not free floating. They find their rationale in the human sciences and are tied to the specifications (for example, of norms) formulated in the human sciences.

This is a generalizable point, for Foucault, and forms part of what he calls 'régimes of truth' (Foucault, 1980b). Where power in some societies is bound to religious forms of truth, he argues, power in modern western societies functions through science. It is subordinated to and subordinates its subjects to the demands of scientific knowledge and truth. The 'mad' are treated, in modern societies, for example, on the grounds that they are 'ill', that is to say, psychiatric discourses provide both a principle through which we perceive particular experiences and behaviours, and a rationale for how we respond to those experiences and behaviours. Another more telling example of this occurs in the contrast between the 'ars erotica' and the 'scientalia sexualis' that Foucault describes in the first volume of his *History of Sexuality* (Foucault, 1984). Where sexuality is thematized in some societies in terms of 'erotic arts' whose aim is maximize sexual pleasure, Foucault notes, western societies have tended to make sex the object of scientific analysis and regulation. Where some societies produce works equivalent to the Karma Sutra, western scientists have been concerned to measure all that can be measured in relation to sex, reducing it to its 'mechanisms' and its scientifically determined function (reproduction), and endeavouring to find ways of bringing those who deviate from these norms into line. In this respect society is scientifically dominated.

The other side of this notion of 'régimes of truth', however, is that particular forms of truth and knowledge are valorized in our society and are kept in their dominant position by means of relations and techniques of power. There are many different frameworks within which knowledge of human beings could be achieved, Foucault observes, but only some of these are sanctioned, legitimated and supported. This might be a matter of divisions in types of knowledge. Science, for example, is generally privileged over other forms of knowledge in our society. However, it may equally work within particular types of knowledge, including sciences. Rose (1985), for example, shows how the fate of different approaches to the study of intelligence in early psychology was determined, to a large extent, by the relative value of those approaches as administrative tools. Administratively useful models were adopted over approaches which had similar or higher intellectual merit but which were not as useful. To this extent, 'truth' is a function of 'power'.

## FURTHER READING

Foucault's work is generally quite easy to follow and interesting. The key texts for this concept are *Discipline and Punish* (Foucault, 1979) and *Power/Knowledge* (Foucault, 1980a). *The Archaeology of Knowledge* (Foucault, 1972) is also interesting and important. A good commentary on certain aspects of Foucault's view of knowledge is Gutting's (1989) *Michel Foucault's Archaeology of Scientific Reason*. Nikolas Rose's work, particularly *The Psychological Complex* (Rose, 1985), provides many examples of the concept of power/knowledge applied in practice.

227

# Public Sphere

Related concepts: **colonization of the lifeworld, discourse, ideal speech situation, system and lifeworld.**

'The public sphere' denotes a space, real or virtual, in which individuals, who otherwise live private lives and have their own private concerns, come together to discuss issues of common concern with the purpose of thrashing out their different views and arriving at a common position. It usually also entails that, in doing this, they generate a pressure for political/legal change by force of either reason or numbers. In this respect, a public sphere is an intermediary between the sphere of the private individual and that of the state. Importantly, however, it is never a part or arm of the state. Many writers who use the concept repeatedly stress that public consultations and debates are only public spheres insofar as they arise from the voluntary initiative of citizens and remain independent of the state. State sponsored consultation exercises and focus group research are not public spheres.

The concept of 'the public sphere' and 'publics' has a long and distinguished history in both philosophy and social science. It has been discussed, directly and indirectly, by a great many important figures. In contemporary debates, however, at least in critical social theory, Jürgen Habermas' (1989) *The Structural Transformation of the Public Sphere*, originally published in Germany in the 1960s, is the usual point of departure for discussion of the concept (although see also Arendt, 1958). In this book, Habermas makes two central claims. The first is that the various social changes of the late eighteenth and nineteenth centuries, in Germany, France and Britain, gave rise, for a short period, to an effective bourgeois public sphere. That is to say, over a relatively brief period, social conditions provoked and facilitated a situation in which large numbers of middle-class men, qua private individuals, came together to engage in reasoned argument over key issues of mutual interest and concern, creating a space in which both new ideas and the practices and discipline of rational public debate were cultivated. The emergence of this new public space, he further claims, both shaped and was shaped by the emergence of a philosophical concept and consciousness of 'publics' and their importance. This is reflected in the work of many key philosophers of the day, including de Tocqueville, Mill, Kant, Hegel and Marx. The second key claim of the book is that conditions effectively served to undermine this public space at almost the moment it came into being, such that the public sphere of the twentieth century – now we might add the twenty-first – is at best problematic and ineffective, if, indeed, it is meaningful to talk of it existing at all.

The dates and precise details of this 'rise and fall' differ between the three national contexts studied by Habermas. However, the general picture is the same in each case. One of the key historical changes facilitating the rise of the public sphere was the increasing differentiation of society and particularly a separation of political authority from what became the private sphere of the individual and domestic family unit.

This was constituted, in part, through the centralization of political power in the national state, a process which made effective political power more remote. The state was 'decoupled', as Habermas (1987a) would later put it, from the intersubjective fabric of everyday life, and indeed also from the normative texture of that fabric. This process, in turn, was greatly enhanced by the separation of state and Church. The reformation effectively freed the state from the moral control of the Church and effected a distinction between the realm of public norms (such as law) and private moral belief. Importantly, this process of differentiation was simultaneous with a large increase in the tax burden imposed by the state (necessitated by an increase in overseas military activity) such that the state was becoming more remote from 'the people' at exactly the same time that it was making greater demands upon them.

This opening gap between the state and its citizens was an important source of pressure for the formation of publics, according to Habermas. The emergence of the state as 'other', simultaneously remote from everyday life and yet impacting and making demands upon it in a multitude of ways, generated a collective demand for accountability. The formation of publics equally presupposes private individuals who come together to form them, however, and, as such, presupposes individualization and privatization of the social agent. This too was increasingly evident in the eighteenth century according to Habermas. At one level he conceives of both home and work as belonging to the newly emerging private realm, since ownership and control of the means of production (in the hands of the newly emerging bourgeois class – see **social class**) were usually fused in the person of a named and known individual (male) who entered into private contracts with his individual workers – a legal arrangement which was itself new. At another level, however, the separation of home and work during the eighteenth century set the scene, particularly amongst the rising bourgeoisie, for an increasing privatization of the family. The family became a private retreat from the 'outside world' and even within the home architecture, increasingly functioned to separate out private from public elements, generating a space in which increasingly privatized individuals and subjectivities could take shape. Finally, Habermas notes that within these private domestic spaces the bourgeoisie were increasingly devoting themselves to projects of self-cultivation. The self was emerging as a cultural theme and individual project. It was against the background of and in contrast to these new manifestations of privacy and individualism that the possibility of publics emerged. Publics were constituted when these newly privatized bourgeois individuals stepped outside of their private sphere to discuss issues of public significance with other private individuals, together forming a new type of collectivity.

In their early forms, publics were largely devoted to literary and artistic criticism. In this respect they were a collective continuation of the above-mentioned projects of self-cultivation. The bourgeoisie were, as Bourdieu (1984) would later note, pursuing their self-formation, cultivation and distinction by way of the constitution of a collective aesthetic sensibility. The famous coffee houses and salons which sprung up in considerable numbers in key urban centres through the course of the eighteenth century were the central locus of these publics.

Once established these publics soon became preoccupied with matters of trade and politics. Literary publics, having established publics as a social form, gave way to political publics. The early, literary publics contributed more than the mere idea of publics to the political forums which followed them, however. Habermas argues that the literary 'jousts', which effectively constituted these publics, functioned to develop and sharpen up the tools of argument which would later be set to work on more political materials. In effect, literary publics gave rise to the rhetorical competence, discipline and 'rules of the game', constitutive of public reason. They were a rationalizing force:

> Public debate was supposed to transform *voluntas* into a *ratio* that in the public competition of private arguments came into being as the consensus about what was practically necessary in the interests of all. (1989: 83, his emphasis)

Having established a taste for and competency at argument in relation to literary reviews, the bourgeoisie were ready to extend the remit of their critical gaze.

The salons were an important social form for the emerging public sphere, but equally important were improvements in printing technologies and the emergence of popular newsletters and journals. Newsletters and journals were an important source of information about the world, which participants in public debate could take as a basis for their arguments and critiques. The prototypes for these journals, Habermas notes, were prompted by the expansion of trade. As trade expanded over greater distances the need for information grew. Traders needed speedy access to the far-flung corners of their various markets and the newsletter emerged to fill this gap. Soon, however, the remit of these newsletters was expanded to include opinions and argument. Along with pamphlets of various sorts, they became the medium through which individuals could express their views and spell out their arguments and critiques. Initially the content of these newsletters was strictly censored by the state. In response to mounting pressure, however, censorship was relaxed and the newsletters became relatively open spaces of debate.

The importance of these developments, for Habermas, is twofold. Firstly, the bourgeois public fostered a critical rationality. They created a space in which the chief operative force was that of the better argument. Secondly, they were important because they were relatively powerful. The ideas generated in these forums had a direct impact upon political life. They created a pressure and a force for change, approximating an ideal to which Habermas subscribes in much of his work, namely, a situation in which the critical reasoning of the public constitutes an effective steering force in both society and polity.

However, the nineteenth-century bourgeois public sphere was only ever an approximation. By the time it had become 'political' it was a predominantly male domain. And it was also predominantly middle class. Furthermore, even in this imperfect form, it was not destined to last.

As when he discusses the emergence of the public sphere, Habermas outlines a range of conditions, too numerous to cover comprehensively here, which have conspired to compromise the public sphere. And as with his account of the emergence of the public sphere, he acknowledges both general trends and regional differences between France, Germany and Britain. For our purposes it will suffice to note three critical factors.

In the first instance, Habermas argues that the sharp delineation of state and society, which formed an essential pre-requisite of the public sphere, qua intermediary between the two, has, if not collapsed, at least become very blurred. The state, as a welfare state, now increasingly intervenes in people's lives, assuming their private concerns and interests as its own. And at the same time, as interest groups have come to occupy an ever greater role within the structure of the state, the state has been infiltrated by a range of private interests. These transformations have various effects, some good but many negative in Habermas' view. Perhaps most important, as he would reiterate in *The Theory of Communicative Action*, the relationship of the individual to the state has increasingly become one of client or consumer of services rather than citizen. Individuals have become dependent upon the state, losing the independence that is central to the citizen role. And by the same route political debate has increasingly lost its political edge by degenerating into utilitarian wrangling over the distribution of resources and private (domestic) interests.

This blurring of state and society has been amplified by a second change. Much of the argument and activity constitutive of the public sphere, having once taken place in society, between private individuals, now takes place within the confines of the state, between professionalized politicians. More to the point, although this may maintain something of the appearance of a public debate, argumentation and debate are now subordinated to the logic of the competition for power between parties. The effect of party-based organization, Habermas argues, is that views tend to be stuck to or strategically manipulated rather than genuinely argued over. Furthermore, the function of argument, at the interface between politicians and their voters, is precisely to win votes rather than engaging the thoughts of voters and, by this means, educating and cultivating them – as the earlier publics had done for their participants. Politics becomes a stage show. This is compounded by the constitution of the electorate. Those who know most about politics, Habermas argues, tend also to know who they will vote for and are inclined to stick with them through thick and thin. The floating voters, who waver and are undecided, also tend to be those least knowledgeable and least interested in politics. And yet these floating voters are precisely the voters whom the politicians are seeking to attract. Consequently debates shift further from the issues and more towards whatever tricks and treats attract the largely disinterested body of floating voters. To use contemporary language, there is a dynamic of 'dumbing down'. Not that tricks and treats work as a means of seducing the politically apathetic. Even in the 1960s there was a noticeable decline in public interest in politics, indicated by, amongst other things, declining electoral turnouts. This fuels the degenerate trend in public political life, for Habermas, but it is also a consequence of it. Although some social groups, particularly those active in civil associations of various kinds, retain an interest in politics, the stage show makes politics less meaningful for many and drives them away from it.

These changes are accompanied, Habermas notes, by a shift in the meaning of public opinion, which has been effected, in large part, by the efforts of professional social scientists. 'Public opinion' is increasingly synonymous with the results of polling surveys (and now 'focus group' research), which politicians use and seek to manipulate for their own ends. There are many problems with these surveys in Habermas' view. Firstly, they are artificial because they solicit 'votes' for pre-determined categories of opinion which may not reflect the categories that those polled would use themselves. Indeed they often induce individuals to select opinions on issues they would not otherwise, and will not subsequently, give thought to. Secondly, they call for an expression of views, seeking out the loudest voice, rather than, as in the public sphere, facilitating a process of discourse in which the 'best argument' can win.

Finally, they treat the loudest voice as a technical variable, rather than engaging it as a moral voice. Here Habermas echoes his forebears, Adorno, Horkheimer and Marcuse, in lamenting the manner in which the 'value neutrality' of positivist social science allows it to become a technical tool in an overly administered society (Adorno et al., 1969; Marcuse, 1968).

Finally, Habermas notes that and how media markets generate problematic dynamics and tendencies within public space. As the mass media began to establish itself as a viable economic market, he argues, it was both hijacked for the purpose of selling goods, via advertising, and became a considerable saleable commodity in its own right. This has meant that public communication, by this means at least, has been moderated by the demands of big business, and it has led to a regressive 'dumbing down' of the level of public debate as editors, ever pursuing new and larger markets, have been inclined to play to the lowest common denominator. Where the early public sphere, as a domain of self-education and cultivation, tended to 'level up', the modern media, in its pursuit of the widest audience, is inclined to 'level down'.

To some degree the thesis of *Structural Transformation* reiterates the pessimism of Habermas' Frankfurt School mentors, and subscribes to their negative view of modern society and subjects – dominated and dumbed down. However, anticipating his own later reflections on the twin currents of modernity, positive and negative, critical and emasculated, his final word is of a world of public life pulled in different directions. The forces of professionalized PR politics and scientized public opinion may have the upper hand in the contemporary world, for Habermas, but they have not completely undermined the forces of rational deliberation and critical argument. This, moreover, is what makes critical theory possible and what makes the presentation of its theses a worthwhile endeavour. The hope behind the project, at a very general level, is that the critical potential of public argument will achieve a wider audience and stimulate the processes of transformation that it calls for, that it will reclaim and reinvigorate the public sphere, as a first step in a wider process of emancipatory social change.

Since the publication of his classic study, Habermas has revisited the concept of the public sphere many times, refining and revising it. Similarly, many social scientists, from different disciplines and theoretical persuasions, have offered critiques and revisions (see Calhoun, 1994; Crossley and Roberts, 2004). In particular Habermas has been criticized for firstly focusing exclusively upon bourgeois publics and thus ignoring both other types of public and the plurality of publics, secondly, for being too prescriptive and overly rationalist (with a monistic conception of rationality)[165] in his conception of public debate, and thirdly, for failing to elaborate sufficiently upon the institutional infrastructure of public debate. Notwithstanding this criticism, however, his position remains the central reference for most debates on this issue.

### FURTHER READING

Habermas' (1989) *Structural Transformation of the Public Sphere* is an accessible and interesting read. Another key text dealing with the public sphere is Hannah Arendt's (1958) *The Human Condition*. For a more sociological spin, there are a number of interesting papers dealing with publics and public opinion in Herbert Blumer's (1986) *Symbolic Interactionism*. Both Arendt and Blumer broadly conceptualize publics in the same way as Habermas but each adds important insights. For a more critical take on Habermas and a consideration of alternative conceptions see the papers in Calhoun's (1994) *Habermas and the Public Sphere*, and in Crossley and Roberts' (2004) *After Habermas: New Perspective on the Public Sphere*.

# Racism(s) and Ethnicity

*Related concepts: hybridity, orientalism.*

Although the term 'racialism' has a longer history, the term 'racism' and its French precursor, 'le racisme', were first used in the late 1930s, largely as a way of making sense of the systematic discrimination against the Jews evident in the rise of fascism (Goldberg, 1993). It is common today to speak of racisms in the plural rather than racism (singular), as the form which identified racism varies widely across different contexts. Different social groups in the same society may be subject to different forms of racism and the same group may find itself subject to different forms of racism across historical time or in different societal contexts. Notwithstanding this, however, at the highest level of abstraction and

---

165 That is, not recognizing different types and forms of rationality that might be operative in different types of 'public'.

*Racism(s) and Ethnicity*

generality the term 'racism' is used to denote social practices (including linguistic practices) which identify or categorize and thereby differentiate a group as a distinct 'race', constituting that group as lower or inferior, and thereby contribute to the exclusion or domination of that group.

The category of 'race' referred to here is often thought of in biological terms. 'Races', as discursive constructions, are rooted in either perceived (for example, skin colour) or imagined (for example, alleged genetic 'stock') biological differences, the presumption being that the human species as a whole sub-divides into various 'natural kinds'[166] along the lines of these differences. Some writers, however, have referred to a 'new racism' which attaches to perceived cultural differences, that is, arguments for segregation and differential/unequal treatment are no longer rooted in claims regarding biological difference but rather in claims regarding cultural differences. It is not uncommon, for example, for groups of the far right to argue that immigrant populations should be expatriated because their culture, an 'inferior culture' in the view of the far right, poses a threat to the indigenous and dominant culture and is not in keeping with it.

The concept of ethnicity, too, tends to be focused upon cultural differences. Where 'racism' denotes an external categorization and judgement of a social group, however, 'ethnicity' tends to be used to refer to different cultural groups as they are defined from the inside, by their own members. Consequently the term tends also to map onto forms of self-identification/identity and a sense of belonging.

It is common to conceptualize racism(s) as manifestations of overt individual prejudice, an individual psychological trait. It is important not to lose sight of this quite crude form of racism, as we explore more subtle and sophisticated forms, as it is still very evident in most western societies. However, many writers claim that racism(s) can be collective or institutional and may be implicit or covert rather than overt; that is to say, the routinized practices of an individual, collective or organization/institution can work in a fashion which systematically differentiates and disadvantages specific social groups, without the agent(s) involved necessarily holding an explicit belief about the inferiority of the disadvantaged group (Gilroy, 1992; Goldberg, 1993). This is a controversial point because the concept of racism seems to suggest 'intention' which, in turn, we are inclined to attribute only to individuals and often only on the basis of their consciously held goals and beliefs. This

---

166 The concept of 'natural kinds' suggests that there are qualities and differences inherent in the nature of certain of the basic components or elements of the world, beyond or in spite of the ways in which we might divide up and categorize the world.

is not the place to engage in a dissection of the concept of intention and its appropriate uses. It must suffice to say that habitual or institutionalized patterns of human behaviour, individual or collective, can have the effect of systematically discriminating against certain groups, with or without the express knowledge and intent of those who engage in them, and that this is what is meant (for better or for worse) by the concept of 'institutionalized racism'. In the case of alleged institutional racism within the police, for example, it may be that police officers are more likely, through force of habit, to see the activities of black youths as suspicious, without even being aware that they see black youths differently, such that they are then, in good faith, more likely to investigate black youths, more likely to discover crimes and thereby, of course, likely to reinforce their habit of viewing black youths with suspicion. Furthermore, in some cases, for example psychiatry, it may be that cultural differences are not recognized as such within institutional processes of classification, and thus become coded or classified under a different heading in a manner which is racist, for example, they are coded as manifestations of mental illness. Members of cultures which practise various forms of witchcraft and which believe in curses, visitation and communication with the dead, and so on may be inclined, perhaps particularly at times when they are distressed, to make claims which a western trained psychiatrist will view as very odd, which they will not be able to understand and which they may consequently deem psychopathological (for a review on the debates over racism in psychiatry see Suman Fernando's (1991) *Mental Health, Race and Culture* or Littlewood and Lipsedge's (1989) *Aliens and Alienists*). The absence of intent in these cases undoubtedly poses problems for legal scholars and professionals who must decide whether parties to institutionalized racism are liable for the injury they cause[167] and whether victims are therefore entitled to compensation. Indeed the concept of institutionalized racism is arguably now as much a legal concept as anything else. In the sociological context, however, where unintended consequences are an important focus and where the need to address the many problems surrounding 'intention' are not nearly so pressing and can often be ignored, the problem is not nearly so great. It does not really matter if racist effects are intended from a sociological point of view so long as we can agree that they are indeed present – as we can in many cases.

Theses on the origin of various forms of racism are varied and there is

---

167 Some legal scholars argue that companies are held responsible for other forms of unintended damage that they cause and could be expected to have foreseen (such as environmental damage), so why not for racism (see Goldberg, 1993)?

little agreement. However, much of the racism against black and Asian groups within Europe should be seen in light of colonialism, a project of economic and political domination and exploitation which generated a context in which many still persistent ideas about biological inferiority took shape. This argument has been developed in a number of ways in the literature and was, for at least some time, strongly associated with Marxist perspectives of racism. In the current climate, however, and particularly in the context of an understanding of the racism suffered by individuals of Middle Eastern origin, Edward Said's thesis of 'orientalism' is a particularly influential version of this thesis (see **orientalism**).

### FURTHER READING

Early influential accounts of racism and its effects include Franz Fanon's important works, *Black Skin/White Mask* (1993) and *The Wretched of the Earth* (1986). More recently Paul Gilroy's (1992) *There Ain't No Black in the Union Jack* is a central text, at least for the UK context, as is his *Black Atlantic* (Gilroy, 1993). Goldberg's (1993) *Racist Culture* is also a useful point of entry into the debates surrounding this issue. For a discussion of contemporary debates on both racism and ethnicity see Mac an Ghaill's (1999) *Contemporary Racisms and Ethnicities.*

# Rationality

237

> Related concepts: **colonization of the lifeworld, ideal speech situation, public sphere, system and lifeworld.**

The concept of rationality has been central to debates in social theory throughout its history. The way that this concept has been used and defined, however, has varied markedly. Here I can only hope to trace out some of the more central trajectories of debate. Specifically I will consider the cost-benefit defintion of rationality posited in 'rational action theory' (RAT), Habermas' (1991a) alternative 'communicative' concept of rationality, and some of the debates concerning the apparent cultural/historical relativity of rationality.

## RATIONALITY AS COST-BENEFIT CALCULATION

One very central use of 'rationality' is found in what is variously referred to as 'rational action theory' (RAT), 'rational actor theory' or 'rational choice theory'. This theory argues that, for methodological purposes at least, social analysis must decompose the social world into the actions of its individual members (this strategy is referred to as 'methodological individualism'),[168] and that it should regard the actions of those members as rational, in a very specific sense of the term. Human action is rational according to RATs insofar as it pursues the specific and individual goals or desires of the agent in an efficient and effective manner, weighing up or at least being sensitive to the various 'costs' and 'benefits' attached to possible courses of action and always opting for the most 'profitable' route. The rational actor, they argue, aims to maximize the rewards of their action and minimize personal costs. Furthermore, this is said to render actions predictable and amenable to causal analysis from the outside perspective of a scientific observer. If we know what counts as a cost to an actor, what counts as a benefit and roughly what 'weight'[169] is attached to these costs and benefits, then we can predict the likely effect on the behaviour of the actor of (perceived) changes in their environment which have a bearing upon these costs and benefits.

Some RATs insist that this model does not imply 'selfishness' on behalf of the agent (for example, an agent may desire the welfare of others) but many concede that it does (and thus that altruism is more apparent than real). Some even go so far as to argue that all goals and desires must, in the final instance, be pre- and asocial. If we are to explain the social world, according to RATs such as Michael Laver (1997), for example, then we cannot presuppose aspects of that world in our theory. We must begin with an account of the pre-social 'atoms' whose actions and desires are generative of the social world as we know it. Those atoms, he maintains, are purely selfish cost-benefit calculating agents. Furthermore, according to Laver and many other RATs, human beings have a range of desires or goals which (in theory) they rank. All things being equal, they argue, the

---

168 For more on this and a critique of it see **relationism**.
169 An agent might regard certain costs as fairly minimal or insignificant, for example, whilst others are deemed considerable and to be avoided in all circumstances. Likewise with benefits and desires, some are 'nice' but not really worth any great effort to pursue, whilst others are to be sought at any cost. Some RAT theorists argue that we can attach a numerical value to the desires and aversions in any given agent's 'portfolio' such that we can work out, mathematically, how they will act in any given situation and what degree of change in a set of circumstances would be necessary to change their behaviour, etc. Not all RATs go as far as this, however.

---

agent will pursue what they most desire, but all things are not equal. Circumstances may make 'top desires' very costly or may facilitate the achievement of two or more lower order desires (whose cumulative value to the agent is greater than the top desire) for a very low cost, in which case the agent will pursue goals lower down on their list of priorities.

How much information agents have to base their decisions upon, how much energy they expend pursuing information and what role interpretation and belief plays in the perception of possible costs/benefits are all matters of contention within RAT (see Goldthorpe, 1998). Suffice it to say, however, that early versions of the theory tended to follow economics in assuming that agents had full and unmediated access to all information relevant to their choices but that most contemporary versions, mindful of the limited predictive value of the earlier models and its intuitive implausibility, have tended to add in a variety of complications which allow for the role of habit, interpretation, the social distribution of information and related factors.

This is not the place to discuss the many criticisms of RAT (see Hindess, 1988; Crossley, 2002: 56–76). It is important, however, to note the dialogue with versions of RAT which has been constitutive of a significant strand of the history of social theory, culminating in the work of the key critical social theorist, Jürgen Habermas (1991a, 1987a). Talcott Parsons is a useful point of departure here. In *The Structure of Social Action*, he observed that the theories of the founders of modern sociology, Durkheim and Weber, were based upon a critique of an early incarnation of RAT, utilitarian philosophy (Parsons, 1968). From the precursor of utilitarianism, Thomas Hobbes (1971), they took the question of how social order is possible but they rejected utilitarian answers to that question.[170] Specifically, and with an eye upon the chief philosophical alternative to utilitarianism offered in the work of Kant (1948, 1993), they argued that human action, whilst partly shaped by selfish desires and the rationality necessary to realize them, is also steered by social norms and a sense of duty. Duty and norms, they continued, are

239

---

170 Writing around the time of the English Civil War, Hobbes had argued that society, in what he calls 'the state of nature', is a 'war of all against all'. Everybody pursues their own selfish goals by whatever means are most efficient (as RAT suggests). This is a very violent state, according to Hobbes, and the violence is only reduced with the formation of a powerful state (which he calls 'Leviathan') which effectively reduces violence and enforces conformity through the threat of its own use of force and violence. Durkheim and Weber, according to Parsons, arrive at a different conclusion from this because they recognize the possibility of moral (that is voluntarily norm oriented) behaviour on behalf of social agents. Human beings are not 'profit machines' in the view of the early sociologists but rather moral beings, capable of engaging in moral relations with one other.

necessary prerequisites of social order. Furthermore, Durkheim in particular argued that duty and norms are irreducibly social, being that we cannot adequately explain norms or their effect upon human action from within a 'methodologically individualistic' framework. Norms and duties emerge out of collective contexts and must necessarily do so. Parsons agreed and this effectively provided the point of departure for the trajectory of his own work, a trajectory which, as is well known, went well beyond these claims into the territory of functionalism and systems theory.

Interestingly, it was in the context of a response to Parsonian functionalism and the attempt to explain aspects of the social world by reference to their functions, that many of the early pioneers of more recent incarnations of RAT within sociology first began to make their case (for example, Homans, 1961, 1973). Attempts to explain the parts of the social world by reference to the whole, via functions, they argued, are problematic on any number of grounds. To adequately explain the parts of the social world we must break them down into further parts, that is, human actions, and we can understand human action in rational, cost-benefit terms. In a further twist in this plot, however, many more sophisticated advocates of RAT have now arrived at the conclusion, like Parsons and Durkheim, that norms play an important role in the organization of social life and are irreducible to 'the individual' (for example, Elster, 1989).

## COMMUNICATIVE RATIONALITY

The latest addition to this twisting and turning plot is the work of the critical theorist, Jürgen Habermas. He adds another and altogether different definition of rationality to the debate. Habermas agrees that at least some human action bears a formal similarity to what RATs describe. He refers to this as 'strategically rational action' or simply 'strategic action'. However, his work advances a wide range of criticisms of RAT. Three are particularly relevant for our purposes. Firstly, he argues that 'strategic action' is contextually bound and must necessarily be so, since it has certain definite limits. The process of socialization, the formation of human identities and the reproduction of knowledge and culture, for example, presuppose something more than the very minimal elements of 'strategic action' and means-end rationality. They presuppose that agents strive to achieve mutual understanding and rapport. Human action only conforms to the model suggested by RAT some of the time for Habermas therefore. Specifically he suggests that we behave as RAT suggests, or at least more like that, when we engage in impersonal economic and political transactions – such as when we buy and sell on markets or when we vote and/or carry out bureaucratic functions.

Secondly, Habermas argues that those (above mentioned) contexts in the social world where strategic action is sufficient and appropriate, have only emerged relatively recently and as a consequence of social changes which have effectively 'decoupled' them from other aspects of the social world. In early societies, he argues, economic and political actions were tightly interwoven in the religious, normative and traditional fabric of society, such that 'strategic action', at least as narrowly conceived, was not possible. It is only in modern societies that the relatively pure form of 'strategic action' noted by the RATs has become possible, and, to reiterate, even that is contextually bound and supported by an institutional and normative framework. We can act like strategic 'atoms' in economic and political life but only insofar as there are economic and political institutions there for us to act within, and only insofar as these institutions are facilitated by a normative (including a legal) framework. There is a very strong sociological critique in what Habermas is arguing here. He effectively follows Durkheim in arguing that the 'rational individual' whom RATs use to explain the social world is a product of the historical development of society.

Thirdly, developing the earlier point about the irreducibility of norms and duties to the strategically rational individual, he argues that norms and duties are aspects of the social world which we can argue over and seek to justify 'rationally', but only in a very different sense of the word 'rational'. Habermas speaks here of 'communicative rationality'. To say that we can argue 'rationally' about norms, rules, right and wrong, and so on, he argues, does not mean that we weigh up costs and benefits but rather that we seek to persuade one another of a particular point of view by reference to logic, evidence, shared assumptions, beliefs, and so on. This is a very different meaning of the term 'rationality' but is no less important than the RAT definition. In a communicatively rational encounter we might point out to our interlocuter that their belief in one thing should lead them to agree with us about something else because the same principle is involved and consistency demands of them that they agree with us. We might say, for example, that the principle of justice which underpins their feminism should also lead them to support campaigns for gay rights or the rights of minority ethnic groups. They might then reply by arguing that their feminism is based upon a different principle, which does not have the same implications, or perhaps by qualifying the principle of justice in such a way that it applies in the case of feminism but not in the other cases. Alternatively, of course, they may allow themselves to be persuaded, claiming that they had not made the connection before but now that it is pointed out find it irresistible (at least to their 'rational side').[171] Similarly, we may present them with some form of evidence from which, we claim, they must logically conclude that we are right. This might be as simple as marching them back into a supermarket to show them that a bag of peas is, as we told them, 65p and not 50p, but it might equally involve reference to complex statistics or results of sophisticated experiments or sociological studies. The point is that we point out evidence which we believe will change their view.

A debate is communicatively rational, for Habermas, to the extent that interlocuters are prepared to be persuaded by the 'reasons' offered by their other and attempt to put themselves in the position of the other, thereby transcending the particularity of their own point of view. Views are accepted or rejected on the basis of the exchange of reasons alone. To the extent that interloctuters lie or otherwise deceive, use or threaten violence, pull rank, and so on a debate is not rational in this communicative sense. Note, however, that this does not preclude arguments becoming heated and 'emotional'. Participants to a debate can become very frustrated when they are struggling to persuade another of their view or to understand the objections of the other.

Like 'strategic rationality', 'communicative rationality' has developed historically according to Habermas. Just as the rational capacities of the individual emerge through a developmental process, so too does the rationality of culture – as we see if we look, for example, at the history of science.[172] For Habermas this is part of the process of 'rationalization' which, following Weber (1930, 1978), he deems central to the definition of modern societies. More to the point it is one of the better aspects of a process which potentiates both positive and negative outcomes. The growth of rationality liberates us from the shackles of tradition, both in the sense that we have the cognitive capacity to question tradition and in the sense that central forms of social and political authority increasingly appeal to 'reasonableness' (rather than tradition or God) for their legitimacy. However, the above-mentioned uncoupling of economic and political life from the normatively bound social community (lifeworld) is

---

171 A person may, of course, find their self forced to concede that an argument is rationally correct but still not much like it and thus only concede to it begrudgingly.
172 The history of science shows relatively clearly that and how contemporary ways of thinking about the world have evolved through a series of 'paradigms', much as our individual capacity for thought and reason can be shown to have done (see Kuhn, 1970, Bachelard, 2002).

also part of this process, and this can have negative effects insofar as those domains tend to grow rapidly, 'colonizing' and undermining other areas of life (see **colonization of the lifeworld**). Reason is our only defence here according to Habermas and he identifies the 'new social movements' (see **new social movements**) as an important manifestation of the power of (communicative) reason to resist this 'colonization of the lifeworld'.

A key aspect of communicative rationality, on Habermas' account, is the distinction which moderns draw between claims to truth, (moral) right and (subjective) truthfulness. Many arguments embody claims of all three types but we separate them out when weighing up these arguments, and treat them differently. We might concede that something is factually true, for example, whilst maintaining that it contradicts moral codes and/or is distasteful to us. Similarly we would maintain a distinction between a claim being wrong and being a lie; in both instances the claim does not correspond to facts in the external world but in the first case there is no intention to deceive where, in the second case, there is. Furthermore, these distinctions are mirrored at the institutional level. Science, for example, deals with matters of fact or truth, independently of matters of value or subjectivity. The truths of modern physics or biology, for example, are deemed true whatever we might feel about them. Similarly, in legal debate we strive to derive rational norms, focusing upon what *ought* to happen in particular situations and distinguishing that from what might currently happen in fact. Finally, in psychotherapy and psychology we strive to explore the truth of our subjective lives (how we feel about things), bracketing out normative judgements about the morality of those feelings or 'objective' judgements about the correspondence or not of those feelings to intersubjectively verifiable states of affairs in the world. Psychoanalysis might reflect upon the 'fact' of my desire to kill another person whom I believe to be persecuting me, for example, without necessarily getting bogged down in the immoral nature of such feelings or the truth-value of my belief that I am being persecuted. What matters is how I feel and experience the world and that is different from the question of how the world actually is and how I ought to act in it.

## RATIONALITY AND RELATIVITY

In making his claims about reason and rationalization Habermas engages with a further 'rationality' debate within sociology and philosophy; a debate from the 1960s focused upon Peter Winch's (1972) claim that rationality is relative to particular societies. Winch arrives at his position through a critique of the anthropologist Evans-Pritchard (1976), who studied the use of sacred oracles in decision-making processes amongst the Azande. For all practical purposes, Evans-Pritchard concluded, oracle magic works as a system of decision-making and it certainly makes sense 'internally', to the Azande, but it is not rational. Winch disagrees. Evans-Pritchard's argument presupposes the definition of rationality posited within contemporary western culture, he argues, but who is to say that this definition is more adequate than the Azande definition? Like oracle magic, western forms of rationality belong to a specific cultural tradition and can appeal to no source of legitimation or authority outside of that tradition. All justifications of western rationality are necessarily internal too. This is true of all forms of rationality, Winch argues; all are rational only in terms of their own internal criteria of rationality and there is no neutral point of observation outside of one culture or another from which competing claims to rationality, such as that made by Evans-Pritchard, could be assessed. Indeed the very notion of a culture-free definition of rationality makes no sense since rationality only emerges in the context of human communities.

Winch's argument provoked many responses (Wilson, 1974; Hindess, 1988), amongst them one from Habermas (1991a), who might be deemed to fall fowl of Winch's critique. Habermas concedes that it is a tall order and perhaps impossible to persuade a die hard relativist out of their position – since the mantra 'well that's relative' can be sung in response to any argument. However, he defends a less relativistic definition, drawing from Piaget's (1961) theory of developmental stages of thought in children, by arguing that the development of rationality involves a succession of stages in which early forms crumble under the weight of their own internal problems, giving rise to new and better forms which encompass all that their predecessor was capable of whilst also overcoming the problems of that predecessor. There is, in short, a learning process in which thought and reason become more encompassing and effective. Western rationality, from this point of view, had its own magical stage several centuries ago but effectively progressed beyond that point when the limitations of magical thinking became apparent 'from within' and collapsed to give way to another more secular form of rationality. Thus western rationality is more advanced than magical forms of reasoning. Needless to say, the court is still out on this debate.

Running alongside the historical emphasis in Habermas' work are a number of arguments which seek to root aspects of rationality transcendentally within language use, that is to say, arguments which claim that certain aspects of our ways of reasoning are necessary and could not be otherwise for language using beings (see especially Habermas, 1991b). This is not the place to explore this quite complex idea here.[173] It must suffice to make three points of criticism with respect to it. Firstly, it is not clear how compatible it is with the more historical emphasis in some of Habermas' work and this begs the question of how much rationality, as Habermas understands it, is owed to history and how much to communicative necessity. Secondly, Habermas' transcendetalism has been criticized by Pierre Bourdieu (1998a, 2000). Whilst Bourdieu, like Habermas, is critical of relativism, he argues that our view of rationality must be entirely historical. Transcendental arguments such as that of Habermas, he argues, universalize historical particularities and rest upon a forgetting of history, that is to say, they assume that what seems absolutely self-evident and necessary now has always done so when historical analysis reveals that this is not so. Whilst Bourdieu agrees with much of what Habermas has to say about rationality he argues that Habermas lacks a proper historical perspective and tends to overstate the universality of conditions which, in fact, are found only in relatively modern societies. Furthermore, a third point of criticism, he argues is that Habermas' tendency to speak of rationality in the singular is insensitive to the many different forms of rationality in contemporary societies. In particular, Bourdieu draws this idea from debates in the philosophy of science where, it is argued, different sciences have given rise, historically, to their own distinct forms of rationality, that is to say, their own distinct ways of making and proving claims, arguing, persuading, and so on.[174]

## FURTHER READING

245

On RAT see Elster's (1989) *Nuts and Bolts for the Social Sciences* and Hindess' (1988) *Choice, Rationality and Social Theory*. Habermas' various discussions of rationality are all quite heavy but the key primary source is the first volume of his *Theory of Communicative Action* (Habermas, 1991b). White's (1988) *The Recent Work of Jürgen Habermas* is a concise and clear secondary account of this and would be a good point of entry for those who do not want to jump in at the deep end. On the 'Winch debate' see Wilson (1974) and Hindess (1988). Habermas' own contribution is in *The Theory of Communicative Action Vol. 1* (1991a).

---

173 For a brief discussion of certain aspects of the idea see **ideal speech situation**.
174 This is a point which Bourdieu takes specifically from the French philosopher of science Gaston Bachelard. For a discussion of Bachelard see **epistemological break**.

---

Bourdieu's contributions are made in his *Practical Reason* and particularly his *Pascalian Meditations* (Bourdieu, 1998a, 2000).

# Realism

> *Related concepts:* **discourse, epistemological break, social constructions/social constructionism.**

Realism is best defined against the background of two other philosophical perspectives which it opposes, positivism and certain forms of constructionism.

## REALISM VS POSITIVISM

Realists share a number of views with positivists. Both agree that there is a world 'out there' that science and social science can attempt to gain knowledge of. Both agree that 'knowledge' in this instance means knowledge of causal relationships which renders the world more predictable or at least understandable. And both tend to agree that the social and natural worlds are equally amenable to scientific analysis. They differ on three crucial points, however. Firstly, they disagree about the nature of causation. For the positivist, following the eighteenth-century philosopher, David Hume (1969), causation is a matter of 'constant conjuncture'; that is, saying 'a causes b' or 'a causes b to do c' means simply that, under certain specific conditions, if a happens then b happens or b does c in a regular and predictable fashion. For the positivist, there is nothing more meaningful that one can say about causation than that, and science is therefore simply a practice of observing and recording these constant conjunctures. The realist disagrees. When we talk of causality, the realist argues, we do not mean only that a follows b. We mean that a brings it about that b happens and that there is some necessity to this. We believe that there is some mechanism that links a and b or that there is something about the nature or essence of a and b which constitutes the causal relationship between them. Science, they continue, is not just a practice of recording constant conjunctures but equally one which offers

246

theoretical accounts of these mechanisms, essences and natures. That is what a scientific explanation is. Furthermore, they argue that this will often involve the scientist making reference to essences, entities and mechanisms which are unobservable. In some cases this may mean things which are unobservable at the moment but could become observable at a later point. Medical scientists, for example, made reference to viruses and genes before the means of visualizing those things was possible. They knew that something must 'be there' to bring about the facts they were observing and were prepared to theorize the existence of such unobservable elements even before they had the means to actually perceive them – and of course they were proved right in these cases. In other cases, however, it may involve reference to things which, for a variety of reasons, are necessarily unobservable in a direct sense. We can see the effects of electricity and magnetic fields, for example, but we cannot directly observe them and there is good reason to believe that we never will be able to. Many aspects of the social world, as relational phenomena, that is, phenomena which have no substantive existence but exist rather in relationships and contrasts between things, arguably fall just into this camp (see **relationalism**). This emphasis upon unobservables constitutes a second point of disagreement between realists and positivists. Positivists are very critical of the idea of unobservables. They believe that reference to unobservables, including 'essences', is metaphysical nonsense and unscientific. This relates, in some cases, to the philosophy of language associated with (logical)[175] positivism, which holds that words are only meaningful to the extent that they correspond with some perceptible datum (see Ayer, 1946). This (positivist) view about unobservables has become increasingly difficult to sustain in recent years as the role of unobservables in modern science has become increasingly apparent. Finally, realists and positivists disagree about scientific method, not least in its application to the social world. Whilst both agree that the social world can and should be studied scientifically, positivists have a very strict notion of the nature of scientific method which, in the view of realists, simply does not match up to the diversity of methodological approaches actually practised by scientists. For the realist, social science can be 'scientific' but this does not mean that it

---

175 Positivism is often associated with the nineteenth-century French philosopher August Comte (who was also an early pioneering sociologist and is credited with coining the term 'sociology'). Logical positivism refers to a later (early twentieth-century) philosophical movement, which was focused very much upon language and the conditions under which statements can be meaningful and true. On positivism see Halfpenny (1982).

---

should attempt to copy any given natural scientific method. Social science, for the realist, must develop its own methods of scientific analysis, as all other sciences have had to do.

## REALISM VS CONSTRUCTIONISM

Realism is also opposed to certain varieties of 'constructionism'. It is a philosophical position which holds that the world exists and has both properties and a form or structure independently of our perceptions and conceptions of it, that is, independently of our constructions of them (though see below for a qualification on this). We cannot know about the world independently of our perceptions and conceptions, of course, but that does not mean that it does not exist, and indeed exist in a specific and determinate form, independently of our perceptions and conceptions. Defined in this way, realism is an ontological rather than an epistemological position; that is, it is a theory about what exists rather than a theory of knowledge and of what we can and cannot know. This is an important distinction for many contemporary realists, not least because they argue that a great deal of criticism of realism relies upon epistemological rather than ontological arguments and, as such, largely misses the point (Bhasker, 1989). Critics of realism, according to realists such as Bhasker (ibid.), endlessly point to the theory-dependence of our knowledge about the world as if this (epistemological) fact about knowledge had some bearing upon the (ontological) question of the existence of a world independently of our knowledge, when it does not. We need to look at this in a little more detail.

Constructionists begin from the arguably well-founded epistemological position that human knowledge is not simply a reflection of a world 'out there' but rather depends upon what the knower him or herself brings to the situation. Different varieties of constructionism identify this 'active ingredient' in different ways. For some it is a matter of human biology. We know the world as we do as a consequence of the hardwired architecture of our brains and perceptual systems. For others, it is a matter of human practice. How we know, it is argued, depends upon the (historically variable) methods of investigating, classifying, and so on, that we have developed. Finally, many theories rest upon an investigation of language and discourse, that is, upon the historically variable conceptual architecture and ways of talking about the world that have emerged in human societies. In all cases, however, it is argued that human knowledge is actively 'constructed', and in the case of the more social varieties of constructionism, historical and cross-cultural variations in perceptions and conceptions of the world are held up as proof of this. If what we perceive and know about the world is simply a reflection of what is there, it is argued, then we would all perceive and know the world in the same way, or at least we would have knock-down arguments against any and all ways of looking at the world other than our own, but we do not. There is much that is contentious in these claims and certainly many philosophers are not happy with constructionism, even as an epistemological position. Many realists and particularly 'critical realists'[176] are prepared to embrace this as an epistemological position, however. What they object to is the inference that some constructionists draw from this, namely, that the world does not exist independently of these human constructs or has no definite form or structure. Here, in the view of the realist, the constructionist slips from a defensible epistemological position into an indefensible ontological position. The realist argues that just because our knowledge of the world is shaped by what we are and do, this does not mean that the world itself is in any way dependent (for its existence or form) on what we are and do. The world and our knowledge of it are two quite different things and we should not confuse the two.

The constructionist, at least if they wanted to pursue this ontological line of argument, might reply to this by asking the realist how they know that the world exists, has a form or structure, and so on. The existence of the world and our knowledge of it may be two different things but we can only know what we know, by definition, and the existence of a world independent of our knowledge (or perception and conception) of it is therefore not something that we can have any knowledge of or even speak meaningfully of. From this point of view realism is, at best, a matter of faith, even if, as many constructionists would concede, it is a faith which we all share most of the time – we certainly act as if the world exists independently of our perception of it. This argument, though perhaps quite fashionable amongst some radical philosophers and social scientists, is by no means new. In many respects it mirrors the line of questioning that Descartes put to himself at the dawn of modern philosophy. Although he was not a constructionist[177], Descartes conceded that, in and

---

176 Critical realism refers to the specific version of realism developed by Roy Bhasker (1979, 1989, 1994) and those influenced by him. I do not have the space here to distinguish this specific variety of realism from others, although much of my discussion is based upon Bhasker's earlier ideas. Bhasker's (1989) *Reclaiming Reality* is a good introduction to critical realism.
177 Insofar as he seeks to establish the existence of a world beyond his own perception of the world, Descartes is clearly a realist. Insofar, however, as he argues for the importance of his rationality in the process whereby he comes to know the world or certain aspects of it, he is also a rationalist or at least a precursor of rationalism (which emerged in its modern forms after his own philosophy).

of themselves, his thoughts and perceptions were not sufficient to prove conclusively that a real world exists beyond his experience of it. He could, after all, be dreaming or hallucinating. Perhaps his experiences were being controlled by an evil demon who wanted to deceive him? Not everything can be doubted by means of arguments of this sort, Descartes claimed. After all, even if he is wrong about everything else, he knows that he exists and that he thinks – an insight which many extreme constructionists are prone to overlook. Deluded people still exist. Indeed, they exist as thinking beings[178] – even if their thoughts are delusional. Nevertheless, it is only after Descartes has 'proven' the existence of God that he feels he has an adequate basis from which to argue convincingly for the existence of an external world corresponding to his knowledge and experience. He reasons that a good God would not allow him to be so fundamentally deceived as he has been imagining. This does not bode well for the atheist who wants also to be a realist.

Many contemporary strands of philosophy have tended to concede the impossibility of rationally arguing one's way out of this puzzle. One cannot, by definition, know what lies beyond one's own knowledge. That does not mean that there is no world beyond our knowledge of the world but only that we cannot know or say anything about it. For some schools of philosophy, including those rooted in Husserl's phenomenology and the work of Wittgenstein, that should really be the end of the matter, a cue for us to move on to other questions that we can hope to answer and learn from. Some contemporary realists believe that there is more to be said on this issue, however. Roy Bhasker, for example, has put forward a 'transcendental' argument for realism. For our purposes, transcendental arguments can be defined as arguments which work back from what we know to what must be the case if what we know is correct. One of the most famous examples of a transcendental argument is found in the work of Kant (1933). Reflecting upon his knowledge and experience, Kant notes that there are aspects and elements to it (for example, its temporal structure) which could not derive from the world itself and so must derive from his own ego, albeit an ego which is not given directly to his own experience and must, to reiterate, be deduced as a necessary prerequisite for his experience being as it is. Interestingly, this argument has had a strong influence on many contemporary strands of constructionism. Constructionists follow Kant in identifying within knowledge and experience, structures and frameworks which play a role

178 The definition of human beings as 'thinking beings' is central to Descartes' philosophy, as is revealed in his famous dictum 'cogito ergo sum' (I think therefore I am).

*Realism*

in our construction of 'the world' but do not derive from that world. Bhasker, however, picking up several threads in Kant's work, runs the argument in the other direction. There are aspects of our knowledge and experience, he argues, which could not derive from us so must derive from the world, such that we can deduce that a world must exist independently of us.

One example of this is the way in which later perceptions correct earlier ones. We are all familiar with the experience of 'thinking' that we have seen one thing, only to later find out that it is something else. Perhaps we think that we see a house in the distance, when walking a country path, but then later find out that it is just a pile of rocks. Perhaps what looks like a person turns out to be a tree upon closer inspection. This demonstrates that our perception involves an active attempt to impose order, just as constructionism suggests. However, what interests the realist is the fact that we are forced to change our construct upon closer inspection. This suggests that there are more active 'ingredients' in human perception than our own interpretative processes. I do not choose to change my interpretation and there is no reason to believe that it changes by virtue of anything other than the 'resistance' which it meets from a world which transcends it. The 'object', to paraphrase Pierre Bourdieu, 'objects' (Bourdieu et al., 1991: 61) (see **epistemological break**). It refuses to let me perceive it in the way that I was initially inclined to do. This is not to deny that 'houses', 'rocks', 'persons' and 'trees' are concepts belonging to the language games of specific societies. Nor is it to suggest, necessarily, that my later perception or interpretation is any better or more real than my earlier one. The pile of bricks that I first took for a house may, on even close inspection, turn out to be a sculpture or a polystyrene model or rocks which blow away just as I attempt to sit on them. It is simply to suggest that my interpretation, or construction, is affected by something other than me, something outside of me that the realist is going to call 'the real world'. At no point do I enjoy direct experience of the real world but the fact that I am forced to shift interpretation, that a perceptual scheme which had seemed valid from one distance no longer does so, offers an indirect proof of its existence. In order to explain my change of interpretation it is necessary to invoke the existence of a world which I interpret, which affords some interpretations under some conditions and resists others. It offers the basis for a transcendental proof.

We might extend this argument into the history of science. The history of science, particularly following the work of Kuhn (1970), is an important source of examples for the constructionist epistemologist. It seemingly shows very clearly that what we know about the world depends upon the practices and assumptions which frame our efforts to come to know about it, not least because these paradigmatic assumptions and practices shift over time. The shifting of these paradigms, with one collapsing and another taking its place, is strong evidence for the constructionist that we can perceive and thus construct the world through a variety of competing perspectives. The realist will concede this much. However, they add that one of the reasons why paradigms shift is that old paradigms sometimes lead to the generation of observations which they cannot accommodate or explain. Things sometimes turn out differently to the way scientists expect and the more such anomalies accumulate the more likely scientists are to seek out or embrace other paradigms. These other paradigms 'construct' reality too, of course. What interests the realist, however, is not the 'fit' between the new paradigm and reality but rather the resistance and anomalies that the older paradigm encounters in its attempt to explain a world which it takes to be independent of it. If 'reality' was simply a construct, realists argue, this would be impossible. The 'facts' would be whatever we defined them as being. Or at least paradigms would not find themselves threatened by dissonant elements. The object would not, to reiterate Bourdieu's felicitous phrase, object. The world would not resist, as it seems to have done so many times in the history of science. The realist is not suggesting that dissonant observations derive from unmediated or unconstructed access to the world. The argument is simply that some interpretations, some of the time, do not work, a state of affairs which forces us to recognize that interpretations must be interpretations of something which exists independently of them.

## THE REALITY OF SOCIETY

Within social science, debates about realism and constructionism have had an additional dimension to them, relating to a slightly different use of the term 'construct'. For realists, society, like the physical world and the psychological world, 'exists'. However, with social things or facts the picture is slightly more complex than is the case for simple physical objects or structures because the social world is, by definition, a 'social construct' in a way which is not true of the physical world. For example, compare the British economy, which is a social construct, with the Planet Jupiter, which is not – at least not in this new sense of 'construct' that I am discussing. The planet Jupiter exists whether or not we think that it does. It existed before we knew it was there and should we ever forget, lose our telescopes or die out as a species, it will, all things being equal,[179] still exist. The British economy is more complex, however, because it involves human behaviour and relationships, and these, in turn, depend upon human perception, conception, understanding, and so on. Part of what we mean by 'the economy', for example, is the money which we routinely exchange in our daily lives. In some cases this has a physical existence, in the form of coins and notes, other times it exists as numbers on cheques, banks statements, computers, and so on. In any of these cases, however, money is a symbolic medium and, as such, depends for its existence upon the way in which we regard and use it. There is nothing about a pound coin or dollar bill that makes it worth a pound or dollar. It is for this reason, of course, that we have to exchange money when visiting a foreign country because our money is not recognized as legal tender in other countries. This is arguably true of our languages, other symbolic systems, norms, roles and much of what makes up the social world. Doctors, for example, do not exist independently of societies, because 'doctor' is both a role and a legal status which, as such, depends upon the 'agreement' of members of a society and upon the law for its existence.

I do not mean that individuals choose to buy into the idea of money or doctors or language. Agreement in these cases is, to paraphrase Wittgenstein (1953), agreement in 'forms of life' rather than an agreement of opinion. We 'agree' in the respect that we all act in the same way towards money, language and doctors but of course we do so without thinking about it, without choosing to and without it occurring to us that we might do otherwise. Money might strike us as being as real as Jupiter and only appears different when we reflect theoretically upon it. Money, doctors and so on, are just so many things that we learn as 'facts of life' in early childhood and seldom call into question. They are, in Bourdieu's terms, 'doxic' (see **doxa**). Furthermore, it would really make very little difference if one or two individuals did refuse to believe in them. As Durkheim says of social facts in general, they impose themselves as coercive facts upon any one of us by virtue of the fact that everybody else behaves in a way which lends them this force. I cannot reject 'money' as a medium because *you* do not; you cannot because *I* do not; we cannot

---

179 I do not mean to suggest that the planet Jupiter will exist for all time, of course. It may be destroyed and could be destroyed by an event which happens also to destroy the Earth and all life on Earth, including human life. The point is that the existence of Jupiter is not dependent upon human beings believing or knowing that it exists, and is thus not dependent upon the existence of human life on Earth.

because the millions of other people in our society do not and so on. The monetary 'system' is held together by a truly enormous chain of human interdependency and one or two dissenters will not suffice to undermine it. An important and related point is that these 'things' are 'emergent properties' of social life, that is to say, they only exist in collective forms of life and are, so to speak, properties of collective life, properties of a shared social fabric rather than of the individual lives that combine in any given collectivity. They are relational phenomena, a point which is crucial for the realist (see **relationalism**). Finally, institutions like money and roles like that of the doctor have become so closely woven into so many aspects of our very complex ways of living that we have become dependent upon them for all sorts of things – some obvious, others not so – and it is therefore not entirely clear how we could 'just decide' to stop believing in them without plunging our (collective) lives into chaos. However, this does not alter the fact that these things depend, for their existence, upon our collective agreement (in forms of life).

So are these things 'real' or 'just constructs'? The only proper answer to this question, I suggest, is that they are 'real constructs', a point which I believe Durkheim was trying to get at with his concept of 'social facts'. Moreover, as Durkheim pointed out, they are real in their effects:

> Our whole social environment seems to us to be filled with forces which really exist only in our own minds. We know what the flag is for the soldier; in itself it is only a piece of cloth. [. . .] A cancelled postage stamp may be worth a fortune; but surely this value is in no way implied in its natural properties. [. . .] collective representations very frequently attribute to the things to which they are attached qualities which do not exist under any form or to any degree. Out of the commonest object, they can make a most powerful sacred being.
>
> Yet the powers which are thus conferred, though purely ideal, act as though they were real; they determine the conduct of men with the same degree of necessity as physical forces. (1915: 259–60)

People will kill in pursuit of 'mere constructs' and/or make themselves ill with worry. Furthermore, just because these social things depend upon our agreement or complicity for their existence, that does not mean that we fully understand their dynamics. I might contribute to the existence of the economy, for example, by acting 'as if' money had value, but that does not mean that I understand how the economy as a whole works, for example, what causes inflation or economic depression. Neither does it mean that the question of how the economy works is a meaningless question. Neither does it mean that I am insulated from the effect of those aspects of the economy that I do not understand. I do not need to

254

know the meaning of 'inflation' or define a situation as inflationary in order to find that I can no longer afford to buy the things that I want or to suffer as a consequence of inflationary tendencies in my society. To invoke Durkheim once more, my life is bound up with that of others, others who are not me, who exist externally to me, and though I may choose how to interpret the fact, this external world can impose all manner of situations upon me.

A very strong version of this realist theory of society is posited by the British social theorist, Margaret Archer (1995). Without denying that society consists in the actions and thus understandings and constructs of interacting social agents, Archer argues that it makes sense to posit an analytic distinction between the individual and society and by way of this to talk of causal relationships passing in both directions between the two. Society is thus said to enjoy an existence or reality, at least in certain respects, beyond the individual and their constructs. I do not have the space to explore her argument here but can certainly recommend it as an engaging read.

### FURTHER READING

Andrew Sayer's (2000) *Realism and Social Science* is the best contemporary account of realism as it applies to social science. It offers a good balance of incisive and complex yet uncluttered and clear argument. Keat and Urry's (1982) *Social Theory as Science* is a slightly older but still relevant and important exposition and defence of realism. Much contemporary realism draws from the work of Bhasker. In my opinion Bhasker's earlier work is better than his later work and it is certainly much clearer. On this basis I recommend *The Possibility of Naturalism* (Bhasker, 1979) and *Reclaiming Reality* (Bhasker, 1989). The key text from Archer, in relation to these debates, is her book, *Realist Social Theory* (Archer, 1995).

255

# Recognition (desire and struggle for)

> Related concepts: alienation, citizenship, freedom, I and me, identity, intersubjectivity.

The importance of 'recognition' as a concept can be traced back, in a variety of guises, through much of the history of Western philosophy and social thought (Fukuyama, 1992). However, the formulation of the concept in the philosophy of Hegel (1979), and in particular the interpretation of that formulation offered in a series of lectures in Paris in the 1930s by Alexandre Kojève (1969), are the key reference points for most contemporary commentators. The usual reference point in Hegel's oeuvre for the concept of recognition is his *The Phenomenology of Spirit* (Hegel, 1979) – which Kojève sought to 'introduce' to French intellectuals in his lectures. The idea is discussed elsewhere in Hegel's work, however, such as his lectures on *The Philosophy of Mind* (Hegel, 1971). Furthermore, the German critical theorist, Axel Honneth (1995), has argued that the most persuasive account is to be found in Hegel's very early (1805–6) 'Jena lectures'. In *The Phenomenology of Spirit*, Honneth argues, Hegel poses the issue of recognition in terms of a 'philosophy of consciousness'. This is very problematic from the point of view of contemporary critical theory, which has criticized and moved beyond the philosophy of consciousness. In Honneth's reading of the Jena lectures, however, Hegel frames the issue of recognition in a different way, a way which is much more compatible with a materialist outlook and, Honneth argues, with the important work of George Herbert Mead (1967) – which, as Honneth observes, takes up Hegelian ideas and develops them in a manner well suited to critical theory (see **I and me**). Honneth is persuasive and there is good reason to follow his preference for the Jena formulation of the concept of recognition. However, *The Phenomenology of Spirit* (and more particularly Kojève's reading of it) is the more usual reference point for contemporary work on recognition. For this reason I will stick with Kojève's reading for this entry. Readers interested in the

Jena lectures will find a clear and interesting secondary discussion in Honneth's (1995) *Struggle for Recognition*.

## THE ORIGINS OF SELF-CONSCIOUSNESS

Hegel raises the issue of recognition in the context of a discussion of self-consciousness. How is it, he asks, that human beings are not merely conscious but are conscious of themselves as conscious beings? Consciousness is usually associated, in the first instance, with the senses and perception. Hegel finds nothing in perception, nor indeed in our capacity to understand, however, which explains self-consciousness. When we perceive we become aware of the things around us, the objects of our perception, but we do not become aware of our perception as such nor of ourselves as perceiving subjects – at least not in any conscious sense.[180] A better starting point, he suggests, is desire. Desire, for Hegel, is 'lack' and entails the experience of 'lack'. The desire for food, for example, derives from a lack of food and it involves an experience of that lack – we feel hungry until we 'fill the gap'. This is important because the experience of lack entails some degree of self-reference and thus self-consciousness. To experience lack is to experience oneself as lacking and thereby to experience oneself, that is, to be conscious of oneself. Such basic desires as the desire for food or sexual desire cannot fully explain human self-consciousness for Hegel, however, because all animals have these desires and yet, in his view, only human beings enjoy self-consciousness. Human self-consciousness, he argues, derives from a desire which is exclusive to human beings, a desire for recognition.

The desire for recognition is quite different from other forms of desire for Hegel because it is a desire for desire itself, that is, a desire to be desired.[181] Human beings desire to be desired by other human beings,

---

180 There are a number of ways in which our perception of objects outside of ourselves, at least as adults, are bound up with a tacit sense of self. Our perception, as Merleau-Ponty (1962) notes, entails a perspectival and relational sense of space. We see things as high, low, near, far, etc. relative to our own bodily position such that our bodily position and bodily existence is therefore necessarily tacitly presupposed. More to the point when we see fast moving projectiles (for example, a falling roof slate) heading towards us we are inclined to move out of the way or adopt some form of defensive gesture. This very clearly suggests that we have a tacit concept of our self within our perception. We move to protect our self. This sense of our self is tacit, however, as we move without thinking in this instance and are not necessarily prompted to reflect deeply upon self as a consequence of such experiences.
181 The desire for desire is sometimes written as 'Desire' in the literature, with an upper case 'D'. I am not going to confuse the matter by adopting that convention here but it is as well to be alert to it, not least as Lacan, following Kojève, sometimes uses it also.

---

that is, to be recognized by those other human beings. This desire is important for Hegel because it elevates human beings into the realm of culture and history. Desire, he argues, leads to the consumption of what is desired, to its negation, and to the transformation of the desiring being into what it desires. Our consumption of food, motivated by our desire for food, for example, very much constitutes us as material, organic beings – akin to the material organisms that we eat. And it involves the destruction or negation of whatever it is that we eat. The desire for recognition is of a higher order, however, since the desire to be desired by others is not focused upon a material object and, as such, does not constitute us in terms of our (obviously inescapable) material, organic nature. To desire 'desire' is not to desire a thing, as 'desire' is not a thing and desiring 'desire' does not thereby constitute one as 'thing-like'. More to the point, as we will see shortly, it requires us to lift ourselves above our basic organic nature and our needs, to project or constitute ourselves into a socio-historical world. At the same time, however, since desire negates, it constitutes a struggle between human beings, each desiring to 'consume' the desire of the other.

Most contemporary writers on recognition argue that this break with our organic nature only comes about by way of our contact with the socio-historical world. Infants, it is argued, do not desire to be recognized because they are not aware of the perspectives of others. They confuse their perception of the world with the world itself, failing to see that their perception is just one perception of the world and that others have perceptions, desires, needs and projects of their own. It is only when, having acquired the capacity to assume the perspective of the other, they experience others as beings with their own perspectives (namely, perceptions, desires, needs and projects), and more particularly when they experience themselves as objects in the perspectives and projects of others, that the struggle for recognition begins:

> . . . the intersubjective world is problematical only for adults. The child lives in a world which he unhesitatingly believes accessible to all around him. He has no awareness of himself or others as private subjectivites. [. . .] For the struggle ever to begin, and for each consciousness to be capable of suspecting the alien presences which it negates, all must necessarily have some common ground and be mindful of their peaceful coexistence in the world of childhood. (Merleau-Ponty, 1962: 355)

It is important to add here, of course, that realization of the existence of others and of a world transcending self is, at the same time, a necessary precondition for a concept of self. We can only truly conceive of our selves to the extent that we are aware of the existence of others who are different and independent from us, that is, to the extent that we can conceive of what is not self (see **I and me**).

Awareness is not the same as recognition, however. Indeed, the gap between awareness of the existence of others and recognition of and by others is at the heart of the 'desire for recognition'. More to the point, having become aware of what Merleau-Ponty (above) calls the 'alien presences' of others, consciousness experiences itself as lacking the confirmation of those others and is driven to seek that confirmation. In both cognitive and affective modalities, the other completes and confirms (or denies and negates) our sense of both who we are and of our worth:

> Self-consciousness exists in and for itself when, and only by the fact that, it so exists for another; that is, it exists only in being acknowledged. (Hegel, 1979: 11)

Achieving awareness of the existence of others teaches us of the incompleteness, particularity and fallibility of our own perspective, motivating us to seek confirmation from others. Furthermore, our sense that we do not exist for them or are not valued for them proves intolerable.

## THE STRUGGLE FOR RECOGNITION: MASTER AND SLAVE

However, recognition is not granted automatically. It gives rise to a struggle for recognition, a struggle between agents in which each seeks the recognition of the other. Indeed, Hegel writes of a 'struggle to the death'. In order to prove themselves to one another, to prove their humanity, he argues, individuals must be prepared to place the prize of recognition above such base, animal desires as the desire for life/survival, and they do this by risking their life in struggle. They fight to the death. In actuality, however, many struggles result in one party succumbing to their will to live and submitting to the other – who is not motivated to kill them because this would deprive them of their source of recognition. The weaker party agrees to recognize the stronger in a situation of domination, effectively becoming a slave to the other's 'master'.

Qua slave the individual is subordinated to the master, lacking recognition and lacking what Hegel refers to as 'citizenship'. They are subordinates. The position of the master is problematic too, however. They are recognized but only by a slave, that is, by one who they do not recognize and who, in their eyes, is therefore not worthy of recognizing them. Recognition is only sought from those whom individuals themselves recognize as worthy of recognizing them. It must be mutual recognition. Moreover, having already staked their life and won the struggle, the master is therefore in an impasse. There is nothing else they can do to secure the recognition that they crave. Only the slave can redeem the situation, by struggling further with the master. Furthermore, because the slave works for the master, they have at their disposal a means of achieving (partial) self-consciousness in Hegel's view. Through work, as Hegel conceives of it, the slave transforms and appropriates nature, thereby mastering nature. They are not slaves to nature, even if they are slaves to a master. In addition, by working to service the master's needs they effectively learn to overcome their own lower appetites and desires, as they should have done in the 'fight to the death', effectively elevating themselves above the animal level and achieving their humanity. They are not mere beasts, slaves to their animal needs; they subordinate those needs in the process of serving their master. Finally, their transformation of the world around them, through work, functions as an externalization of their subjectivity and consciousness which, in turn, affords them an opportunity for self-consciousness. The objects they produce reflect back to them their consciousness, as the consciousness of the other would in relations of mutual recognition. They see in the objects of their labour a reflection or sign of their own humanity and creativity,[182] or rather, almost so. The slave struggles for recognition from the master, according to Hegel, and the dynamic of the relationship of masters to slaves is effectively the dynamic of human history. This is one of the key aspects of Hegel's work that was to inspire Marx. Echoing Hegel's view of history as a struggle of masters and slaves, Marx famously declared class struggle to be the motor of history. And the same might be said of Hegel's account of work, which is echoed quite strongly in some of Marx's earlier work, albeit in a more critical and materialist form.

## STRUGGLES IN HISTORY

As he analyses the situation of master and slave, Hegel shifts his focus away from an account of abstract individuals towards an account of concrete collectivities. He maps his story onto the contours of human history, as known in his day, and thereby derives a concrete philosophy of history. His account is largely an account of successive forms of ideology which serve to mask and perpetuate relations of lordship and bondage

---

182 This Hegelian view of work is an important influence on the Marxist concept of alienation. See **alienation**.

---

(masters and slaves). The account ends, however, with the French Revolution of 1789. This, for Hegel, was the moment in history where relations of mutual recognition were first historically instituted. The point at which history, as a struggle for recognition, came to an end – because mutual recognition was achieved.

This success story was echoed in an updated form recently, with due reference to Hegel and Kojève, by the right-wing political commentator Francis Fukuyama (1992). He declared the dominance of liberal capitalism at the end of the twentieth century to be 'the end of history' (namely because history is constituted through the struggle for recognition and must therefore come to an end when mutual recognition is achieved). Needless to say, many critics, also inspired by Hegel, disagree. Following Marx, they see the class relationships of contemporary capitalist societies as a major obstacle to full recognition. And going beyond Marx they identify a range of social relationships and social struggles which belie an unresolved politics of recognition, for example, in gender relations, between sexualities and between ethnic groups.

## OBJECTS OF DESIRE

The struggle for recognition is a struggle between individuals or groups but it is also one which can be mediated by objects and symbols. Objects can become desirable for one individual because they are desirable to another or rather they are desired by individuals because they are desired by the group and represent the desire of the group. Things become desirable not because of some intrinsic property that they possess but because they symbolize the desire of the other.[183] Kojève (1969) discusses the importance of flags in military struggles in this vein. A flag is just a piece of cloth, he observes, but soldiers are often prepared to lay down their lives attempting to variously seize or defend a flag because of the

---

183 This may seem to the beg the question of how something becomes desirable in the first place. Surely somebody must desire the thing intrinsically in order for it then to become desirable for others. This may be true in some cases. It may be, for example, that what has instrumental value for one party (or is perceived to do so) comes to have symbolic value to another party on account of its (perceived) value to the first party. However, it is also conceivable that competitive struggles precede the desired objects that come to play a role in them, with the latter being drawn upon simply as a means of exercising distinction – as agents cast about in search of anything which might be invested with the capacity to grant distinction. Mead (1967), for example, argues that individuals seize upon seemingly quite arbitrary and random aspects of personal appearance in a strategic effort to distinguish themselves, investing such aspects with a value which they did not previously have either for the individual or anybody else prior to this appropriation.

---

*Recognition (desire and struggle for)*

symbolic value it acquires in the context of struggle. In consumer societies, many objects may be invested in much the same way. Consumer objects become 'status symbols' – desired because they are desirable. Furthermore, individuals will risk life and limb to perform feats (such as climb unclimbed mountains, fly higher, dive lower, and so on) which, on the face of it are quite arbitrary and have no intrinsic value or point but which symbolize distinction (see **illusio**).

## LEVELS OF ANALYSIS

The jump which Hegel makes from a discussion of abstract individuals to a discussion of concrete collectives is one of a number of problematic moves in his argument. There are steps missing in the argument to say the least. One way round this problem is to be found in Axel Honneth's aforementioned study, *The Struggle for Recognition*. In effect, Honneth subdivides the desire and struggle for recognition into three elements. In the first instance, he argues, human beings need love and their struggle for this form of recognition is played out in the family and personal relationships (leaving its mark on the personality of the individual). On this level he cites a number of psychoanalytic authors who have either explicitly appropriated Hegel's idea of recognition in their own work (for example, Benjamin, 1991) or arrived at very similar conclusions independently (for example, Winnicott, 1971). The psychoanalysts quoted by Honneth belong to the branch of psychoanalysis referred to as 'object-relations' (on account of the role which it accorded to relationships in its account of the development of the psyche). However, he might equally have referred to the Lacanian school, which also draws strongly from the work of Hegel and Kojève (Lacan, 1989). Secondly, at a more collective level, Honneth identifies a desire for formal equality and social membership. The motivating drive of this desire is evident in many of the key struggles which divide our societies, past and present, he argues. He singles out T.H. Marshall's account of the gradual emergence and transformation of the institution of citizenship as one key example of this, however (Marshall and Bottomore, 1992) (see **citizenship**). Finally, beyond this level of formal equality, he discusses the human desire for individual distinction, as played out in sport, fashion and various other social status 'contests'. The work of Pierre Bourdieu (especially Bourdieu, 1984), though not cited by Honneth in this context, is a good example of how this idea can be developed sociologically. In his study, *Distinction*, he precisely shows how consumption and leisure activities serve as markers of status distinction. Bourdieu does not theorize this explicitly in terms of

*Recognition (desire and struggle for)*

'recognition' but there are periodic references to 'recognition' and 'struggles for recognition' in this and other of his works.

## THE FRENCH CONNECTION

In addition to the tradition of German critical theory, to which Honneth belongs, Hegel's theory of recognition, and more particularly Kojève's rendering of it, has been of particular significance in the trajectory of French social theory during the latter half of the twentieth century, particularly in the existentialism of Jean-Paul Sartre (1969), Simone de Beauvoir (1988) and Maurice Merleau-Ponty (1962).[184] The Hegelian claim, discussed earlier, that the desire for recognition elevates human beings above their animal nature is given an extreme form in Sartre's early work, particularly *Being and Nothingness*. He attributes a radical and uncompromising form of freedom to human beings, defining human being as 'transcendence'.[185] Similarly, the idea of the struggle for recognition is central to his philosophy and is interpreted in a radical fashion. *Being and Nothingness* presents an almost paranoid vision of human relationships, in which agents either dominate the other or find themselves dominated. When the other looks at me, Sartre claims, I feel myself caught up, trapped in their gaze. I am alienated. And when they look at other objects I experience that as a loss to myself. They are 'consuming' the objects and meaning of 'my' visual field. Simone de Beauvoir and Merleau-Ponty were equally influenced by Hegel. They each attempt to balance Sartre's account, however. In the first instance, they seek to draw important implications about human interdependency and the potential of mutual recognition from Hegel's work. If others are a potential source of alienation for us, they argue, it is only because they are also our sole source of genuine fulfilment. It may be, as Sartre (1947) says in his play, *Huis Clos*, that 'Hell is other people' but so too is heaven. Indeed others can only be 'hell' for us because our true fulfilment ('heaven') is dependent upon them. Secondly, in different ways each attempts to temper Sartre's claims about the transcendence of human beings by way of an exploration of 'imminence', that is, they seek to show

184 For further discussion of some of the ideas of these philosophers see the entries on **body-subject** and **freedom**.
185 I do not have the space to go into the technicalities of the concept of 'transcendence' here. Suffice it to say that Sartre means that human beings are capable of going beyond what is given to them in the world. They can imagine and create forms of life which go beyond the world as they currently find it.

*Recognition (desire and struggle for)*

that and how individuals cannot enjoy the type of freedom and disconnection he describes. Without denying the reality of choice and projects, they seek to show how these transcendent aspects of human beings necessarily take shape within a context shaped by both material nature and the social world (see **freedom**).

In a slightly different vein, Merleau-Ponty (1962) also begins to explore the relationship between recognition, language and communication. His argument is that relations of mutual recognition can be achieved by way of genuine communication. The alienation that Sartre describes, he suggests, is an effect of non-communication, a refusal to communicate which, qua refusal, 'communicates'[186] aggression and objectification. This alienation is overcome when agents communicate openly and thereby express, directly and indirectly, their recognition of the other. This is a theme also taken up by the French psychoanalyst, Jacques Lacan (1989). In his early papers Lacan appears to take a similar line to Merleau-Ponty. He suggests that genuine communication effects relations of mutual recognition and he claims that speech is motivated by the desire for recognition; every utterance calls for a response and thus for a confirmation or sign of recognition. In his later work, however, Lacan becomes more sceptical. Sounding rather more like Sartre, at least in his pessimism regarding human relationships, he reflects upon the essential ambiguities of language and the many ways in which the meanings of speech are elusive. If a person says that they love me, for example, do they mean it? Do they mean that they love me but . . .? Are they just pacifying me or trying to get something from me? How can I ever know for sure? For the later Lacan we are driven into speech by our desire for recognition but we will never find our solution in there. There will always be doubt about recognition and the desire for it will therefore never be satisfied.

There is a great deal wrong with the concept of recognition, whichever formulation we latch on to. At the same time, however, there is something irresistible about it as an idea. It captures certain undeniable aspects of human behaviour and for that reason is echoed throughout a great many different perspectives in social science. One does not have to dig too deep into the work of even the most hardened of utilitarian or materialist thinkers to find them making reference to the human need for 'status', 'approval', 'acceptance', 'respect', 'distinction' or some other synonym of 'recognition'. And notions such as 'status contests' are staple in many

---

186 The refusal to communicate is still a form of communication for Merleau-Ponty (1962). One cannot, at least if one lives amongst others (as we all do) fail to communicate to them by virtue of what one does.

---

*Recognition (desire and struggle for)*

sociological approaches. Furthermore, the notion of recognition is not merely an explanatory concept. As Honneth has argued, it is equally a key concept for moral theory. Struggles for recognition are moral struggles and relations of mutual recognition are moral relations. More to the point, recognition is arguably a fundamental 'good' which, through the process of struggle, agents have sought to establish as a 'right' (see Honneth, 1995 for an extended discussion of the implications of this argument). This combination of moral and explanatory aspects makes the concept of recognition a particularly valuable one for critical theory.

### FURTHER READING

Kojève's (1969) *Introduction to the Reading of Hegel* is quite straightforward. This book also includes a reproduction of the relevant section from Hegel's (1979) *The Phenomenology of Spirit*, so one can at least get a feel for Hegel's own manner of expressing his ideas (*The Phenomenology of Spirit* as a whole is very heavy going by anybody's standards but the section reproduced by Kojève is relatively clear). Kelly's (1965) paper 'Notes on Hegel's lordship and bondage' is a useful article for putting Kojève's specific reading of Hegel into perspective and suggesting other readings. Honneth's (1995) *The Struggle for Recognition* also offers a slightly different (and more detailed) reading of Hegel, and shows clearly how the idea can be developed within the context of critical social science. It is a 'must read' for anybody interested in this concept. Finally, though flawed in its central thesis, Fukuyama's (1992) *The End of History and the Last Man* is a very entertaining and lively account which illustrates how the idea of recognition might be applied historically. It offers food for thought.

**265**

# Relationism (vs Substantialism)

Related concepts: *field, intersubjectivity, power, social space I and II.*

A key polarity within sociological theory is that between individualist and holistic approaches, that is, between those approaches, such as rational action theory (see **rationality**), which reduce 'society' to the individuals comprising it and those, such as functionalism, which seek to explain the 'parts' of society (for example, rituals, institutions, cultural patterns, and so on) in terms of the whole and its 'needs' or 'functional pre-requisites'. From a relational point of view both of these approaches commit the error of substantialism, and both must be rejected. 'Substantialism' entails that elements studied within science are attributed fixed and stable qualities, which are then used as a basis of explanation. It also means that these elements are regarded independently of the context of their relationship to other elements. In the history of the natural sciences substantialism has proved to be a problem and some philosophers of science have argued that the advanced science we have today only became possible when it was exorcized from theoretical discourse. Gaston Bachelard (2002), for example, writes of substantialism as an 'epistemological obstacle' which hindered early developments in physics (see **epistemological break**), whilst Ernst Cassirer (1923) argues that the move from substantialism to relationalism was fundamental to the birth of modern physics. A growing number of social scientists argue that this same transition is necessary in social science (see especially Mead, 1967; Elias, 1978; Blumer, 1986; Emirbayer, 1997; Bourdieu, 1998).

So what is relationalism? In the context of social science, or perhaps rather of sociology,[187] relationalism entails that we take neither individuals nor society as fixed entities which can be used to explain aspects of the social world but rather focus upon interactions and relationships between agents. Moreover, the relational claim is that these relationships and interactions are constitutive of both 'individuals' and 'society'. In other words, it is not 'society', at least as an overarching 'thing', which makes individuals, and it is not individuals, as independent beings, which make society. Interaction is the primary datum, and interaction shapes both the individual and society (see Figure 1).

This double process of creation (i.e. of both individual and society) might take more or less durable forms. Interaction, in the form of socialization, can have a relatively lasting impact upon the agent, for

187 Other social sciences might be relational too, but different sciences will focus upon different relations and interactions and I cannot begin to enumerate them all here.

*Relationism (vs Substantialism)*

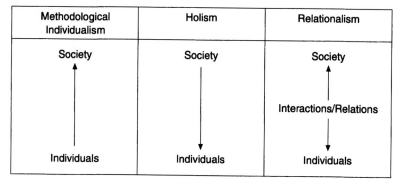

Figure 1 *Individual, society and social relations*

example, shaping their habitus (see **habitus**) in a relatively durable way. However, many interactions are fleeting and only shape the individual implicated in them over a short space of time.[188] Similarly, interactions can become stabilized in institutionalized patterns, giving rise to seemingly durable aspects ('structures') of society, or can be much more fluid, constantly evolving even over the short term. In the final instance, however, relationalists tend to call for a more dynamic form of sociology. 'Interaction', they insist, implies temporality, movement and process, such that nothing stays the same, or at least that which appears relatively static does so only in virtue of ongoing interactions which perpetuate its relatively stable form.

Furthermore, they insist that interaction is irreducible. To take a simple case, if the action of one agent 'a' is a reaction to the actions of another 'b' and the action of the second 'b' is, in turn, a reaction to the actions of the first 'a', then the two 'a,b' form an irreducible whole. The interaction is a structure which may be studied as such and which cannot be reduced back to its component parts. Needless to say this is even more so when complex network patterns are involved as a pattern of relationships may itself generate effects upon action. If a, b and c know each other, for example, then the dynamic of their interactions is able to unfold in different ways to a situation in which a and b know one another and b and

188 It is tempting to say that these more fleeting interactions do not shape the individual but only certain of their actions. Relationists such as Elias (1978), however, challenge this tendency to separate the agent from their action. The agent, they argue, is in constant motion, constant action, and to that extent is always in process (and changing). One is what one does, not some 'substance' or thing lying behind the action. This is quite a radical point and might take a little thought before it can be fully appreciated.

*Relationism (vs Substantialism)*

c know one another but a and c do not know one another. The pattern of established relationships makes a difference.

Relationalism also calls upon us to think about the 'entities' we refer to in social science in different ways, and encourages a very specific way of interpreting the findings of our studies. 'The working class', for example, exist only relative to 'the middle class', as 'males' exist only relative to 'females', and we need to be mindful about this when making claims about either of them. There is a temptation to imagine that we are referring to a 'thing' when in fact we are referring to a relationship. Norbert Elias (1978) illustrates this nicely in his discussion of power (see also **power**). We are tempted, he argues, to think of power as a 'thing' which particular (powerful) groups or individuals 'possess'. However, it is better thought of as a relation which holds between two (or more) sets of interdependent agents or groups of agents. A powerful individual is only powerful relative to another individual or group whose links to him or her enable them to influence their conduct, and it is perfectly conceivable that they are powerful in the context of this particular relationship but not in others. Furthermore, power is never wholly on one side of a relationship. It always exists in the form of a balance or 'ratio'. A young child is able to influence the behaviour of its parents, for example, at least insofar as its parents care about it, and to that extent the relationship of child to parent is one of power, favouring the child. But the parents also have effective control over many of the resources desired by the child and are in a position to influence its conduct in a variety of ways, such that they too have power over the child. Indeed, any two interacting agents influence the conduct of one another, for Elias, such that there is always a two-way power relationship between them. Finally, balances of power shift as a consequence of any number of factors, including the constant interaction within the networks in which they take shape. Children get older and become less dependent, for example, whilst parents get older and become more dependent. Scarce resources sometimes become common place and the advantage of those who possess them diminishes. Divided groups form alliances; aligned groups split, and so on. One interesting illustration of this is to be found in Elias' (1984) *Civilizing Process*. Integral to Elias' argument in this book is an account of the increasing shift in the balance of political/military power towards the centralized state. Centralized power was impossible in the Middle Ages, Elias argues, because society was geographically fragmented and the centre had no leverage through which to exert control. As geographical areas became more socially interdependent, however, a perceived recognition of the need for a powerful centre began to take shape and the centralized state was thus able to develop. The power of the centralized state, from this point of view, is not a property or belonging of the state but rather of a function of its strategic location within relations of interdependency between different geographical locations of a given territory.

Although the term 'relationalism' might have a relatively new ring to it, the spirit underlying this argument is anything but new. One can find echoes of it in many of the classic statements on sociology, even if 'the founding fathers' are not consistent in practice with the view. Georges Simmel (for example, 1971), in particular, has been identified as the key early advocate of the view. In the contemporary context, there are a number of important strands of relational thinking. One key strand, in my view at least, is symbolic interactionism. Many of the programmatic claims in recent 'relational' arguments are to be found in interactionism. Interactionists argue that (symbolic) meaning, identity, self-hood, action, social institutions and society as a whole are all constructed in and through ongoing social interactions. Another key contemporary source of relational thinking is Norbert Elias, whose concept of 'figurations' captures nicely the notion of the various webs of interaction and mutual interdependency which interweave within society, and whose emphasis on process is a constant reminder that neither individual nor society are static or unchanging phenomena but rather are both in a process of ongoing flux. Similarly, Pierre Bourdieu, through his concepts of both 'social space' and 'fields', has sought to advocate a relational view of the social world – indeed Bourdieu (1998a) argued explicitly in favour of 'relationalism' as a philosophy of science (see **social space I** and **field**). Finally, social network theories provide an important source of much relational thinking. Social network theories, in effect, have provided an important set of techniques for actually mapping the relational figurations which relational theory more generally argues constitute the social world (see **social space II**).

### FURTHER READING

Elias' (1978) *What is Sociology?* is one of the best accounts of relationism that I have come across. Bourdieu outlines his relationism at various points in his work (though always in a fragmented way). I suggest that his *Practical Reason* (Bourdieu, 1998a) is the best place to start. For a good overall account see Emirbayer (1997). The symbolic interactionists did not necessarily dress up their ideas in quite the same way as the above thinkers but what they advocated is very much the same. Herbert

Blumer's (1986) *Symbolic Interactionism* is a good starting point for getting into this literature, but note that much of Blumer's position is draw from G.H. Mead's (1967) *Mind, Self and Society*. Howard Becker's important study, *Art Worlds* (1984), is a good example of the relationism of interactionism in action. John Scott's (1991) *Social Network Analysis: A Handbook* is an excellent discussion of the mechanics of network analysis (and the history of the techniques associated with it).

# Repertoires of Contention

Related concepts: *cycles of contention, new social movements, social movements.*

The concept of 'repertoires of contention' derives from the work of Charles Tilly. Studying 'contentious politics'[189] and protest across different societies during long historical spans, Tilly observed that the ways in which people protest varies across time and place. Each society, seemingly, has a different 'repertoire' of techniques of protest (a different 'repertoire of contention') that its members draw upon in struggle. In modern societies these repertoires tend to be national and are even shared across nations. In the early stages of the industrial revolution, many were much more geographically localized and specific, and for that reason much more obvious as distinct and variable 'repertoires' to the historical eye.

Tilly first formulated the concept of repertoires in a paper which surveyed and compared forms of contentious political action in the Burgundy region of France over a 300-year period (Tilly, 1977). Since

---

189 The label 'contentious politics' is one which Tilly and his followers give to any form of politics which takes place outside of, or which challenges the official and 'normal' political process. The concept was formulated in the context of the analysis of social movements but it represents Tilly's explicit intention to broader his focus beyond social movements to focus on a wide range of 'contentious' political phenomena including revolutions, riots, strikes, acts of sabotage and many others.

---

then he has revisited and revised the concept many times (Tilly, 1978, 1986, 1995a), as have many others (see Traugott, 1995a, b; Beissinger, 1998; Chabot, 2000; Mueller, 1999; Szabó, 1996; Steinberg, 1995, 1999). The best discussion of the concept in his own work, in my view, is in a paper of 1995. Here he defines the concept in the following way:

> The word *repertoire* identifies a limited set of routines that are learnt, shared and acted out through a relatively deliberate process of choice. Repertoires are learnt cultural creations, but they do not descend from abstract philosophy or take shape as a result of political propaganda; they emerge from struggle. People learn to break windows in protest, attack pilloried prisoners, tear down dishonoured houses, stage public marches, petition, hold formal meetings, organize special-interest associations. At any particular point in history, however, they learn only a rather small number of alternative ways to act collectively. (1995: 26)

Five points are noteworthy from this definition. Firstly, there is a suggestion that repertoires constrain behaviour and choice. Although Tilly elsewhere makes reference to improvization in relation to repertoires, it is evident that he believes protest to be bounded by the repertoires that protestors have learnt. Indeed, one of his hypotheses with respect to repertoires is that: 'the prior history of contention [in a given geographical/social arena] constrains the choices of action currently available, in partial independence of the identities and interests that participants bring to the action' (ibid.: 29). Secondly, on the other side of this same point, there is a tacit recognition of the know-how or acquired competence involved in specific forms of protest. Protesting requires a certain degree of skill in specific techniques of protest. Thirdly, there is an emphasis upon the practical constitution of repertoires. They do not emerge out of abstract thinking but rather out of struggle and the activities of everyday life. Traugott's (1995b) study of barricades illustrates this well. The use of the barricade in popular protest, most famously associated with the French revolution, he shows, developed out of a routine and everyday method of 'neighbourhood protection' in sixteenth-century Paris. Fourthly, a notion of deliberate but constrained choice is introduced. Protesters choose their repertoire from the available stock. Finally, to reiterate the main point, repertoires are identified with specific historical periods.

Repertoires are not so much forms of action as of interaction, however. They connect and belong to sets of actors:

> The action takes its meaning and effectiveness from shared understandings, memories, and agreements, however grudging, among the parties. In that sense, then, a repertoire of actions resembles not individual consciousness but a language; although individuals

Tilly's reference here to shared understandings, memories and agreements suggests that contention is, in certain respects, the expected punishment to which elites are subject when they overstep a culturally determined mark. And this entails a sense that the aggrieved have a 'right', however grudgingly accorded them, to defend their interests in this way. In addition, there is a sense both that the protest follows an expected path and that it works, in part, by way of a communicative power which is afforded it by the aforementioned shared expectations. In effect, repertoires are legitimate or accepted moves in a game which all parties, perhaps unwittingly, adhere to. This entails that repertoires are, to a degree, institutionalized, and Tilly extends this notion by noting the 'fit' between repertoires and other institutionalized aspects of the social world, for example, 'police practices, laws of assembly, rules of association, routines for informal gatherings, ways of displaying symbols of affiliation, opposition . . . means of reporting news and so on' (1995: 26–7). Repertoires are shaped by these other institutions, he argues, but they also play a part in shaping those institutions. Or rather, the institutionalized space for legitimate protest is carved out by way of protest itself. As an example of this Tilly (ibid.) makes reference to the struggles in Britain during the nineteenth century over what counted as acceptable and legal forms of strike activity. Contemporary strike activities take place in the 'space' forged by these earlier struggles.[190]

Given the emphasis that Tilly puts upon historical differences and comparison it is obvious that he will need some account of how new forms emerge within a repertoire and how old ones either die away or are modified. He actually says relatively little with respect to this issue, but insofar as he does, his focus is upon innovation. Activists are constantly innovating, he argues, but this is usually at the 'perimeter' of existing repertoires. Moreover, even when they do generate new forms of protest these forms will often fail. If, however, they are successful and other actors perceive them to be so and appropriate them, then they will enter and modify the repertoire. Other writers have argued that peaks in 'cycles of contention' (see **cycles of contention**) tend to produce high levels of innovation in repertoires.

---

190  Of course laws regarding protest and strike action change frequently and have changed many times since the eighteenth and nineteenth centuries.

---

**Repertoires of Contention**

The concept of repertoires clearly involves linguistic or discursive forms of behaviour. The act of petitioning is a form of discourse, for example, as is the chanting which often occurs on marches. Steinberg (1995, 1999) has extended this further by focusing on the various forms of rhetoric and argumentative strategy which seem to become institutionalized in various types of struggle. One can identify acquired rhetorical forms of argument within and across struggles as surely as one can identify acquired behavioural forms of protest, he argues. Similarly one can trace the history of contention that has shaped these 'fighting words'. Thus the concept of repertoires must be expanded to incorporate these forms of talk. We must be alert to the phenomena of 'discursive repertoires'.

### FURTHER READING

Tilly's (1995) paper, 'Contentious repertoires in Great Britain, 1758–1834' is his best exposition of the concept in my view. The paper is in Mark Traugott's (1995) edited collection, *Repertoires and Cycles of Collective Action*, which in itself is an excellent resource for those with an interest in both repertoires and cycles of contention, and a great place to start for those who find these ideas of interest. There is paper by Steinberg in that collection which lays out the basic idea of discursive repertoires.

# Repression (psychoanalysis)

273

> *Related concepts: body-power/bio-power, id, ego and superego, imaginary, symbolic and real, mirror stage and the ego, power, power-knowledge, unconscious (the).*

The concept of repression is central to psychoanalysis and psychoanalytic social theory. As noted in my entry on 'the unconscious' (see **unconscious (the)**), this mental realm is generated, according to the founder of psychoanalysis, Sigmund Freud, through force of repression. Socially unacceptable thoughts, desires, memories, and so on, are actively pushed out of consciousness, such that we only catch a glimpse of them, in disguised form, in our dreams, parapraxes[191] and neuroses. For Freud himself, repression is necessary for civilization. Human nature involves sexual and aggressive drives which are uncivilized and anti-social, and which must be controlled and repressed if an orderly and civilized life is to be achieved (Freud, 1986). The only qualification to this which we find in his own work is in the form of a claim that excessive repression, such as characterized the social circles of the Victorian middle-classes, to which he and his patients belonged, gives rise to neurotic symptoms. Excessive repression, in other words, is potentially damaging. A number of more radical theorists have seized upon this basic idea of repression, however, as a means of exploring what they take to be the psychologically stultifying nature of capitalist societies.

Herbert Marcuse (1987) provides one early example of this. Overlaying Freud's ideas with those of Marx, he distinguishes between what he deems 'socially necessary repression', that is, repression necessary to any kind of civilized and fulfilling life, and 'surplus repression', that is, the additional repression necessary to the maintenance of specifically capitalist societies, with their excessive concerns for profit and efficiency, and their specifically exploitative character.[192] Capitalist societies do not simply repress negative aspects of human nature which, arguably, should be repressed, Marcuse argues, they also repress more positive (empathic,

191 In psychoanalytic parlance 'parapraxes' are behaviours which seem accidental but which, in the view of psychoanalysts, reveal elements of our unconscious (and thus 'repressed') desires, feelings, beliefs, etc. The obvious example of this is slips of the tongue (commonly called 'Freudian slips', after the founder of psychoanalysis, Sigmund Freud), where we say something other than 'what we mean' but which potentially has a meaning in the situation we are in. To give a Freudian example, we might say 'mother' when we mean 'lover'. Such a slip would be highly significant in the eyes of a psychoanalyst. They would suggest that a small part of our unconscious had just come into view – perhaps we think of our mother as our lover, as Freud's theory of the Oedipus Complex suggests. In addition to slips, psychoanalysts claim to be able (potentially) to read unconscious significance in bungled actions, memory lapses, the forgetting or mixing up of names and many other 'accidents' of conduct. All are parapraxes. See **unconscious (the)**.

192 In any society, for example, it is necessary for people to work, which requires that they defer gratification, suspending the pursuit of pleasure for periods of what may, in some cases, prove to be hard, boring or otherwise unpleasant activity. Even the 'best' jobs will have some element of this. Thus repression is always necessary in some measure – workers must keep their 'pleasure principle' under control. In capitalist societies, however, Marcuse argues, the working class have to work much harder (since their wages do not reflect the true value of their labour – see **social class**) and they work under much harsher working conditions than they otherwise might. In this context a much higher level of repression is required from them – what Marcuse, echoing Marx's account of 'surplus value', refers to as 'surplus repression'.

**Repression (psychoanalysis)**

creative and aesthetic) aspects of our nature, which, given free reign, might provide the key to a better way of living. The balance of repression is precarious, according to Marcuse, however, and these repressed energies might also provide the impetus to revolutionary action, such as that prefigured in the 'sexual revolution' and counter-culture of the 1960s. In a slightly different vein, but not unrelated, the work of such contemporary feminists as Julia Kristeva (1980) hinges upon the idea that the symbolic order of contemporary societies is founded only upon the basis of a repression of more feminine aspects of our nature which, again, might constitute a basis for a more fulfilling way of living.

Another interesting development of this idea, more historically rooted but less explicitly political, is Norbert Elias' (1984) analysis of 'the civilizing process'. Through an examination of a variety of historical sources, principally etiquette manuals, Elias shows that and how a variety of forms of human behaviour have been transformed over the last 400 years, becoming more 'civilized',[193] and how levels of self-control have increased. This analysis is very clearly influenced by Freud's thesis. It goes beyond Freud, however, in the respect that it considers empirical-historical evidence has a much more sophisticated theoretical apparatus for analysing this historical-social process than we find in Freud, and offers a variety of criticisms of the tendency towards reification in Freudian models of both 'mind' and 'individual-society' relations (Elias, 1978, 1984).

Given the centrality of the concept of repression to psychoanalysis it is surprising, as Billig (1999) has noted, to find that it is nowhere adequately explained by Freud or his followers. It is nowhere explored or unpacked. It is simply presented, dressed in mechanistic metaphors, as a fact of psychological life. Psychological mechanisms, we are asked to believe, block out socially or personally disturbing material, relegating it to the unconscious and keeping conscious mental functioning unburdened. To accept this view, as such, we would have to buy into an extremely reified concept of mind. Moreover, if we seek to avoid reification, as many have done, we are forced to confront a perplexing paradox noted by Sartre (Sartre, 1969) amongst others. In order to repress unacceptable thoughts, desires and memories, Sartre argues, consciousness must be aware of them and aware that they are unacceptable. How else could it keep them out? But if it is aware of them then they are not unconscious, rather they are ideas that we consciously hold at a distance.

---

193 Elias is also clear to stress that the very idea of 'civilization' and 'civilized behaviour' belongs to this historical process.

It might make sense to talk of repression, from this point of view, but not an 'unconscious', and repression would be conceived of as a necessarily conscious rather than unconscious process.

The most persuasive way of thinking through this and other problems, to my mind, has been suggested by Michael Billig (1999). Billig conceives of repression in terms of habit and routine. We are all aware at some times, he notes, of the way in which we push unacceptable thoughts out of our minds or cover them over with rationalizations. We are also aware of the way in which we tailor and censor our thoughts in accordance with specific situational norms. The way we talk to our lecturers or parents, for example, is different from the way in which we talk to our friends. There is nothing mysterious about this and also nothing hidden. We know that we are doing it. We are aware of 'biting our tongue', forcing back laughter, 'restraining' ourselves or thinking of 'acceptable' ways of saying things that, presently, are occurring to us in a way likely to cause offence. It is for this reason that the concept of repression has a common sense appeal and plausibility. We know that we do it sometimes because we are conscious of doing so.

Like anything else that we do repeatedly, however, such acts of repression can become routinized and habitual, such that we do them without realizing that we are. And we can become quite emotionally attached to these habits of repression insofar as they make our lives easier and keep us relatively free of anxiety. Moreover, we can be explicitly trained to repress in these ways. Learning to speak, for example, as Billig argues, is not merely a matter of learning what to say but also learning what not to say, and learning, as Bourdieu (1992b) has argued, to euphemize. This might explain the difficulty Freud's patients experienced in talking about sex – an experience which led him to the ideas of repression and the unconscious. They were finding themselves drawn into discussion about issues which they had learned to avoid talking about. However, in a fascinating twist of the argument, Billig argues also that it explains Freud's studious avoidance of a range of social and political issues which were having a considerable and negative impact upon the life of both himself and his patients at the time that much of his case material was being gathered and his key works being written – chiefly the persecution of the Jews in Germany and Austria. Freud may have been relatively open about sex, Billig notes, but he was seemingly quite repressed when it came to matters of political persecution. He refused to face up to it or consider it as a factor affecting the psychological health of his (Jewish) patients. We do not need to limit our understanding of repression to the repression of supposedly 'primary'

*Repression (psychoanalysis)*

psychological drives, Billig continues; we can equally consider the repression of historically contingent social and political issues. Furthermore, this time agreeing with Freud, he acknowledges that some repression is desirable. Those who are inclined, for whatever reason, towards sexist and racist ways of thinking, for example, might do better to learn to repress these impulses and channel their frustrations elsewhere.

This argument presupposes a rather different model of the agent from that proposed by Sartre, or Freud for that matter. To accept the model we must be prepared to accept, as Freud (1985) suggested, that consciousness does not pre-empt our mental life. Our psychology is not the sum of that which we are conscious of at any time. Rather than following psychoanalysis in hypothesizing the existence of an inner mechanical sanctum of the mind, however, Billig suggests that what underlies our consciousness is embodied and habitual human action. What we think is erected upon the basis of a whole range of things that we do without thinking, and consciousness is, so to speak, the effect rather than the cause of our actions. For Billig, as a psychologist with a strong interest in discourse and rhetoric, much of this is a matter of speech; of learning to talk and thus think about issues in socially acceptable ways. The habits of primary interest to Billig are habits of speech and discourse (see **discourse**). He also identifies an important role for daily routines, however, focusing on Freud's daily routines in particular. Such routines, he argues, are the way in which we organize our lives, habitually and without thought, so as to regulate our own conduct and affect what we expose ourselves to. Again this habitual behaviour mirrors our more conscious behaviour. One relatively conscious way in which we 'push things out of our minds' is to 'make ourselves busy'.

Where does this leave the concept of the unconscious? I believe that it steers us away from any reified and naïvely substantialist or animistic understandings of the unconscious as a 'real' place somewhere inside the individual, bursting to get out. It may be that, in particular situations, our habits of civilized and appropriate conduct encounter real resistance in the form of strong affective responses or inarticulate impulses to act otherwise than we 'should'. But we would have to say that such impulses or emotions were responses to a situation rather than long-standing and ever present drives. I am not constantly fighting the aggressive impulse to hit other people or seduce them. These impulses might take a grip some of the time but they are not permanent fixtures of my psychological life (conscious or unconscious). Similarly, it may be that our forms of talk constitute polite misrepresentations and misunderstandings of forms of conduct which would be better described differently – namely it might be that our self-understanding does not bear close scrutiny and that our dispositions, actions and 'motives' would be better described in other terms. Indeed, integral to Billig's model, I suggest, is a break with the Cartesian notion that individuals have an immediate self-understanding. He opens the door to the possibility of motivated self-deception, and to the possibility that there are aspects of ourselves and our histories that we are unaware of. I might not understand why I am an anxious person or am afraid of dark spaces, for example, and might have repressed episodes in my personal history which best explain those dispositions. I might need psychotherapy or psychoanalysis to help me to remember them. This does not mean that I have lost memories wandering around my head for large periods of my life, however. Memories presuppose a process of remembering, a reconstructive social and linguistic process. They do not exist outside of this process, 'unconsciously' or consciously. I might still be affected by aspects of my past that I have forgotten, that is, episodes which I have forgotten as explicit memories but which nevertheless had a formative influence upon me and thus still 'shape' my present. That is not the same thing as having 'repressed memories' lurking around in a hypothetical mental ether, however.

Billig's model connects nicely with a number of other critical engagements with psychoanalysis. His work connects with the philosophy of Merleau-Ponty (1962, 1965), who also struggles to make psychoanalytic ideas more plausible. And it connects with the work of Bourdieu, whose 'habitus' (like Merleau-Ponty's 'body-subject') mirrors aspects of Billig's model of agency, and who also seeks to recast key psychoanalytic concepts in a more social light (see **habitus** and **body-subject**). Finally, it connects with an important reflection upon 'habits of self-constraint' which runs through a variety of key social thinkers including Durkheim, Elias and, again, Bourdieu. Through the work of these various writers, I suggest, we may find useful ways of operationalizing psychoanalytic ideas within critical social science.

As a final note on the concept of repression we should briefly mention Foucault's (1984) critique of 'the repressive hypothesis'. Without wanting to deny that society places prohibitions on sexual conduct or that this was particularly so in the Victorian context addressed by Freud, Foucault questions the validity of understanding the relationship between sexuality and society in terms of 'repression'. The Victorians did not so much repress sexuality as 'invent' it Foucault argues. At one level this argument is centred upon the fact that the Victorian era marked a period of transition in the history of human self-understanding. It was the time when the concept of sexuality, in its modern form, and the related notion of human beings as sexual animals (consisting of various sexual types – 'perverts', 'inverts', and so on) whose 'truth' lay in their 'sexuality', first emerged. More to the point, however, Foucault argues that the Victorians, having 'invented' the concept of sexuality, became obsessed with it. They talked incessantly of it, saw it everywhere and attempted to regulate it everywhere. It became a key principle of social organization – in architecture, pedagogy, psychiatry, and so on. Moreover, Foucault even suggests that the various attempts to regulate sexuality and evade regulation generated a degree of excitement and pleasure – which we might deem 'sexual'. Sexuality was, in this sense, produced by régimes of power/knowledge (see **power/knowledge**), rather than repressed. Furthermore, the ideas of Freud, Marcuse, and so on, take shape within this régime of power/knowledge according to Foucault. They belong to the apparatus of power in modern societies and are thus not nearly so radical as they pretend – this is particularly true of psychoanalysis as a therapeutic practice. This point resonates with Foucault's wider claims that power in modern societies is productive and related to attempts to know and understand human beings (see **body-power/bio-power, power,** and **power/knowledge**).

### FURTHER READING

As noted above, there is no good, clear discussion of repression in Freud's work – though he refers to it constantly. However, his *Civilization and its Discontents* (which is included in the collection *Civilization, Society and Religion* (Freud, 1986)) is the key text on the relationship of repression to civilized society. His *Introductory Lectures on Psychoanalysis* (Freud, 1973) are also a good source for getting an overall picture of psychoanalysis – and like all of Freud's work they are very clearly presented. Elias' (1984) *The Civilizing Process* is a fascinating read which is very relevant to this issue. Billig's (1999) *Freudian Repression* is also an excellent book, very clear and very interesting (although perhaps more so for those who already have some interest in Freud and some familiarity with the debates in psychoanalysis). Foucault's (1984) *History of Sexuality Vol. 1* is also a very relevant and interesting study.

279

# Sex/Gender Distinction

> *Related concepts:* **body-power/bio-power, patriarchy, performativity, power/knowledge, social constructions/social constructionism.**

Many early academic feminists, such as Simone de Beauvoir (1988) and Ann Oakley (1972), and also more conservative 'sex role' theorists (see Connell, 1987), sought to establish a distinction between 'sex' as a biological reality and 'gender' as a cultural, psychological and historical reality. There is a biological difference between the sexes, it was argued, and most people are born (albeit with a few ambiguous cases in between) as one sex or another. However, having been born into one sex or another, it was argued, individuals are then socialized according to specific gender expectations and roles. Biological males learn to take on masculine roles and to think and act in masculine ways, whilst biological females learn to take on feminine roles and to think and act in feminine ways. This is captured in de Beauvoir's much cited claim that, to paraphrase, one is not born a woman but becomes one.

The evidence for this distinction came from a number of sources. On the one hand, for example, much historical and anthropological evidence was gathered to demonstrate that what is 'typically' male or female varies considerably between societies – whilst biological differences remain relatively constant.[194] Roles or attributes that one society allocates and attributes to males might be allocated and attributed to females in another society, and vice versa. What seems naturally masculine to us, therefore, may in fact be relatively culture-bound and certainly not typical of men in other cultures or times. On the other hand, a number of cases were identified where individuals had, by force of some quirk of birth, developed the 'wrong' gender for their sex, and had at some point changed their gender on account of, for example, an ambivalence regarding their biological sex. In other words, individuals appear capable

---

194 I say 'relatively' here since human social agents are, of course, biological beings and how they act can affect their biological constitution. There is, in effect, a two-way relationship between 'biology' and 'society', mediated by action; our biology affects how we act and thus affects our social relationships but our social relationships also affect how we act and thus affects our biology.

of changing their gender, whilst their biological constitution remains constant.

This set the scene for a powerful feminist critique. The distinction between sex and gender is often overlooked, feminists argued. We assume many of the variable features of gender to be fixed facts of nature (sex). Cultural or social 'facts' are (mis)understood to be biological facts, such that gender relations are 'naturalized' and persistent inequalities between the sexes are portrayed as legitimate because they are inevitable. These claims sparked a series of (now well-known and well-rehearsed) nature/nurture debates, simultaneously scientific and political, in which the evidence for and against a particular attribute being biologically or socially caused would be mounted up.

The later history of academic feminism, however, has spawned various critiques of this early feminist position. On the one hand, for example, some feminists have argued that there is an implicit and wrong assumption in some of these sex/gender arguments that the roles and attributes of men are better or more preferable. The point of feminism should not be to establish that women can be like men, they continue, but rather to challenge the ideology which disvalues feminine attributes and roles in the first place, and uses them as an excuse to debar women from life opportunities that they might wish to pursue. The biological differences between the sexes may indeed explain certain differences in psychology and social role, from this point of view, but that is largely beside the point. I will not explore this criticism here. Rather, I will focus upon a further and currently more influential criticism, associated primarily with the work of Judith Butler (1990, 1993, 1994).

The implication of the sex/gender distinction, Butler argues, is that sex comes first and is natural. Gender is perceived as a secondary construct which is imposed over the top of this 'natural' distinction. Against this Butler argues that 'sex' itself is a social category, that is to say, the distinction between 'male' and 'female' is a human, social distinction. It belongs to our particular way of perceiving the world and dividing it up. In this respect 'sex' is as much a matter of culture as is gender. Indeed, it might be deemed secondary to it as 'sex' is a category shaped by 'gendered' discourse (see **discourse**). Or rather, the distinction between sex and gender itself collapses. Although Butler does not discuss them in detail, debates and shifts in the scientific (biological) meaning and definition of sex are an importance source of evidence for this argument, since they indicate that the category of sex is theoretically rooted, historically variable and has shifted over time (on this see Laqueur, 1990). It is not unproblematic, as one might assume. Furthermore, Butler and others revisit the aforementioned instances of individuals whose biological sex at birth is unclear and cannot be decided on the basis of conventional procedures.[195] These cases, she believes, blur and problematize sexual categories. They suggest that these categories are, in some degree at least, arbitrary.

In making this claim, Butler does not seek to deny that there are demonstrable (biological) differences between 'the sexes' in most cases. Her concern, rather, is that 'biology' itself, as a scientific discipline, is a social system of representation and more importantly that there are any number of differences between human beings but only some become a basis for dividing human beings into distinct 'types'. In other words, even if we accept that there are basic differences between 'the sexes' there is no necessity that these differences should serve as a basis for dividing human beings into groups (namely, sexes), that is to say, there is no logical or rational reason for doing so, independently of the social and political contexts within which this operation has been performed.

'Sex' is not merely an analytic category, Butler continues. It is equally a normative category, that is, it does not merely stipulate what women and men are, it stipulates what they ought to be. It formulates a law or regulation. Drawing upon Foucault (1980a) she claims that knowledge of sex is intimately bound up with forms of power for regulating and controlling it (see **power/knowledge**). This is very apparent in the aforementioned ambiguous cases, where an individual's 'sex' cannot be decided on biological grounds. In such cases there is no question that such individuals be allowed to remain without a sex or between sexes, as a purely analytic and dispassionate investigation might suggest. Rather it is insisted that they must have, or rather be a sex. A sex is allocated to them and in many cases biological ambiguities are removed by way of surgery.[196] This is an extreme example but, again, it illustrates a more general point for Butler, namely, that the category of 'sex' has a normative content and does not so much describe a pre-given reality as orient practices which produce sex. This relates to her further concern with the 'performativity' of sex and gender (see **performativity**).

This normative discourse on sex, Butler continues, is intimately interwoven with a normative discourse on sexuality, which again divides individuals into types (heterosexual, homosexual, bisexual, and so on) and stipulates, often seemingly on biological grounds, how they ought to

195 Some individuals, for example, are born with both male and female sex organs, or with an organ which falls ambiguously between the two.
196 An individual who has both male and female genitals, for example, might be castrated.

identify and behave. The heterosexual 'norm' in what Butler, in her early work, refers to as the 'heterosexual matrix', is a strategic centre around which forms of classification and regulation which seek to discipline human agents circulate. Sexuality, sex and gender are interconnected normative models from this point of view, which are enforced at numerous points throughout the social body.

The underlying message of Butler's argument would appear to be that the static and pre-emptive categories of sex and sexuality both fail to capture the degree of fluidity and difference within the populations that they categorize and, at the same time, function within régimes of regulation which seek to discipline and regulate that fluidity and difference. On this issue, moreover, she is critical of other feminists and gay and lesbian writers who seek in some way to clarify or elaborate female or gay identities. Such work, she suggests, contributes to normalization processes which seek to fit fluid and heterogenous lives and practices into neat regulated 'boxes' and thereby to shape and discipline social agents. At the very least, she argues, by seeking out the essence of sex or sexuality they ignore the diversity amongst women and lesbians which derives from diverse racial, class and geographical positions.

None of this seeks to challenge what the earlier feminists had argued about the socialization of children along gendered lines – although Butler does have her own specific take on this (see **performativity**). Having been categorized as a specific 'sex', the argument goes, infants are then subject (in varying degrees) to a range of gendered expectations regarding their behaviour and to a gendered socialization trajectory. Where the argument departs from the earlier feminist position, to reiterate, is in questioning the 'given-ness' of 'sex' as a bedrock upon which gender is constructed.

### FURTHER READING

Butler is a notoriously difficult writer who does not state her claims in the form of clear arguments. However, in an interview in 1994, in the *Radical Philosophy* journal, she does explain her key ideas (as they were at that time) in a relatively clear fashion, including her ideas on sex and gender (Butler, 1994). The key reference that I have used in this entry is *Gender Trouble* (Butler, 1990) but her later text, *Bodies that Matter* is arguably as important in respect of this issue. Both books are discussed in the aforementioned interview. Bob Connell (1987) offers an excellent discussion of questions of gender in his *Gender and Power*, which traces a different path through the literature and arrives at a slightly different (arguably more persuasive and more sociological) position. I have not

283

discussed Connell here due to space restrictions and the greater infamy of Butler, but I do strongly recommend his work as key reading.

# Social Capital

> Related concepts: capital, field, social space I and II.

The concept of social capital is relatively new to social theory, having only come into popular use in the late 1980s. However, it has managed over this short period to attract a sufficient number of competing definitions, controversies and ambiguities to compare with many more traditional concepts. In this entry I am going to focus upon the key work of Robert Putnam (1993, 2000) and some of the debate it has attracted, as well as the rather different approach that appears in the work of Pierre Bourdieu.[197]

Part of the ambiguity associated with the concept of social capital stems from the fact that it began life, in the work of James Coleman (1988), as something of an umbrella concept. Coleman is a rational choice theorist and, as such, is committed to methodological individualism. He believes that, for methodological purposes at least, society can be decomposed into the activities of self-interested individuals who use a variety of resources that they have available to them to pursue their individual aims and goals, and who enter into relationships of exchange with one another, trading resources in the pursuit of profit. Unlike other methodological individualists, however, he believes that certain of the resources available to individuals in specific situations are 'social' in the respect that they derive from and are properties of relationships between individuals, which cannot be reduced back to the individual, for example, norms, trust, networks, and so on.[198] Furthermore, he is interested not just

---

197 See also **capital** for a discussion of Bourdieu's concept of social capital and its relationship to the various other forms of capital referred to in his theory.
198 In making this claim Coleman goes beyond the boundaries of what is conventionally thought of as 'methodological individualism'. However, in other respects he does remain very much committed to an approach to analysis which is focused upon the individual.

---

in individual behaviour but in social systems,[199] and he believes that the resources at work in these systems include some which are 'social' in the above sense. 'Social capital' is the name which Coleman gives to these various resources, and it was his work on this form of capital, which examined the relationship between educational success and a supportive family background (a form of social capital), which first launched the concept into prominence. From this point of view 'social capital' is anything inherently and irreducibly social or collective in nature that an individual can use to their advantage in the pursuit of their projects, namely that they can use as a resource.

It was the work of Robert Putnam, who draws upon Coleman, however, which made the concept of social capital a household name in social science. Putnam's early work was focused upon Italian society and, in particular, the discrepancy in rates of development between the north (which has developed well, relatively speaking) and the south (which has developed less well) (Putnam, 1993). Putnam's question is as to why this is so and his answer lies in 'social capital'. The traditions of northern Italy, tracing right back into the Middle Ages, entail a much stronger involvement in civic associations and forms of voluntary public activity, he notes, and this activity or rather the level of trust, reciprocity and networking it engenders, spills over into and provides an infrastructure for other spheres of activity. It is this social infrastructure, this concentration of social capital, which explains the relative success of the north. Northern Italy has a higher level of social capital than southern Italy and it has prospered as a consequence.[200]

The implication of this study is that social capital accrues over many hundreds of years and cannot, as such, be engineered. It is the centuries old traditions of northern Italy which allowed it to prosper relative to the south, according to Putnam, traditions which emerged gradually over a long period. However, his later and more famous study, *Bowling Alone*, paints a rather different picture. Focusing upon contemporary US society, he bemoans the decline of strong forms of public association which create strong community ties, forms typified, in his view, by the bowling alley

---

199 This may seem an odd focus for a methodological individualist and perhaps is, but the key, for Coleman, is that, whilst it makes sense to speak of and focus upon social systems, they can in the final instance be broken down into the individuals who compose them and can in fact only be adequately analysed and understood from this point of view.
200 Putnam's empirical work has been subject to a considerable amount of criticism, both substantive and methodological, but that is not our concern in this conceptual exposition. For an introduction to some of the criticism see Fine (2001).

and the networks which used to form around it. This decline, he claims, has taken place in only a few decades and both he and many after him see this as a key source of a range of social ills, including crime, political apathy, poor physical and mental health, and again poor levels of economic development. It is necessary, Putnam argues, to start rebuilding social capital.

It is the claim that social capital is declining which appears to have really captured the imagination of social researchers. There have been a large number of studies which have sought to trace this decline in different national contexts or to invoke it in explanations of a range of social ills or perhaps again to contest the very idea of decline.

There is something very peculiar about this version of the social capital concept. It derives from a very individualistic form of social theory, deeply embedded in economic forms of theorizing, which has traditionally been very critical of structuralist forms of sociology and their notion that society is sui generis and irreducible to individuals qua individuals. And yet that is precisely what the concept of social capital entails. The term 'capital' suggests that we are dealing with a resource that agents might mobilize, and we will see that the concept can be used in a fashion more consonant with this notion, but in Putnam's version we are talking about what other social theorists have called social integration, a structural property of society sui generis. Individuals might benefit from this integration and might rely upon it in various ways in their projects but it is not, as the term 'capital' suggests, something which they possess. It is a property of the social networks to which they belong. Furthermore, the thesis regarding the decline of social capital and the various social ills stemming from that is very similar to Durkheim's (1952) classic argument in *Suicide* and his more general emphasis upon the dangers associated with the breakdown of organic forms of social solidarity (see **anomie**). In this respect the concept of social capital is a reinvention or rediscovery of much older sociological ideas –albeit very important ideas – and, indeed, one which is both confusing and dishonest because it attempts to disguise what it is doing in order to remain within its 'rational action' framework. This is not to deny that there is something empirically impressive about the work generated by Putnam and his followers. There is much to be learnt from their empirical work, from their measures and from the methods of social network analysis that they have played an important part in rediscovering. But it is my view that this would all make a lot more sense if it were relocated in a different theoretical framework, a framework which breaks more decisively and clearly with individualism.[201] It might also make more sense to drop the confusing term 'social capital'.

There is another version of the concept of social capital, however, which does have a more individual/'resource' focus and which develops that in a coherent and useful way. From this point of view an agent's own individual (ego-centred) 'ties' or 'contacts' are a resource which they can draw upon to further whatever ends they have in view[202]. 'Social capital', when used in this way, is a sociological version of the common sense thesis that it is *who* and not *what* you know' that counts for getting on in life. Mark Granovetter's (1973) classic early study of the role of 'weak' ties in the process whereby agents secure employment is a very good example of this. He shows that and how agents mobilize their personal connections to secure the information they need to get a job, emphasizing that more dispersed contacts, who are often only weakly linked to the agent, are particularly valuable in this context. It is the work of Pierre Bourdieu,[203] however, which really formalizes this approach, setting 'social capital' alongside a variety of other forms of capital (economic, cultural and symbolic) (see **capital**). Bourdieu's understanding of social capital resonates with the 'who you know' thesis but also with the notion of 'old boy' networks connecting agents who have been to elite schools and universities. We all have some sort of network of friends, family and colleagues, and we all rely upon that network to some extent for a variety of 'services', but some of us have 'friends in high places' or rather friends in higher places whose services may be of a 'higher' order too. These are the links that Bourdieu is really interested in. Who has connections that allow them access to power and/or which help them up the social ladder? Furthermore, he notes that friends in high places are usually met in high places, or at least when *en route* for high places. They are friends met at Oxford, Harvard or the Sorbonne, at Eton, Harrow or perhaps an exclusive gentleman's club. In this respect social capital is much more closely embedded in the class structure and much more closely tied to the

---

201 This need not entail an abandonment of the individual altogether or indeed of a notion that individuals are, in some part, motivated by utilitarian impulses. It would simply involve more clarity regarding those phenomena which transcend the individual. It is my belief that classic social theorists, such as Durkheim and G.H. Mead are actually much clearer in this respect – although, having said that, they are often misread on these points.

202 In other words, rather than looking, as Putnam did, at the general level of community integration and the advantages it may generate for those within it, we can look at who specific agents know and whose services they are able to call upon.

203 There is no obvious reference for this in Bourdieu's work but the concept crops up in a number of his studies.

other forms of capital than certain definitions of social capital might suggest. Being born in a 'high place' considerably increases one's likelihood of having friends in high places.

Having said this, given Bourdieu's view that the social world is differentiated into distinct fields (see **field**), we must take the view that social capital, to an extent, is differentiated also. For example, the connections which might help an individual make their way in international banking are not the same as the ones which might pave the way in areas of sport or the arts or in street gangs. 'Who you know' may be as important to survival in a violent inner city estate as in the upper echelons of the banking or academic worlds but the 'who' in question will be quite different.

Structural and resource versions of the concept of social capital, at least if we reduce the structural to its network element, are not necessarily incompatible. What individual agents 'have' in the way of social capital positions them within a network structure which, in turn, has its own (analysable) properties. To illustrate this consider the small-scale hypothetical networks below:

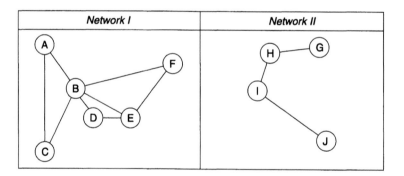

We can study these networks from a structural point of view (see **social space II**). Comparatively, for example, we might say that Network I is more 'centred'[204] (as all points converge on point B) than Network II (in which points H and I are more central than G and J, having two

204 To say that a network is centred or rather to speak of its degree of centredness is to reflect upon the extent to which its constituent members are each connected to a core member or members. This, in turn, has a mathematical definition which is discussed both in Scott (1991) and Degenne and Forsé (1999).

connections rather than one, but no point is very central). Furthermore, we might compare what network theorists call the density of the two networks, that is, the number of actual connections between points as a proportion of the number of possible connections.[205] These are useful structural comparisons which have at least some bearing upon questions of social integration, such as we discussed briefly in relation to Putnam.[206] Given the greater degree of centrality in Network I we might say, using the language of 'social capital', that it has a greater concentration of social capital than Network II – alternatively, given the greater precision of the concepts of 'centrality' and 'density' we might stick to these. However, we might also compare individuals in the network, treating their position in the network as an individual resource for them. Agent B in Network I, for example, is very central and very well connected (five connections) compared to agent A, who is out on a limb and has only two connections. Thus B has more social capital relative to this network than A. The structural and personal-resource definitions of social capital are two sides of the same coin from this point of view.

## FURTHER READING

Putnam's work is quite clear and is worth reading first hand, particularly *Bowling Alone* (Putnam, 2000). Granovetter's (1973) 'The strength of weak ties' is a classic and well worth a read. For a good critique of 'social capital theory' see Fine's (2001) *Social Capital Versus Social Theory*. For a discussion of social capital in the context of social network theory see Degenne and Forsé's (1999) *Introducing Social Networks*. The latter authors also introduce the key concepts of the social network approach, as does Scott (1991). I find Scott clearer in relation to key concepts and methods but Degenne and Forsé offer more discussion of certain specific theories sometimes associated with network research.

205 In Network I there are 8 connecting lines out of a possible 15, giving a density score of 8/15 = 0.533. For Network II, interestingly, there are 3 connections out of a possible 6, giving a very similar density score of 3/6 = 0.5.
206 I am not suggesting that either density or centrality are direct 'measures' of integration but they clearly say something about the degree to which a network is tightly knit and thus integrated.

# Social Class

Related concepts: **capital, crisis, habitus, ideology, power, social space I.**

Like most of the concepts discussed in this book, the concept of social class is much debated and contested, and is subject to various competing definitions. The obvious starting point for our brief outline, however, is Marx. Most key discussions of class, particularly in the critical literature, point back to Marx.

## MARX

Marx's theory of class is related to his broader theory of history and in particular to his concepts, 'forces of production', 'relations of production' and 'modes of production'. Different historical epochs, he claimed, are characterized by different modes of production. Modes of production comprise, firstly, the means by which that society produces its essential material goods (means or forces of production) and secondly, the social relationships of members of society to those forces of production and, via the forces of production, to one another (relations of production). In capitalist societies, he continues, the means of production are industrial, comprising large production units such as factories and large extraction units such as mines. The social relations investing these forces tend to divide society into two distinct groups. One relatively small group, whom Marx calls 'the bourgeoisie', both own and control the means of production (for example, they are factory or mine owners). The other much larger group, whom Marx calls 'the proletariat', neither own nor control the forces of production. They own only their own potential labour power as workers and to survive they must sell their labour power to the bourgeoisie in return for what Marx deems a subsistence wage, that is, a wage which, combined with that of other family members, just about keeps their family alive and available for work. The bourgeoisie and the proletariat are thus each defined by their relationship to the forces of production, and this relationship, in turn, mediates their relationship to one another; the bourgeoisie need the proletariat to work in their factories and down their mines, and so on. The proletariat are forced to sell their labour power to the bourgeoisie as they depend upon paid work for their own survival. This relationship of interdependency is, at the same time, a relationship of exploitation according to Marx, however. The value of the products produced in factories, and so on, is an effect of the labour put into them (this is the key claim of Marx's 'labour theory of value'). It is a function of the work of the proletariat. And yet the proletariat receive only a tiny amount of this value back in the form of wages. The difference, which Marx terms 'surplus value', is appropriated by the bourgeoisie. Put bluntly, they get rich by exploiting the labour power of the proletariat.

The bourgeoisie and the proletariat are not the only social classes in capitalist societies, according to Marx. On one hand, for example, notwithstanding his views of revolution (see below), he recognizes that societies do not change all at once, and that any society will retain elements of old modes of production and perhaps also the seeds of future modes. Most capitalist societies of western Europe contain traces of their feudal past for example. The monarchy in the United Kingdom and the aristocratic relations connected to it are one illustration of this. Furthermore, Marx recognizes the existence of both a 'petit bourgeoisie', who own and control the means of their own production but do not employ others, and a 'lumpen proletariat' who exist outside of the labour market and, in Marx's view, are particularly prone to crime and disorder. However, the bourgeoisie and the proletariat are the major social groupings in capitalist society and they are the important groupings because it is their relationship, and particularly its impact upon the proletariat, which drives the 'motor' of history. Society is driven by the conflict between the bourgeoisie and the proletariat and this conflict, Marx predicts, will result in a revolution in which the proletariat take the forces of production into common ownership, thereby effecting a transition from capitalism to a socialist or communist society. Marx is famously vague on the question of how this revolution will start and what the new society will look like (see **crises**). However, integral to his account is a prediction that the dynamics of competition within the bourgeoisie will result in a situation where the rate of exploitation of the proletariat is greater (since the 'costs' of competition will be offset by a lowering of wages) and capital is concentrated into fewer and fewer hands (as smaller capitalists are forced out of business by bigger players in the market place). The capitalist economy is anarchic, crisis ridden and fiercely competitive, Marx argues, such that only a small number of the bourgeoisie can survive, with the gap between the survivors and the proletariat becoming ever wider and more polarized (see **crises**). At the

291

same time, however, the concentration of capital will be mirrored by the greater concentration of the proletariat into bigger factories and industrial centres, a process which increases the chances of the members of the proletariat becoming aware of their common social situation, transforming the proletariat from a 'class in itself' to a 'class for itself'[207] and fulfilling the basic revolutionary precondition of 'class consciousness'.

Numerous social changes in the period since Marx was writing (and of course the conspicuous lack of revolutionary change) have posed problems for this schema. Although one can make a case that capital is increasingly concentrated in a few hands, for example, ownership and control of the means of production are often separated now, owners do not control. They delegate to managers and these managers constitute an in-between class strata which is distinct from Marx's own petite bourgeoisie. Furthermore, ownership has become blurred because of the practice of both share ownership and government ownership (with their related stock schemes). Most large companies are now part-owned by a number of shareholders, who are even further removed from matters of day-to-day running than a single dedicated owner who has delegated managerial responsibility. Finally, as societies have developed from the industrial period analysed by Marx, the nature of work has changed. The transition to 'post-industrialism', for example, has generated categories of workers, such as public sector professionals, who do not neatly fit the Marxist schema, and has involved the displacement of much traditional 'proletarian' work into the third world.

## WEBER

These changes have generated a great deal of debate. Even before many of them surfaced, however, other sociologists had begun to criticize,

---

207 A class 'in itself' is a group which objectively meets the Marxist criteria of 'class', that is, a group whose members objectively have the same relationship to the means of production but who are not subjectively aware of this such that 'class' is not a salient aspect of their self-identification (either individually or collectively). A class 'for itself' is a class whose members recognize that they form a class, who identify as a class. A class for itself is also said to be 'class conscious' as it is conscious of itself as a class. Class consciousness is a key precondition of revolutionary action, according to Marxists, although there is considerable argument about the extent to which classes will develop a 'revolutionary consciousness' (that is, a conscious readiness to engage in revolution) spontaneously. Lenin (1918) and those who follow him, generally maintain that a workers' party is necessary to transform spontaneous manifestations of class consciousness into revolutionary class consciousness.

question and modify the Marxist schema. Max Weber (1978), for example, called for a much more nuanced view of class. Weber accepted the basic parameters of the Marxian schema but introduced three important innovations. First, whilst he accepted that there is basic distinction between those who own the means of production and those who sell their labour, he noted that labour skills can have a very different market value, resulting in different groups of workers yielding very different rewards, or having different 'life chances'.[208] A medical doctor and a shop floor assistant both sell their labour, for example, but the doctor gets a better price for her labour than the shop floor assistant and has greater life chances. More possibilities are open to her and she can expect to enjoy a greater range of 'goods'. Some functionalist theories of class have suggested that this reflects underlying social values and needs – they suggest that the skills of the doctor are more important and hard come by than those of the shop floor assistant and that this is reflected in the differential rewards attached to these roles (for example, see Davis and Moore, 1945). Weberians are generally more critical, however. Much Weberian-inspired work has examined both the way in which professional groups limit access to and supply of their skills, thus increasing the market value of those skills and, in a critique of the implications of the functionalist view that occupational position is a reflection of talent and motivation (which enable one to get into the 'best' jobs) alone, they have explored the activities which effect 'closure' around and limit mobility between specific occupations – or clusters of occupations (see below). Getting a highly-paid and well-respected job is not as easy as having a great deal of talent and motivation, at least not for everyone, Weberians argue. For those born into the 'right' circumstances it is much easier than this and for those born into the 'wrong' circumstances it is much more difficult. The reasons for this are numerous and cannot be discussed here.

One of the consequences of Weber's arguments regarding the market value of occupational skills is that the class structure can seem to decompose down into individuals, all of whom have slightly different market values and thus slightly different 'class situations', as Weber calls them. However, as noted above, Weber believes that 'class situations' tend to cluster into groupings of individuals and occupations which afford broadly similar life chances and life experiences, and around which a

293

---

208 An individual's life chances are the opportunities, risks, constraints, etc. that they are likely to face in their lifetime, given their social location.

degree of 'closure' and thus lack of social mobility is effected.[209] These clusterings and this closure form the basis of what Weber calls 'social class'.

So defined, Weber continues, class is also a basis for distinctive lifestyles. Groups who are closer together in 'social space' are more likely to associate with one another and, combined with the fact that they have similar life chances, they are therefore likely to lead similar sorts of lives. This point echoes, in some measure, Marx and Engels' various reflections upon class cultures (see especially Engels, 1969), but it constitutes a key theme of the Weberian approach and is more elaborated therein.

The third and related key innovation of Weber was to introduce considerations of status and party into debates on social stratification. The power and life chances of human agents are not shaped by their class position and market capacity alone, he maintained, but equally by the status groups to which they belong and their access to the political machinery of the state. Of course these things overlap as occupational groups are also status groups, but their configuration is socially variable and they can be teased apart. An agent's gender status or status as a member of an ethnic minority might clearly affect their occupational opportunities, for example, and thus their social class position. But certain status differentials will persist even if an individual succeeds in securing a high occupation/class position, and, of course, there are many individuals who do not belong to disadvantaged status groups who nevertheless occupy a disadvantaged class position and, in some respects, do not fare as well as agents from disadvantaged status groups who are in high class positions. Both class and status are important and they overlap, but we must be mindful of the distinction between them.

## CONTEMPORARY DEBATES

In contemporary debates upon class the spectres of both Marx and Weber still loom large. Indeed, the two key theories of class which dominate

---

209 So, for example, a skilled manual worker may change jobs and/or the child of a skilled manual worker may take a different job from that of their parent(s), but in both cases movement is likely to be within the skilled manual bracket and, specifically, is unlikely (or at least less likely) to involve upward movement into, for example, the professional bracket. The professional sphere is likely to prove relatively closed to all but those who have professional parents and are born into it. That, at least, is the bare bones of the argument. The account becomes more complex when we consider that recent social changes have tended to involve an expansion of the professional sector, such that a certain degree of upward mobility has been facilitated for some.

contemporary debate, that of Erik Wright and that of John Goldthorpe, whilst innovative in many respects, echo much in Marx and Weber respectively. On one side, Wright (1985, 1989, 1997) has done much to rehabilitate the Marxist position, seeking to address social changes such as those noted above and to argue for its continued relevance. On the other side, though perhaps less explicitly, there is an indentifiable Weberian lineage to the work of Goldthorpe and his colleagues (for example, Goldthorpe et al., 1980). Both Wright and Goldthorpe offer complex accounts of the nature of class – too detailed to outline here – and the debate between them continues. (For good critical discussions of these positions see Crompton, 1998 and Savage, 2000.)

Another important contemporary figure in debates about class is Bourdieu. Though inspired by Marx in certain respects, his position on class is more Weberian. Like Weber, he believes that individuals are positioned in 'social space' in accordance with their possession of a variety of forms of 'capital', chiefly economic capital (namely money and goods with a potential monetary value), cultural capital (such as competence, skills and qualifications with a cultural and market value), symbolic capital (status) and social capital (useful ties and connections) (see **capital** and **social space** I). Furthermore, like Weber – and also the Durkheimian sociologist Maurice Halbwachs (1958) – he is interested both in the clusters and closure which take shape around distributions of these forms of capital and the lifestyle and class habitus (see **habitus**) which takes shape within these clusters. Bourdieu's explicit definition of class is not greatly elaborated and his work does not, therefore, feature strongly in the 'Wright versus Goldthorpe' debates (although see Crompton, 1998; Savage, 2000). However, some theorists of class have argued that debates on the subject cannot continue without the proper consideration of culture that his perspective is uniquely placed to offer (see especially Savage, 2000). Furthermore, this argument seems vindicated by the fact that some more culturally oriented sociologists, who are critical of the relative neglect of issues of class in their research domain, often turn to Bourdieu as a key source for bringing class into focus (for example, Skeggs, 1997; Charlesworth, 2000).

The dominance of class in earlier phases of sociology's development and the tendency for definitions and measures of it to ignore other important sources of social division, such as gender and race, have been a source of much criticism by some recent sociologists. This criticism was undoubtedly justified and problems of understanding the interpenetration of class, gender and race remain. However, as a number of critics have argued, we must be wary not to let the issue of class slip out of mainstream sociology (whether into a more specialized field of debate or oblivion) (Savage, 2000). Whilst there are other equally important sources of social division, class counts (to quote the title of one of Wright's books) and it is important to preserve it as a category of mainstream social analysis. How we do that, of course, will remain an issue of contention.

### FURTHER READING

The best introduction to and discussion of contemporary debates on class analysis is Mike Savage's (2000) *Class Analysis and Social Transformation*. A slightly different but also interesting and persuasive line is taken by Rosemary Crompton (1998). For an excellent discussion of the classicial theories of class see John Scott (1996).

# Social Construction/ Social Constructionism

*Related concepts: **performativity, realism, sex/gender.***

The concept of 'social construction' has become very fashionable recently in the social sciences, as has the tendency to say that one is a social constructionist and that this, that and most things are 'social constructions' or 'social constructs'. The use to which these labels are put varies widely, however, as do the various attempts of 'social constructionists' to legislate with respect to their use. Consequently, I propose to do no more here than list the main uses I have encountered in the literature, adding the proviso that in some cases these uses may overlap but need not do so.

One relatively straightforward use of the term 'social construction' occurs in those instances where we wish to indicate that some part of the social world (a role, institution, practice, form of behaviour and so on) is better explained in social rather than biological or (individual) psychological terms. To say, 'it's a social construct', in this context, means that we believe the phenomenon in question to be a product of our particular society or societies like it, rather than being something which is natural or inevitable, hard-wired into our biological constitution and invariant. This is part of what Durkheim (1965) meant when he referred to 'social facts'. Importantly, this use does not imply that everything is a social construct. Some things are and some things are not because some things depend upon society for their existence, where other things do not. Democracy, for example, is a social construction, both because it is a form of social organization and because it only emerges in some societies, but mountains, rivers and sheep are not, because, though affected ecologically by the life of human societies, their existence, as such, is not dependent upon the existence of human societies. They are not emergent properties of the social world. We explain how they emerge by reference to biology, geology, and so on.

The implication of the above use is that social constructs are specific to particular societies. We might find a particular role or practice in our society but we would not expect to find it in every society, and we perhaps have historical or cross-cultural evidence to show that the said role or practice does not exist in other societies. Indeed, to make our case persuasively we would need just that kind of evidence. However, it may be that some things are 'social constructions' even if we find them in all societies. Although languages and moral codes or norms vary across societies, for example, it is a reasonable assumption that one will find (versions of) them in all societies. Different societies have different languages but all societies have languages. Similarly, different societies live by different moral codes but all societies have moral codes. The apparent universality of such institutions denies to us the usual method of proving that they are social constructions. We cannot point to the fact that they only exist in certain types of society. Yet it seems equally reasonable to claim, with Durkheim again, that they are emergent properties of societies, that is, that they emerge out of collective life and, as such, are social constructions. Moral rules, for example, regulate our relationships and interactions with other people, so they can only emerge in contexts where there are other people. Robinson Crusoe (who of course grew up in a society and benefited from its nurturing environment) may develop his own individual habits but he must wait for Man Friday to arrive before norms begins to emerge, since it is only when he must co-ordinate his life with that of another that rules or norms become necessary. As with the first definition of social constructions, this definition does not imply that everything is a social construct. Assumedly everybody could agree that some things are social constructions by this definition and that other things are not.

297

*Social Construction/Social Constructionism*

Another way in which 'social construction' has been used in the literature is to stress the activity-dependency of certain social 'things'. For example, those who embrace 'constructionism', in this sense, might argue that the tendency to talk in reifed terms of such 'things' as 'the state', 'the media' or 'patriarchy' within social science obscures the fact that these 'things' are not things at all but rather ensembles of human interactivity and interdependence. They are 'constructed' by means of human activity and can be 'deconstructed' or perhaps constructed differently. The purpose of social science, from this point of view, is to explore these processes of construction; to explore how agents 'do' patriarchy, 'do' the state, and so on. We also see this in some psychological variations of social constructionism, where the tendency to reify mental life is challenged by reference to the active social processes it involves (Potter and Wetherell, 1987). For example, rather than treating 'memory' as a strictly individual store of images, somewhere in the head, constructionist psychologists explore the real world social contexts wherein memories are recalled and discussed, often for quite specific purposes. Memory is not a simple matter of recall, from this point of view, but is rather a matter of active re-construction. Furthermore, re-construction, in turn, is often social in nature, in the respect that it is performed collectively, drawing upon contextual clues and often orienting to social purposes (for example, we reminisce together as a means of re-establishing our relationships, attributing blame, formulating 'lessons' for others to learn from, and so on). It makes sense, in this respect, to speak of constructionism as a distinct social scientific perspective, as one might believe that all or most of social and psychological reality must be understood in terms of such social activities. Still, however, this does not imply that everything is socially constructed, since not everything is activity or context dependent in this way. To return to the above example, trees and mountains are not social constructions from this point of view since they do not need to be 'done' in social contexts in order to exist.

Having said this, to pre-empt my discussion below, some variants of this approach would argue that 'trees', 'mountains', and so on, only enter into the social world insofar as they feature within human projects and that they are constituted as meaningful objects in relationship to human projects, such that they too are 'constructed' after a fashion. 'Mountains', for example, are 'constructed' in terms of the human capacity and desire to either cross them or climb and 'conquer' them, and so on. Arguing this, however, involves a slippage in the meaning of 'construction' which we must be wary of. This calls for more discussion.

It is my contention that in each of the above cases, with the exception of that discussed in the very last paragraph before this, 'social construction' is used in an ontological fashion; that is, we are saying that the existence or manner of existence of a thing is dependent, in some substantial part, upon the social world. This does not preclude the possibility that some things are not socially constructed, nor does it preclude the fact that those things which are socially constructed may equally well depend upon other, non-social aspects of the world for their existence. Indeed, if we follow Durkheim we would be forced to conclude that the existence of the social world, though sui generis and therefore strictly irreducible to such lower order structures as those of biology and psychology, nevertheless depends upon these structures for its own existence. We are always simultaneously psychological and biological, indeed chemical and physical beings, for Durkheim, even if these facts about ourselves tell us relatively little about the things that we, as sociologists, are interested in.

'Social construction' has also been used in a more epistemological vain, however, to indicate that the way in which we come to know the world is also shaped by social factors, for example, by social-linguistic categories, by procedures and practices of knowledge production and by technologies which, in turn, embody irreducibly social relations and ideas. Again Durkheim (1915) lies at the root of this use, given his concern with 'social representations'. He sought to show that the way in which we classify and come to know the world is shaped by the social relations of our society. This is a fascinating and very important use of 'social construction' but it is also potentially problematic if misunderstood, particularly in relation to the question of whether everything in the world is socially constructed. Ontological and epistemological claims can very easily become confused (see **realism**). It is not uncommon, for example, for social constructionists to argue, with critical or provocative intent, that all manner of illnesses, death, indeed everything under the sun (including the sun) is a social construct. If what is meant here is that the way in which we define and come to know these things is shaped by classificatory schemas, and so on, which are products of our specific society, then this is undoubtedly true. Unfortunately, however, the debate sometimes slides into more ontological territory; constructionists appear to suggest that the very existence of a variety of objects belonging to the natural world are somehow dependent upon our labelling of them, such that we might be tempted to believe that our world would not be blighted by a variety of illnesses and natural disasters if we had not given life to these phenomena by naming them. Clearly we have no good reason to believe that this is true and every good reason to suppose that it is not.

*Social Construction/Social Constructionism*

The world and our knowledge of it are two different things. The former pre-dates the latter considerably, and will in all likelihood outlive it also.

Having said this, as indicated above, analyses can move between epistemological and ontological uses of 'construction', and this movement can lead to interesting results. The important point, in my view, is that we remain aware and clear that we are moving between definitions and uses of 'construction' when we do so. If we fail to do this then we end up with accounts which are silly and intellectually dishonest in equal measure.

### FURTHER READING

Berger and Luckmann's (1979) *The Social Construction of Reality* is an excellent introduction to the constructionist position. On the constructionist position in psychology, see Potter and Wetherell (1987). For a detailed discussion of the ontology/epistemology issue, see Bhasker's (1989) *Reclaiming Reality*.

# Social Movements

> *Related concepts:* **crises, cycles of contention, new social movements, repertoires of contention.**

It is a lot easier to think of examples of social movements than it is to come up with a clear and effective definition of them. There is no disagreement that environmentalism, feminism, animal rights, the labour movement, fascism, and so on, constitute movements. When it comes to specifying the precise characteristics that qualify them as movements, however, there is considerable disagreement. Much of what 'social movements' have in common they also share with other social forms. Yet any attempt to narrow down the definition risks excluding empirical cases that many would want to include in the category of social movements. And the situation is muddied by two further points. Firstly, any neat theoretical definition which we might be able construct will inevitably fall foul of the enormous amount of empirical work in the area of social movement studies, which embodies a wide ranging number of operational definitions, some of which even blur seemingly basic divisions between social, religious, political and even lifestyle/fashion movements. In other words, we might be able to devise a watertight definition of movements for present purposes but that would be a relatively insignificant victory as it would not correspond with many definitions used in the sociological literature, not least because there is no consensus amongst the definitions in the literature. Secondly, the many definitions that one finds in the literature not only conflict but also often draw upon terms that are themselves fuzzy, ambiguous and in need of further definition, for example, 'collective', 'political', 'protest.'[210] I have responded to this semantic minefield elsewhere by suggesting that the concept of social movements belongs to everyday discourse, is subject to the fuzzy and contextual logic of everyday discourse and, as such, identifies a 'family resemblance' between social forms rather than essential characteristics (Crossley, 2002a), that is to say, different movements share different characteristics with other movements, without any one central set of characteristics being both sufficiently inclusive and sufficiently exclusive to constitute a watertight definition. This does not preclude us from formulating specific definitions for the purposes of specific research projects. That is necessary and unavoidable. But it does preclude a general all-purpose definition.

This is perhaps not such a satisfactory conclusion. However, if we cannot offer a watertight definition of social movements we can at least offer a model which will apply in many cases and which allows us to begin to think about what movements involve. The model I am going to propose is my own model of movements as 'fields of contention' (see Crossley, 2002a, 2003b), a model which draws both upon Pierre Bourdieu's concept of fields (see **field**) and also upon a number of models of social movements outlined in the literature. I will begin with a brief discussion of Zald and McCarthy's (1994) model of movement fields.

Zald and McCarthy use the term 'social movement' in a very vague and minimal way, to designate a basic desire or demand in society for some sort of change. If there is a general feeling in society that some part

---

210 What, for example, defines an activity as collective? Are two people enough to constitute a collective and thus a social movement? Should there be three? And what constitutes 'protest'? Is it necessary to wave a placard? Is that enough? Must one parade outside of parliament? Each of these terms, and many others which get included in definitions of social movements, are extremely slippery (see Crossley, 2002a).

of it is problematic and in need of change then, in Zald and McCarthy's terms, there is a social movement. In order to include more conservative and reactionary movements in this definition we should perhaps add to that also a desire or demand to stop certain sorts of change and keep society the same (or even return to the ways of the past). Furthermore, Zald and McCarthy add to this a notion of 'counter-movements', which are defined as a shared demand or desire which opposes that of a social movement. So, for example, in many societies we find pro- and anti-abortion sentiments, fascist and anti-fascist sentiments, pro- and anti-hunting sentiments, and so on. These are movements and counter-movements – movements being whichever of the two opposing camps comes first, counter-movements being the later development which reacts to (counters) it.

More important than these 'sentiment pools', according to Zald and McCarthy, however, are the 'social movement organizations' (SMOs) which 'carry' the movement. The contemporary environmental movement, defined simply as a shared desire to protect and enhance the environment, for example, is 'carried' at a national level in the United Kingdom by such SMOs as Earth First, Reclaim the Streets, Friends of the Earth and Greenpeace. Zald and McCarthy conceptualize the relationship between movements and SMOs in terms of 'supply and demand'. SMOs emerge in response to and/or seek to foster a collective demand for change. Furthermore, they are prepared and/or able to do so insofar as that demand takes the form of 'adherents' and 'constituents' who are prepared to donate money, time and other resources to them, to make their actions possible and, in some cases at least, to reward them for taking the trouble.

Here we get to the crux of Zald and McCarthy's model. SMOs can only survive, organize and take part in protests if they are able to mobilize the resources necessary to do so. They may get those resources from a variety of sources but in many contemporary cases they get them, chiefly in the form of money donations, from individuals in the wider society who not only support their goals (adherents) but are prepared to act upon their belief by way of some form of material donation (constituents). Greenpeace for example, are able to do what they do for the environment to the extent that they receive outside donations and the annual subscriptions of their supporters.

The relationship between SMOs, their adherents and their constituents is an important dynamic. So too, however, is the relationship between all of the SMOs in what Zald and McCarthy term a 'social movement industry'. Industries are clusters of SMOs who are in pursuit of similar goals. We might speak, for example, of an environmental industry, a feminist industry, a peace industry, and so on. SMOs in the industry necessarily interact or at least have an impact upon one another, not least as they tend to draw from the same pool of potential adherents/constituents and the same pools of potential resources. This can lead to co-operation between SMOs, under certain circumstances, but it can also lead to conflict and competition. Furthermore, these various forms of interaction generate a pressure upon SMOs to change and adapt. For example, if they are too similar to another organization, which tends to take 'their' constituents, then they will need to find an alternative niche. If other successful SMOs manage to redefine central issues, they may need to do so also in an effort to keep up. The interrelationship of SMOs in an industry may be direct. As network analysis has shown, explicit collaborations, exchanges of resources, overlapping memberships and direct avenues of communication all allow us to trace direct lines of connection between them. Interactions may also be less direct (and perhaps unintended), however. For example, the failure of potential constituents or indeed authorities to distinguish between SMOs in an industry can mean that a successful campaigns by one generates increased support for another. Conversely, a controversial act by one might lower support for the industry as a whole. Historical research on the British suffragettes, for example, shows that disruptive protests by more militant organizations reduced support for all organizations in the female suffrage 'sector', and effectively reduced the bargaining power of the less militant organizations. In a slightly different vein, the dominance that one SMO achieves in relation to certain types of intervention may necessitate that other SMOs find alternative strategies – even if this was not the intention of the first SMO. Reflecting upon these complex dynamics leads Zald and McCarthy themselves to talk (albeit in a non-Bourdieusian sense) of 'fields': '. . . all of the SMOs of a social movement industry must be seen as part of an interacting field.' (Zald and McCarthy, 1994: 120).

I will suggest my own version of this 'field' idea shortly. Firstly, however, we should note that, for Zald and McCarthy, there is also a relationship of competition between social movement industries. Potential adherents and constituents do not have infinite amounts of time and money and may thus have to choose not only between the SMOs in a particular industry but also between industries. They might decide, for example, to focus their time, money and energy on feminist causes rather than environmental ones, or perhaps they will give less to feminism, reducing the power of feminist SMOs, in an effort to give something to environmentalism. Furthermore, the 'social movement sector', which comprises all social movement industries collectively, must compete with the voluntary, public and private sectors of the economy. It is for this reason, Zald and McCarthy argue, that social movement activity tends to increase during times of economic boom. In boom times, individuals ordinarily enjoy a greater surplus in their finances, after they have paid their taxes into the public sector and bought what they want from the private sector, and are thus better placed to donate goods into the voluntary and movement sectors. This increased level of donation funds higher levels of activity amongst SMOs and perhaps encourages would-be 'movement entrepreneurs' to form new organizations.

There is much that is important about this model. In particular it invites us to 'open up' social movements and to look at the various different positions and relationships (for example, across SMOs and between SMOs and their constituents) they tend to entail. Furthermore, we can differentiate between types of SMO, different types of constituent (for example, those who just give money, those who give time) and so on. Finally, the economic metaphor which underlies their approach is helpful for allowing us to grasp the dynamics of exchange which, to some extent, generate protest and mobilization. However, their economism is also the source of the main problem with their approach. At some points in their work they identify clear differences between SMOs and economic organizations, flagging up the often symbolic nature of movement activism:

> Although we think the parallel with economic processes is striking, we should remember that there are differences. In particular, competition for dominance amongst SMOs is often for symbolic dominance, for defining the terms of social movement action. Social movement leaders are seeking symbolic hegemony. At some point social movement analysis must join with cultural and linguistic analysis if it is to understand fully co-operation and conflict in its socially specific forms. (Zald and McCarthy, 1994: 180)

I agree absolutely with this. Furthermore, it is noteworthy that, when looking at actual examples of SMOs, Zald and McCarthy recognize the often 'decentred' nature of these organizations, thereby meeting the objection levelled by some critics, that they tend to portray SMOs in an overly unified and 'rational' fashion. SMOs might be central loci of movement activism but, as Zald and McCarthy acknowledge, some SMO clusters are characterized by high levels of overlapping membership, such that their boundaries are very blurred. And many become subject to internal conflicts and factions, such that they lack internal agreement or coherence. There are problems with Zald and McCarthy's work however. Firstly, they pay little more than lip service to most of these points and certainly do not elaborate upon their reference to more symbolic/cultural elements. Secondly, much of their work effectively brackets out these wider considerations, positing a relatively narrow economistic model in which SMOs, qua economically rational agents, act as fundraisers. Thirdly, this leads them to ignore, in their concept of SMOs, networks and movement 'experiments' which do not conform to their basic organizational model. Finally, their account simultaneously presupposes a 'rational action' model of human agency (see **rationality**) and key concepts which lie outside of and contradict that model. The rational action model assumes, for example, that actors act only in pursuit of their own, selfish material ends – a notion which has been very explicitly discussed in social movement analysis, following Olson's (1971) work, and which Zald and McCarthy appear to endorse as a working assumption – and yet they refer also to 'conscience constituents' and 'purposive incentives', seeming to suggest that agents become involved in social movement activity for altruistic and other, non-material, non-selfish reasons. They assume both selfish materialism and its contrary in the same model, seeking to use elements of both to explain activism. Moreover they do so without in any way explaining how they propose to combine these seemingly opposing assumptions.

It is my claim that we might be able to begin to square some of these circles in the context of the broader and more culturally oriented concept of 'fields' suggested by Bourdieu – I have also argued elsewhere, that Bourdieu's concept of the habitus helps us to address related problems stemming from the use of 'rational action' concepts in models such as those of Zald and McCarthy (Crossley, 2002a, 2003b). This model would include many of the same elements as that of Zald and McCarthy, albeit perhaps more widely defined (for example, SMOs, adherents, constituents) but it would seek,  at the very least, to explore more thoroughly: firstly, the cultural framework(s) in which activist actions and exchanges take place; secondly, the attunement of activists to their 'field' at the level of the habitus (see **habitus**) and the role of 'belief in the game' (see **illusio**); and thirdly, the role of symbolic and cultural (as well as economic and temporal)  resources in the exchanges and interactions constitutive of the field (see **capital**). These are all important aspects of Bourdieu's concept of fields (see **field**).

This is not something that we need begin from scratch, however. In addition to Bourdieu, who is a crucial resource, we find that, from the early work of Blumer  (1969) through to the more recent work of Melucci (1986, 1996) and various 'collective identity theorists' (for example, Della Porta and Diani, 1999), there is a considerable literature which allows us to begin to make sense of the cultural fabric and contests that constitute movement fields. If we can successfully map the findings of this work on to the concept of 'movement fields' or 'fields of contention' that I have begun to outline here, utilizing also the important innovations of Bourdieu, then we will have taken considerable steps forward towards a powerful model of social movements.

### FURTHER READING

For a broader discussion of the field of social movement research see my *Making Sense of Social Movements* (Crossley, 2002a). I outline my own ideas more thoroughly in this book, and from another angle in Crossley (2003b). Alternatively see Della Porta and Diani's (1999) *Social Movements*. Zald and McCarthy's (1994) *Social Movements in an Organizational Society* is also a fascinating book in my view.

# Social Space I
# (Bourdieu)

> *Related concepts:* **field, habitus, relationalism, social class, social space II.**

The concept of social space has (at least) two distinct uses in the work of Pierre Bourdieu, both of which relate to his desire to develop ways of visualizing society and social relationships. On the one hand, he refers to social fields as social spaces, allowing us to think of society along the lines of a geographical map, with different regions corresponding to different spheres of activity (see **field**). On the other hand, he sometimes refers to 'the' social space – a synonym, seemingly, for a particular conception of a national society taken as a whole. It is this latter use that I am concerned with here. Social space, in this sense, is constituted by way of the distribution of the key forms of capital identified in Bourdieu's sociology, for example, economic capital, cultural capital, symbolic capital and social capital (see **capital**). These forms of capital can be thought of as individual resources. Individuals 'have' certain quantities of money and culture. However, insofar as individuals can be placed or positioned along a continuum in accordance with their possession of these various forms of capital, we can begin to think of these general resources, or rather their axes of distribution, as dimensions of an (at least)[211] four-dimensional space.[212]

To begin to unpack some of this let us think about a two-dimensional space, comprising economic and cultural capital. Some agents are rich in both money and cultural credentials. Some are culturally rich but do not have much money. Some have money but lack cultural credentials, and some people are poor in terms of both. We can visualize this in the form of scatterplot or 'perceptual map':

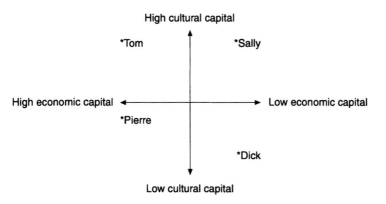

Figure 1 *Two-dimensional social space*

In the above diagram Tom occupies the most privileged position, being rich in both cultural and economic capital. Dick is in the opposite position; he is low in both forms of capital. Sally is high in cultural capital but less so in economic capital. Pierre is very high in economic capital (higher than Tom) but only middling in cultural terms. This is not merely

---

211 The more forms of capital we identify, which can be thought of in terms of a continuum, the more dimensions we can include. I am sticking with four, for purposes of exposition, because this corresponds to Bourdieu's basic typology of the types of capital but there is no necessity for doing so – and clearly, as I go on to explain, one might wish to stick to two dimensions.

212 The idea of four-dimensional space may seem odd. It is quite common in contemporary mathematics and geometry, however, to theorize in terms of many dimensional spaces – certainly more than four. Furthermore, it is recognized that the social sciences are one good field of application for these ideas. Bourdieu was certainly influenced by these newer mathematical ideas. For an interesting and accessible introduction to some of these ideas, in their mathematical context, see Gowers' (2002) *Mathematics: A Very Short Introduction.*

an illustrative exercise. Using such statistical techniques as factor analysis, principal components analysis, multi-dimensional scaling or, more particularly in Bourdieu's case, (multiple) correspondence analysis, it is possible for us plot members of a given population in just this way.[213] Furthermore, we are not restricted to plotting agents. Assuming a relatively large sample which allows us to examine the relationship between agents' practices and their forms of capital, we can map practices and preferences in this way too, as Bourdieu famously does in *Distinction* (see Figure 2).[214]

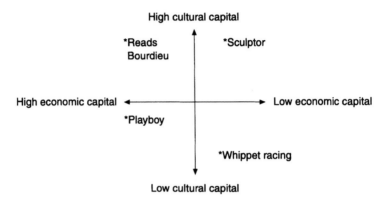

Figure 2 *Practices and occupations in two-dimensional space (hypothetical)*

*Distinction*, contains a number of diagrams of this sort (though with many more practices and occupations mapped on to them), based upon a correspondence analysis of proper data. These maps allow us to see how practices (and occupations) are positioned relative to one another within 'social space'.

In addition to these basic maps, it is possible to map agents, occupations and practices in accordance with their total volume and composition of capital – indeed this is usually what Bourdieu does. This

213 A number of texts which explain these new techniques are now available. Note also that these techniques are included in most of the basic statistical software packages available to students, including the more recent versions of SPSS. See Kruskal and Wish (1978), Hair et.al., (1984), Clausen (1998) and Andersen (1997).

214 Although note that Bourdieu tends to use a slightly more complex 'correspondence map' which plots composition of capital against volume of capital; that is, rather than present an axis of levels of cultural capital and one of economic capital, Bourdieu tends to have one axis representing total level of capital (cultural and economic capital combined) and then one representing the balance of agents' 'portfolio' of capital between economic and cultural – for example, the extent to which they are higher in one than the other.

involves one axis of social space representing the combined amount of capital (economic and cultural) that attaches to an occupation, agent or practice, whilst the other represents the ratio of cultural to economic capital. In Figure 3, for example, the far left side of the map represents a ratio of economic to cultural capital strongly weighted in the direction of the former, whilst the right hand side of the map represents the opposite ratio.

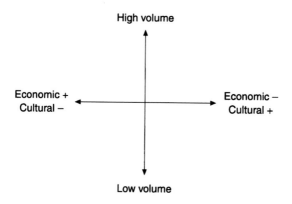

Figure 3 *Volume and composition of capital*

Of course the relative distributions of economic and cultural capital are only two dimensions of what Bourdieu effectively describes as a four-dimensional space (corresponding to his four main types of capital). We need also to consider symbolic capital and social capital. Furthermore, we may wish to add a fifth dimension: change through time. However, most of Bourdieu's analyses tend to focus on the two-dimensional space constituted by economic and cultural capital, and they do so for three principal reasons in my view. Firstly, the diagrams tend to be two-dimensional because it is difficult to represent positions in three-dimensional space within the two dimensional space of a book or journal page (see Figure 4). And it is impossible to represent any more than that in a single diagram, other than as a composition of interacting two-dimensional models.[215] Furthermore, these maps are supposed to make patterns and relationships easier to spot than tables of figures would, and the more difficult they are on the eye the less they serve that purpose.

---

215 Gowers (2002) gives an example of this in his aforementioned introduction to advanced maths.

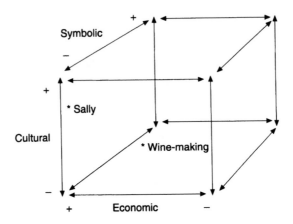

Figure 4 *A three-dimensional plot of social space*

Secondly, economic and cultural capital are easier to quantify in a meaningful way, and time, in particular, is very difficult to include on a perceptual map of the kind used by Bourdieu.[216] Finally, and more positively, I think that Bourdieu believes that economic and cultural capital, as they are configured at any point in time, are the most reliable and important dimensions of social space. They are the forms of capital which really make a difference in the social world.

But why are they important? What is the point of mapping social space in this way? On one level I think the answer to this is that Bourdieu believes, with good reason, that these dimensions are key underlying structures of society which shape other aspects of the social world and can be used to explain them. Following Weber (1978) and Maurice Halbwachs (1958) he believes that levels of economic and cultural capital shape both life chances (what an individual can hope to achieve in life) and lifestyles (in the form of the habitus)[217] (see **social class** and **habitus**). Agents with a similar profile of economic and cultural assets will enjoy

216 One can, of course, map past and present positions, with an arrow connecting them, but this makes things very difficult indeed to read.
217 Bourdieu can sound quite deterministic in his account of this. However, I think that it makes more sense to see the link between habitus and social position as an index of the combination of collective agency and creativity of actors on the one side and the restraints imposed by lack of resources and location in particular types of networks and relationships (such as employment relationships) on the other. Class will tend to 'give rise' to habitus, in this sense, both because their members interact together and because those members find themselves subject to very similar conditions (social and material) and restraints in their efforts to make a life for themselves.

*Social Space I (Bourdieu)*

similar resources and a similar level of power, and will tend to endure/enjoy similar formative experiences (for example, the threat of redundancy or going to a private school, having lots of money or having none). Furthermore, distributions of these 'capitals' constitute an effective basis of group formation. Being at a similar position in social space increases the chances that people will come into contact with each other and that, when they do, they will identify with each other on the basis of common experiences and the common 'habitus' this has given rise to.

### FURTHER READING

*Distinction* (Bourdieu, 1984) is the obvious text to consult in relation with this issue, although the first chapter of *Practical Reason* (Bourdieu, 1998a) may prove useful too.

# Social Space II (networks)

> *Related concepts: relationalism, social capital, social space I.*

In addition to the important conception of social space outlined in the work of Bourdieu and discussed both in my last entry and the entry on fields (see **Social Space I** and **Field**), there is an additional conception of social space related to the concept of 'networks' and, more specifically, to developments in formal social network theory. Network theory attempts to map and explore patterns of social relationships between such entities as human individuals, organizations, nation states and other social entities that might be related. These relationships are plotted by a series of 'dots' or 'nodes',[218] which represent the agents or elements connected in a network, and 'lines'[219] which represent the connections between them

---

218 Also referred to sometimes as 'vertices'.
219 Also referred to as either 'edges' or 'arcs'.

(see Figure 1). How connections are defined is a matter for researchers to decide. It depends upon the research question[220] and the data available or potentially gatherable.[221] In some cases, such as the weighted model in Figure 1, lines carry a number representing the strength of the relationship, as measured by the researcher. They might also or alternatively carry an arrow, as in the directed model, indicating the direction of the relationship (or interaction). If we were using social network analysis for epidemiological purposes, for example, and tracing the spread of a virus, the arrow would indicate who 'gave' the virus to whom.

How we map a network, the methodological decisions about inclusion/exclusion and presence/absence of ties, is clearly very important. Most of the work on network analysis, however, is concerned with the manner in which, having mapped a network, we can analyse its structural properties and study its effects. Needless to say, whole books have been written about this and I can only hope to give a brief outline here. However, we can consider a few brief structural properties of the hypothetical network outlined in Figure 1, so as to bring the idea to life a bit. To keep things simple, I will limit my discussion to the basic model, discarding both weights and directions.

Firstly, we can consider the property of 'density'. This concept compares the actual amount of links between nodes in a network with the potential number. In a network of 9 nodes, such as we have opposite, for example, if everybody was in a relationship with everybody else (by whatever definition of 'related' we use), there would be 36 relationships in total (that is, 36 connecting lines on the graph). A quick way of working this out is to multiply the number of nodes (9 in this case) by one minus the number of nodes (8) and then halve it (= $(9 \times 8)/2 = 72/2 = 36$).[222] However, not

220 If we were interested in the social basis of 'taste', for example, the edges might represent patterns of interaction and relating which involve discussion of aesthetic matters or the seeking of opinions. If we were interested in questions of social integration and stability, by contrast, we might be looking to define the lines in terms of levels of trust, mutual recognition and perhaps mutual support. If we were interested in the spread of sexually transmitted diseases we would only link people who had engaged in sexual activity together but if we were interested in the spread of flu we might link people who happen to use the same bus, whether or not they know each other in any meaningful way. Finally, if the dots were companies, we might be linking those with overlapping directorships or those who trade regularly.

221 It is actually very difficult in practice to gather good data on social networks for all sorts of reasons. Much research is forced by pragmatic pressures to define networks in accordance with the data available.

222 In a directed network we would not perform the final operation of halving our total (at least not necessarily) because each relationship is potentially a two-way relationship and could thus count twice.

312

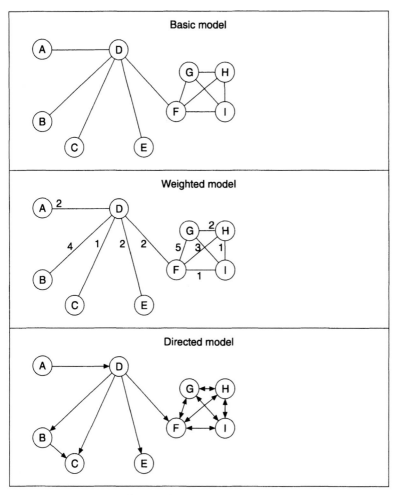

Figure 1  *A social network diagram*

everybody is related to everybody else. There are only 12 lines on the graph. The density of the network, therefore, is 12 divided by 36, which equals 0.333.[223] The formula for density then, is the number of actual relationships (or 'lines') divided by the potential number of relationships (or lines), which

223  The maximum density for a network is 1.00 since the maximum number of actual ties in a network can only ever equal (never exceed) the maximum potential number, by definition (in our case 36 out of 36). When actual and potential ties are the same, the one divided by the other is equal to 1.

is, in turn, calculated by multiplying the number of nodes by the number of nodes minus one and then halving it. Or:

$$\frac{l}{n(n-1)/2}$$

(where $l$ (as in 'lines') is the number of lines present)

Whether the density of a network has any significance and, if so, what the significance is, will clearly vary in accordance with the issue we are examining and the way in which we define relationships, but one can readily imagine situations where it might make a difference. If we were predicting the likelihood that our network would engage in collective action of some sort, for example, we might assume that a high density would increase this likelihood as solidarity is likely to be greater in a group who all know each other, and the process of organizing a collective response would be easier. Similarly, we might predict that information would move more quickly through a dense network as it has many more possible channels to move through and is likely to be reinforced through repetition, as in situations where every one of your friends in succession 'surprises' you with the same great revelation. How easy these hypotheses are to test will again vary considerably but a comparison of identically defined networks with different densities would allow us to begin to explore these possibilities.

Our network is not particularly dense. However, if we look at the sub-group composed of F, G, H and I in Figure 1, we have a situation in which each node is connected to all of the others. There is a density here of 1.00, the maximum possible, and we thus have what network theorists call a 'clique'. Again one cannot make generalized statements about the significance of a clique. That depends upon what sort of a clique it is (namely, how the relationships are defined). But again it is not difficult to imagine that, under certain circumstances, the presence of a clique will be important. We might expect more solidarity within a clique, for example, or at least in a biggish clique, since each member of that clique will find their behaviour influenced in the same way by a number of people. For the same reason we might expect a higher degree of homogeneity. And we might expect that the members of a clique could organize themselves more quickly and to a greater degree than others as each member in the clique is able to pass on information to every other member. Ideas do not have to pass through a chain of intermediaries before reaching certain members of the network.

314

Looking at density and cliques focuses us upon the pattern across the network as a whole. When we measure these variables we adopt a structural approach. We might equally well look at the position of individual nodes within the network, however. We might note, for example, that where A and E each have only one connection, and B and C only two, D has five connections and is thus much more central to the network. Indeed, D is the hub in a wheel; that is, D is the only point connecting A and E to each other and, in turn, connecting them to B and C (who are related to each other). This assumedly makes D quite powerful within the network – although it may also create conflicts of interest and stress for D. F has fewer total connections, at four, but has a very significant position as the bridge between the clique (F, G, H, I) and the wider network (A, B, C, D, E, F). If our network is a business network, this might give company F a great deal of power because they control the flow of information between two halves of an industry. Or perhaps rather the power is concentrated on the relationship between D and F, each of whom has access to a network.

There is a great deal more that could be said about the different ways in which networks can be analysed, and the many methodological issues and problems this type of analysis throws up. Enough has been said, however, to briefly introduce this very fruitful and interesting way of mapping social space.

### FURTHER READING

John Scott's (1991) *Social Network Analysis: A Handbook* is the best introduction to the area, certainly in terms of explaining the basic technical concepts and also the history of the approach. Scott explains the ideas very clearly, getting you to a point where you are ready to have a go. Because he is a sociologist with a lot of experience in the field, he is also able to bring the approach alive and root it in contexts and examples that most sociologists will understand. Degenne and Forsé's (1999) *Introducing Social Networks* is also a good introduction. It is more focused upon the idea of social network *theory* as a branch of social theory – where Scott tends to stick to the notion of network analysis as a set of techniques which proponents of different theoretical approaches might be tempted to use. I would suggest that it is worth looking at the theory discussed by Degenne and Forsé but I am more inclined to recommend Scott's take on network analysis, not least because there are any number of interesting approaches to sociology which have not been taken up by many network theorists (at least not yet) and which do not themselves use network theory (as such) but which theorize the social world in terms of networks and have a great a deal to offer an understanding of them. Indeed, in this vein I would recommend both Norbert Elias' (1978) *What is Sociology?* and Howard Becker's (1984) *Art Worlds* as excellent reading for anybody interested in 'network' issues.

# Symbolic Power/ Symbolic Violence

> *Related concepts:* **field, capital, doxa, discourse, habitus, power, power/knowledge.**

In the work of Pierre Bourdieu, who first formulated these concepts, symbolic power and symbolic violence are used interchangeably. I will suggest here that we can usefully use the two terms to refer to and distinguish two quite different phenomena but first we must consider Bourdieu's singular usage.

Symbolic power is a concept which Bourdieu uses to challenge both the neglect of questions of representation and symbolic culture in many analyses of power, politics and inequality, and the neglect of questions of power and politics in many analyses of representation and symbolic culture. Language, discourse (see **discourse**) and symbolic culture play a crucial role in our society in defining situations or 'framing' reality and thereby shaping social practices and institutions, he notes, but the practice of defining and constructing is by no means an open or equal process. Some social positions and social groups are sanctioned to make definitions. Others are not. The medical profession is sanctioned to define individuals as 'ill' or 'well', for example, and in some cases 'sane' or 'insane', often with quite considerable consequences. Officially defining an individual 'ill' (in the form of a doctor's note), for example, thereby grants them the legal right to take time off work without fear of punishment. If a lay member of the public makes the same diagnosis it has no equivalent weight. Similarly, if a psychiatrist (or in terms of UK law, two psychiatrists) defines an individual 'mentally ill', and specifically if they suggest that the individual would benefit from treatment, that individual can be compulsorily detained in a mental hospital for up to six months and compulsorily treated. If, by contrast, the diagnosed individual declares that they are sane or perhaps that it is the psychiatrist who is ill, their definition does not carry the same weight. Some agents, to reiterate, are sanctioned to make judgements and impose definitions/categories so that their words, at least within the domains where they are sanctioned, carry more power than those of others.

There is a clear overlap here with Foucault's arguments on 'power/knowledge' and 'régimes of truth' (see **power/knowledge**). Bourdieu is more concerned, however, to engage with the philosophical theory of speech acts and with the appropriation of that idea within sociology. The theory of speech acts suggests that words 'do things', that speaking is a way of acting and indeed is the form assumed by most action, including acts of great social significance. Many discourse and conversation analysts have argued, with a critical eye on their counterparts in 'macro-sociology', that most of the key 'big' processes of the social world are achieved through talk (see **discourse**). Wars are declared, parliaments dissolved, laws changed, and so on, all by way of talk. Bourdieu agrees with this, on one level, but has a number of reservations. In the first instance, though, for example, wars may be officially started with a declaration of war – 'we declare war on you' – what is often of more significance for social science is the background context of factors which lead up to a situation of conflict where such a declaration might be made. More importantly for us here, however, Bourdieu is concerned that the words 'we declare war on you' only have the effect of starting a war if one happens to be a political or military leader, sanctioned by the 'we' to take this decision and publicly declare it.[224] On this point Bourdieu takes his lead from the original philosophical theorist of speech acts, J.L. Austin (1971), who referred to the 'felicity conditions' presupposed by such acts. All it takes to name a ship, Austin notes, is utterance of the words 'I name this ship the good ship whatever', but for those words to do the trick, to work their magic, certain (felicity) conditions must have been met. Principally one must be the person appointed to name the ship. What Austin identifies here, Bourdieu notes,

---

224 It may also be necessary, of course, that the agent in question has gone through a series of specified procedures before performing their (speech) act. The sanction to perform certain acts and make certain decisions is usually subject to the proviso that they are made in particular ways, following particular safeguards.

---

**Symbolic Power/Symbolic Violence**

is the existence and importance of a whole web of institutional conditions which invest speech acts and lend them their performative magic. This web of connections is the basis of symbolic power.

If we return to the example of the psychiatrist, for example, his or her power depends upon the fact that s/he is officially sanctioned by the psychiatric and medical establishment to practise psychiatry, a sanction which, in turn, is conditional upon him or her having completed an officially recognized education in psychiatry and general medicine. The psychiatrist has been examined numerous times over by the medical authorities before they are granted the certificate that affords them the power to get a job which, in turn, affords them the power to deprive others of their liberty. And the medical establishment itself has to be recognized by the state, which exercises an effective monopoly on the legitimate use of violence (which psychiatry calls upon sometimes to enforce its decisions) and symbolic power. The right of the psychiatric establishment to sanction its practioners to act in particular ways is itself sanctioned by the state, which itself, of course, at least nominally seeks a sanction from the wider public (who recognize its power and sanction specific managerial elites by way of their vote). The history of psychiatry is, to some extent, a history of struggle by medics to achieve this sanction and fend off the claims of competing authorities (for example, legal and religious professionals) (Scull, 1993; Busfield, 1989; Porter, 1987).

In making these claims Bourdieu is walking a thin but very important line. On one hand he is arguing that symbolic power, in the final instance, depends upon recognition, or perhaps rather 'misrecognition', by those subject to it. Its power is that of a self-fulfilling prophecy and is dependent upon our unwitting complicity and legitimation. Certain social agents are empowered, in part, by our belief that they are powerful. On the other hand, however, Bourdieu is seeking to challenge those who would seek to reduce, for example, the power of the psychiatrist over his/her patient to the interactional dynamics effected between them in any particular encounter. The power of the psychiatrist derives from their position in a dynamic, historically evolving field. In making this point, Bourdieu is seeking to challenge what he takes to be a naïve over-emphasis on language and symbolism in interactionist sociology, linguistic philosophy and, more recently, the post-structuralism of Judith Butler.[225] Moreover, his argument stems from his philosophy of science. Many discourse analysts, following what can only be described as a positivist and

---

225 Butler criticizes Bourdieu's emphasis on institutions in her *Excitable Speech* (Butler, 1997b). Her emphasis is much more upon the performativity of power in situ. To my mind

behaviourist conception of social science, justify their tendency to ignore wider institutional conditions of discourse on the grounds that analysis can only focus upon conditions which are visible and thus observable. If 'institutions' are important, they argue, then we should be able to see (or hear) that in the 'real' interactions between agents. Bourdieu, rightly in my view, views this as an out-moded view of science, an 'epistemological obstacle', to use Bachelard's (2002) term (see **epistemological break**). Modern science is preoccupied with the invisible, he notes. It is constituted by the discovery of hidden forces behind the world of immediate perception. And sociology should be too. Of course, we have to prove the existence and efficacy of these forces, but that does not mean limiting our focus to the minutia of discourse.

As noted above, Bourdieu tends to use the terms 'symbolic power' and 'symbolic violence' interchangeably to describe this power. If there is any difference in his usage it is that 'symbolic violence' sometimes emphasizes the way in which social agents, by virtue of their socialization and historical symbolic struggles, come to accept the catgeories and symbolic systems which, in turn, are imposed upon them – and whose power they unwittingly sanction. However, I would like to suggest that we reserve the term 'symbolic power' for this, and that we use the term 'symbolic violence' to denote instances where particular groups are systematically denied the degree of recognition enjoyed by others (see **recognition**), that is, instances where they are devalued or stigmatized. It seems to me confusing to have two terms applying to the same thing, without any obvious distinction, and 'symbolic violence' is not always well suited to situations which cause no obvious pain (psychological or physical) to those subject to it. By contrast 'symbolic violence' does seem an appropriate term to capture the felt and/or lived suffering of those devalued, stigmatized or otherwise denied a basic level of recognition by their wider society. Bourdieu's later study, *The Weight of the World* provides many examples of this lived sense of devaluation, as indeed do Goffman's (1961, 1969) studies of *Asylums* and *Stigma*.

319

she makes just the error Bourdieu is pointing to, in a major way. Although there is some element of reply to Butler in Bourdieu's *Masculine Domination* he died before this argument could be resolved. Although I accept Butler's point that Bourdieu's schema sometimes leaves little room for resistance, recent work has suggested that resistance is not as free of 'sanction' as Butler suggests (Lovell, 2003) and my vote is squarely with Bourdieu on this matter. For some discussion of Butler's ideas see the entries on **performativity** and **sex/gender distinction**.

**Symbolic Power/Symbolic Violence**

The two key texts of Bourdieu's on these issues are *Reproduction* (Bourdieu and Passeron, 1996) which tends to use the language of 'symbolic violence' and *Language and Symbolic Power* (Bourdieu, 1992b), which tends to use the language of 'symbolic power'. John Austin's (1971) *How to Do Things With Words* is a fascinating read and an important background text for a proper understanding of Bourdieu's conception of symbolic power.

# System and Lifeworld

*Related concepts:* **colonization of the lifeworld, lifeworld, new social movements, public sphere.**

Earlier in this collection I discussed the concept of the lifeworld as it was developed in the work of the phenomenologists. Here I discuss Habermas' conception of the lifeworld and his contrasting conception of 'the system'. Habermas' conception of the lifeworld borrows much from the phenomenological version but I will not explore those links here. For present purposes it would make more sense to regard them as two quite distinct concepts.

Habermas draws the distinction between 'system' and 'lifeworld' in two ways. System and lifeworld are two different 'parts' of society, in his work, but he also draws an epistemological distinction between systemic and lifeworld modes of analysis. This generates some potential for confusion and that potential is increased by virtue of the fact that the lifeworld can be regarded as a part of the system from the point of view of a systemic analysis. I will try to unpick these various conceptual tangles in this entry but it is best to be forewarned of them before we begin. I will begin by considering the lifeworld as a distinct part of society.

All of society, system and lifeworld, consists in interaction for Habermas. However, interaction can assume different forms and contexts, thus giving rise to different levels of social organization. The lifeworld consists in 'symbolic' or communicative interactions which are co-ordinated at a face-to-face level by way of the mutual understanding achieved between agents, in dialogue, and their common orientation towards shared norms and values. The lifeworld is held together by traditions and the various obligations and duties they impose and, qua communicative space, is also the area of society wherein those traditions, along with other aspects of culture, knowledge and identity, are reproduced.

As a site of symbolic interaction, the lifeworld invites hermeneutic[226] analysis. This is what Habermas means by a 'lifeworld analysis'. Lifeworld analysis can involve either an investigation, for sociological purposes, of the meanings which social actions have for the agents who engage in them or, for more philosophical purposes, an investigation of the basic logic and grammar of important concepts and/or communicative forms. As noted above, however, Habermas believes that the lifeworld is amenable to a systems analysis too. This broadly amounts to a functional analysis, after the fashion of Talcott Parsons (1966); that is to say, Habermas believes that we can analyse the lifeworld not only from the point of view of the meanings and interpretations of the agents whose intereactions comprise it, but equally from the point of view of the functions which it serves for the preservation of wider society. Habermas' own schema of functional analysis comes very close to that of Parsons. The lifeworld, in effect, assumes the 'integration' and 'latency' functions of Parsons' (1966) AGIL[227] schema. It is conceived of as a normative order, that is a system of rules or norms (explicit and tacit, official and unofficial) which co-ordinates interaction at the ground level ('integration'), and also as a communicative order which reproduces the cultural patterns, dispositions and resources, such as language, which make social life possible and which other 'parts' of society require ('latency'). This systemic analysis can be posited in very general terms. We may say, for example, that any society must have a system of norms which co-ordinate or 'integrate' its constitutive interactions, and that it must have a means of reproducing its basic cultural stock (such as language, beliefs, and so on). The analysis may also be more specific, however, in respect that we may argue that 'this' type of society presupposes 'this' kind of social organization and therefore these kinds of norms and cultural patterns. We might argue, for example,

---

226 That is, an analysis focused upon ascertaining the meaning of what agents do and say.
227 Parsons argues that every social system must satisfy four basic 'functional prerequisites' if it is to survive. It must adapt (A) to its external environment, formulate and attain goals (G), achieve internal integration (I) and reproduce its latent cultural patterns (L). This is known as his AGIL schema.

that capitalist societies require some form of work ethic that motivates their members into productive economic activities, and that representative democracies presuppose a specific form and degree of interest in politics on the behalf of their citizens.

Where Habermas differs from Parsons is that he draws attention to the possibility of crisis tendencies within the lifeworld, when considered as a social-cultural system (Habermas, 1988). Specifically he refers to the possibility of 'legitimation crises', wherein norms are brought into question and contested, losing their integrative power to a degree which the political system is incapable of dealing with, and also to 'motivation crises', in which the lifeworld ceases to reproduce the basic dispositions, such as the work ethic, required by the societal system as a whole (see **crisis**).

The lifeworld is constituted through 'communicative action'. This, to reiterate, is a form of linguistic interaction oriented towards the achievement of mutual understanding and agreement. Habermas divides this action type into two sub-categories, norm-conformative action and discourse. As its name suggests, norm-conformative action involves a more or less habitual and unnoticed adherence to shared social norms. Agents conform to the shared social expectations which apply to whatever types of interaction they are involved in. Discourse, by contrast, designates those moments at which agents reflexively turn back upon their habits and assumptions to subject them to a communicatively rational interrogation and evaluation (see **discourse**). It entails a contest between agents in which each attempts to persuade the other of their view by recourse to logic and the exchange of reasons alone.

Habermas (1987a) situates his account of communicative rationality within a broader account of historical rationalization (see **rationality**). Communicative rationality is, he argues, a historical achievement. As the history of science most clearly demonstrates, our ways of reasoning, arguing and making sense belong to the realm of culture and the learning processes evident within the history of culture. The ways that we reason today differ from the ways in which we used to reason. The advent of modern patterns of reasoning, he continues, has made a discursive democracy possible. It has opened up the possibility of a society whose norms, including most centrally its laws, are the outcome of a genuinely communicatively rational debate. Furthermore, areas of social life once deemed 'beyond argument', particularly those pertaining to power and authority, are now open to argument and contestation. Prior to rationalization and enlightenment political structures and laws were rooted in and legitimated by reference to religion, which was itself not open to question or argument. The feudal king did not claim legitimacy for his láws by reference to their reasonableness, which would have left them open to question by reasonable subjects, but by reference to God, whom nobody was entitled to question. Through the process of rationalization, this changed and political elites increasingly claimed legitimacy for their authority and decisions by reference to their reasonableness. The laws of the land are not the laws of God but rather what any reasonable individual would accept as fair and appropriate, or at least that is the ideal. In practice, Habermas argues, democratic societies fall well short of the ideals they are founded upon and appeal to for their legitimacy (see **crisis** and **public sphere**).

The process of rationalization is also central to what Habermas refers to as the 'system' part of society. In traditional societies, he observes, all aspects of society were subsumed within the lifeworld. This meant that both political and economic activities were strongly regulated by religion and tradition, which lent them a framework of meaning and morality. One did not trade freely with the highest bidder in one's economic transactions, for example. Goods tended to be passed around in accordance with tradition and obligation. Integral to the process of rationalization, however, has been an uncoupling of these two forms of activities from the normative core of society, such that each has become an arena for relatively free utilitarian action, rooted in instrumentally rational calculation. As political and economic agents, in modern societies, we make a choice about what is best for us and then pursue that choice in a strategic fashion. We are not, or at least need not, be bound by normative considerations or traditions. Furthermore, each of these domains of life, economy and polity, has been further rationalized through the emergence of new communicative media peculiar to them, namely, money in the case of the economy and rationalized political power in the case of the polity. These new media have transformed economic and political relations in both quantitative and qualitative ways, Habermas notes. The emergence of a standardized national currency, for example, links all of the members of a nation much more tightly than previously in a mutually affective network and thereby gives rise to a whole range of new social dynamics. The numbers of people linked through a common currency is much greater, as is the strength of the link, and the ways in which people (indirectly) affect and impact upon one another is transformed.

The net effect of all of this, for Habermas, is that a new form of societal integration, which he terms 'system integration', has emerged. The lifeworld, to reiterate, is integrated by virtue of the mutual understanding achieved between interlocuters in local interactions. This is 'social integration'. System integration, by contrast, is a more impersonal matter of balance being achieved between inputs and outputs, supply and demand, at the macro-cosmic level. In the political system, for example, every citizen has a degree of power which they 'spend' at elections and other participation contexts, in whatever way they wish. This constitutes a transfer of power to the state, which in turn is then mandated to impose policies and laws upon those same citizens. Integration is achieved to the extent that the state accumulates a sufficient mandate to execute whatever policies it is required to make. Similarly in the economy, every economic actor is freed to pursue wealth and then spend it in whatever way they wish. They act, or at least can act, selfishly and without a thought for anybody else. The system is integrated to the extent that people are sufficiently motivated by the desire for wealth to supply the goods that others demand in sufficient amounts that these two sides of the picture, supply and demand, balance.

As with his concept of the lifeworld, Habermas does not believe the (systemic) 'integration' of the system is automatic or assured. To the contrary, he identifies two distinct crisis tendencies within the systemic aspect of the system of modern societies, economic crisis tendencies and rationality crisis tendencies (see **crisis**). His understanding of economic crisis tendencies is essentially Marxist in orientation. If unfettered, he believes, the economy is subject to a trend of declining profit and periodic crises of over-production. Moreover, insofar as this results in unemployment, declining wages and increased poverty amongst the working classes, he bolsters the Marxist position by noting that economic crisis tendencies can easily give rise to legitimation and motivation crises, in the form of working-class opposition to capitalism and radical class consciousness. Where he departs from Marx, using the advantage of historical hindsight, is in recognizing the capacity of the state to intervene in society in such a way as to stabilize economic crisis tendencies and pacify, or at least control, worker uprising – such as gathered in pace in many European societies throughout the nineteenth century and the earlier part of the twentieth. Specifically the state has assumed increased responsibility for economic management and, via social policy and the welfare state, for the welfare of its citizens and the smooth running of civil life. Furthermore, the franchise has been extended, such that the state now claims to be the democratic representative of all adult members of society. This has not resolved the crisis tendencies of capitalism in Habermas' view, however, so much as displaced them. The economy may be less prone to independent crises, since it is now managed and lacks independence, but this does not prevent 'crises of crisis management' or what Habermas calls 'rationality crises' (see **crisis**). The state in modern societies elects to balance the books, alongside the demands and needs of its citizens, but this is no guarantee that it is able to do so and thus the prospect of an administrative or 'rationality' crisis is a constant threat. The rapid decline of the postwar consensus, Keynesian approaches to economic management and the rise of neo-liberal modes of governance in the late 1970s, in both the United Kingdom and the United States, may be taken as examples of this sort of crisis.

To sum up then, Habermas distinguishes system and lifeworld as two forms of analysis. Systems analysis is 'functional' in nature, whilst lifeworld analysis is interpretative or hermeneutic in nature. However, lifeworld and system also refer to two distinct levels of social integration; one (the lifeworld) focused on mutual agreement between people, achieved by way of norms and understanding (social integration), the other (system) based upon unintended harmony between the various parts of the social world, wherein functional prerequisites are met (system integration). Finally, however, the system is particularly associated with the 'uncoupling' of the economy and the state, from the lifeworld, in the context of modern societies – a process which has allowed these parts of society to operate more freely, in accordance with their own systemic nature, and which has created a space wherein a different action orientation is expected of agents. The lifeworld is constituted by communicative ('communicatively rational') action, oriented towards understanding. The economic and political systems are characterized by strategic and strategically rational action (see **rationality**), mediated by money and power and oriented towards the achievement of individual goals.

### FURTHER READING

The key text for this is Volume 2 of Habermas' (1987b) *Theory of Communicative Action*. This is quite a difficult text, however, and it might be easier to begin with White's (1988) *The Recent Work of Jürgen Habermas* or Outhwaite's (1993) *Habermas*.

# Unconscious (the)

> **Related concepts: id, ego and superego, imaginary, symbolic and real, mirror stage and the ego, repression.**

The concept of the unconscious can and has been traced back deeply into the history of western culture and philosophy. In contemporary terms, however, it is generally associated with the discipline of psychoanalysis and specifically with the founder of that discipline, Sigmund Freud. Freud was critical of the philosophers and psychologists of his time for, as he saw it, equating 'the mind' or 'psychology' with consciousness; that is, with human conscious awareness of both self and world. That human psychology is not exhausted by consciousness is quite clearly revealed, he argued, by the evidence of what he called the 'pre-conscious'. This involves everything of which the individual is not aware, at a particular moment, but which they can readily recall if they either need or desire to. For example, I am not permanently thinking/conscious of my telephone number or home address but I can readily bring either to consciousness (I can recall them in words and say them) if I desire to and/or am required to. These 'facts' are pre-conscious in the respect that they are not in consciousness now but could become conscious at any time. They are instructive because they suggest that there is more to mental life than that of which we are conscious at any time, and thus that consciousness is but the tip of a psychological iceberg.

More relevant and important still than the pre-conscious, for Freud, however, is what he terms the 'unconscious'. The unconscious, he argues, consists of mental phenomena, chiefly memories and representations, which we cannot bring to consciousness, at least readily and in ordinary contexts, and yet which we can surmise both to exist and to exert an effect on our conscious experience and behaviour. Freud arrived at this idea in the context of developing a specific psychotherapeutic practice (psychoanalysis). Neurotic problems seem to be explained, he argued, by experiences (real or imagined) which the individual cannot bring to consciousness but which have effects.[228] The 'proof'[229] for the idea was

---

228 Psychoanalytic psychotherapy, so its practitioners claim, draws these unconscious elements into consciousness in the attempt to either exorcise them or at least reconcile the individual with their misery.

---

and is thus, in part, clinical. However, he also sought to develop his proof for the idea by reference to certain of the phenomena of 'normal' and 'ordinary' experience too – what he calls the 'psychopathology of everyday life' (Freud, 1976).

On one hand he pointed to the evidence of what he termed 'parapraxes'. These are the sorts of everyday and mundane 'mistakes' that most of us routinely make. Slips of the tongue, in which we accidently say something inappropriate, are perhaps the most famous examples of this, and have acquired the title 'Freudian slips', but Freud gives many other examples, including the forgetting of names and appointments, the bungling of actions and the mishearing of words. We are inclined, Freud argues, to think of such slips as just that, slips or accidents. But he suggests an alternative view. If we look at many of our slips in detail, he argues, they reveal features that are not readily reconciled with the notion that they are accidental or the result of (bio-psychological) 'machine failure'. We do not simply fail to say a word. For example, we say another word, often a word quite unlike the word that we should have said. And this word is often meaningful in the context in which we say it, even if its meaning opposes or contradicts what we were 'trying to say'. In other words, we do not just fail to perform a meaningful act; we perform another meaningful act contrary to it and contrary to our conscious intention. In these case, Freud argues, we mix up two intentions, one of which we are aware of and the other of which we are not, that is, one of which is unconscious. It is common today for us to attribute meaning to this, supposing, for example, that we did indeed intend to say what 'slipped out', albeit perhaps unconsciously, and we more or less follow Freud in doing this. The coherence and meaningfulness of the slip suggests that it is not quite so 'accidental' as we might like to believe. More specifically, it is at least suggestive of an aspect of our psychological life which is ordinarily well hidden but which periodically forces its way to the surface in the form of our slips and blunders.

In addition to parapraxes, Freud finds evidence of an unconscious psychological life in the phenomenon of dreams. Dreams, like parapraxes, are a 'disturbance' according to Freud. They disturb our sleep. And like parapraxes, they reveal unconscious wishes, albeit often in disguised ways. Any dream, Freud argues, has a manifest meaning. I might dream, for example, that I am running for my life down a tunnel which gets longer the more I run, so that I will never get to the end of it. In this case the

---

229 The validity of Freud's ideas are much contested and it has become something of a paradigm case for illustrating the difficulties of 'proving' things in interpretative social science.

---

*Unconsious (the)*

manifest meaning of the dream is 'I am running along a corridor etc. etc.' But why I am having this dream? What has running along a corridor got to do with anything? Why am I dreaming about that and not, for example, about the events of my day or about my forthcoming breakfast? When we ask this question we begin to consider what Freud calls the latent meaning of the dream, what it 'really' means. Freud argues that the impetus for the dream must have come from somewhere. In some cases this impetus is external to us. Events in the room in which we are sleeping, such as loud bangs, sometimes feature in our dreams in a coded fashion (for example, as the bang of a gun). In many cases, however, they are internal. One sub-class of these internal factors involves appetites or desires that we are usually aware of in our conscious state. If I am hungry, for example, I often dream of food. And if my bladder is full I sometimes dream of water or relieving myself. The key interference that explains much of my dream content, according to Freud, however, is interference from the unconscious, and the key to explaining the latent content of my dream – unlocking the code – is tracing the dream back to this unconscious interference. Specifically, he argues that dreams are an aspect of 'wish fulfilment',[230] that is, they reflect our unconscious wishes or desires and the various anxieties, fears and concerns that are bound up with those wishes. To return to my 'long corridor', for example, it may be that I wish to get on in life and strive to do so but seem to be getting further away from my goal with every effort I make to move myself forward. Perhaps I do not allow myself to think in this way consciously but the concern is there, in my unconscious, and it returns in the form of a dream, embedded as a theme in a story – just as my full bladder and desire to pee emerges in my dream as an image of flowing water.

There is more to it than this, however. Failure to achieve one's goals is an unpleasant experience and one that we do not much like to admit to ourselves, hence we might not be inclined to admit it to ourselves and it may only find outlet in the metaphorical form of the corridor in the dream. But it is recognized, understood, tolerated and perhaps even sympathized with in many social contexts. This is not true of most contents of the unconscious in the classic Freudian schema, and for this reason the metaphoric form which unconscious wishes might assume in the dream-text are understood, in many cases, as quite explicit forms of euphemization. In our everyday life and indeed our literature and myths, Freud notes, we are prone to euphemism when dealing with socially

---

230 This is true of some of the other cases too, of course, such as the hungry sleeper who dreams of food or the dreamer whose bladder inclines them to dream of water or release.

---

*Unconsious (the)*

sensitive and particularly sexual matters (note that 'socially sensitive' is, in this context, itself a euphemism for 'sexual'). In literature, for example, sexual initiation is sometimes indicated, symbolically, by way of a character crossing over another, more literal 'line', or in film, by a train passing through a tunnel. And we have hundreds of words which allow us to avoid the embarrassment of referring to our sexual organs and/or practices, for example 'bit of ows yer father', 'old man', 'Mary Jane', 'Arthur, J. Rank'. So it is, says Freud, with the unconscious wishes that make it into our dreams. The relaxed state of sleep brings these wishes closer to the surface, they begin to intrude on the dream state, but even in this case they do so in a disguised or euphemized way which sanitizes and somewhat disguises them.

This point takes us to a number of questions at the heart of the Freudain enterprise, namely, why do we have an unconscious and how is it formed? The answer, for Freud, lies in the conflict between our basic state of nature and the demands of life in a society, and particularly in a civilized society such as our own. Specifically, Freud believes that, by nature, our sexual inclinations do not accord with the morals of our society. We are, by nature, 'polymorphous and perverse' (Freud, 1973); that is, we can derive sexual pleasure in a wide variety of ways and have little natural inclination towards the rules of polite and moral society. If it feels good and it is in our power to do it we are inclined to do so. Furthermore, we are equally inclined towards forms of aggression which are incompatible with group life and, again, with civilized life in particular. Consequently, Freud argues, we have to learn to repress these desires and the experiences and memories of the earlier period of our life when they were in control of our psychological life (see **repression**). Furthermore, when we have achieved such a state of civilization and repression, these desires might prove quite shocking and upsetting to us if we were to become aware of them, thus generating a greater incentive towards repression. This process of repression does not eliminate these desires and memories, however, it just keeps them out of consciousness. It creates an unconscious in the specifically psychoanalytic sense.

A seminal moment in this process, for Freud, is what he calls the oedipal stage of childhood development.[231] The sexual history of the infant, he argues, begins with a focus upon the mouth. Very young infants put everything that will fit into their mouths and seemingly enjoy the sensation of doing so. As they get older, this seems to give way to a range

---

231 This is said to occur at around five years of age.

of anal pleasures and to a struggle between parents and children over 'the potty'. Children initially exercise no control over their bowels and have no inhibition about playing with their faeces. Indeed, Freud suggests that they delight in playing in this way. Needless to say, they have to learn to master their bowels and they have to develop a distaste for their faeces. When this has been achieved, however, attention shifts to the genitals. Moreover, this coincides with a period in which, in Freud's view, children are overly identified with their mother and develop a strong (sexual)[232] attraction to her. This is contrary to one of the strongest social taboos, the incest taboo and, Freud argues, mobilizes the father to intervene. In the case of boys in particular this causes the child to repress their sexual desire for the mother, to identify with the father and thus to take on the (civilized) attitudes and dispositions of the father. In other words, it is a radical break during which the child succumbs to the demands of civilization and thereby develops an unconscious. This theory has any number of problems, not least concerning the fate of little girls in all of this, and has been criticized, reinterpreted and reformulated many times. Most psychoanalysts, as far as one can tell, do not subscribe to quite this 'just so' story, but the basic idea is still widely adhered to by many psychoanalysts, and is tied closely to the idea of the unconscious. The unconscious is deemed the product of the oedipal conflict.

The credibility of the wider aspects of psychoanalytic theory, and the theory of the unconscious more particularly, is difficult to assess. Freud has proved to be a tremendous inspiration to many social theorists. Some have seen his model of the psyche as a powerful critique of conventional views of the social agents. Others have turned his analysis of sexual repression into a critique of social/political repression (see **repression**). There are good reasons to be cautious in our reception of Freud and wider psychoanalysis, however. Many social theorists, for example, would agree that human agents are not conscious of all of the motives, events, and so on, which shape their actions. And many might also agree that agents are capable of concealing from themselves motives which they might not wish to admit to (see **repression**). But one can concede all of this without necessarily buying into the Freudian account. Furthermore, the Freudian model raises all sorts of problems. On the one hand, for example, the complex picture of unconscious mental processes painted by

---

232 Psychoanalysts differ in the extent to which this represents the sexual attraction in 'adult' terms. Some go to lengths to explain that the sexual attraction which the child experiences is very different from adult sexual attraction but others more or less equate it with adult desire (if only by default). Freud, by and large, falls into the latter camp.

---

psychoanalysis can seem somewhat overly 'mentalistic'[233] and somewhat implausible. On the other hand, much of Freud's own work is both extremely mechanistic and deterministic, and very much tied to an outdated image of society and social relations. Finally, psychoanalytic explanations are often difficult to accept because they are neither testable nor parsimonious.[234] At the best one would have to say that the jury is still out on this particular source of social theory.

## FURTHER READING

In contrast to many key critical theorists (and particularly many psychoanalysts), Freud is wonderful to read. He is clear and makes strong (if not always persuasive), rational arguments in defence of his position. His clearest exposition of the idea of the unconscious is to be found in his metapsychology (Freud, 1985). His introductory lectures on psychoanalysis are also very good, however, as they provide a general overview of psychoanalysis as he conceived of it (Freud, 1973).

331

233 Many writers argue that references to our mind and 'inner worlds' are really metaphors and that our mental life, in fact, consists largely in our 'outward' behaviours and perceptions. From this point of view, psychoanalytic references to complex 'internal' mental processes are, at best, elaborate metaphors but unfortunately ones which psychoanalysts themselves mistake for literal descriptions.

234 That is to say, they are by no means the most obvious or simplest of explanations. This would not matter if they could be tested and 'proved' but they cannot . Similarly, their untestable nature would not be such a problem if the explanations psychoanalysis offered were the most straightforward and obvious (i.e. parsimonious). Falling between these two stools does make the account problematic however.

# bibliography

Adorno, T. ed. (1969) *The Positivist Dispute in German Sociology*. London: Heinemann.

Adorno, T. and Horkheimer, M. (1983) *The Dialectic of Enlightenment*. London: Verso.

Althusser, L. (1969) *For Marx*. London: Verso.

Althusser, L. (1971) 'Ideology and State Ideological Apparatuses', in *Essays on Ideology*. London: Verso. pp.1–60.

Althusser, L. and Balibar, E. (1979) *Reading Capital*. London: Verso.

Andersen, E. (1997) *Introduction to the Statistical Analysis of Categorical Data*. New York: Springer.

Archer, M. (1995) *Realist Social Theory: the Morphogenetic Approach*. Cambridge: Cambridge University Press.

Arendt, H. (1958) *The Human Condition*. Chicago: University of Chicago Press.

Aristotle (1955) *The Ethics*. Harmondsworth: Penguin.

Austin, J. (1971) *How To Do Things With Words*. Oxford: Oxford University Press.

Ayer, A. (1946) *Language, Truth and Logic*. London: Gollancz.

Bacharac, P. and Baratz, M. (1970) *Power and Poverty*. New York: Oxford University Press.

Bachelard, G. (1970) *Le Rationalisme Appliqué*. Paris: Presses Universitaires de France.

Bachelard, G. (1984) *The New Scientific Spirit*. Boston: Beacon.

Bachelard, G. (2002) *The Formation of the Scientific Mind*. Manchester: Clinamen.

Bagguley, P. (1995) 'Middle class radicalism revisited', in T. Butler and M. Savage *Social Change and the Middle Classes*. London: UCL.

Barrett, M. (1991) *The Politics of Truth*. Cambridge: Polity.

Beck, U. (1992) *The Risk Society*. London: Sage.

Becker, G. (1996) *Accounting for Tastes*. Cambridge: Harvard University Press.

Becker, H. (1960) 'Notes on the concept of commitment', *American Journal of Sociology*, 66.

Becker, H. (1984) *Art Worlds*. California: University of California Press.

Becker, H. (1993) *Outsiders*. New York: Free Press.

Beissinger, M. (1998) 'Nationalist violence and the state: political authority and contentious repertoires in the former USSR', *Comparative Politics* 30: 401–33.

Bell, V. (ed.) (1999) 'Performativity and Belonging', *Theory, Culture and Society* (special issue) 16 (2).

Benjamin, J. (1991) *The Bonds of Love*. London: Virago.

Benvenuto, B. and Kennedy, R. (1986) *The Works of Jacques Lacan*. London: Free Association Books.

Berger, P. and Luckmann, T. (1979) *The Social Construction of Reality*. Harmondsworth: Penguin.

Bernstein, J. (1995) *Recovering Ethical Life*. London: Routledge.

Beynon, J. and Dunkerley, D. (2000) *Globalisation; The Reader*. London: Athlone.

Bhabha, H. (1994) *The Place of Culture*. London: Routledge.

Bhasker, R. (1979) *The Possibility of Naturalism*. Brighton: Harvester.

Bhasker, R. (1989) *Reclaiming Reality*. London: Verso.

Bhasker, R. (1994) *Plato Etc*. London: Verso.

Billig, M. (1999) *Freudian Repression*. Cambridge: Cambridge University Press.

Blauner, R. (1964) *Alienation and Freedom*. Chicago: University of Chicago Press.

Blumer, H. (1969) 'Collective Behaviour', in A. McClung-Lee *Principles of Sociology*. New York: Barnes and Noble. pp. 67–121.

Blumer, H. (1986) *Symbolic Interactionism*. Berkeley, University of California Press.

Bourdieu, P. (1977) *Outline of a Theory of Practice*. Cambridge: Cambridge University Press.

Bourdieu, P. (1983) 'The forms of capital', in J. Richardson *The Handbook of Theory and Research for the Sociology of Education*. New York: Greenwood Press. pp. 241–58.

Bourdieu, P. (1984) *Distinction*. London: RKP.

Bourdieu, P. (1986) *Homo Academicus*. Cambridge: Polity.

Bourdieu, P. (1988) 'Vive la Crise!', *Theory and Society* 17 (5): 773–88.

Bourdieu, P. (1990a) *In other words*. Cambridge: Polity.

Bourdieu, P. (1990b) *Photography: A Middle-Brow Art*. Cambridge: Polity.

Bourdieu, P. (1992a) *The Logic of Practice.*, Cambridge: Polity.

Bourdieu, P. (1992b) *Language and Symbolic Power*. Cambridge: Polity.

Bourdieu, P. (1993) *Sociology in Question*. London: Sage.

Bourdieu, P. (1996) *The State Nobility*. Cambridge: Polity.

Bourdieu, P. (1998a) *Practical Reason*. Cambridge: Polity.

Bourdieu, P. (1998b) *On Television and Journalism*. London: Pluto.

Bourdieu, P. et al. (1999) *The Weight of the World*. Cambridge: Polity.

Bourdieu, P. (2000) *Pascalian Meditations*. Cambridge: Polity.

Bourdieu, P. Chamboredon, J-C and Passeron, J-C (1991) *The Craft of Sociology*. Berlin: Walter de Gruyter.

Bourdieu, P., Darbel, A and Schnapper, D. (1990) *The Love of Art*. Cambridge: Polity.

Bourdieu, P. and Haakce, H. (1995) *Free Exchange*. Cambridge: Polity.

Bourdieu, P. and Passeron, J. (1996) *Reproduction*. London: Sage.

Bourdieu, P. and Wacquant, L. (1992) *An Invitation to Reflexive Sociology*. Cambridge: Polity.

Bowie, M. (1991) *Lacan*. London: Fontana.

Burkitt, I. (1991) *Social Selves.*, London: Sage.

Burkitt, I. (1999) *Bodies of Thought*. London: Sage.

Busfield, J. (1989) *Managing Madness*. London: Unwin Hyman.

Butler, J. (1989) 'Sexual ideology and phenomenological description: a feminist critique of Merleau-Ponty's *Phenomenology of Perception*', in J. Allen and I. Young *The Thinking Muse*. Bloomington: Indiana University Press.

Butler, J. (1990) *Gender Trouble*. London: Routledge.

Butler, J. (1993) *Bodies That Matter*. London: Routledge.

Butler, J. (1994) (with Osborne, P. and Segal, L.) 'Gender as performance: an interview with Judith Butler', *Radical Philosophy* 67: 32–9.

Butler, J. (1997a) *The Psychic Life of Power*. Stanford, CA: Stanford University Press.

Butler, J. (1997b) *Excitable Speech*. London: Routledge.

Buytendijk, F. (1974) *Prolegomena to an Anthropological Physiology*. Pittsburgh, Duquesne University press.

Byrne, P. (1997) *Social Movements in Britain*. London: Routledge.

Calhoun, C. (1994) (ed.) *Habermas and the Public Sphere*. Cambridge: MIT.

Calhoun, C. (1995) '"New Social Movements" of the early nineteenth century', in M. Traugott *Repertoires and Cycles of Contention*. London: Duke University Press. pp.173–216.

Callinicos, A. (2003) *An Anti-Capitalist Manifesto*. Cambridge: Polity.

Camic, C. (1986) 'The matter of habit', *American Journal of Sociology* 91: 1039–87.

Camus, A. (1948) *The Plague*. Harmondsworth: Penguin.

Camus, A. (1975) *The Myth of Sisyphus*. Harmondsworth: Penguin.

Camus, A. (1982) *The Outsider*. Harmondsworth: Penguin.

Canguilhem, G. (1980) 'What is Psychology?' in *I&C* 7: 37–50.

Canguilhem, G. (1991) *The Normal and the Pathological*. New York: Zone.

Cassirer, E. (1923) *Substance and Function* and *Einstein's Theory of Relativity*. London: Open Court Publishers.

Chabot, S. (2000) 'Transnational diffusion and the African American reinvention of the ghandian repertoire', *Mobilisation* 5: 201–16.

Charlesworth, S. (2000) *A Phenomenology of Working Class Experience*. Cambridge: Cambridge University Press.

Chester, G. and Dickey, J. (1988) *Feminism and Censorship*. Dorset, Prism Press.

Clausen, S-E. (1998) *Applied Correspondence Analysis*. London: Sage.

Clegg, S. (1989) *Frameworks of Power*. London: Sage.

Coleman, J. (1988) *Foundations of Social Theory*. Cambridge: Harvard University Press.

Connell, R. (1987) *Gender and Power*. Cambridge: Polity.

Cooke, M. (1997) *Language and Reason: A Study of Habermas' Pragmatics*. Cambridge, MA: MIT Press.

Cooley, C. (1902) *Human Nature and the Social Order*. New York: Charles Scribner's Sons.

Coulter, J. (1979) *The Social Construction of Mind*. London: Macmillan.

Crenson, M. (1971) *The Un-Politics of Air Pollution*. Baltimore: John Hopkins University Press.

Crompton, R. (1998) *Class and Stratification*. Cambridge: Polity.

Crossley, N. (1994) *The Politics of Subjectivity: Between Foucault and Merleau-Ponty*. Ashgate: Aldershot.

Crossley, N. (1995) 'Body techniques, agency and intercorporeality', *Sociology* 29 (1): 133–50.

Crossley, N. (1996a) *Intersubjectivity: The Fabric of Social Becoming*. London: Sage.

Crossley, N. (1996b) 'Body-subject/body-power', *Body and Society* 2 (2): 91–116.

Crossley, N. (1998) 'R.D. Laing and the British anti-psychiatry movement: a socio-historical analysis', *Social Science and Medicine* 47 (7): 877–89.

Crossley, N. (1999) 'Working utopias and social movements: an investigation using case study materials from radical mental health movements in Britain', *Sociology* 33 (4): 809–30.

Crossley, N. (2001a) *The Social Body: Habit, Identity and Desire*. London: Sage.

Crossley, N. (2001b) 'The phenomenological habitus and its construction', *Theory and Society*, 30: 81–120.

Crossley, N. (2001c) 'Citizenship, intersubjectivity and the lifeworld' in N. Stevenson *Culture and Citizenship*. London: Sage.

Crossley, N. (2001d) 'Merleau-Ponty', in B. Turner and A. Elliott *Profiles in Contemporary Social Theory*, London: Sage, pp.30–42.

Crossley, N. (2002a) *Making Sense of Social Movements*. Buckingham: Open University Press.

Crossley, N. (2002b) 'Global anti-corporate struggle: a preliminary analysis', *British Journal of Sociology* 53 (4): 667–91.

Crossley, N. (2002c) 'Habitus, agency and change: engaging with Bourdieu', *Gendai Shakai-Riron Kenku* (Journal of Studies in Contemporary Social Theory) 12: 329–57.

Crossley, N. (2003a) 'Even Newer Social Movements', *Organisation* 10 (4): 287–305.

Crossley, N. (2003b) 'From reproduction to transformation: social movement fields and the radical habitus', *Theory, Culture and Society* 20 (6): 43–68.

334

Crossley, N. (2004a) 'Phenomenology, structuralism and history: Merleau-Ponty's social theory', *Theoria* 103: 88–21.

Crossley, N. (2004b) 'The circuit trainer's habitus: reflexive body techniques and the sociality of the workout', *Body and Society* 10 (1): 37–69.

Crossley, N. and Roberts, J.M. (2004) *After Habermas: New Perspective on the Public Sphere.* Oxford: Blackwell.

Cutler, A, Hindess, B., Hirst, P. and Hussain, A. (1977) *Marx's Capital and Capitalism Today.* London: RKP.

Dahl, R. (1961) *Who Governs?* New York: Yale University Press.

Danaher, K. (2001) *10 Reasons to Abolish the IMF and World Bank.* New York: Seven Stories Press.

Davidson, D. (1980) *Essays on Actions and Events.* Oxford: Clarendon Press.

Davis, K. and Moore, W. (1945) 'Some Principles of Stratification', *American Sociological Review* 10.

de Beauvoir, S. (1948) *Pyrrus and Cinéas.* Paris: Gallimard.

de Beauvoir, S. (1962) *The Prime of Life.* Harmondsworth: Penguin.

de Beauvoir, S. (1967) *The Ethics of Ambiguity.* New York: Citadel.

de Beauvoir, S. (1988) *The Second Sex.* London: Picador.

Degenne, A. and Forsé, M. (1999) *Introducing Social Networks.* London: Sage.

Della Porta, D. and Diani, M. (1999) *Social Movements: An Introduction.* Oxford: Blackwell.

Derrida, J. (1973) *Speech and Phenomena.* Evanston, Il: Northwestern University Press.

Derrida, J. (1978) *Of Grammatology.* Baltimore: Johns Hopkins University Press.

Derrida, J. (1982) *Margins of Philosophy.* Brighton: Harvester.

Derrida, J. (1989) *Edmund Husserl's Origin of Geometry: An Introduction.* New York: Bison Books.

Derrida, J. (1994) *Spectres of Marx.* London: Routledge.

Descartes, R. (1969) *Discourse on Method and The Meditations.* Harmondsworth: Penguin.

Dews, P. (1987) *The Logics of Disintegration.* London: Verso.

Dews, P. (1995) *The Limits of Disenchantment.* London: Verso.

Dreyfus, H. and Rabinow, P. (1982) *Michel Foucault: Beyond Structuralism and Hermeneutics,* Brighton: Harvester.

Durkheim, E. (1915) *The Elementary Forms of Religious Life.* New York: Free Press.

Durkheim, E. (1952) *Suicide.* London: RKP.

Durkheim, E. (1964) *The Division of Labour.* New York: Free Press.

Durkheim, E. (1965) *The Rules of Sociological Method.* New York: Free Press.

Durkheim, E. (1973) 'The dualism of human nature and its social conditions', in *Émile Durkheim: On Morality and Society.* Chicago: Chicago University Press. pp.149–66.

Durkheim, E. (1974) *Sociology and Philosophy.* New York: Free Press.

Durkheim, E. (1982) *The Rules of Sociological Method.* New York: Free Press.

Durkheim, E. (2002) *Moral Education.* New York: Dover Publications.

Dworkin, A. (1981) *Pornography.* London: The Women's Press.

Edwards, G. (2004) 'Habermas and new social movements: what's new', in N. Crossley and J.M. Roberts *After Habermas: New Perspectives on the Public Sphere.* Oxford: Blackwell.

Elias, N. (1978) *What is Sociology?* London: Hutchinson.

Elias, N. (1984) *The Civilising Process.* Oxford: Blackwell.

Elias, N. (1996) *The Germans.* Oxford: Blackwell.

Elster, J. (1989) *Nuts and Bolts for the Social Sciences.* Cambridge: Cambridge University Press.

335

Emirbayer, M. (1997) 'Manifesto for a Relational Sociology', *American Journal of Sociology* 99(6): 1411–54.

Engels, F. (1969) *The Condition of the Working Class in England*. St Albans: Panther.

Evans-Pritchard, E. (1976) *Witchcraft, Oracles and Magic Amongst the Azande*. Oxford: Clarendon.

Eyerman, R and Jamison, A. (1991) *Social Movements: A Cognitive Approach*. Cambridge: Polity.

Fairclough, N. (1994) *Language and Power*. London: Longman.

Fanon, F. (1986) *The Wretched of the Earth*. Harmondsworth: Penguin.

Fanon, F. (1993) *Black Skins, White Masks*. London: Pluto.

Fernando, S. (1991) *Mental Health, Race and Culture*. London: Macmillan.

Fine, B. (2001) *Social Capital versus Social Theory*. London: Routledge.

Foucault, M. (1965) *Madness and Civilisation*. London: Tavistock.

Foucault, M. (1970) *The Order of Things*. London: Tavistock.

Foucault, M. (1972) *The Archaeology of Knowledge*. London: Tavistock.

Foucault, M. (1973) *Birth of the Clinic*. London: Tavistock.

Foucault, M. (1978) 'Politics and the study of discourse', *Ideology and Consciousness* 3: 7–26.

Foucault, M. (1979) *Discipline and Punish*. Harmondsworth: Penguin.

Foucault, M. (1980a) *Power/Knowledge*. Brighton: Harvester.

Foucault, M. (1980b) *Language, Counter-Memory, Practice*. New York: Cornell University Press.

Foucault, M. (1982) 'The subject and power', in H. Dreyfus and P. Rabinow *Michel Foucault: Beyond Structuralism and Hermeneutics*. Brighton: Harvester. pp. 208–26.

Foucault, M. (1984) *The History of Sexuality Vol I*, Harmondsworth: Penguin.

Foucault, M. (1988) 'Truth, Power, Self: An Interview', in Martin, L., Gutman, H. and Hutton, P. *Technologies of the Self*. London: Tavistock. pp.9–16.

Frankfurt, H. (1982) 'Freedom of the will and the concept of the person', in G. Watson *Free Will*. Oxford: Oxford University Press. pp.81–95.

Freud, A. (1968) *The Ego and the Mechanisms of Defence*. London: Hogarth.

Freud, S. (1973) *Introductory Lectures on Psychoanalysis*. (Pelican Freud Library Vol. 1) Harmondsworth: Penguin.

Freud, S. (1985) *On Metapsychology* (Pelican Freud Library Vol. 11): Harmondsworth: Penguin.

Freud, S. (1986) *Civilisation, Society and Religion*. (Pelican Freud Library Vol. 12): Harmondsworth: Penguin.

Fukuyama, F. (1992) *The End of History and the Last Man*. Harmondsworth: Penguin.

Giddens, A. (1984) *The Constitution of Society*. Cambridge: Polity.

Giddens, A. (1990) *The Consequences of Modernity*. Cambridge: Polity.

Giddens, A. (1991) *Modernity and Self-Identity*. Cambridge: Polity.

Gilroy, P. (1992) *There Ain't No Black in the Union Jack*. London: Routledge.

Gilroy, P. (1993) *The Black Atlantic*. London: Verso.

Goffman, E. (1959) *Presentation of Self in Everyday Life*. Harmondsworth: Penguin.

Goffman, E. (1961) *Asylums*. Harmondsworth: Penguin.

Goffman, E. (1969) *Stigma*. Harmondsworth: Penguin.

Goldberg, D. (1993) *Racist Culture*. Oxford: Blackwell.

Goldstein, K. (2000) *The Organism*. New York: Zone.

Goldthorpe, J. (1998) 'Rational actor theory for sociology', *British Journal of Sociology* 49 (2): 167–92.

Goldthorpe, J. (2000) *On Sociology*. Oxford: Oxford University Press.

Gowers, T. (2002) *Mathematics: A Very Short Introduction*. Oxford: Oxford University Press.

Gramsci, A. (1971) *Selections From Prison Notebooks*. London: Lawrence and Wishart.

Granovetter, M. (1973) 'The strength of weak ties', *American Journal of Sociology* 78.

Grehan, K. (2002) *Gramsci, Culture and Anthropology*. London: Pluto.

Grosz, E. (1990) *Jacques Lacan: A Feminist Introduction*. London: Routledge.

Gutting, G. (1989) *Michel Foucault's Archaeology of Scientific Reason*. Cambridge: Cambridge University Press.

Habermas, J. (1970a) 'On systematically distorted communication', *Inquiry* 13 (3): 205–18.

Habermas, J. (1970b) 'Towards a theory of communicative competence', *Inquiry* 13 (4): 360–75.

Habermas, J. (1972) *Knowledge and Human Interests*. London: Heinemann.

Habermas, J. (1981) 'New social movements', *Telos* 49: 33–7.

Habermas, J. (1987a) *Towards a Rational Society*. Cambridge: Polity.

Habermas, J. (1987b) *The Theory of Communicative Action Vol. II*. Cambridge: Polity.

Habermas, J. (1988) *Legitimation Crisis*. Cambridge: Polity.

Habermas, J. (1989) *Structural Transformation of the Public Sphere*. Cambridge: Polity.

Habermas, J. (1989b) *Toward a Rational Society*. Cambridge: Polity.

Habermas, J. (1991a) *The Theory of Communicative Action: Reason and the Rationalisation of Society* (Vol. 1). Cambridge: Polity.

Habermas, J. (1991b) *Communication and the Evolution of Society*. Cambridge: Polity.

Habermas, J. (1992) *Moral Consciousness and Communicative Action*. Cambridge: Polity.

Habermas, J. (1993) *Justification and Application*. Cambridge: Polity.

Hair, J., Anderson, R., Tatham, R. and Black, W. (1984) *Multivariate Data Analysis*. London: Prentice Hall.

Halbwachs, M. (1958) *The Psychology of Social Class*. London: Heinemann.

Halfpenny, P. (1982) *Positivism and Sociology*. London: Allen and Unwin.

Hall, S. (1987) 'Gramsci and Us', *Marxism Today* (June): 16–21.

Hammond, M., Howarth, J. and Keat, R. (1991) *Understanding Phenomenology*. Oxford: Blackwell.

Hegel, G. (1971) *The Philosophy of Mind*. Oxford: Clarendon Press.

Hegel, G. (1979) *The Phenomenology of Spirit*. Oxford: Oxford University Press.

Heidegger, M. (1962) *Being and Time*. Oxford: Blackwell.

Heidegger, M. (1978) 'A letter on humanism', in *Basic Writings*. London: RKP. pp. 190–242.

Held, D. (1980) *Introduction to Critical Theory: Horkheimer to Habermas*. Cambridge: Polity.

Held, D. and McGrew, A. (2002) *Globalisation/Anti-Globalisation*. Cambridge: Polity.

Heritage, J. (1984) *Garfinkel and Ethnomethdology*. Cambridge: Polity.

Hertz, N. (2001) *The Silent Takeover*. London: Heinemann.

Hindess, B. (1982) 'Power, interests and the outcome of struggles', *Sociology* 16 (4): 498–511.

Hindess, B. (1998) *Choice, Rationality and Social Theory*. London: Unwin Hyman.

Hindess, B. and Hirst, P. (1977) *Mode of Production and Social Formation*. London: Macmillan.

Hirschman, A. (2002) *Shifting Involvements*. Princeton: Princeton University Press.

Hirst, P. (1979) *On Law and Ideology*. London: Macmillan.

Hobbes, T. (1971) *Leviathan*. Harmondsworth: Penguin.

Homans, G. (1961) *Social Behaviour*. London: RKP.

Homans, G. (1973) 'Bringing men back in', in A. Ryan *The Philosophy of Social Explanation*. Oxford: Oxford University Press. pp.50–64.

Honderich, T. (1973) *Essays on Freedom of Action*. London: RKP.
Honneth, A. (1995) *The Struggle For Recognition*. Cambridge: Polity.
Howells, C. (1999) *Derrida*. Cambridge: Polity.
Hume, D. (1969) *A Treatise of Human Nature*. Harmondsworth: Penguin.
Husserl, E. (1970a) *The Crisis of the European Sciences and Transcendental Phenomenology*. Evanston, IL: Northwestern University Press.
Husserl, E. (1970b) 'The origin of geometry', in E. Husserl *The Crisis of the European Sciences and Transcendental Phenomenology*. Evanston, IL: Northwestern University Press. pp.353–78.
Husserl, E. (1973) *Experience and Judgement*. Evanston, IL: Northwestern University Press.
Husserl, E. (1989) *Ideas Pertaining to a Pure Phenomenology and to a Phenomenological Philosophy; Second Book*. Dordrecht: Kluwer.
Husserl, E. (1991) *Cartesian Meditations*. Dordrecht: Kluwer.
Hutchby, I. and Wooffitt, R. (1988) *Conversation Analysis*. Cambridge: Polity.
Jamison, A., Eyerman, R., Cramer, J. and Laessoe, J. (1990) *The Making of the New Environmental Consciousness*. Edinburgh: Edinburgh University Press.
Jay, M. (1996) *The Dialectical Imagination*. Berkeley: California University Press.
Jenkins, R. (1987) *Social Identity*. London: Routledge.
Joas, H. (1985) *G.H.Mead*. Cambridge: Polity.
Kant, I. (1933) *Critique of Pure Reason*. London: Macmillan.
Kant, I. (1948) *The Moral Law: Groundwork of a Metaphysic of Morals*. London: Routledge.
Kant, I. (1993) *Critique of Practical Reason*. New Jersey: Prentice Hall.
Kappeler, S. (1986) *The Pornography of Representation*. Cambridge: Polity.
Keat, R. and Urry, J. (1982) *Social Theory As Science*. London: RKP.
Kelly, G.A. (1965) 'Notes on Hegel's lordship and bondage', *Review of Metaphysics* 19: 780–802.
Kemp, S. and Squires, J. (1997) *Feminisms*. Oxford: Oxford University Press.
Kingsnorth, P. (2003) *One No, Many Yeses*. London: Free Press.
Klein, M. (1993) *Envy and Gratitude*. London: Virago.
Klein, N. (2000) *No Logo*. London: HarperCollins.
Kojève, A. (1969) *Introduction to the Reading of Hegel*. New York: Basic Books.
Koopmans, R. (1993) 'The dynamics of protest waves', *American Sociological Review* 58: 637–58.
Kristeva, J. (1980) *Desire in Language*. New York: Columbia University Press.
Kruks, S. (1990) *Situation and Human Existence*. London: Unwin Hyman.
Kruskal, J. and Wish, M. (1978) *Multidimensional Scaling*. London: Sage.
Kuhn, T. (1970) *The Structure of Scientific Revolutions*. Chicago: Chicago University Press.
Lacan, J. (1989) *Écrits*. London: Routledge.
Laclau, E. and Mouffe, C. (1986) *Hegemony and Socialist Strategy*. London: Verso.
Laqueur, T. (1990) *Making Sex*. Cambridge: Harvard University Press.
Larrain, J. (1979) *The Concept of Ideology*. London: Hutchinson.
Laver, M. (1997) *Private Desires, Political Action*. London: Sage.
Leder, D. (1990) *The Absent Body*. Chicago, University of Chicago Press.
Leder, D. (1998) 'A tale of two bodies', in B. Welton *Body and Flesh*. Oxford: Blackwell. pp.117–30.
Lenin, V.I. (1918) *State and Revolution*. Moscow: Foreign Language Publishing.
Lenin, V.I. (1973) *What is to be Done?* London: Progress.
Levin, D. (1989) 'The body politics: the embodiment of praxis in Foucault and Habermas', *Praxis International* 9 (1/2): 112–33.
Littlewood, R. and Lipsedge, M. (1989) *Aliens and Alienists*. London: Unwin Hyman.

Levi-Strauss, C. (1966) *The Savage Mind*. Chicago: Chicago University Press.

Levi-Strauss, C. (1969) *The Elementary Forms of Kinship*. Boston: Beacon.

Levi-Strauss, C. (1987) *Introduction to the Work of Marcel Mauss*. London: Routledge.

Lloyd, M. (1999) 'Performativity, parody, politics', *Theory, Culture and Society* 16 (2): 195–213.

Lockwood, D. (1964) 'Social integration and system integration', in G. Zollschan and W. Hirsch *Explorations in Social Change*. London: RKP.

Lovell, T. (2003) 'Resisting with authority'. *Theory, Culture and Society* 20 (1): 1–19.

Lukács, G. (1971) *History and Class Consciousness*. London: Merlin.

Lukes, S. (1974) *Power: A Radical View*. London: Macmillan.

Lukes, S. (1986) *Power*. Oxford: Blackwell.

Luxemburg, R. (1986) *The Mass Strike*. London: Harper Torchbooks.

Mac an Ghaill, M. (1999) *Contemporary Racisms and Ethnicities*. Buckingham: Open University Press.

Mandel, E. (1970) *Introduction to Marxist Economic Theory*. New York: Pathfinder.

Marcuse, H. (1968) *Negations*. Boston: Beacon.

Marcuse, H. (1986) *One-Dimensional Man*. London: Arc.

Marcuse, H. (1987) *Eros and Civilisation*. London: Arc.

Marshall, T.H. and Bottomore, T. (1992) *Citizenship and Social Class*. London: Pluto.

Marx, K. (1959) *Economic and Philosophical Manuscripts of 1844*. Moscow: Progress Publishers.

Marx, K. (1976) *Capital* (Vol. 1): Harmondsworth: Penguin.

Marx, K. and Engels, F. (1967) *The Communist Manifesto*. Harmondsworth: Penguin.

Marx, K. and Engels, F. (1970) *The German Ideology*. London: Lawrence and Wishart.

Mauss, M. (1979) *Sociology and Psychology*. London: RKP.

McAdam, D. (1995) "Initiator' and 'Spin-Off' Movements', in Traugott, M. *Repertoires and Cycles of Collective Action*. London: Duke. pp.217–40.

McAdam, D., Tarrow, S. and Tilly, C. (2002) *Dynamics of Contention*. Cambridge: Cambridge University Press.

McAllester Jones, M. (1991) *Gaston Bachelard: Subversive Humanist*. Madison: University of Wisconsin Press.

Mead, G. (1967) *Mind, Self and Society*. Chicago: Chicago University Press.

Melucci, A. (1986) *Nomads of the Present*. London: Radius.

Melucci, A. (1996) *Challenging Codes*. Cambridge: Cambridge University Press.

Merleau-Ponty, M. (1962) *The Phenomenology of Perception*. London: RKP.

Merleau-Ponty, M. (1964) *Signs*. Evanston, IL: Northwestern University Press.

Merleau-Ponty, M. (1965) *The Structure of Behaviour*. London: Methuen.

Merleau-Ponty, M. (1968a) *The Visible and the Invisible*. Evanston, IL: Northwestern University Press.

Merleau-Ponty, M. (1968b) *The Primacy of Perception and Other Essays*. Evanston, IL: Northwestern University Press.

Merleau-Ponty, M. (1969) *Humanism and Terror*. Beacon: Boston.

Merleau-Ponty, M. (1971) *Sense and Non-Sense*. Evanston, IL: Northwestern University Press.

Merleau-Ponty, M. (1973) *Adventures of the Dialectic*. Evanston, IL: Northwestern University Press.

Merleau-Ponty, M. (1974) *The Prose of the World*. London: Heinemann.

Merleau-Ponty, M. (1988) *In Praise of Philosophy and Themes From the Lectures at the College De France*. Evanston, IL: Northwestern University Press.

Merleau-Ponty, M. (1992) *Texts and Dialogues*. New Jersey: Humanities Press.

Merton, R. (1964) *Social Theory and Social Structure*. Glencoe: Free Press.

339

Michels, R. (1949) *Political Parties*. Glencoe: Free Press.

Monbiot, G. (2001) *Captive State*. London: Macmillan.

Mueller, C. (1999) 'Escape from the GDR, 1961–1989: hybrid repertoires in a disintegrating Leninist regime'. *American Journal of Sociology* 105: 697–735.

Neale, J. (2002) *You are G8, We are 6 Billion*. London: Vision.

Nietzsche, F. (1967) *The Genealogy of Morals and Ecce Homo*. New York: Vintage.

Norris, C. (1987) *Derrida*. London: Fontana.

Mills, C.W. (1974) *Power, Politics and People: the Collected Essays of C.W. Mills*. London: Oxford University Press.

Oakley, A. (1972) *Sex, Gender and Society*. London: Temple Smith.

Offe, C. (1985) 'New social movements: challenging the boundaries of institutional politics'. *Social Research* 52 (4): 817–68.

Offe, C. (1993) *Structural Contradictions of the Welfare State*. Cambridge: MIT Press.

Olson, M. (1971) *The Logic of Collective Action*. Cambridge, MA: Harvard University Press.

Orwell, G. (1978) *Nineteen Eighty-Four*. Harmondsworth: Penguin.

Outhwaite, W. (1993) *Habermas*. Cambridge: Polity.

Parsons, T. (1951) *The Social System*. New York: Free Press.

Parsons, T. (1966) *Societies*. New Jersey: Prentice Hall.

Parsons, T. (1968) *The Structure of Social Action* (2 Vols). New York: Free Press.

Pascal, B. (1972) *Pensées*. Harmondsworth: Penguin.

Piaget, J. (1961) *The Language and Thought of the Child*. London: RKP.

Piaget, J. (1962) *Play, Dreams and Imitation in Childhood*. New York: W.W. Norton.

Porter, R. (1987) *Mind Forg'd Manacles*. Harmondsworth: Penguin.

Potter, J. and Wetherell, M. (1987) *Discourse and Social Psychology*. London: Sage.

Psathas, G. (1995) *Conversation Analysis*. London: Sage.

Pusey, M. (1987) *Jürgen Habermas*. London: Routledge.

Putnam, R. (1993) *Making Democracy Work*. Princeton: Princeton University Press.

Putnam, R. (2000) *Bowling Alone*. New York: Touchstone.

Rabinow, P. (1987) *The Foucault Reader*. Harmondsworth: Penguin.

Robertson, R. (1992) *Globalisation: Social Theory and Global Culture*. London: Sage.

Roche, M. (1992) *Rethinking Citizenship*. Cambridge: Polity.

Rootes, C. (1995) 'A new class? The higher educated and the new politics', in L. Maheu *Social Movements and Social Classes*. London: Sage.

Rose, N. (1985) *The Psychological Complex*. London: RKP.

Rose, N. (1989) *Governing the Soul*. London: Routledge.

Rowbotham, S. (1973) *Woman's Consciousness Man's World*. Harmondsworth: Penguin.

Ryle, G. (1949) *The Concept of Mind*. Harmondsworth: Penguin.

Said, E. (1978) *Orientalism*. Harmondsworth: Penguin.

Said, E. (1994) *Culture and Imperialism*. New York: Vintage.

Sartre, J-P. (1947) 'Huis clos', in *Théâtre I*. Paris: Gallimard.

Sartre, J-P. (1948) *Existentialism and Humanism*. London: Methuen.

Sartre, J-P. (1965) *Nausea*. Harmondsworth: Penguin.

Sartre, J-P. (1969) *Being and Nothingness*. London: Routledge.

Sartre, J-P. (1972) *The Psychology of Imagination*. London: Methuen.

Sartre, J-P (1973) *The Age of Reason*. Harmondsworth: Penguin.

Sartre, J-P. (1976) *The Critique of Dialectical Reason*. London: New Left Books.

Sartre, J-P. (1993) *The Emotions: Outline of A Theory*. New York: Citadel.

Saussure, F. de (1959) *Course in General Linguistics*. New York: The Philosophical Library.

Savage, M. (2000) *Class Analysis and Social Transformation*. Milton Keynes: Open University Press.

340

Sayer, A. (2000) *Realism and Social Science*. London: Sage.
Schutz, A. (1964a) *Collected Papers I: The Problem of Social Reality*. The Hague: Martinus Nijhoff.
Schutz, A. (1964b) *Collected Papers II: Studies in Social Theory*. The Hague: Martinus Nijhoff.
Schutz, A. (1970) *Reflections on the Problem of Relevance*. New Haven, CT: Yale University Press.
Schutz, A. (1971) *Collected Papers III: Studies in Phenomenological Philosophy*. The Hague: Martinus Nijhoff.
Schutz, A. (1972) *The Phenomenology of the Social World*. Evanston, IL: Northwestern University Press.
Scott, J. (1991) *Social Network Analysis: A Handbook*. London: Sage.
Scott, J. (1996) *Stratification and Power*. Cambridge: Polity.
Scull, A. (1993) *The Most Solitary of Afflictions*. New York: Yale University Press.
Sharrock, W. and Anderson, B. (1986) *The Ethnomethodologists*. Chichester: Ellis Harwood.
Simmel, G. (1971) *Individuality and Social Forms*. Chicago: University of Chicago Press.
Simmel, G. (1990) *The Philosophy of Money*. London: Routledge.
Skeggs, B. (1997) *Formations of Class and Gender*. London: Sage.
Sloan, T. (1996) *Damaged Life*. London: Routledge.
Smart, B. (1983) *Foucault, Marxism and Critique*. London: RKP.
Smith, J. (2001b) 'Globalising Resistance,' *Mobilisation* 6 (1): 1–20.
Snow, D., Zurcher, L. and Ekland-Olson, S. (1980) 'Social networks and social movements', *American Sociological Review* 45 (5): 787–801.
Starr, A. (2001) *Naming the Enemy*. London: Zed Books.
Steinberg, M. (1995) 'The roar of the crowd', in M. Traugott *Repertoires and Cycles of Collective Action*. London: Duke University Press. pp.57–88.
Steinberg, M. (1999) 'The talk and back talk of collective action: a dialogic analysis of repertoires of discourse among nineteenth-century english cotton spinners', *American Journal of Sociology* 105 (3): 736–80.
Stevenson, N. (2001) *Culture and Citizenship*. London: Sage.
Strauss, A. (1997) *Mirrors and Masks*. New Brunswick: Transaction.
Szabó, M. (1996) 'Repertoires of contention in post-communist protest cultures', *Social Research* 63 (4): 1155–82.
Tarrow, S. (1989) *Democracy and Disorder*. Oxford: Oxford University Press.
Tarrow, S. (1995) 'Cycles of collective action', in M. Traugott *Repertoires and Cycles of Collective Action*, London: Duke University Press. pp.89–116.
Tarrow, S. (1998) *Power in Movement*. Cambridge: Cambridge University Press.
Tilly, C. (1977) 'Getting it together in Burgundy'. *Theory and Society* 4: 479–504.
Tilly, C. (1978) *From Mobilisation to Revolution*. Reading: Addison Wesley.
Tilly, C. (1986) 'European violence and collective violence since 1700'. *Social Research* 53: 159–84.
Tilly, C. (1995) 'Contentious repertoires in Great Britain, 1758–1834', in M. Traugott *Repertoires and Cycles of Collective Action*. London: Duke University Press. pp. 15–42.
Touraine, A. (1981) *The Voice and the Eye*. New York: Cambridge University Press.
Traugott, M. (1995a) *Repertoires and Cycles of Collective Action*. London: Duke University Press.
Traugott, M. (1995b) 'Barricades as repertoire', in M. Traugott *Repertoires and Cycles of Collective Action*. London: Duke University Press. pp.43–56.
Tucker, K. (1991) 'How new are the new social movements?' *Theory, Culture and Society* 8 (2): 75–98.

341

Turner, B. (1986) *Citizenship and Capitalism*. London: Allen and Unwin.
Wacquant.L. (1995) 'Pugs at Work', *Body and Society* 1 (1): 65–94.
Wainwright, H. (2003) *Reclaim the State*. London: Verso.
Walby, S. (1986) *Patriarchy at Work*. Cambridge: Polity.
Wallach, L. and Sforza, M. (1999) *The WTO*. New York: Seven Stories Press.
Waters, M. (1995) *Globalisation*. London: Routledge.
Watson, G. (1982) *Free Will*. Oxford: Oxford University Press
Weber, M. (1930) *The Protestant Ethic and the Spirit of Capitalism*. London: Allen and Unwin.
Weber, M. (1978) *Economy and Society* (2 Vols): New York: Bedminster Press.
Westwood, S. (1999) *Power and the Social*. London: Routledge.
White, S. (1988) *The Recent Work of Jürgen Habermas*. Cambridge: Cambridge University Press.
Wilson, B. (1974) *Rationality*. Oxford: Blackwell.
Winch, P. (1958) *The Idea of a Social Science*. London: RKP.
Winch, P. (1972) 'Understanding a primitive society', in *Ethics and Action*. London: RKP. pp.8–49.
Winnicott, D. (1971) *Playing and Reality*. London: Tavistock.
Wittgenstein, L. (1953) *Philosophical Investigations*. Oxford: Blackwell.
Woodward, K. (1997) *Identity and Difference*. London: Sage.
Wright, E. (1985) *Classes*. London: Verso.
Wright, E. (ed.) (1989) *The Debate on Classes*. London: Verso.
Wright, E. (1997) *Class Counts*. Oxford: Oxford University Press.
Wrong, D. (1961) 'The over-socialised conception of man in modern sociology', *American Sociological Review* 26: 184–93.
Young, I. (1980) 'Throwing like a girl', *Human Studies* 3: 137–56.
Young, I. (1998) 'Pregnant Embodiment', in D. Welton *Body and Flesh*. Oxford: Blackwell. pp.274–85.
Zald, M. and McCarthy, J. (1994) *Social Movements in an Organisational Society*. New Brunswick: Transaction Press.
Zolberg, A. (1972) 'Moments of madness', *Politics and Society* (Winter): 183–207.